CAPTAIN AMERICA:
TRUTH

WRITER
ROBERT MORALES

ARTIST
KYLE BAKER

LETTERERS
JG, RS & COMICRAFT'S WES ABBOTT

ASSISTANT EDITORS
JOHN MIESEGAES, WARREN SIMONS & JENNY HUANG

EDITOR
AXEL ALONSO

CAPTAIN AMERICA: TRUTH. Contains material originally published in magazine form as TRUTH: RED, WHITE & BLACK (2002) #1-7. Second edition. First printing 2021. ISBN 978-1-302-93427-9. Published by MARVEL WORLDWIDE, INC., a subsidiary of MARVEL ENTERTAINMENT, LLC. OFFICE OF PUBLICATION: 1290 Avenue of the Americas, New York, NY 10104. © 2021 MARVEL No similarity between any of the names, characters, persons, and/or institutions in this book with those of any living or dead person or institution is intended, and any such similarity which may exist is purely coincidental. **Printed in Canada.** KEVIN FEIGE, Chief Creative Officer; DAN BUCKLEY, President, Marvel Entertainment; JOE QUESADA, EVP & Creative Director; DAVID BOGART, Associate Publisher & SVP of Talent Affairs; TOM BREVOORT, VP, Executive Editor; NICK LOWE, Executive Editor, VP of Content, Digital Publishing; DAVID GABRIEL, VP of Print & Digital Publishing; JEFF YOUNGQUIST, VP of Production & Special Projects; ALEX MORALES, Director of Publishing Operations; DAN EDINGTON, Managing Editor; RICKEY PURDIN, Director of Talent Relations; JENNIFER GRÜNWALD, Senior Editor, Special Projects; SUSAN CRESPI, Production Manager; STAN LEE, Chairman Emeritus. For information regarding advertising in Marvel Comics or on Marvel.com, please contact Vit DeBellis, Custom Solutions & Integrated Advertising Manager, at vdebellis@marvel.com. For Marvel subscription inquiries, please call 888-511-5480. **Manufactured between 11/12/2021 and 12/14/2021 by SOLISCO PRINTERS, SCOTT, QC, CANADA.**

10 9 8 7 6 5 4 3 2 1

CAPTAIN AMERICA
CREATED BY
JOE SIMON
& JACK KIRBY

Collection Editor
Jennifer Grünwald
Assistant Editor
Daniel Kirchhoffer
Assistant Managing Editor
Maia Loy
Assistant Managing Editor
Lisa Montalbano
VP Production & Special Projects
Jeff Youngquist
SVP Print, Sales & Marketing
David Gabriel
Editor in Chief
C.B. Cebulski

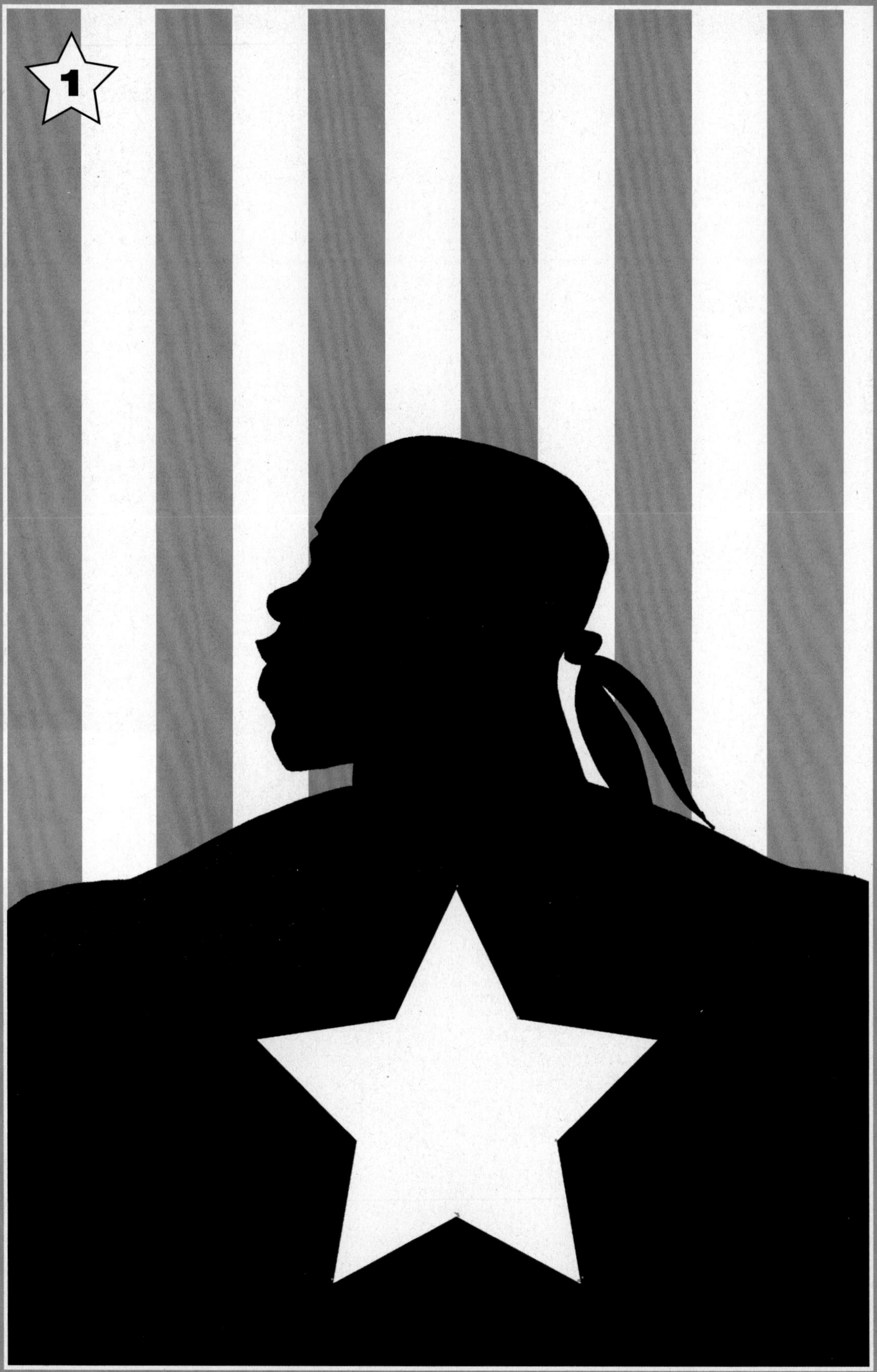
1

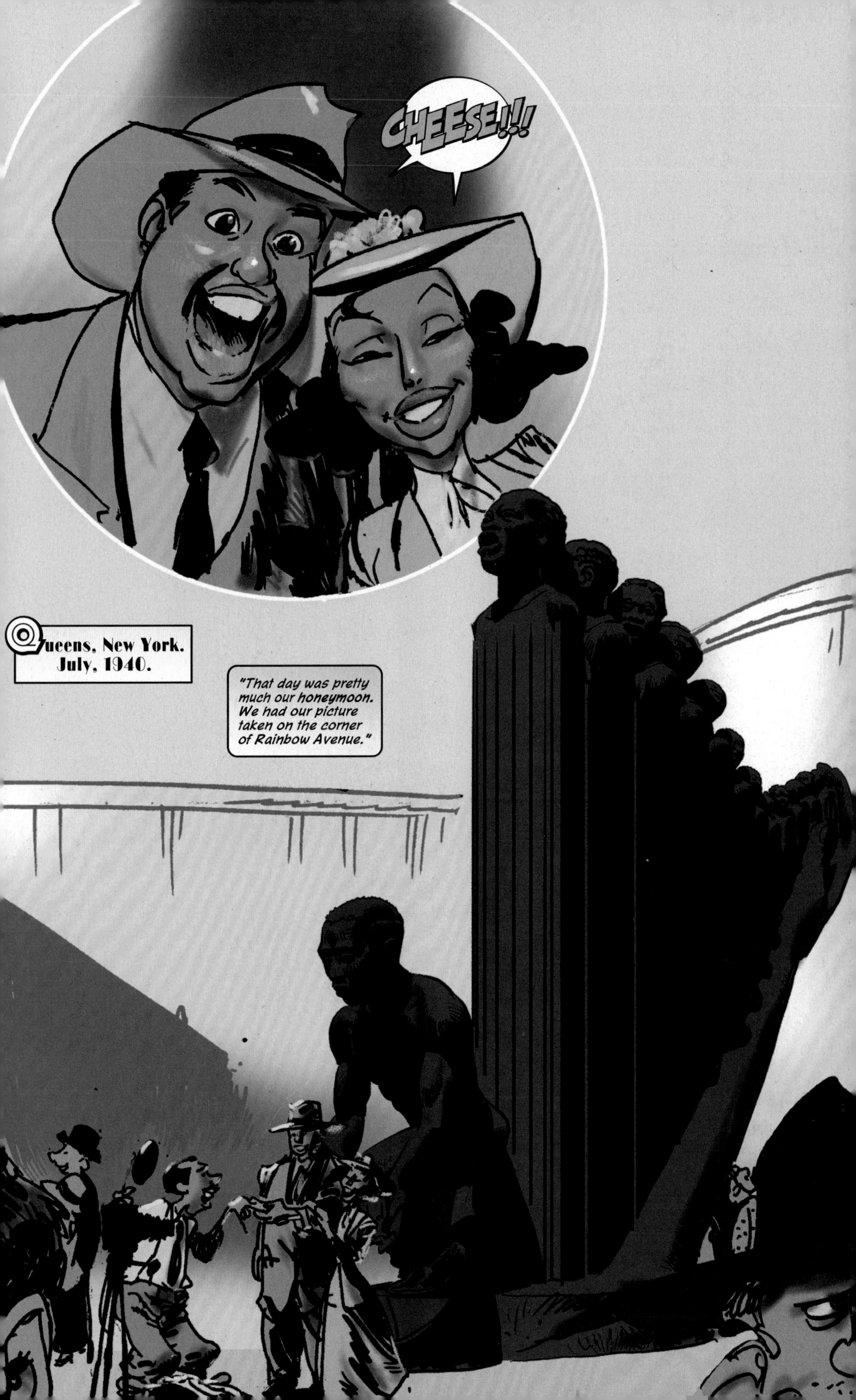
CHEESE!!!
Queens, New York.
July, 1940.
"That day was pretty much our honeymoon. We had our picture taken on the corner of Rainbow Avenue."

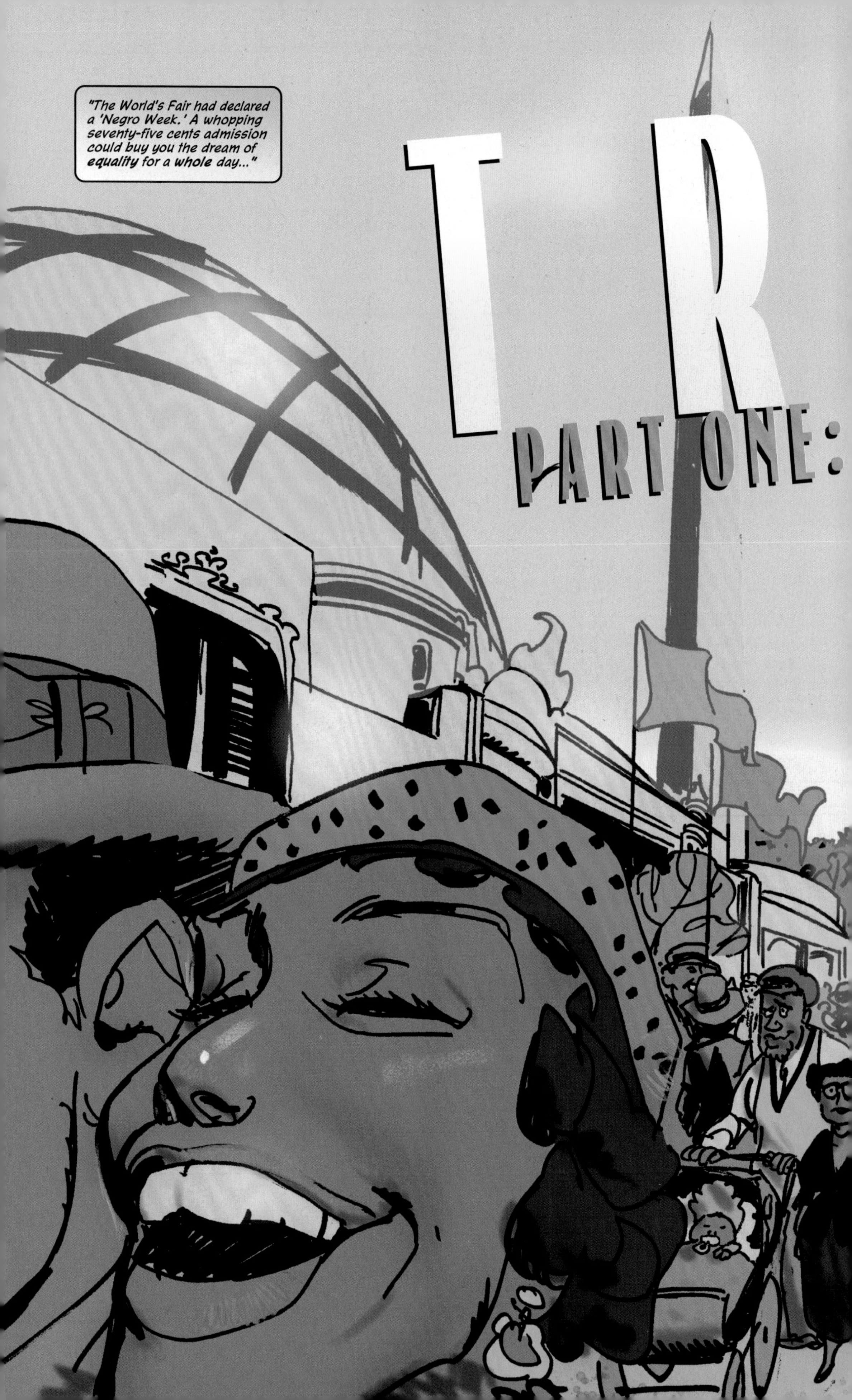
"The World's Fair had declared a 'Negro Week.' A whopping seventy-five cents admission could buy you the dream of equality for a whole day..."
T R
PART ONE:

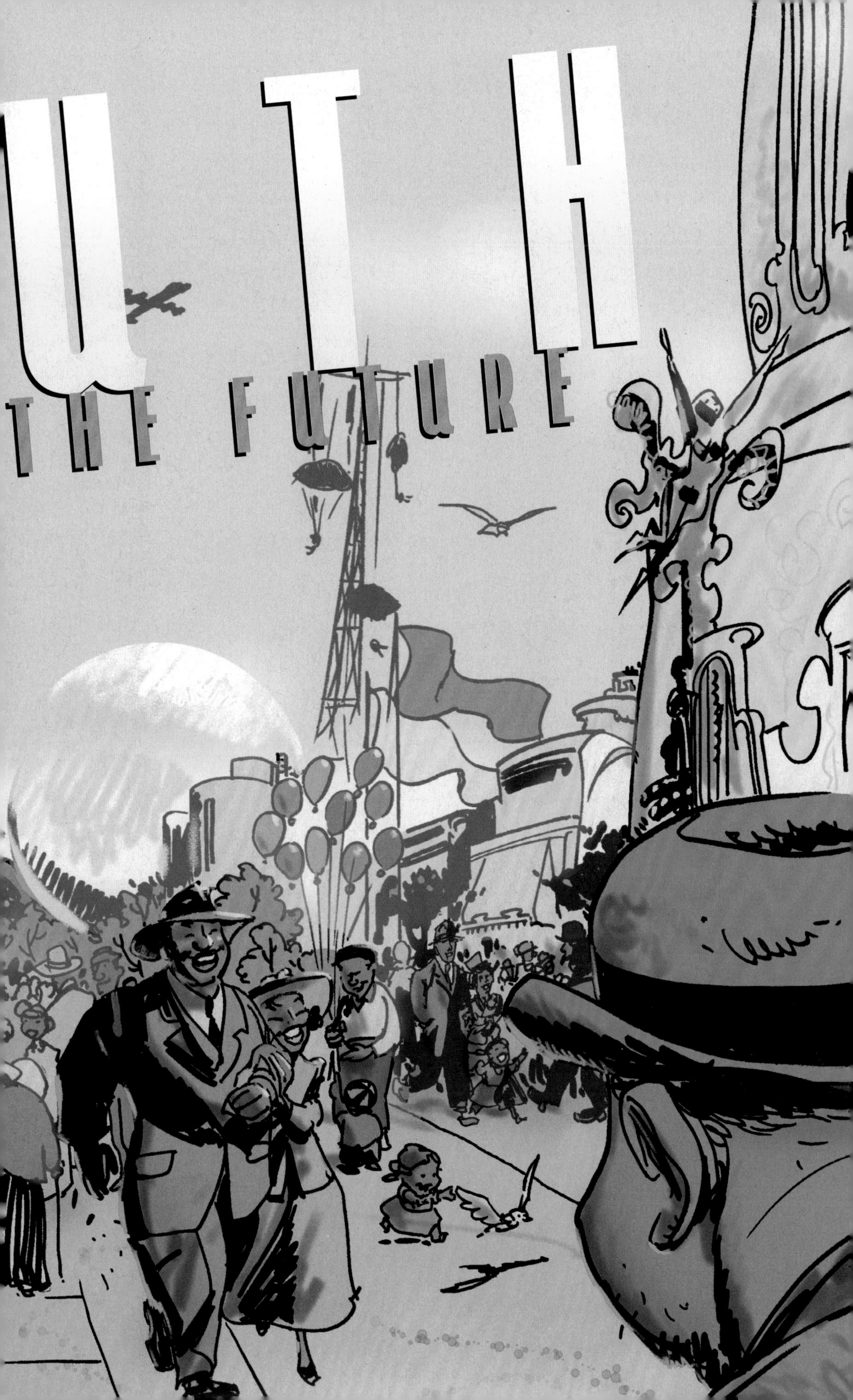
U T H
THE FUTURE

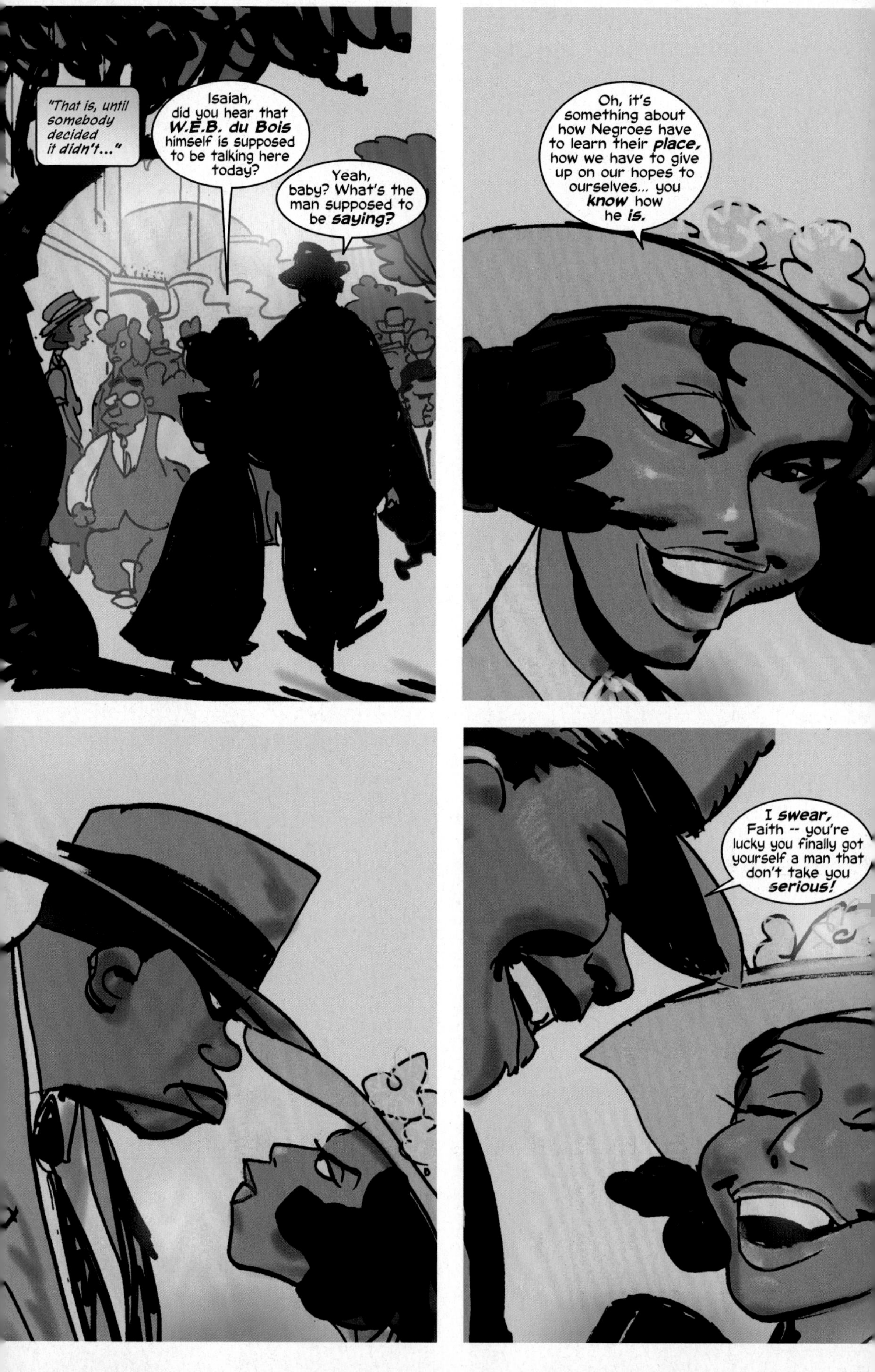
"That is, until somebody decided it *didn't...*"
Isaiah, did you hear that **W.E.B. du Bois** himself is supposed to be talking here today?
Yeah, baby? What's the man supposed to be **saying?**
Oh, it's something about how Negroes have to learn their **place,** how we have to give up on our hopes to ourselves... you **know** how he **is.**
I **swear,** Faith -- you're lucky you finally got yourself a man that don't take you **serious!**

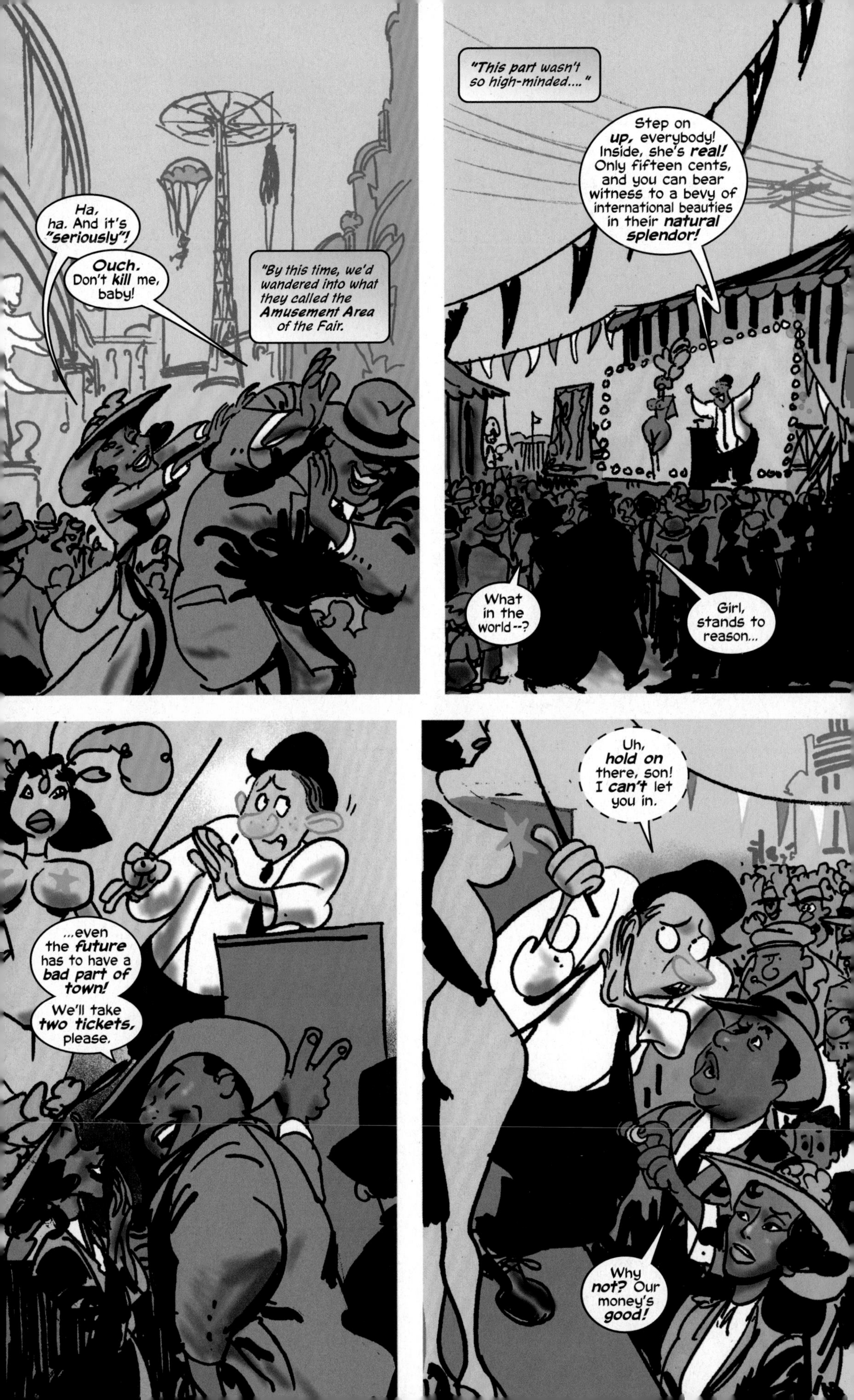

Ha, ha. And it's "seriously"!
Ouch. Don't kill me, baby!
"By this time, we'd wandered into what they called the Amusement Area of the Fair.
"This part wasn't so high-minded...."
Step on up, everybody! Inside, she's real! Only fifteen cents, and you can bear witness to a bevy of international beauties in their natural splendor!
What in the world--?
Girl, stands to reason...
...even the future has to have a bad part of town!
We'll take two tickets, please.
Uh, hold on there, son! I can't let you in.
Why not? Our money's good!

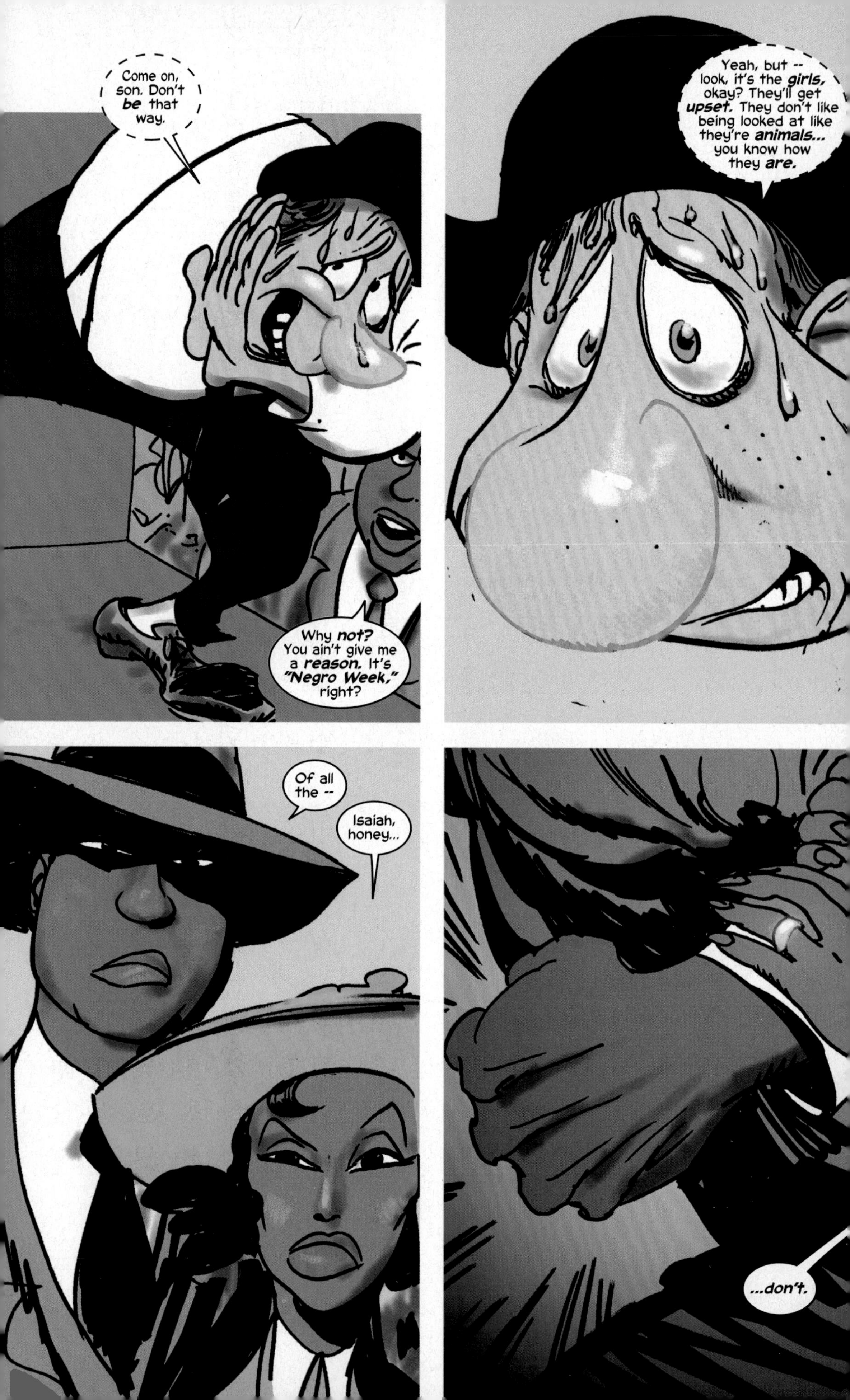
Come on, son. Don't be that way.
Why not? You ain't give me a reason. It's "Negro Week," right?
Yeah, but -- look, it's the girls, okay? They'll get upset. They don't like being looked at like they're animals... you know how they are.
Of all the --
Isaiah, honey...
...don't.

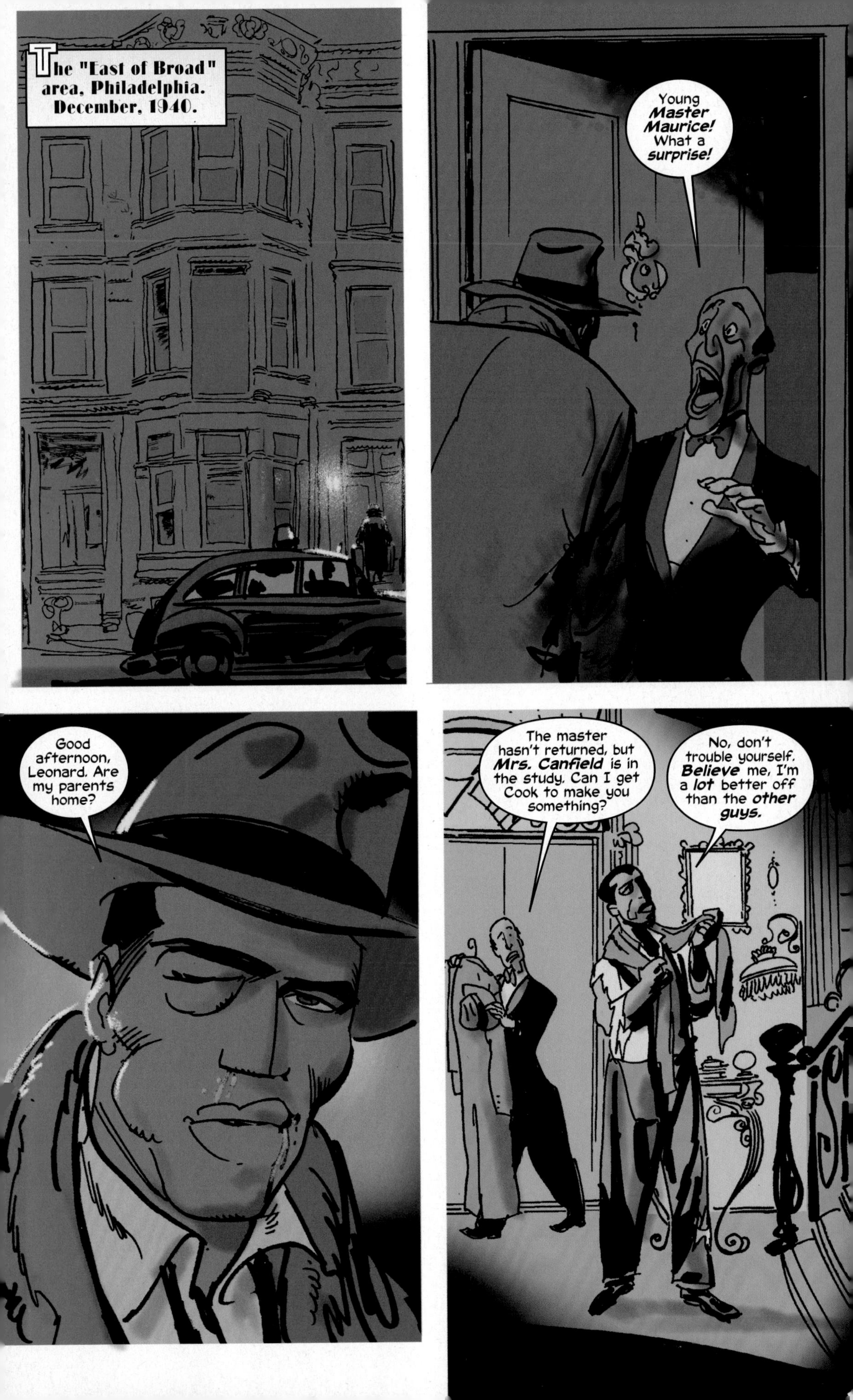
The "East of Broad" area, Philadelphia. December, 1940.
Young Master Maurice! What a surprise!
Good afternoon, Leonard. Are my parents home?
The master hasn't returned, but Mrs. Canfield is in the study. Can I get Cook to make you something?
No, don't trouble yourself. Believe me, I'm a lot better off than the other guys.

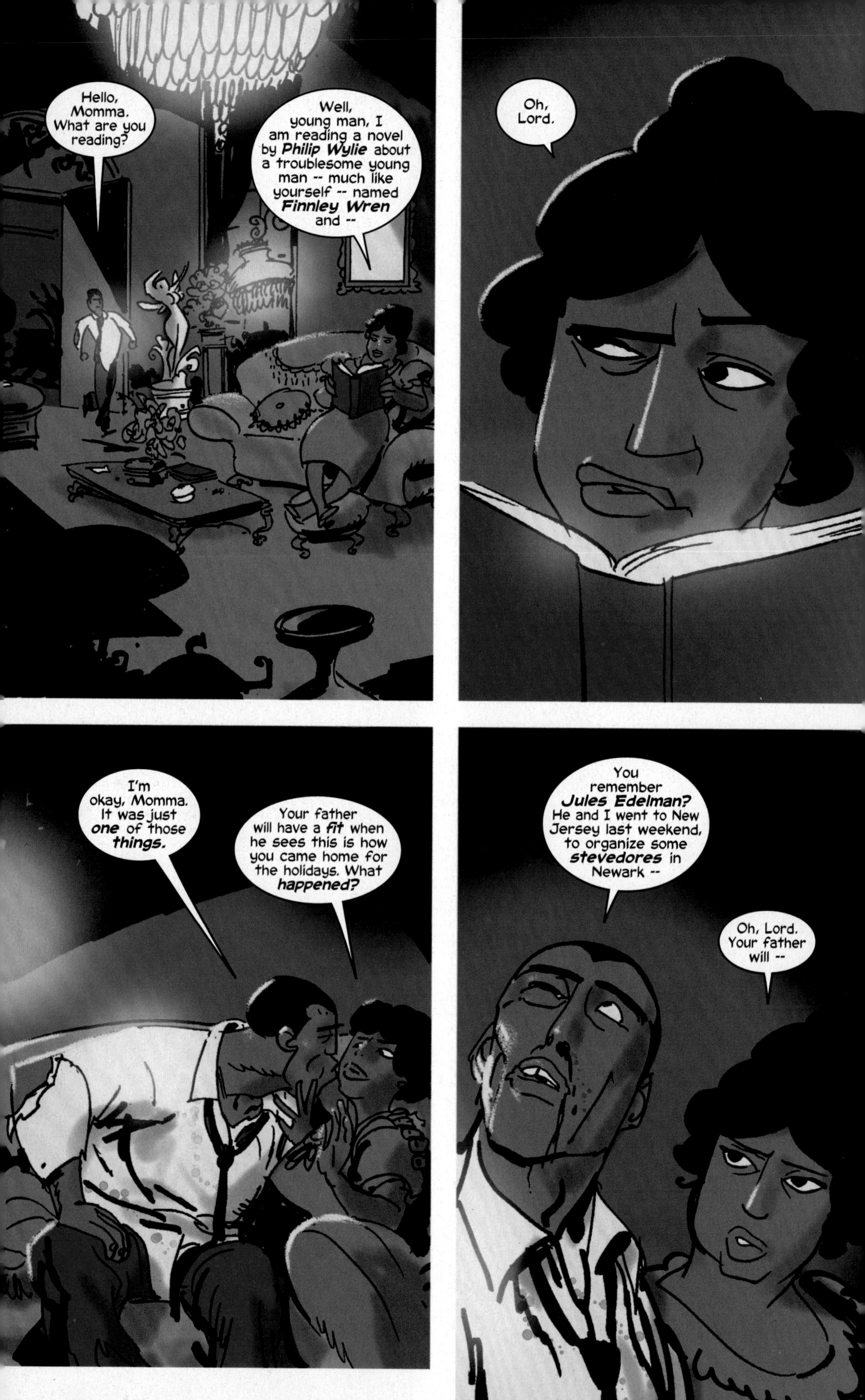
Hello, Momma. What are you reading?
Well, young man, I am reading a novel by Philip Wylie about a troublesome young man -- much like yourself -- named Finnley Wren and --
Oh, Lord.
I'm okay, Momma. It was just one of those things.
Your father will have a fit when he sees this is how you came home for the holidays. What happened?
You remember Jules Edelman? He and I went to New Jersey last weekend, to organize some stevedores in Newark --
Oh, Lord. Your father will --

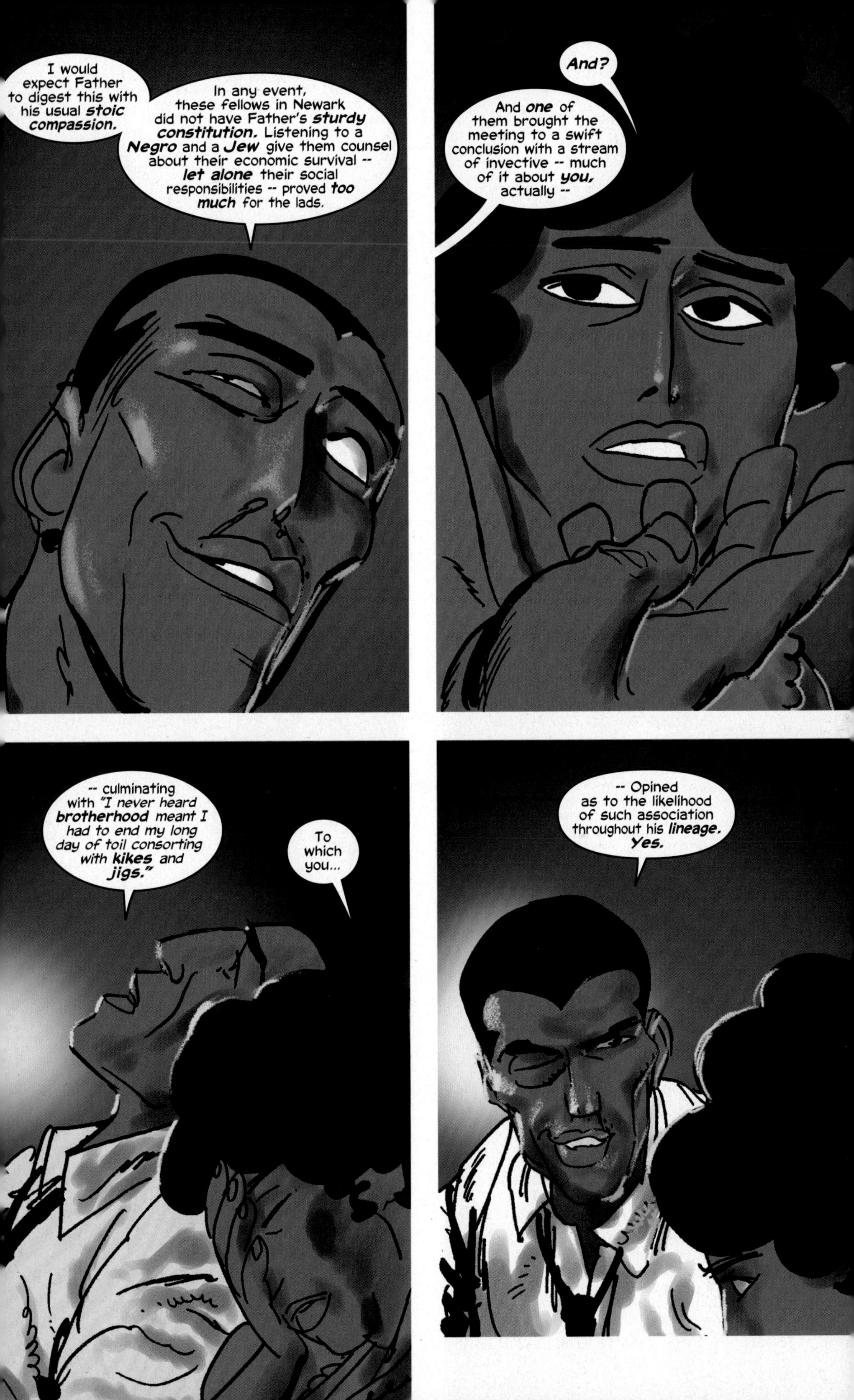
I would expect Father to digest this with his usual *stoic compassion.*
In any event, these fellows in Newark did not have Father's *sturdy constitution.* Listening to a *Negro* and a *Jew* give them counsel about their economic survival -- *let alone* their social responsibilities -- proved *too much* for the lads.
And?
And *one* of them brought the meeting to a swift conclusion with a stream of invective -- much of it about *you,* actually --
-- culminating with *"I never heard* ***brotherhood*** *meant I had to end my long day of toil consorting with* ***kikes*** *and* ***jigs."***
To which you...
-- Opined as to the likelihood of such association throughout his *lineage.* ***Yes.***

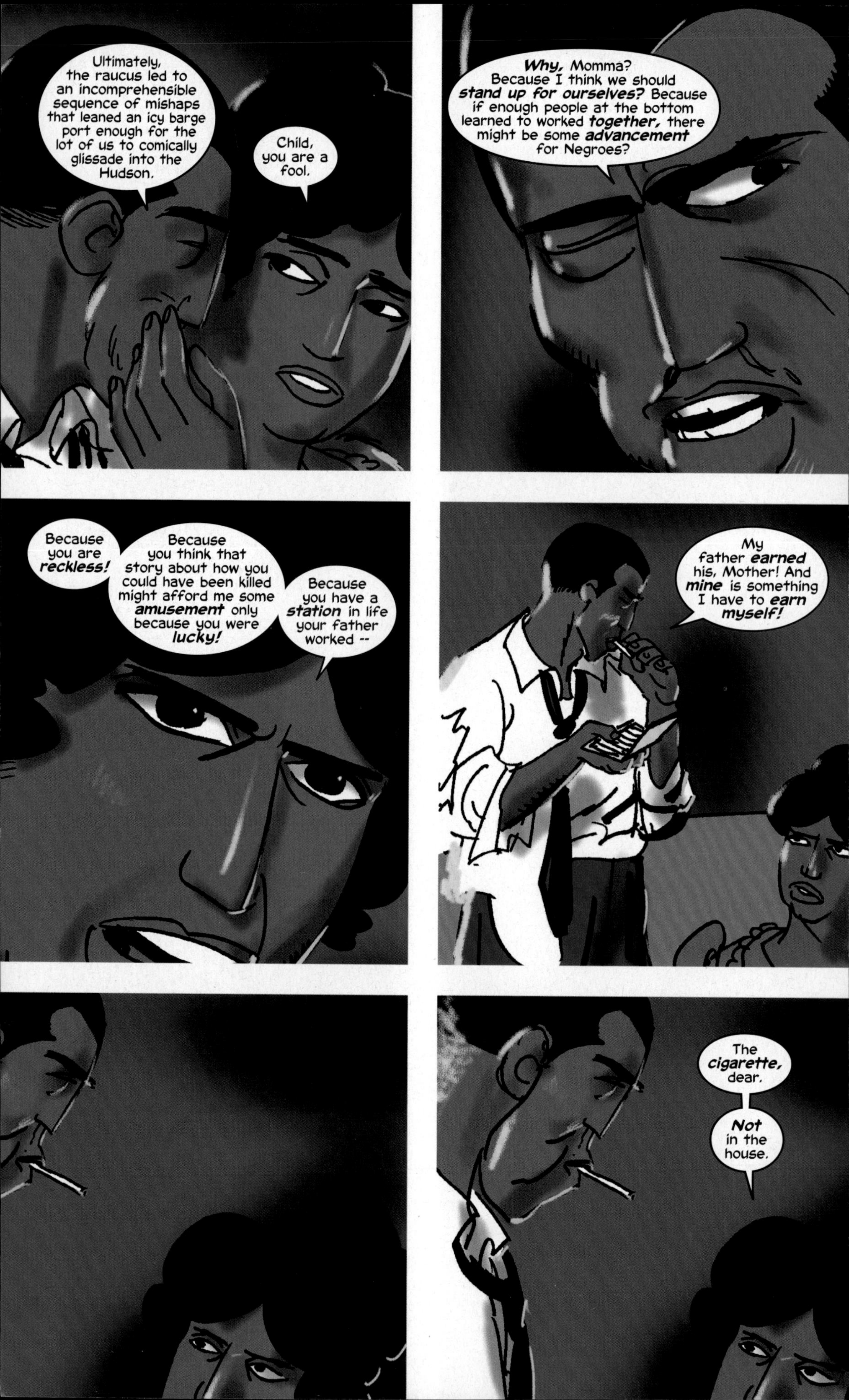

Ultimately, the raucus led to an incomprehensible sequence of mishaps that leaned an icy barge port enough for the lot of us to comically glissade into the Hudson.
Child, you are a fool.
Why, Momma? Because I think we should stand up for ourselves? Because if enough people at the bottom learned to worked together, there might be some advancement for Negroes?
Because you are reckless!
Because you think that story about how you could have been killed might afford me some amusement only because you were lucky!
Because you have a station in life your father worked --
My father earned his, Mother! And mine is something I have to earn myself!
The cigarette, dear.
Not in the house.

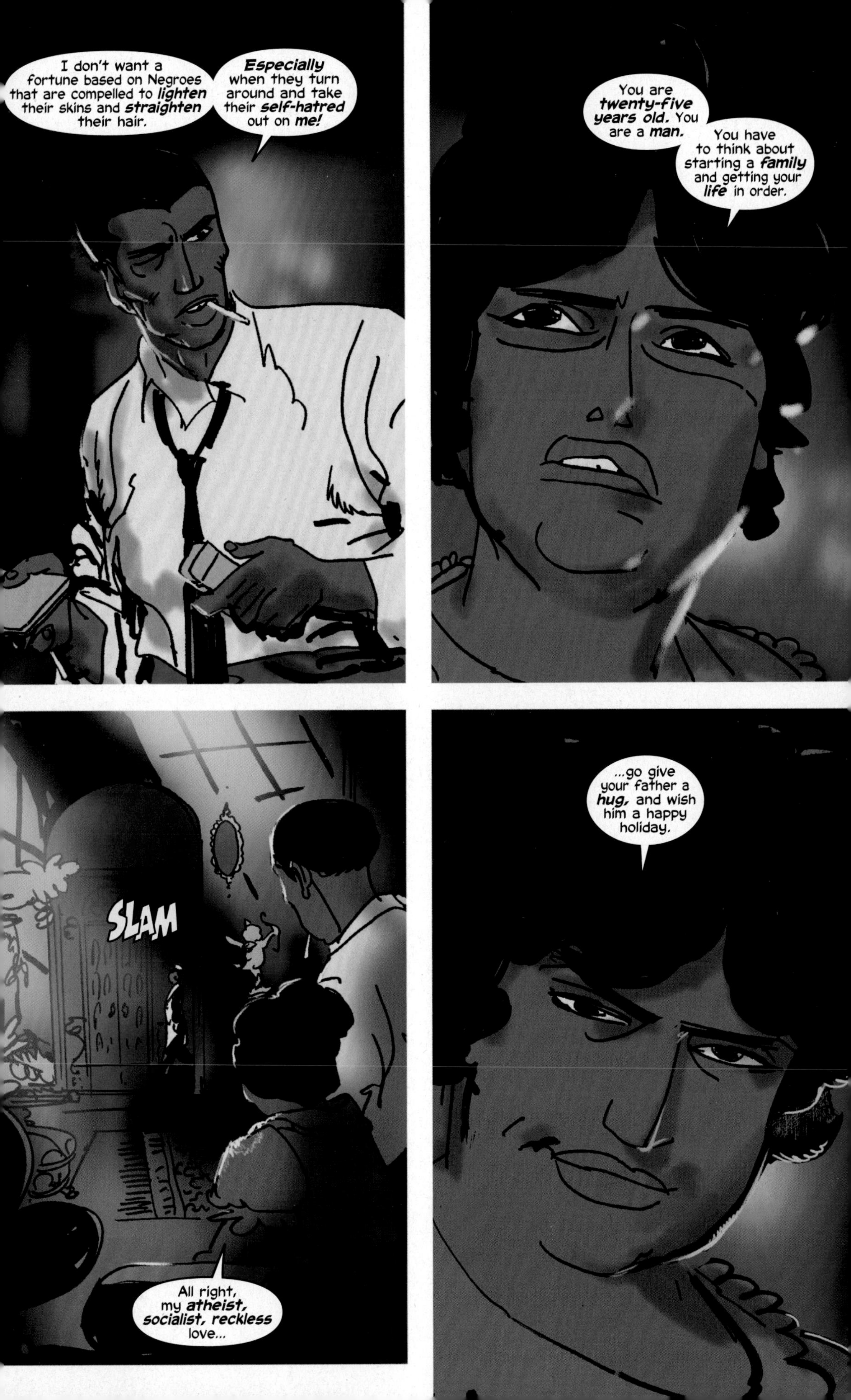
I don't want a fortune based on Negroes that are compelled to *lighten* their skins and *straighten* their hair.
Especially when they turn around and take their *self-hatred* out on *me!*
You are *twenty-five years old.* You are a *man.*
You have to think about starting a *family* and getting your *life* in order.
SLAM
All right, my *atheist, socialist, reckless* love...
...go give your father a *hug,* and wish him a happy holiday.

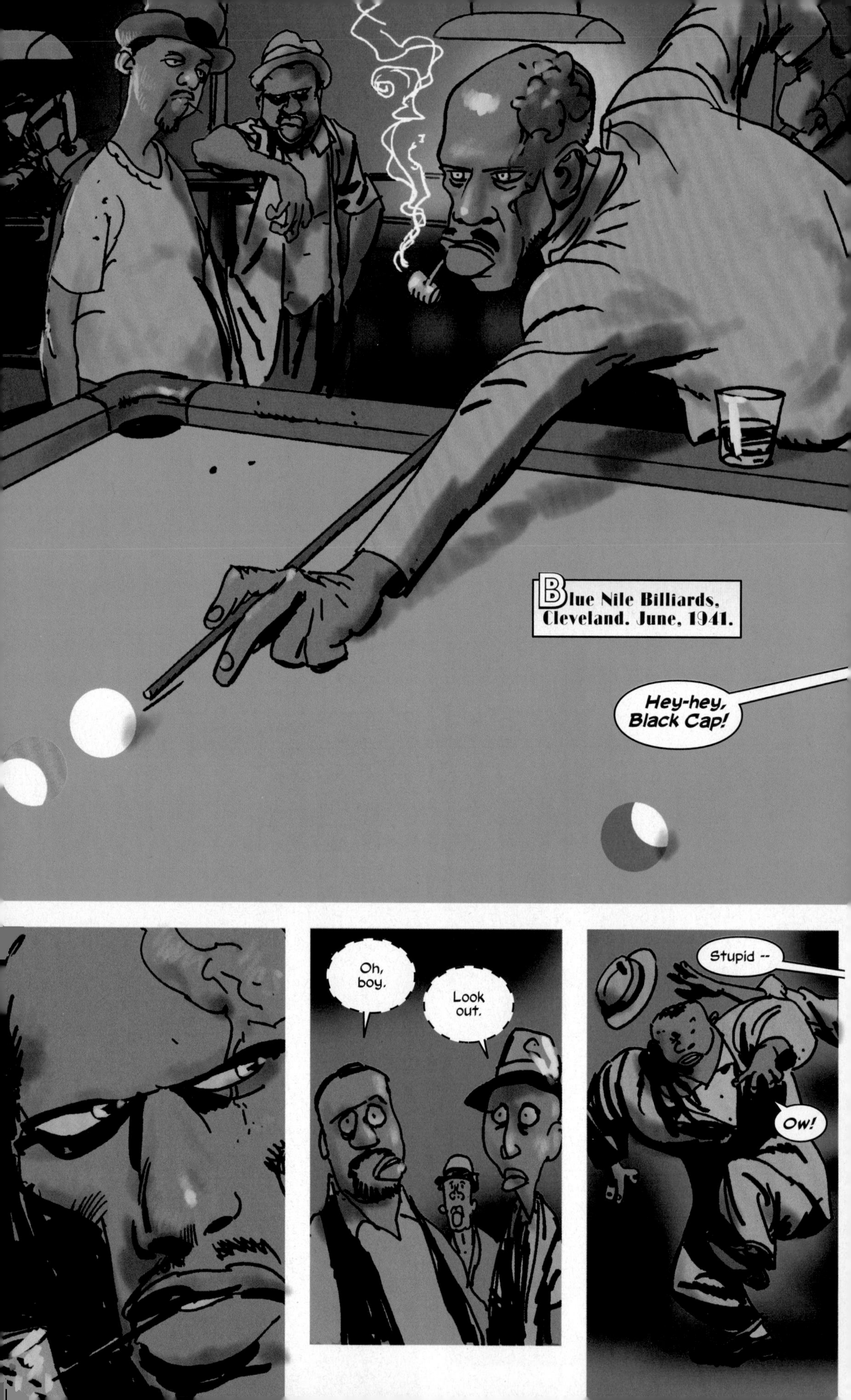
Blue Nile Billiards,
Cleveland. June, 1941.
Hey-hey, Black Cap!
Oh, boy.
Look out.
Stupid --
Ow!

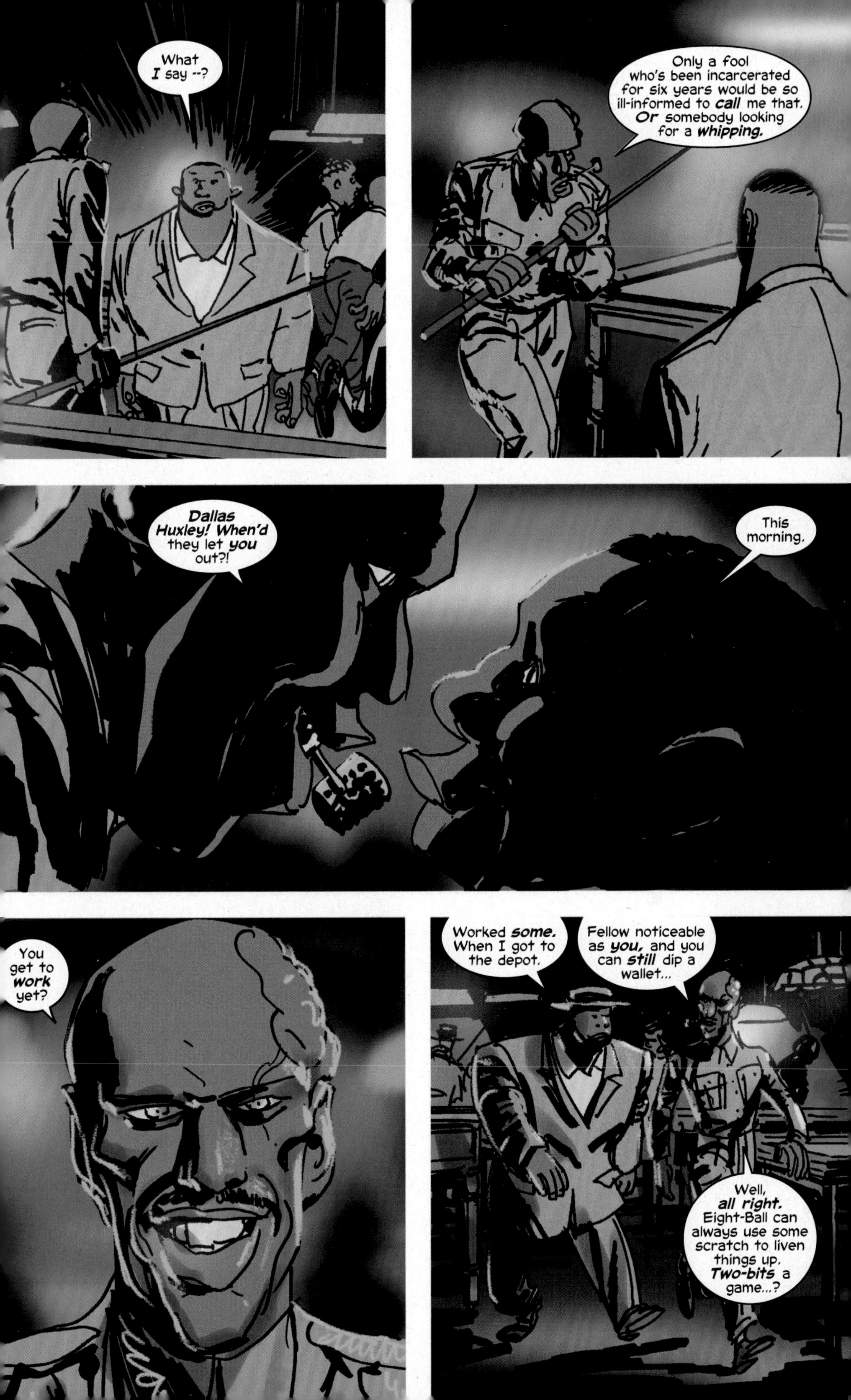
What I say --?
Only a fool who's been incarcerated for six years would be so ill-informed to call me that. Or somebody looking for a whipping.
Dallas Huxley! When'd they let you out?!
This morning.
You get to work yet?
Worked some. When I got to the depot.
Fellow noticeable as you, and you can still dip a wallet...
Well, all right. Eight-Ball can always use some scratch to liven things up. Two-bits a game...?

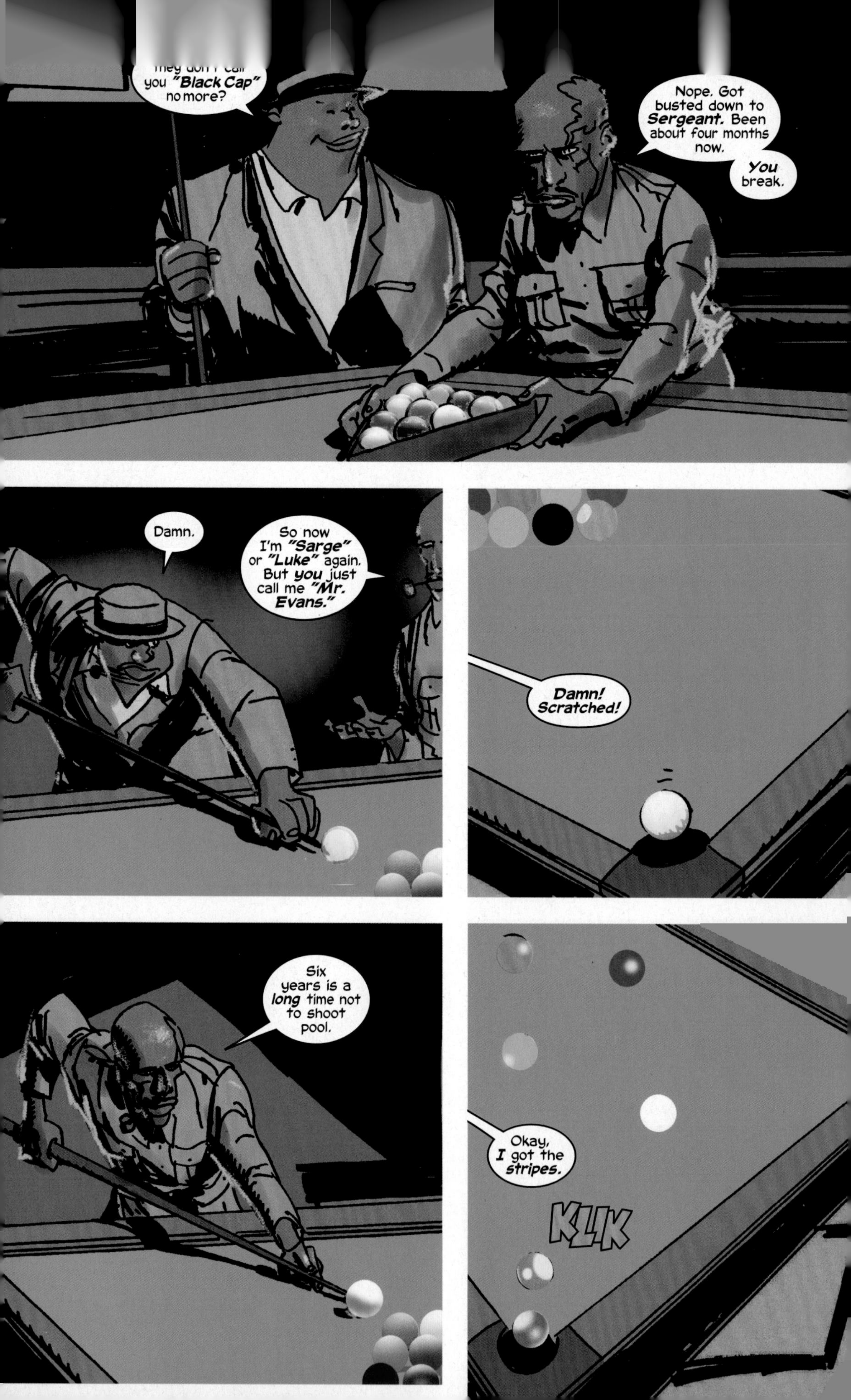
you "Black Cap" no more?
Nope. Got busted down to Sergeant. Been about four months now.
You break.
Damn.
So now I'm "Sarge" or "Luke" again. But you just call me "Mr. Evans."
Damn! Scratched!
Six years is a long time not to shoot pool.
Okay, I got the stripes.
KLIK

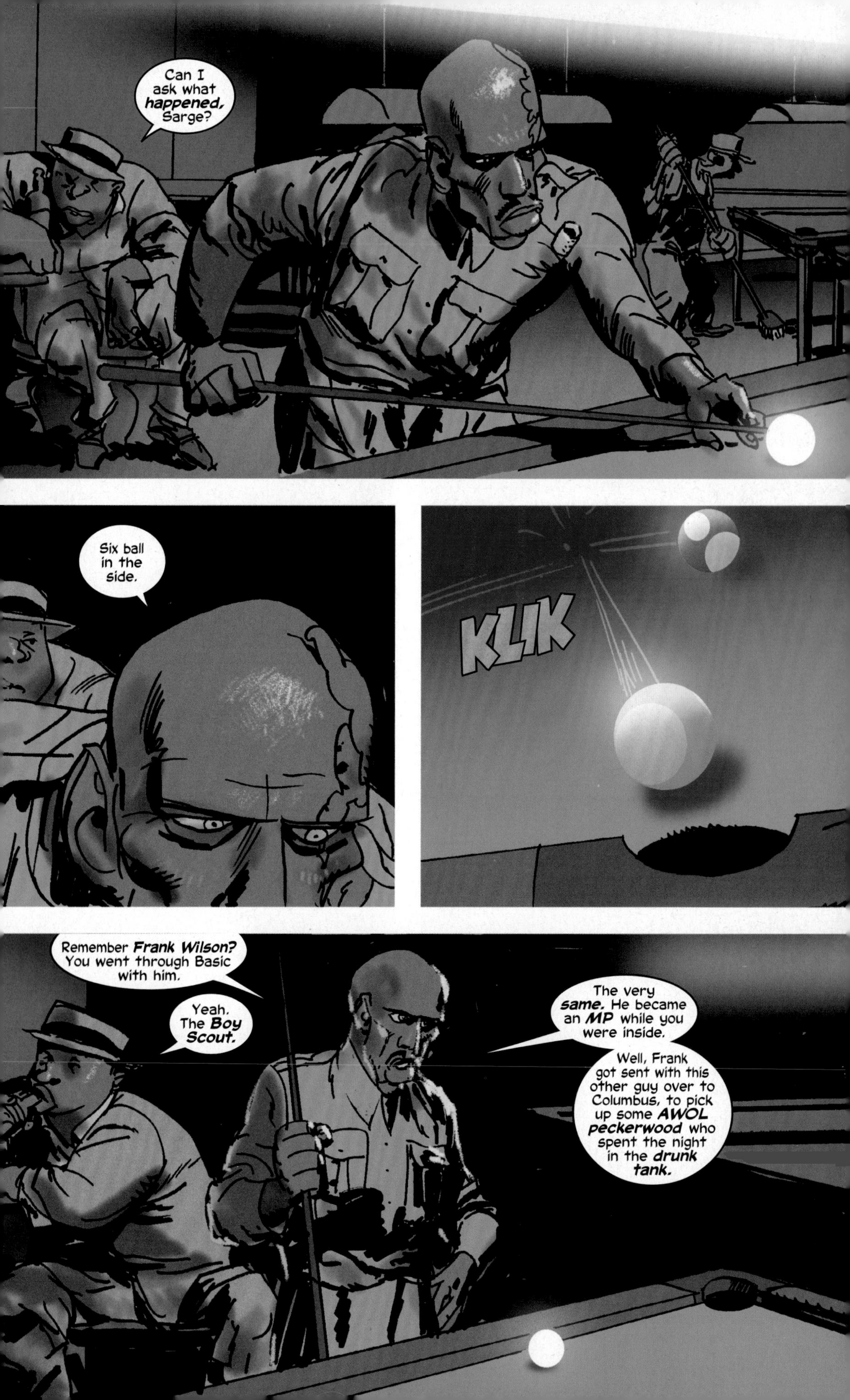
Can I ask what *happened,* Sarge?
Six ball in the side.
KLIK
Remember *Frank Wilson?* You went through Basic with him.
Yeah. The *Boy Scout.*
The very *same.* He became an *MP* while you were inside.
Well, Frank got sent with this other guy over to Columbus, to pick up some *AWOL peckerwood* who spent the night in the *drunk tank.*

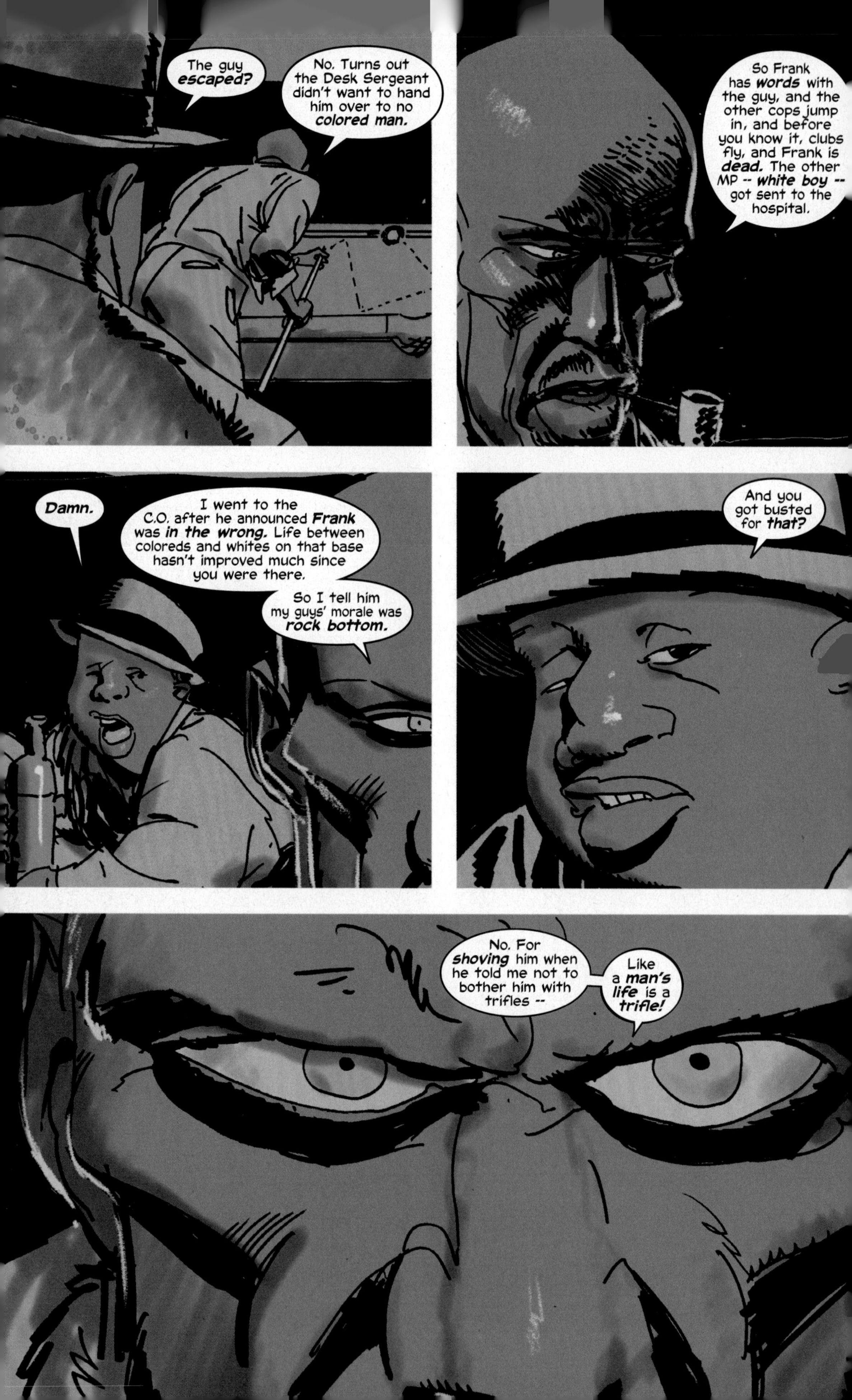
The guy *escaped?*
No. Turns out the Desk Sergeant didn't want to hand him over to no *colored man.*
So Frank has *words* with the guy, and the other cops jump in, and before you know it, clubs fly, and Frank is *dead.* The other MP -- *white boy* -- got sent to the hospital.
Damn.
I went to the C.O. after he announced *Frank* was *in the wrong.* Life between coloreds and whites on that base hasn't improved much since you were there.
So I tell him my guys' morale was *rock bottom.*
And you got busted for *that?*
No. For *shoving* him when he told me not to bother him with trifles --
Like a *man's life* is a *trifle!*

Damn, I gotta *make water.*

That's a *bad* break, man.

It *is* what it *is.* Maybe I'll make Captain again in another seventeen years.

If anything, I learned something --

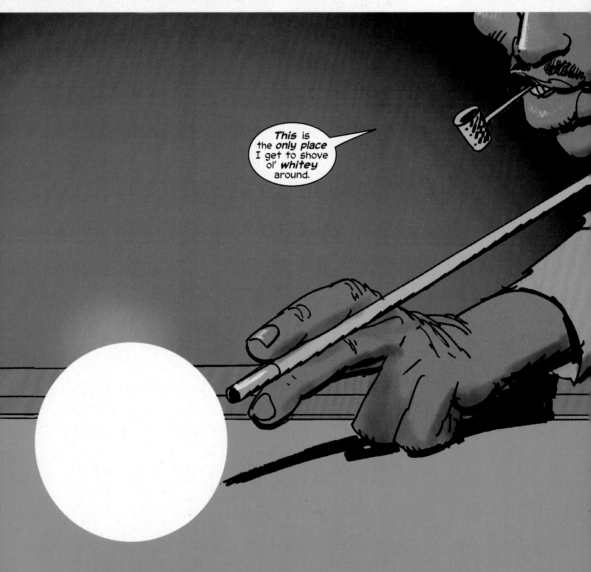

This is the *only place* I get to shove ol' *whitey* around.

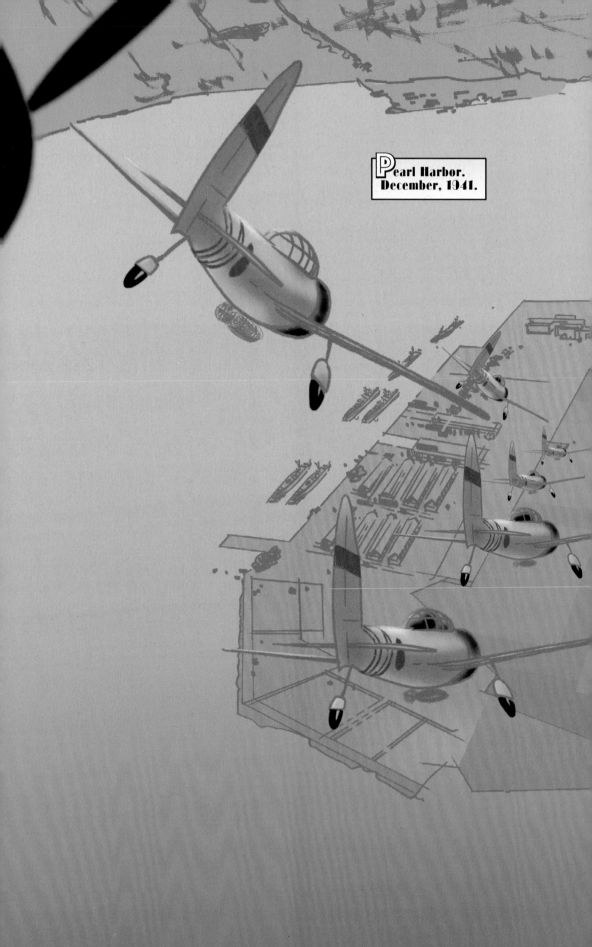

Pearl Harbor.
December, 1941.

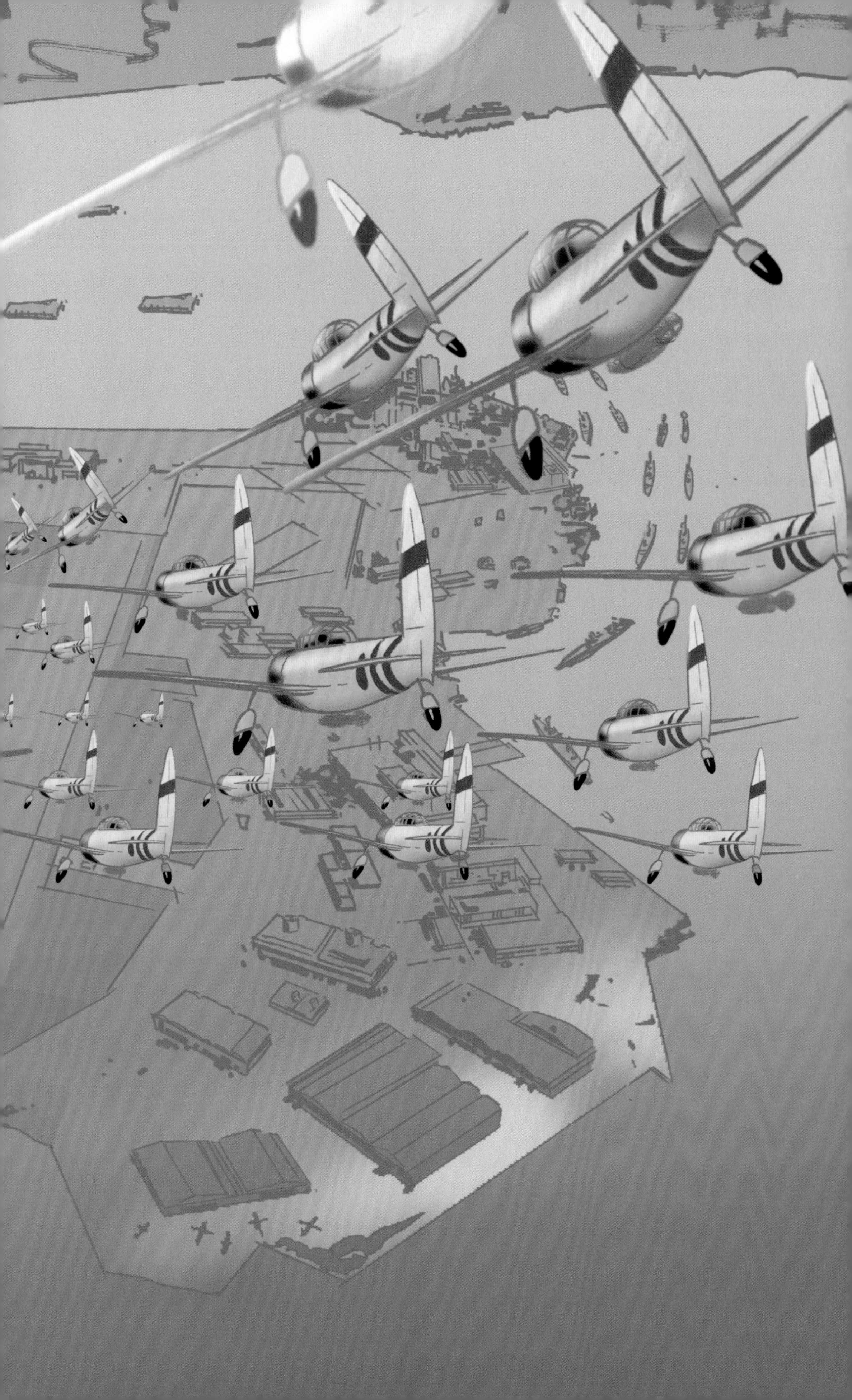

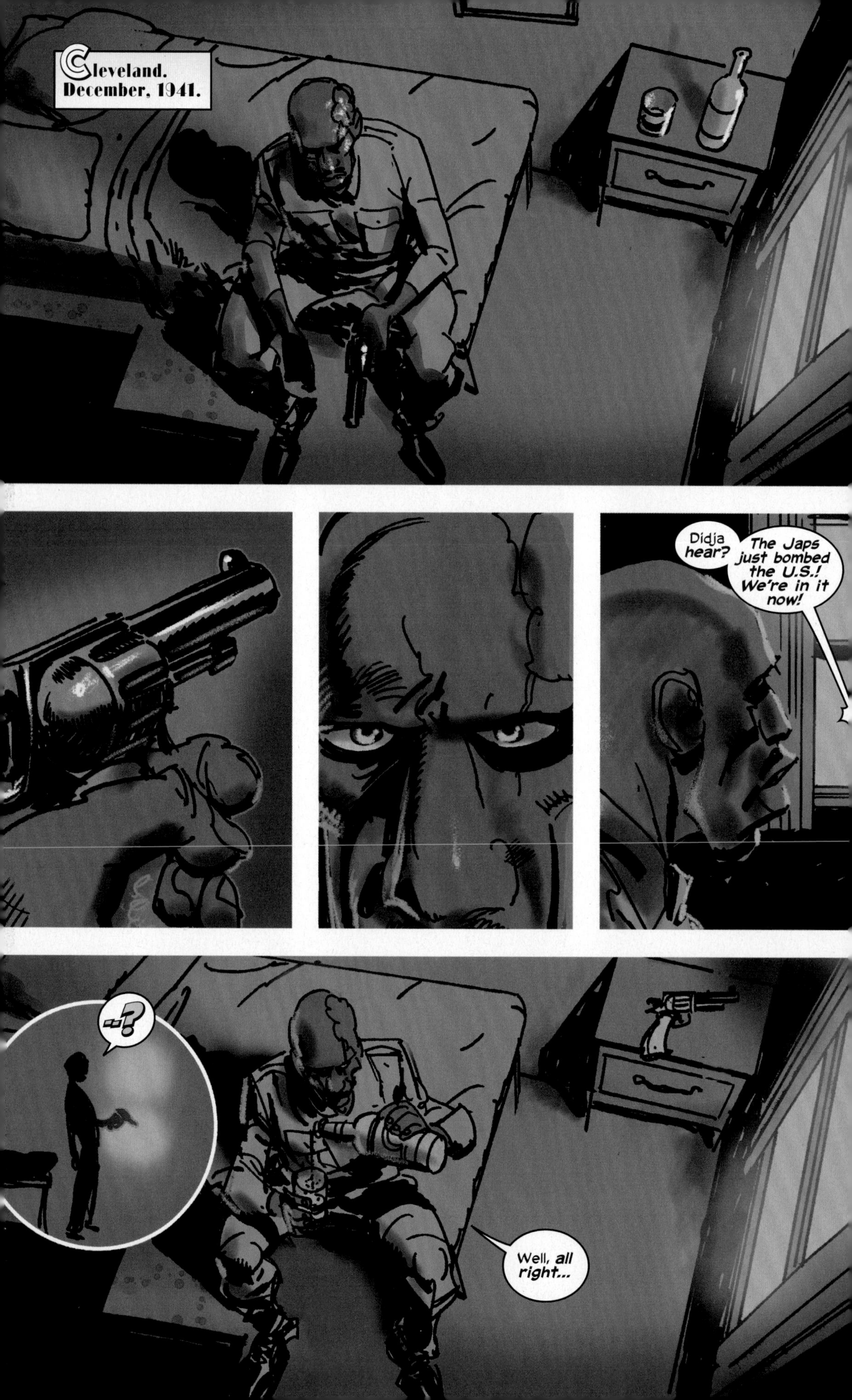
Cleveland. December, 1941.
Didja hear?
The Japs just bombed the U.S.! We're in it now!
--?
Well, all right...

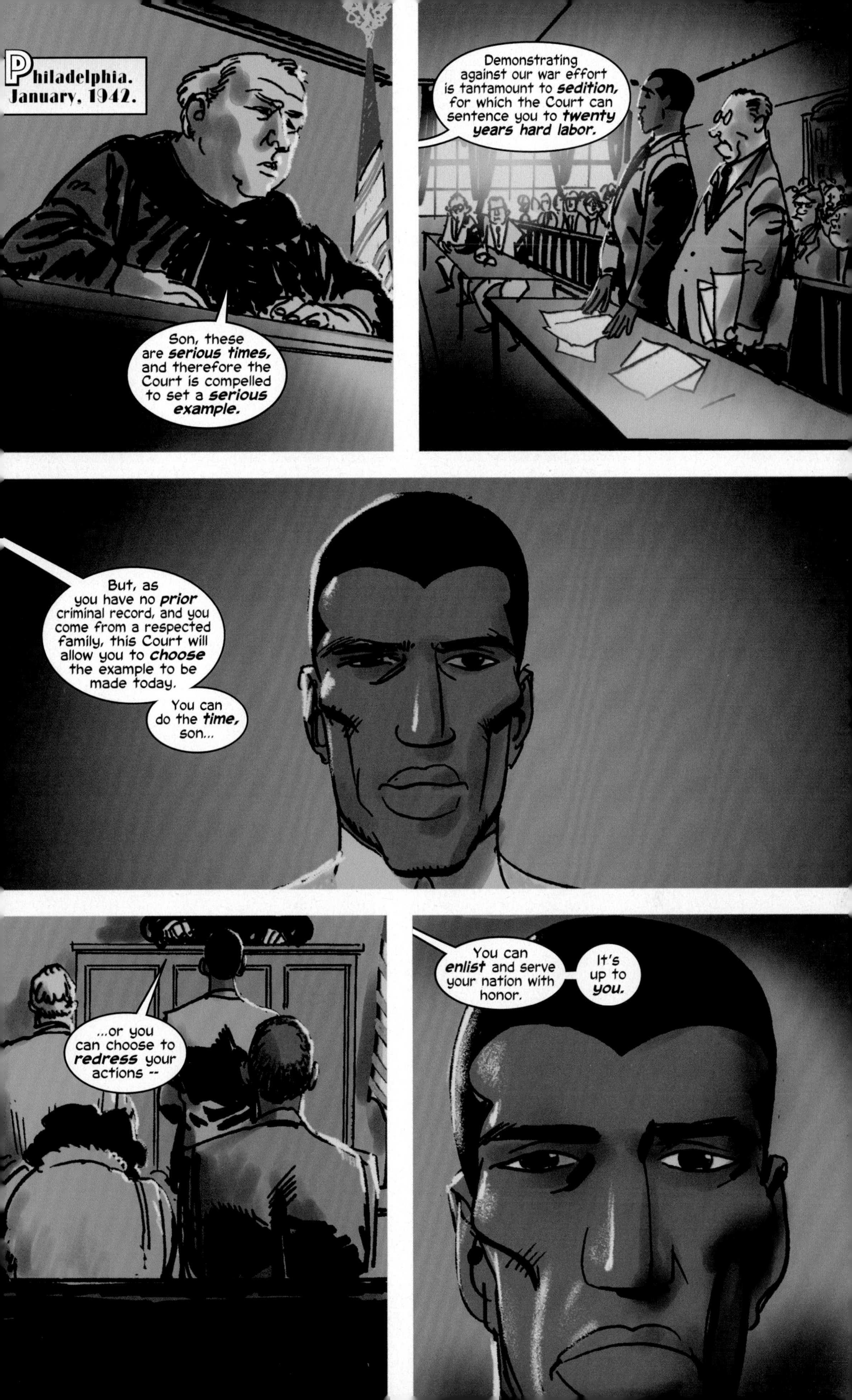
Philadelphia. January, 1942.
Son, these are serious times, and therefore the Court is compelled to set a serious example.
Demonstrating against our war effort is tantamount to sedition, for which the Court can sentence you to twenty years hard labor.
But, as you have no prior criminal record, and you come from a respected family, this Court will allow you to choose the example to be made today.
You can do the time, son...
...or you can choose to redress your actions --
You can enlist and serve your nation with honor.
It's up to you.

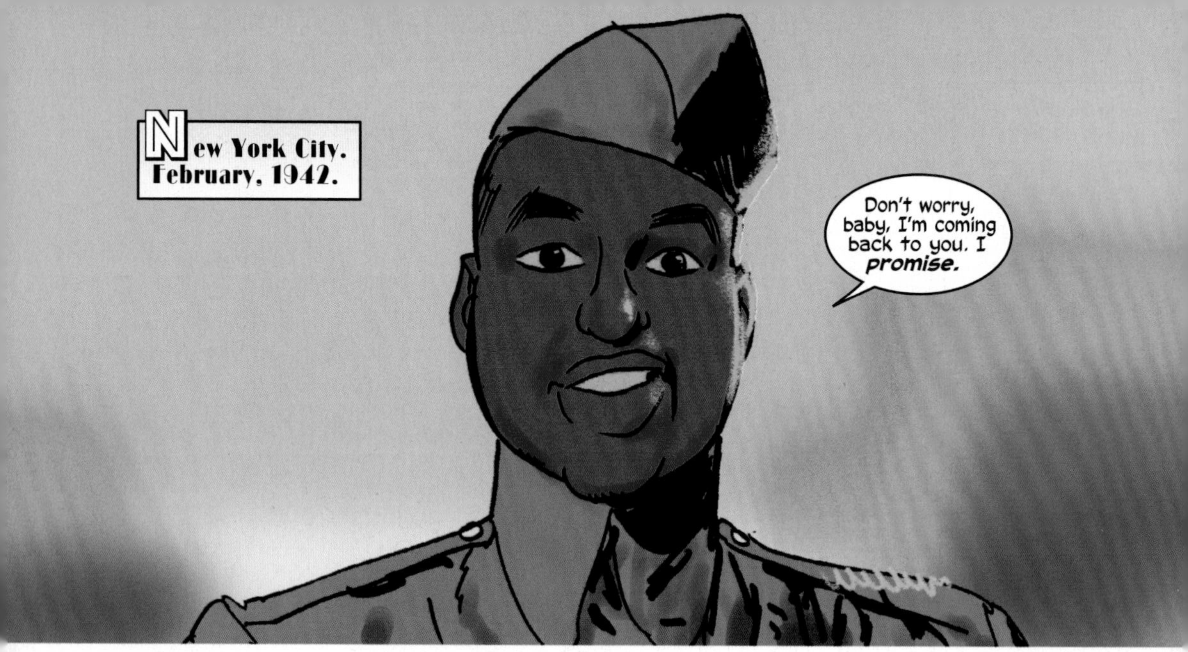
New York City.
February, 1942.
Don't worry, baby, I'm coming back to you. I promise.

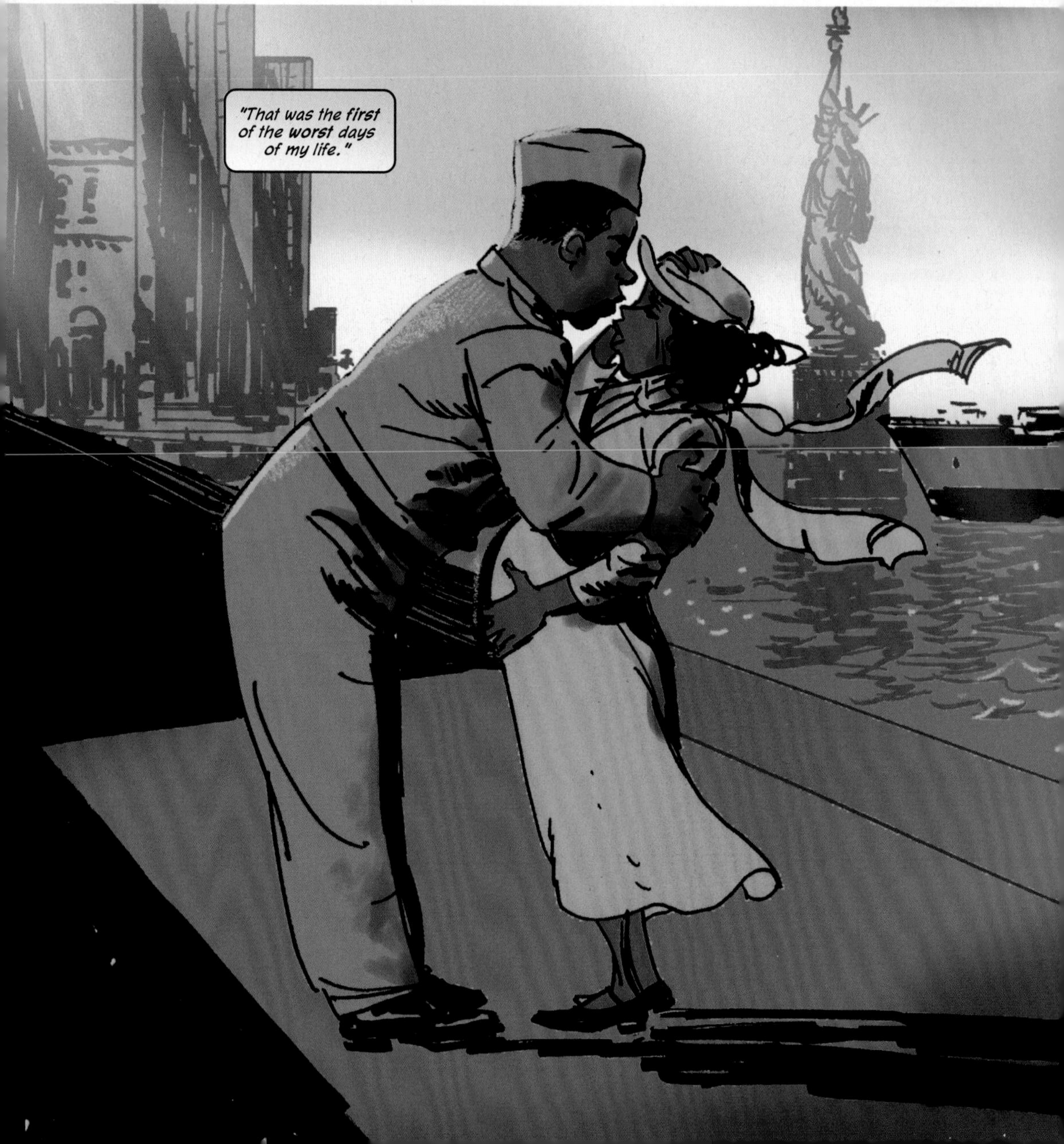
"That was the first of the worst days of my life."

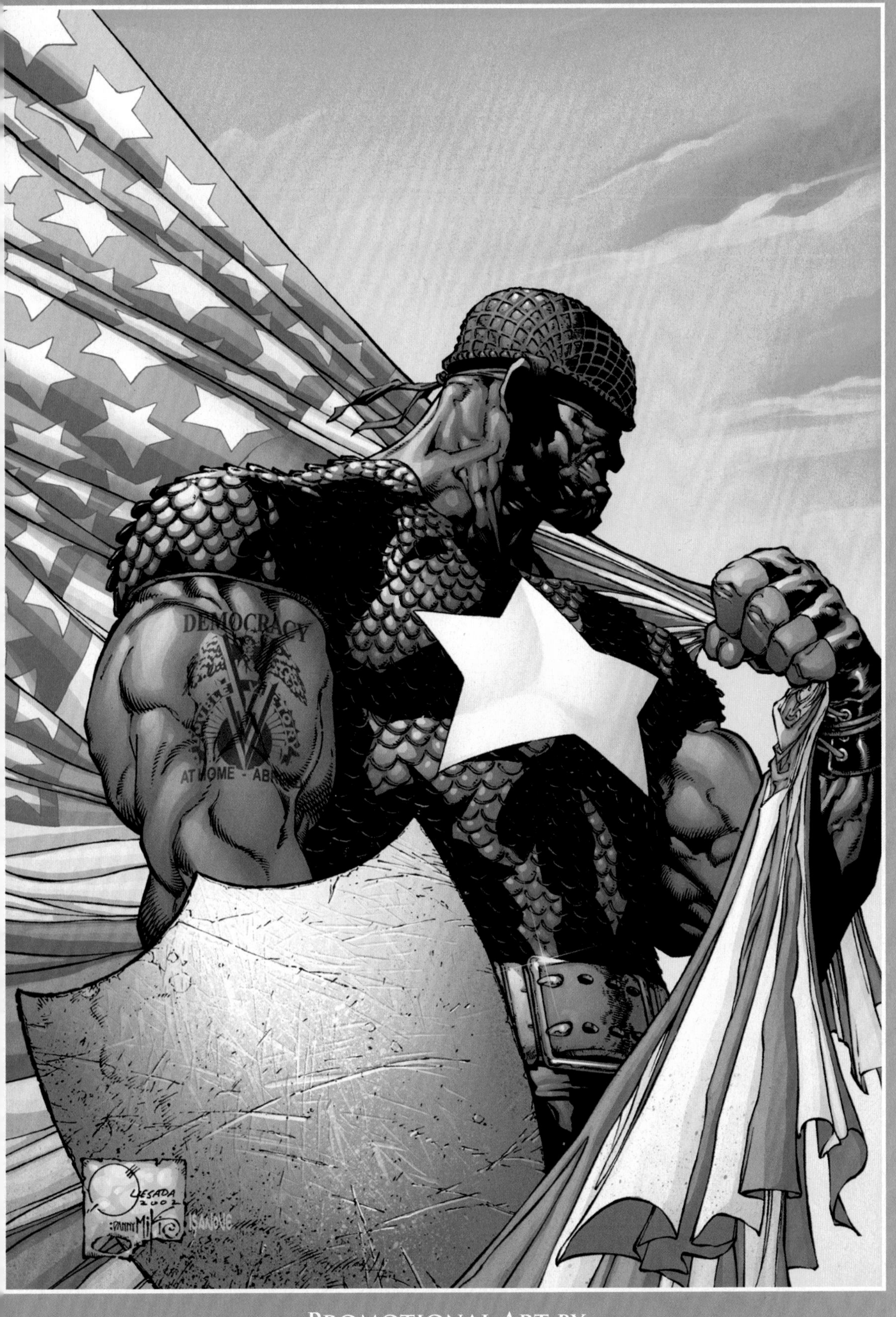
DEMOCRACY
AT HOME - ABR
QUESADA 2002
DANNY MIKI
ISANOVE

PROMOTIONAL ART BY
JOE QUESADA, DANNY MIKI & RICHARD ISANOVE

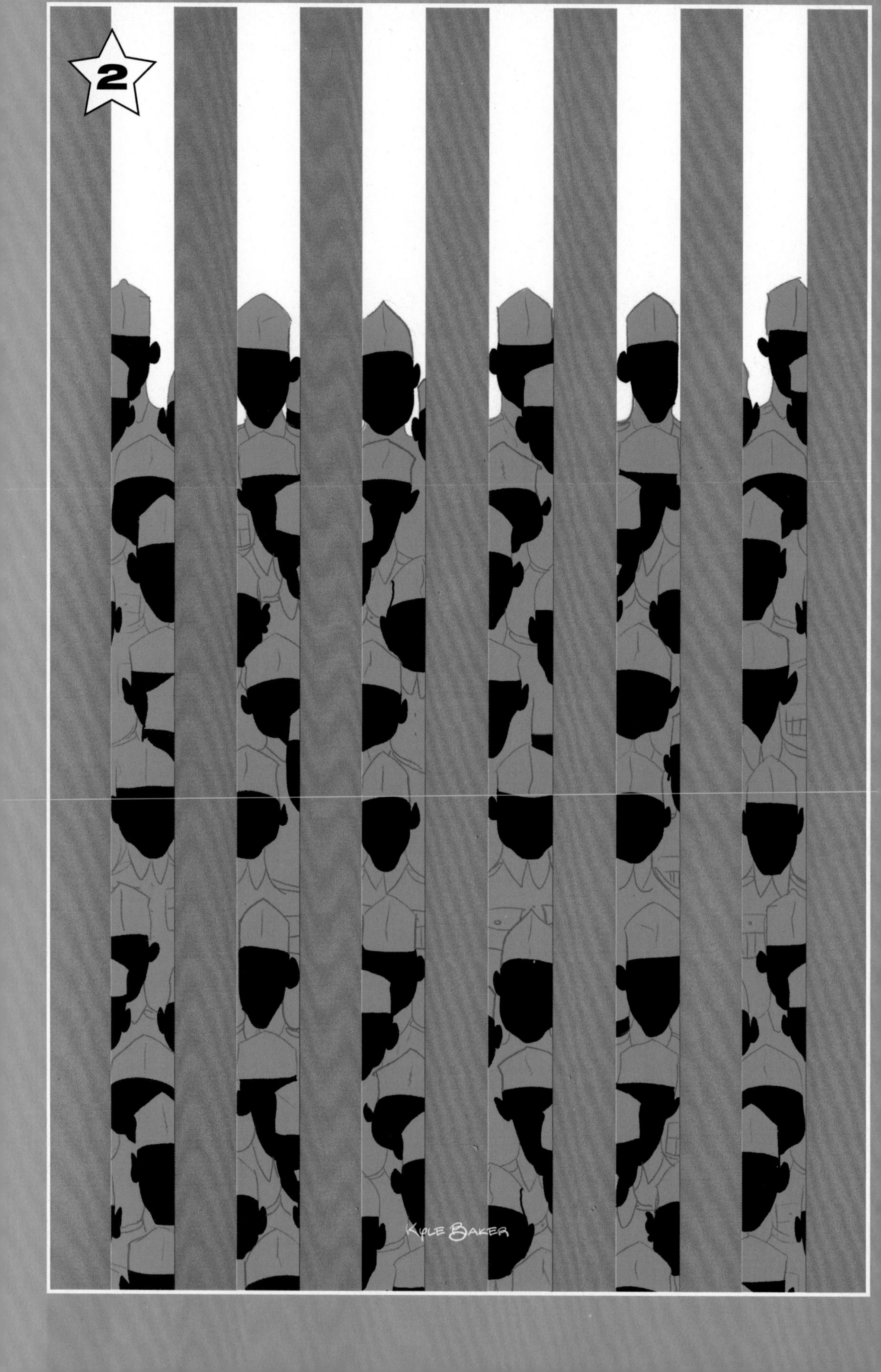
2
KYLE BAKER

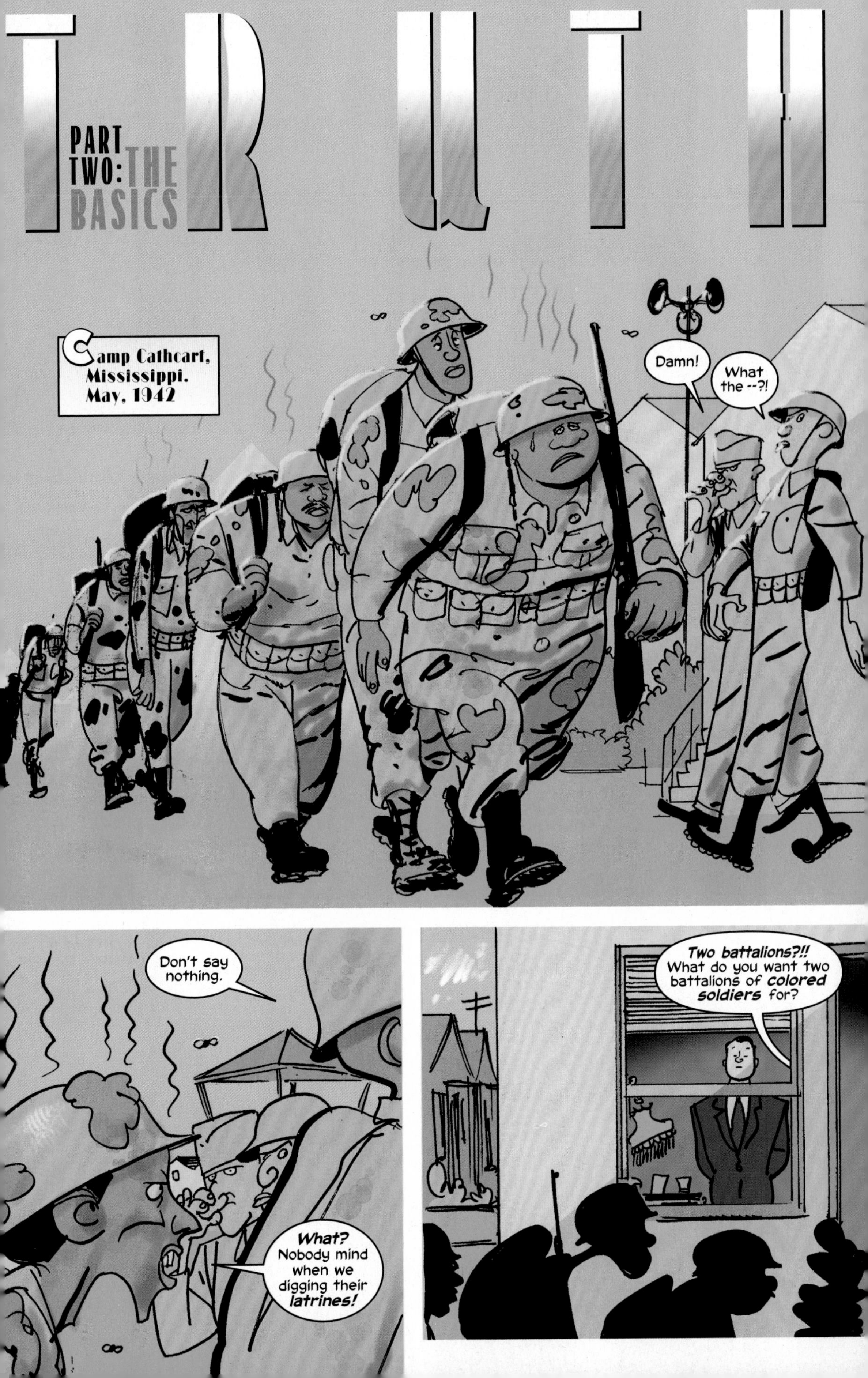
TRUTH
PART TWO: THE BASICS
Camp Cathcart, Mississippi. May, 1942
Damn!
What the --?!
Don't say nothing.
What? Nobody mind when we digging their latrines!
Two battalions?!! What do you want two battalions of colored soldiers for?

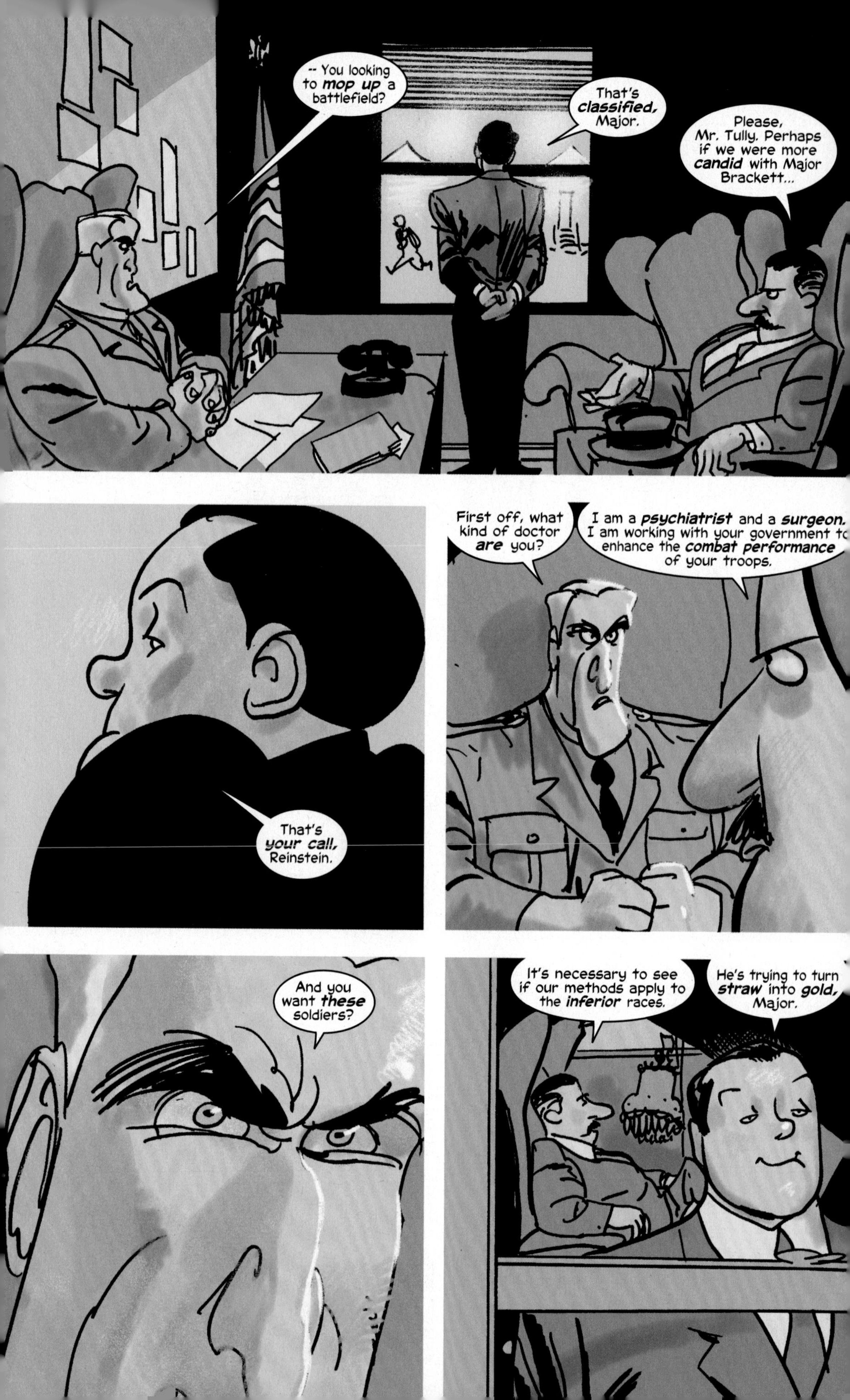
-- You looking to mop up a battlefield?
That's classified, Major.
Please, Mr. Tully. Perhaps if we were more candid with Major Brackett...
That's your call, Reinstein.
First off, what kind of doctor are you?
I am a psychiatrist and a surgeon. I am working with your government to enhance the combat performance of your troops.
And you want these soldiers?
It's necessary to see if our methods apply to the inferior races.
He's trying to turn straw into gold, Major.

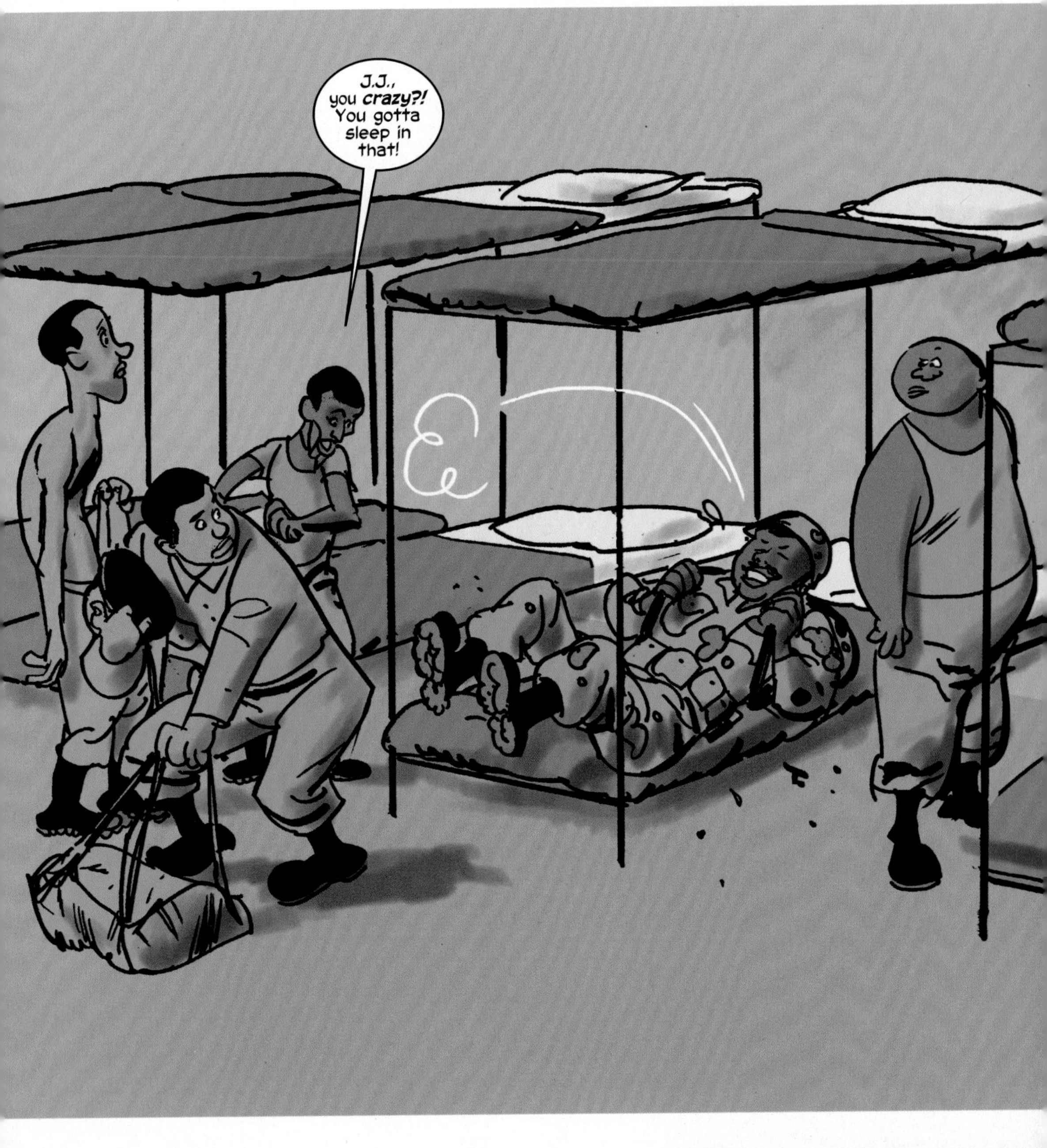
J.J., you crazy?! You gotta sleep in that!

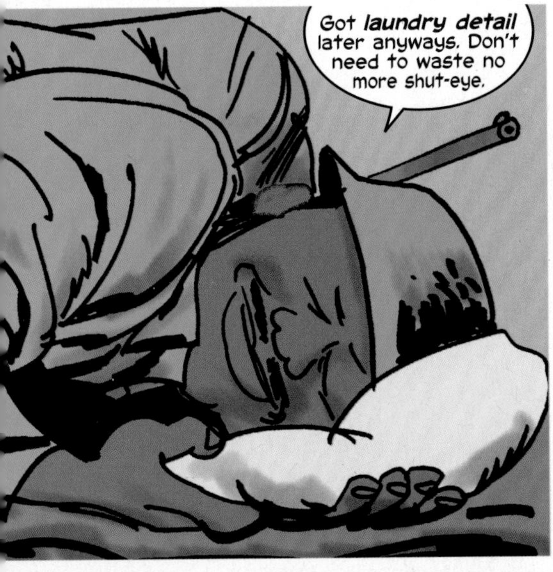
Got laundry detail later anyways. Don't need to waste no more shut-eye.

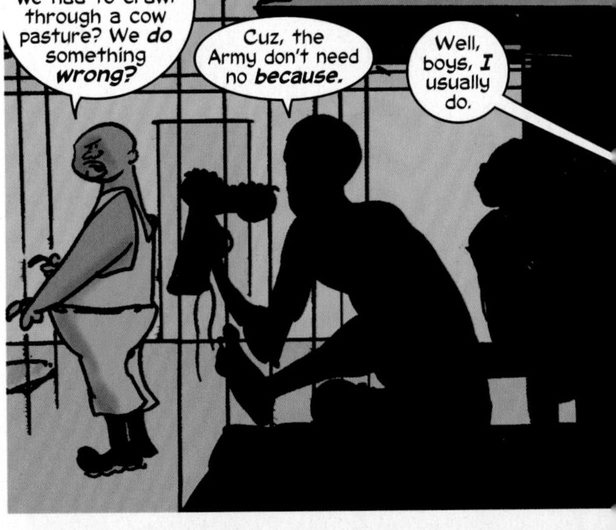
Guys, how come we had to crawl through a cow pasture? We do something wrong?
Cuz, the Army don't need no because.
Well, boys, I usually do.

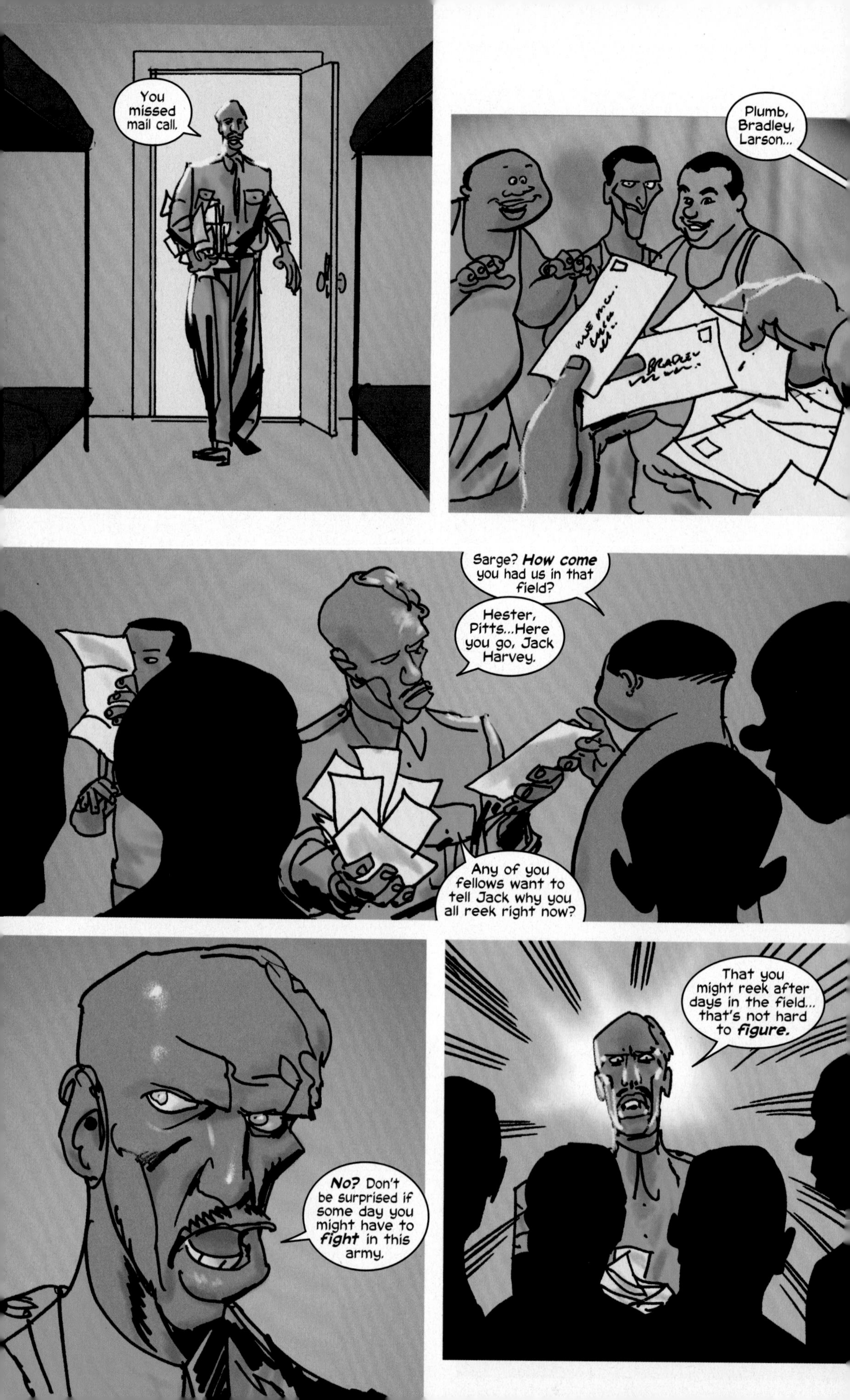
You missed mail call.
Plumb, Bradley, Larson...
Sarge? **How come** you had us in that field?
Hester, Pitts...Here you go, Jack Harvey.
Any of you fellows want to tell Jack why you all reek right now?
No? Don't be surprised if some day you might have to ***fight*** in this army.
That you might reek after days in the field... that's not hard to ***figure.***

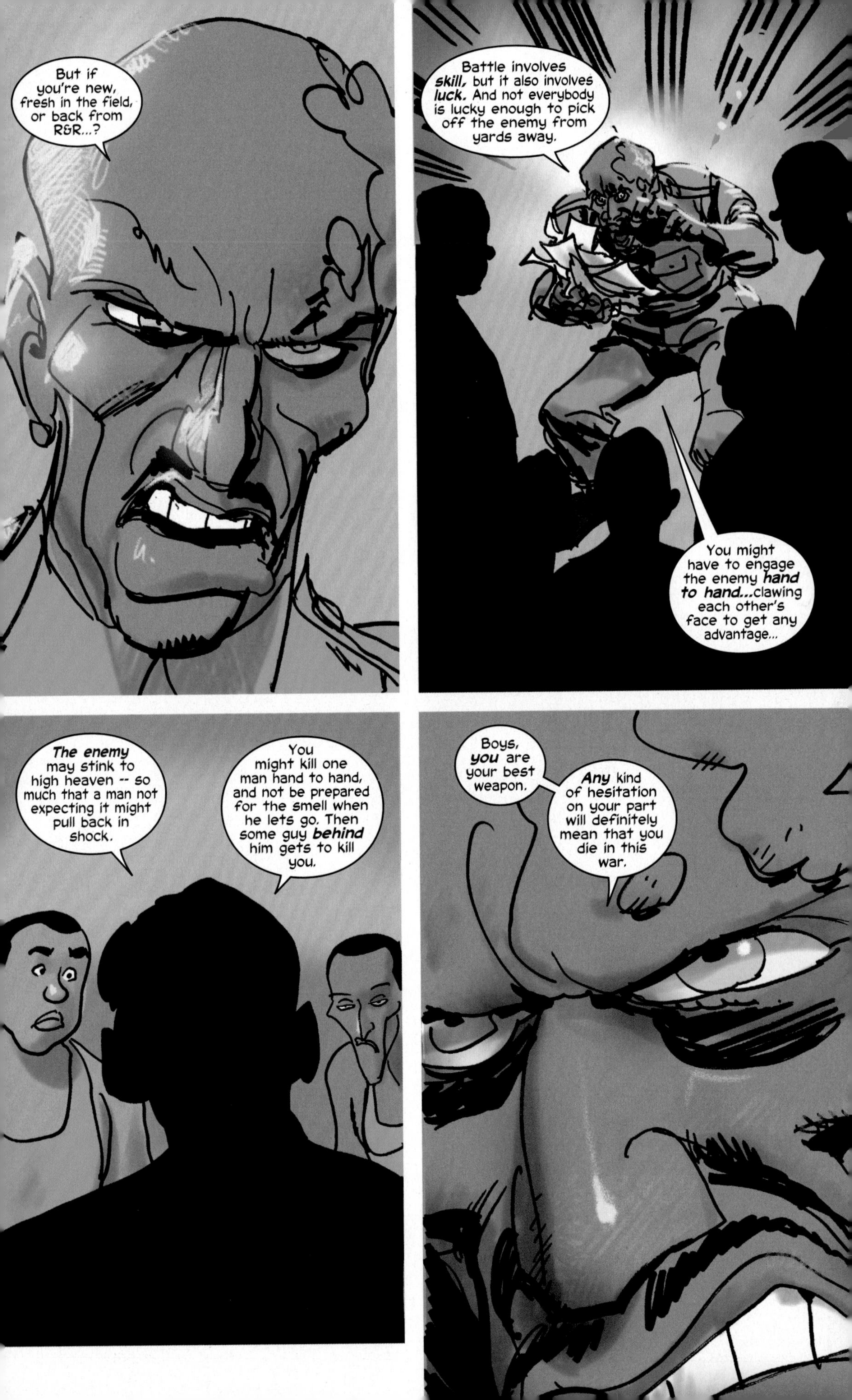
But if you're new, fresh in the field, or back from R&R...?
Battle involves **skill,** but it also involves **luck.** And not everybody is lucky enough to pick off the enemy from yards away.
You might have to engage the enemy **hand to hand...**clawing each other's face to get any advantage...
The enemy may stink to high heaven -- so much that a man not expecting it might pull back in shock.
You might kill one man hand to hand, and not be prepared for the smell when he lets go. Then some guy **behind** him gets to kill you.
Boys, **you** are your best weapon.
Any kind of hesitation on your part will definitely mean that you die in this war.

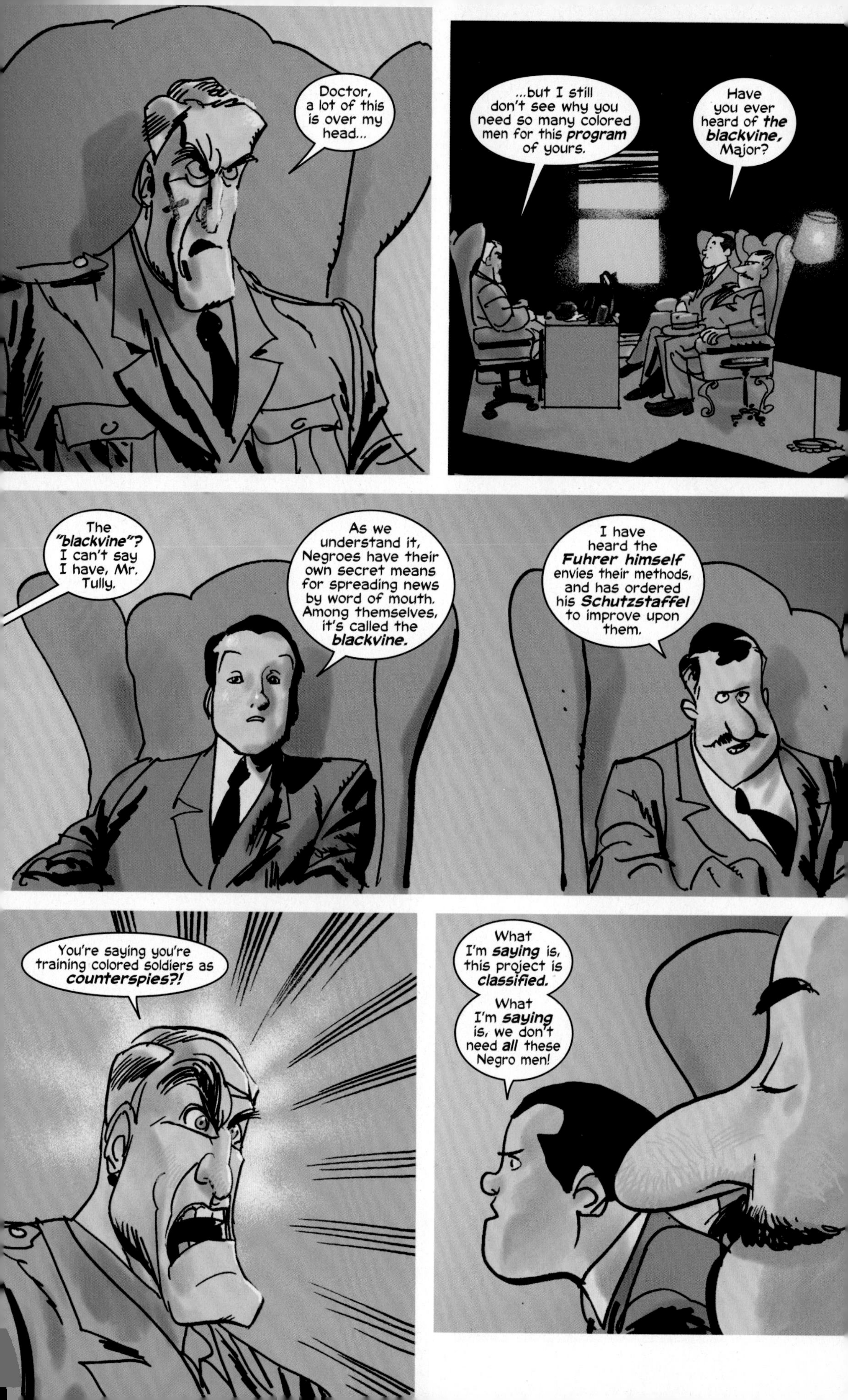
Doctor, a lot of this is over my head...
...but I still don't see why you need so many colored men for this *program* of yours.
Have you ever heard of ***the blackvine,*** Major?
The ***"blackvine"?*** I can't say I have, Mr. Tully.
As we understand it, Negroes have their own secret means for spreading news by word of mouth. Among themselves, it's called the ***blackvine.***
I have heard the ***Fuhrer himself*** envies their methods, and has ordered his ***Schutzstaffel*** to improve upon them.
You're saying you're training colored soldiers as ***counterspies?!***
What I'm ***saying*** is, this project is ***classified.***
What I'm ***saying*** is, we don't need ***all*** these Negro men!

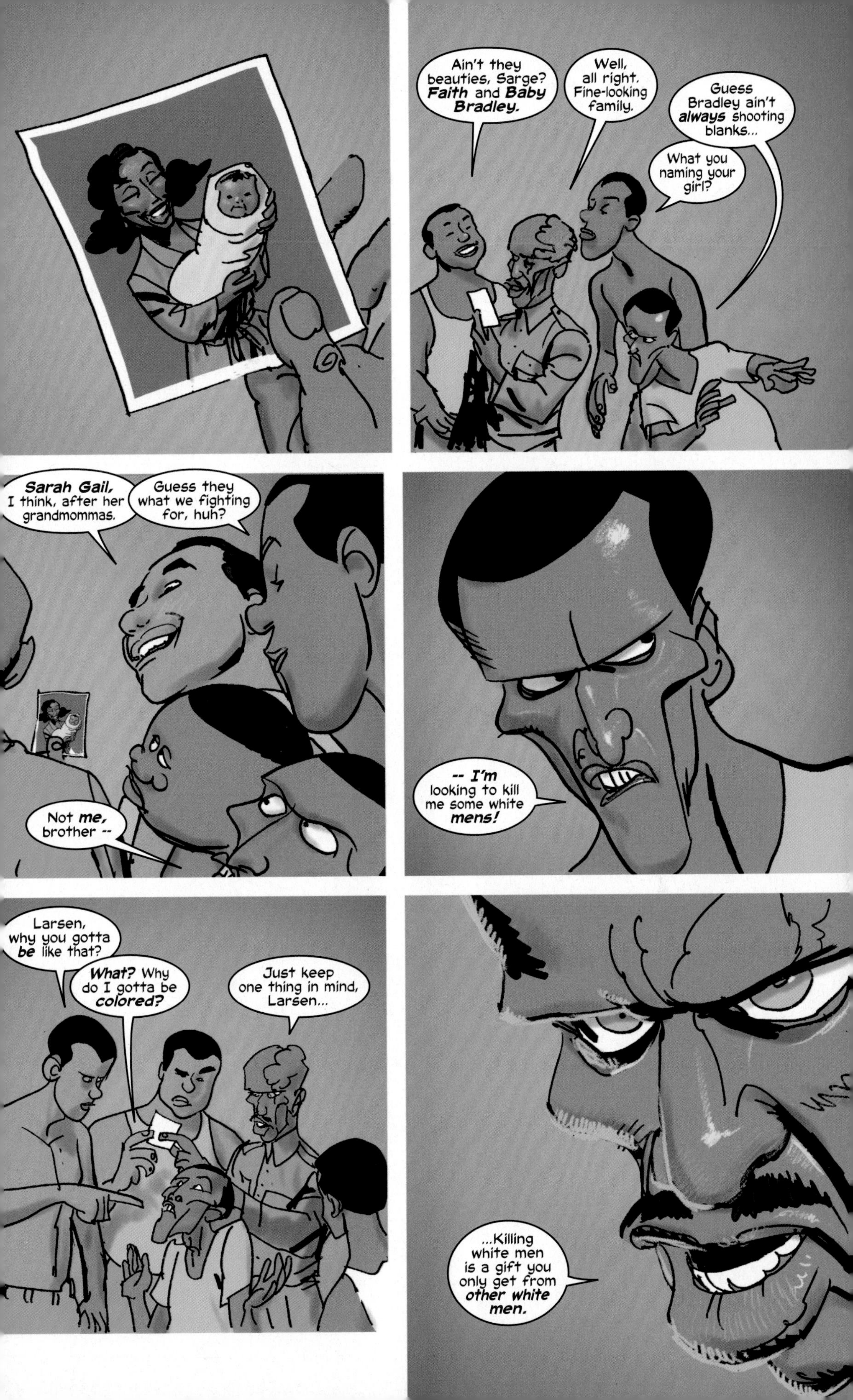

Ain't they beauties, Sarge? Faith and Baby Bradley.
Well, all right. Fine-looking family.
Guess Bradley ain't always shooting blanks...
What you naming your girl?
Sarah Gail, I think, after her grandmommas.
Guess they what we fighting for, huh?
Not me, brother --
-- I'm looking to kill me some white mens!
Larsen, why you gotta be like that?
What? Why do I gotta be colored?
Just keep one thing in mind, Larsen...
...Killing white men is a gift you only get from other white men.

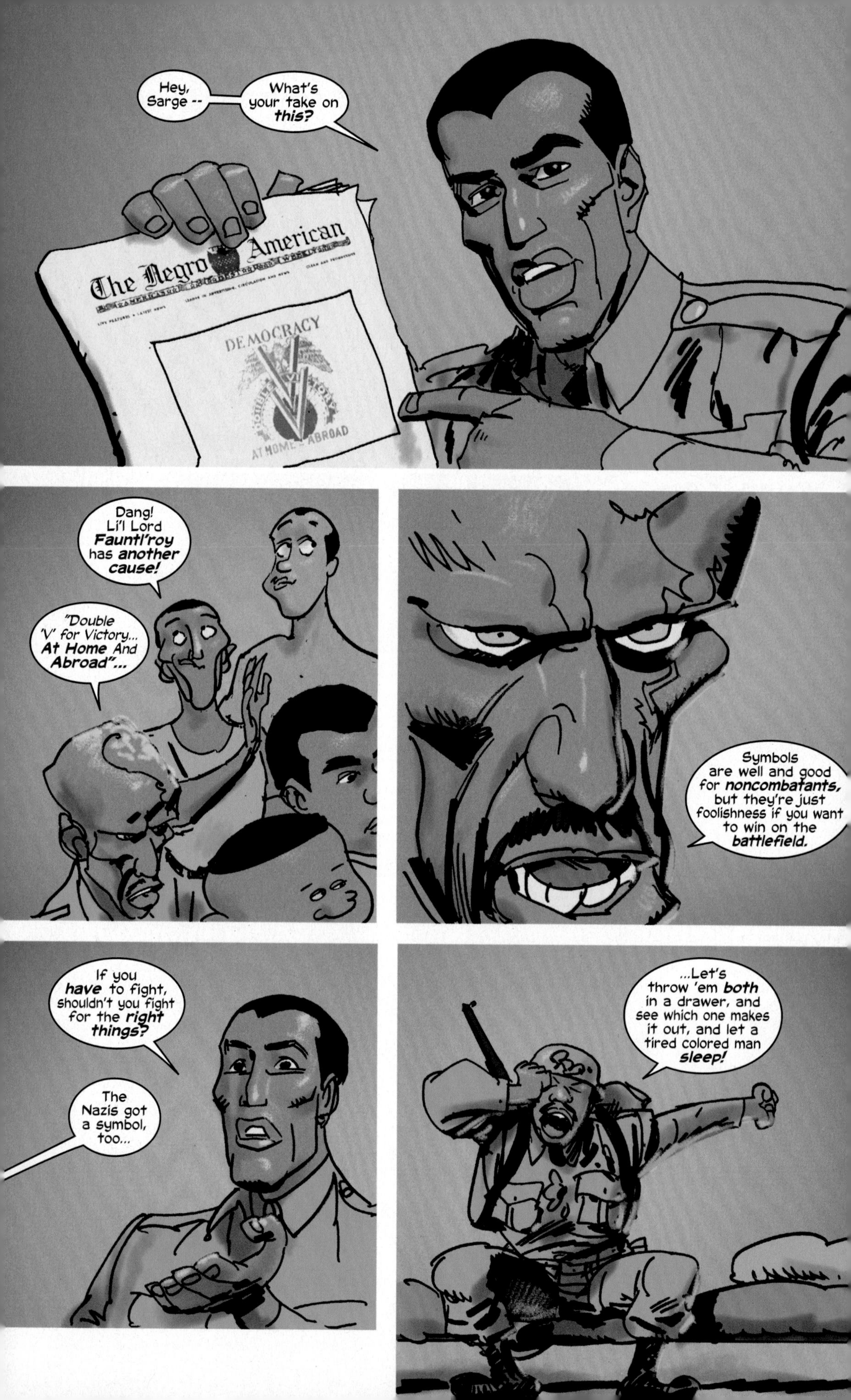

Hey, Sarge --
What's your take on *this?*
The Negro American
DEMOCRACY
Dang! Li'l Lord *Fauntl'roy* has *another cause!*
"Double 'V' for Victory... **At Home** And **Abroad"...**
Symbols are well and good for **noncombatants,** but they're just foolishness if you want to win on the ***battlefield.***
If you ***have*** to fight, shouldn't you fight for the ***right things?***
The Nazis got a symbol, too...
...Let's throw 'em ***both*** in a drawer, and see which one makes it out, and let a tired colored man ***sleep!***

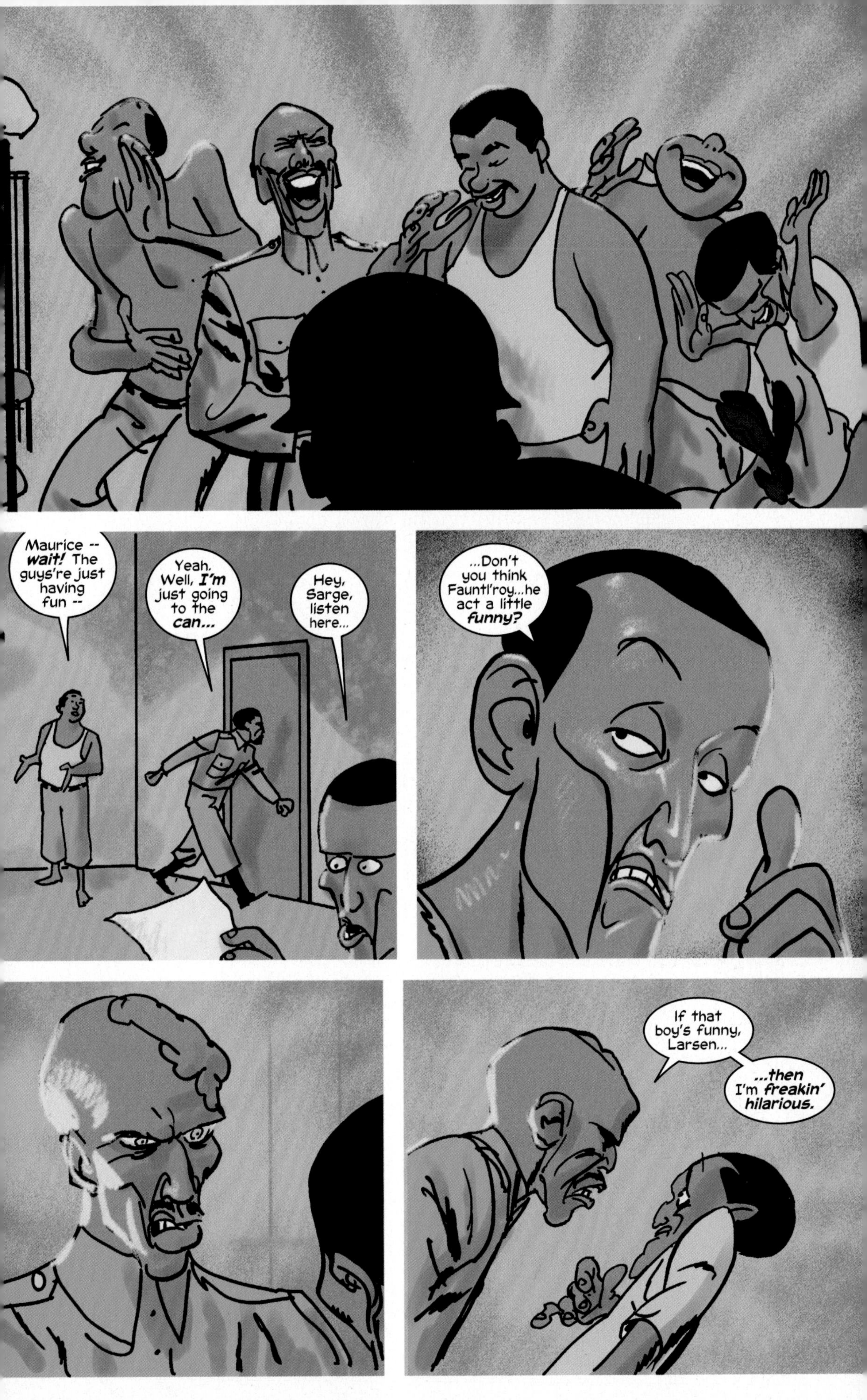
Maurice -- wait! The guys're just having fun --
Yeah. Well, I'm just going to the can...
Hey, Sarge, listen here...
...Don't you think Fauntl'roy...he act a little funny?
If that boy's funny, Larsen...
...then I'm freakin' hilarious.

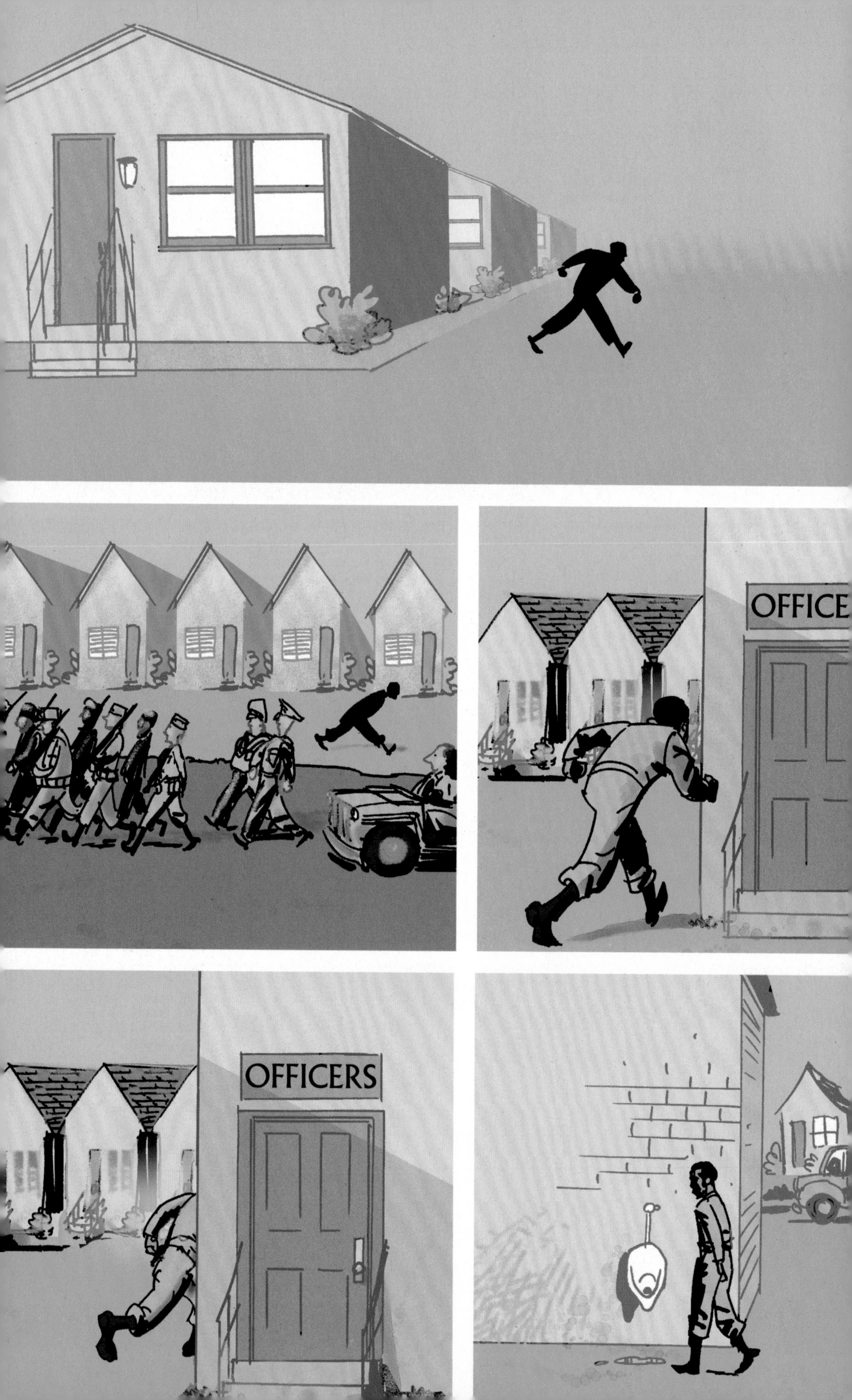
OFFICE
OFFICERS

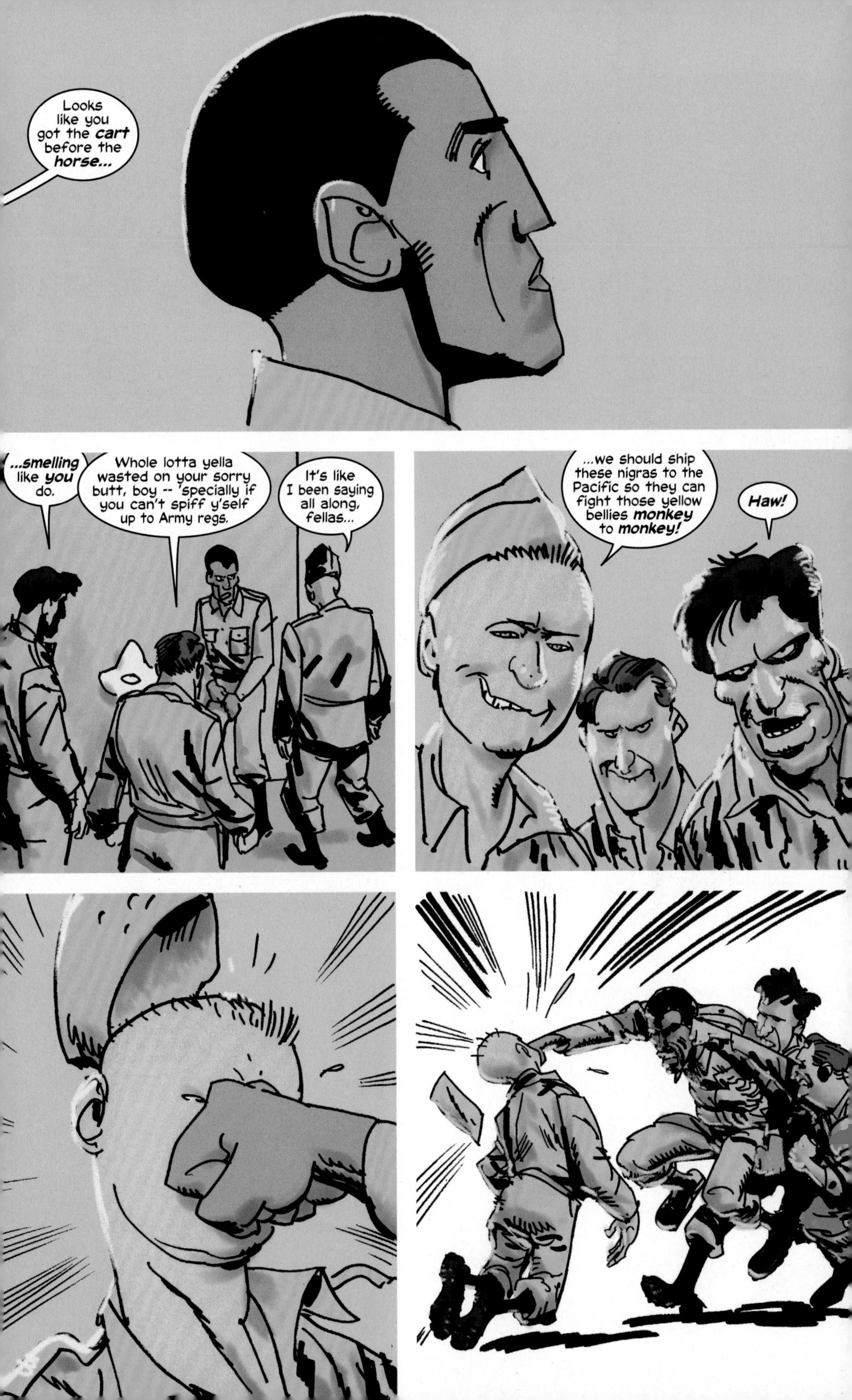
Looks like you got the *cart* before the *horse...*
...smelling like *you* do.
Whole lotta yella wasted on your sorry butt, boy -- 'specially if you can't spiff y'self up to Army regs.
It's like I been saying all along, fellas...
...we should ship these nigras to the Pacific so they can fight those yellow bellies *monkey* to *monkey!*
Haw!

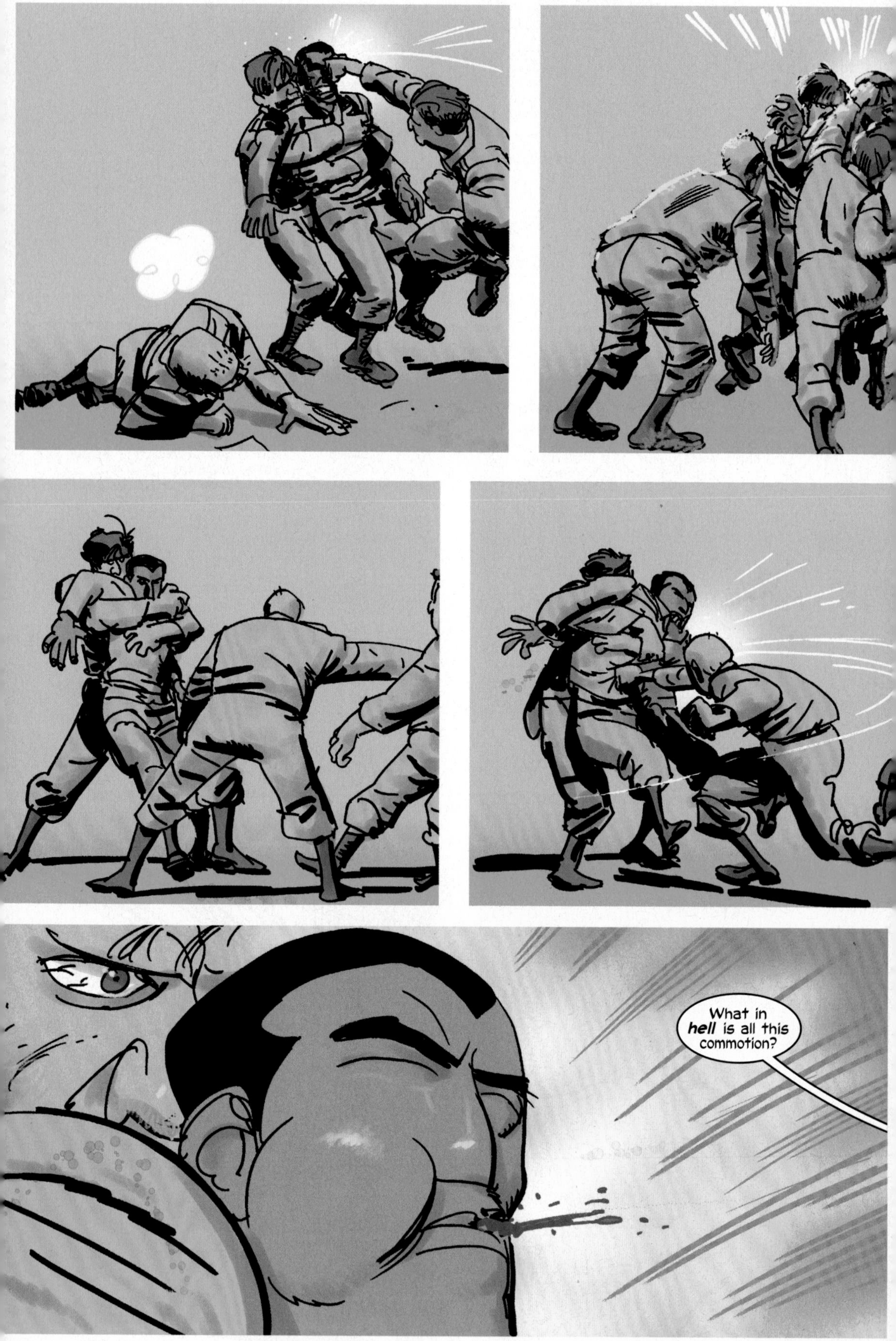
What in
hell is all this
commotion?

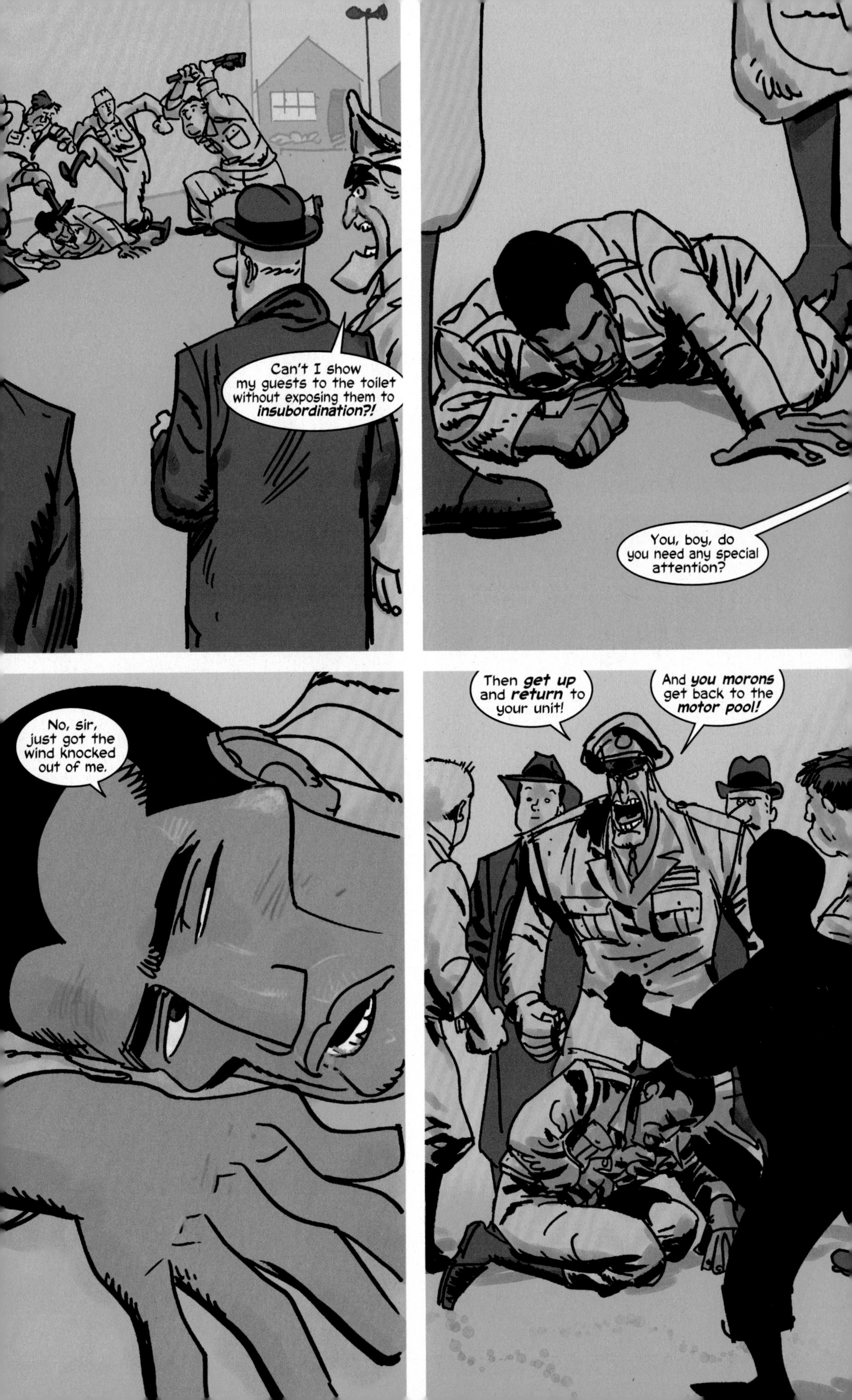
Can't I show my guests to the toilet without exposing them to *insubordination?!*
You, boy, do you need any special attention?
No, sir, just got the wind knocked out of me.
Then *get up* and *return* to your unit!
And *you morons* get back to the *motor pool!*

What you *do* to get'm mad?

Larsen --

What the hell *happened* to *you*, Canfield?

I got set upon by those unable to comprehend the *plumbing* needs of the average Negro soldier.

No fooling? They *see* anything?

Well, Sarge -- honestly, how could they *not?*

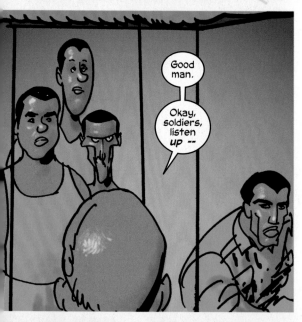

Good man.

Okay, soldiers, listen *up --*

At 2300 hours tonight, we are to take part in a special *night training exercise.*

We'll be traveling light, without weapons or gear, to a *classified* location where we will then receive further orders.

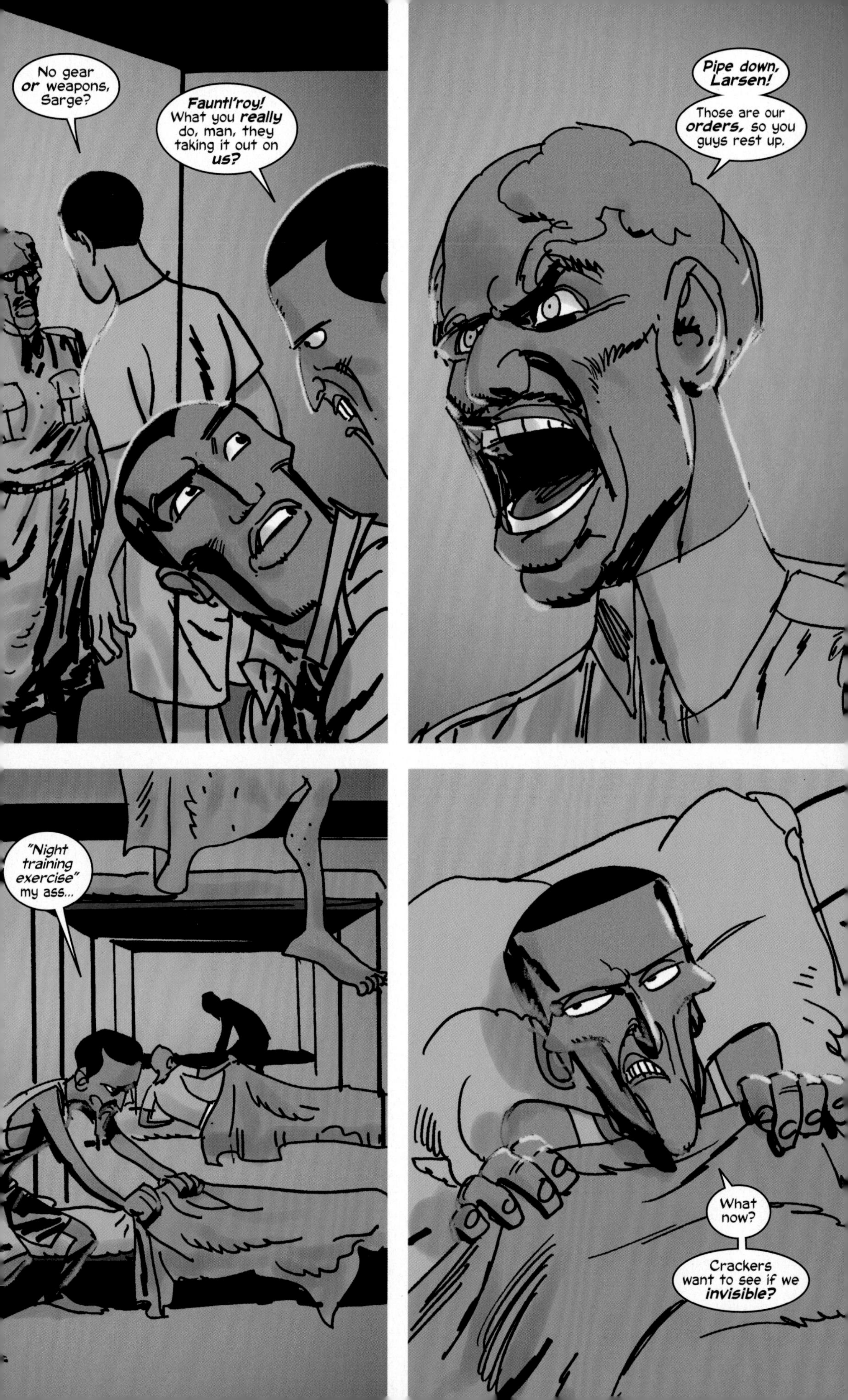
No gear **or** weapons, Sarge?
Fauntl'roy! What you **really** do, man, they taking it out on **us?**
Pipe down, Larsen!
Those are our **orders,** so you guys rest up.
"Night training exercise" my ass...
What now?
Crackers want to see if we **invisible?**

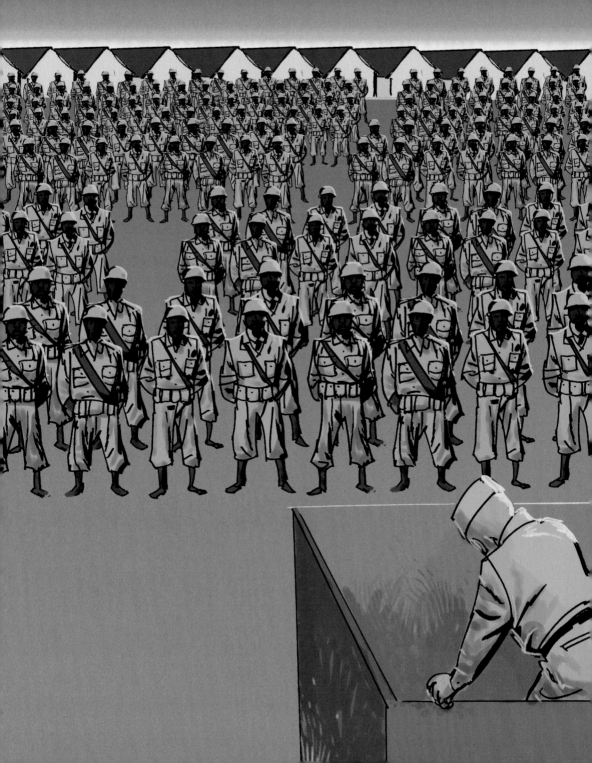

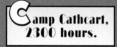

Camp Cathcart,
2300 hours.

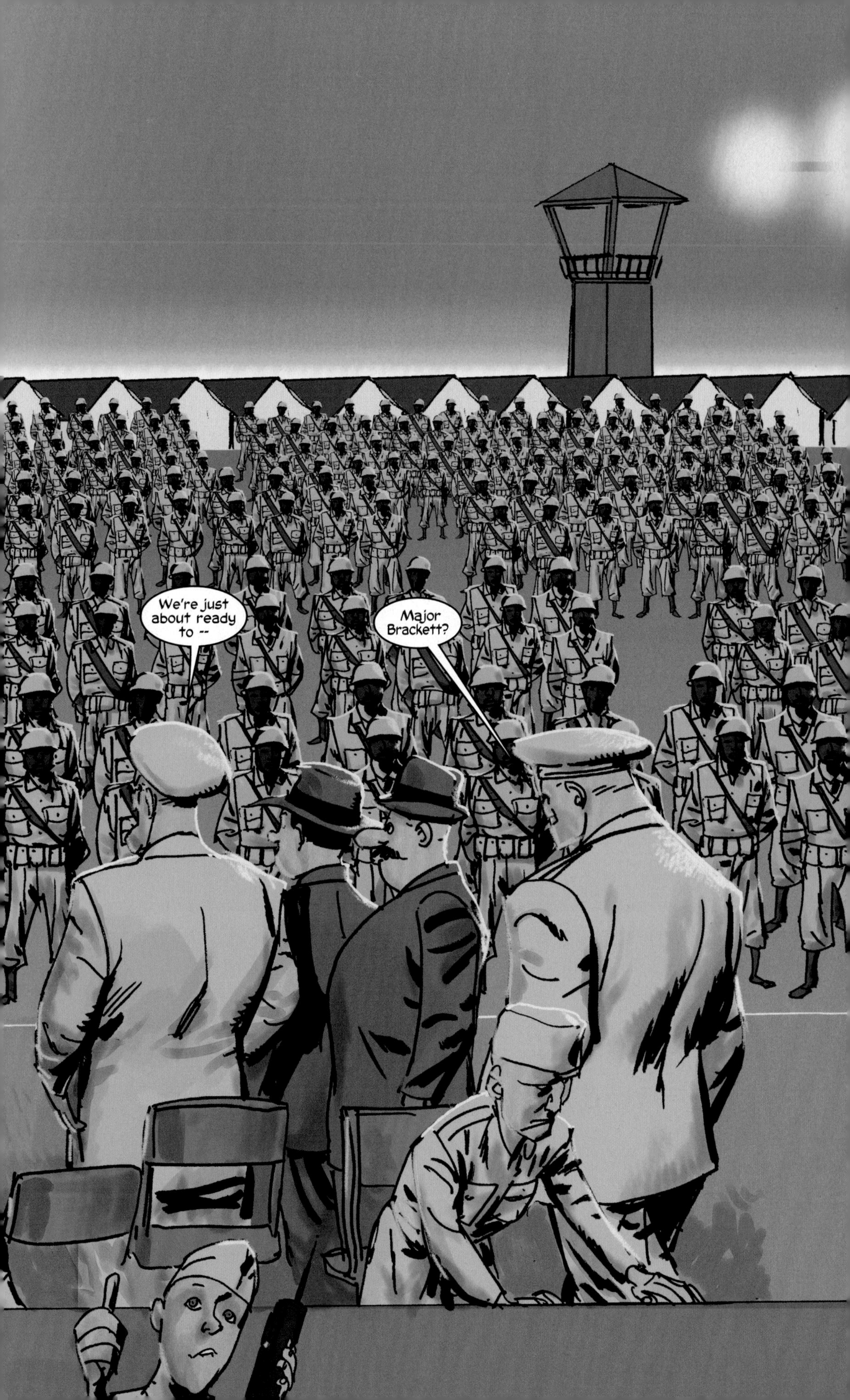

We're just about ready to --
Major Brackett?

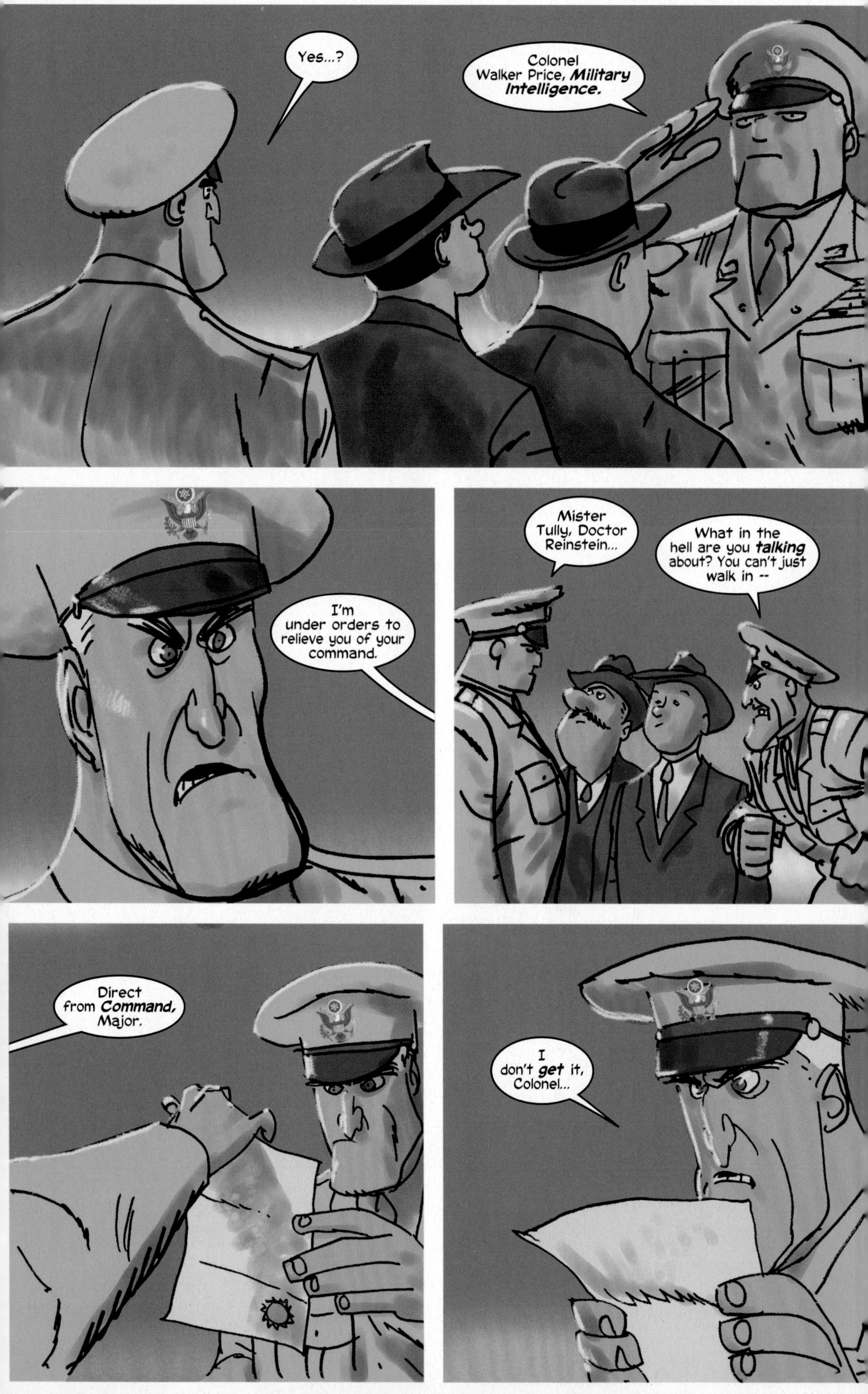
Yes...?
Colonel Walker Price, **Military Intelligence.**
I'm under orders to relieve you of your command.
Mister Tully, Doctor Reinstein...
What in the hell are you **talking** about? You can't just walk in --
Direct from **Command,** Major.
I don't **get** it, Colonel...

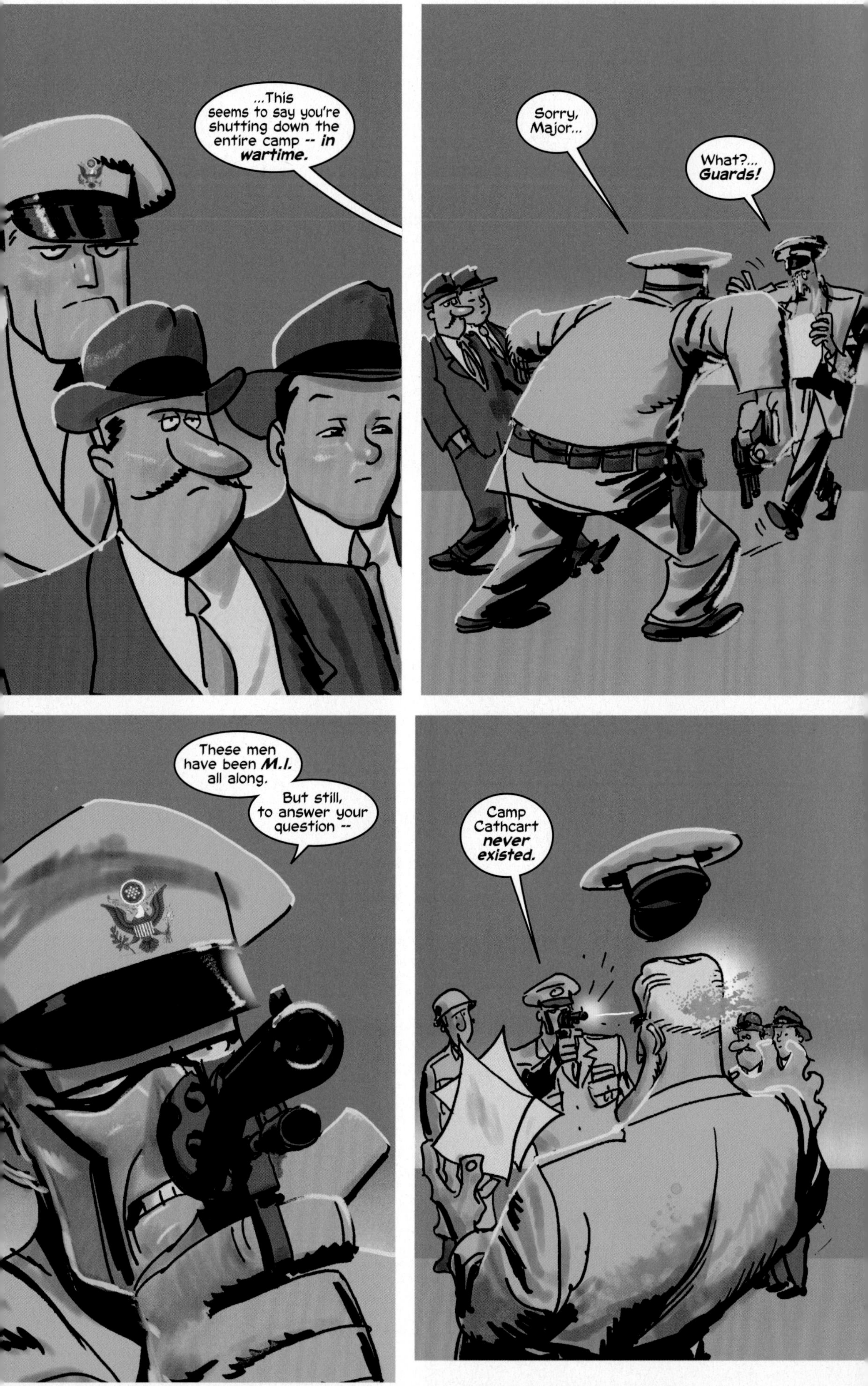
...This seems to say you're shutting down the entire camp -- ***in wartime.***
Sorry, Major...
What?... ***Guards!***
These men have been ***M.I.*** all along.
But still, to answer your question --
Camp Cathcart ***never existed.***

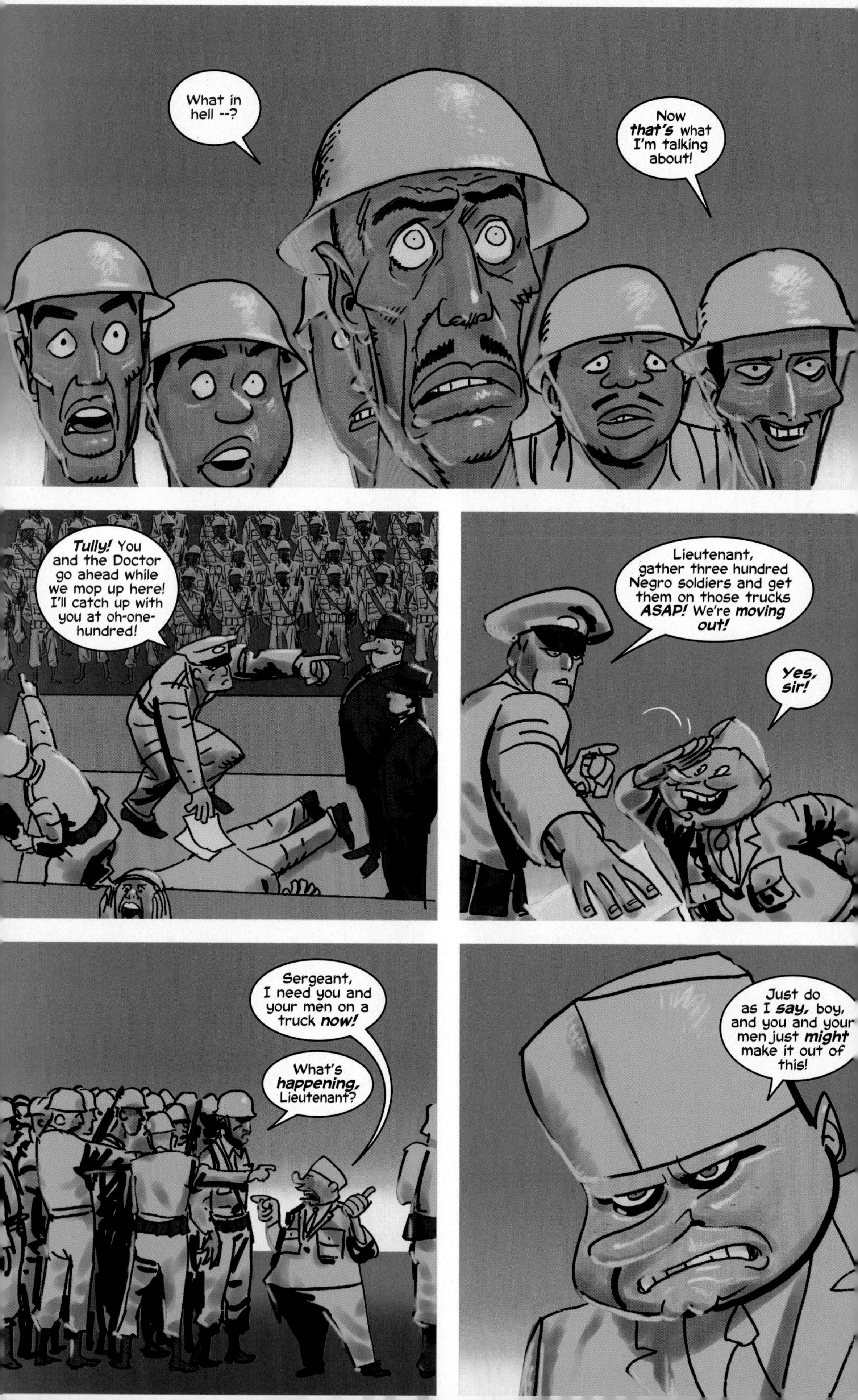
What in hell --?
Now ***that's*** what I'm talking about!
Tully! You and the Doctor go ahead while we mop up here! I'll catch up with you at oh-one-hundred!
Lieutenant, gather three hundred Negro soldiers and get them on those trucks ***ASAP!*** We're ***moving out!***
Yes, sir!
Sergeant, I need you and your men on a truck ***now!***
What's ***happening,*** Lieutenant?
Just do as I ***say,*** boy, and you and your men just ***might*** make it out of this!

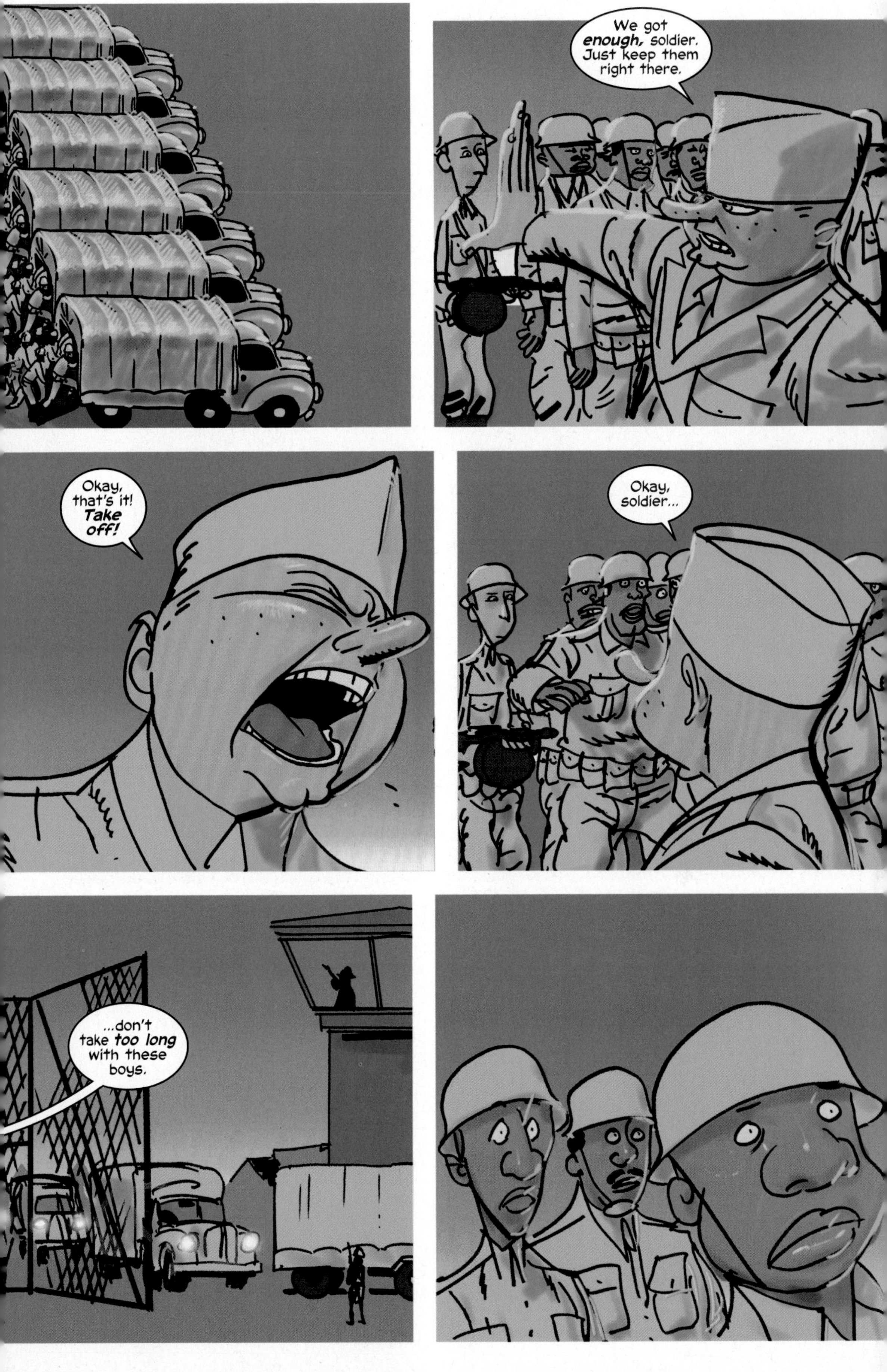
We got enough, soldier. Just keep them right there.
Okay, that's it! Take off!
Okay, soldier...
...don't take too long with these boys.

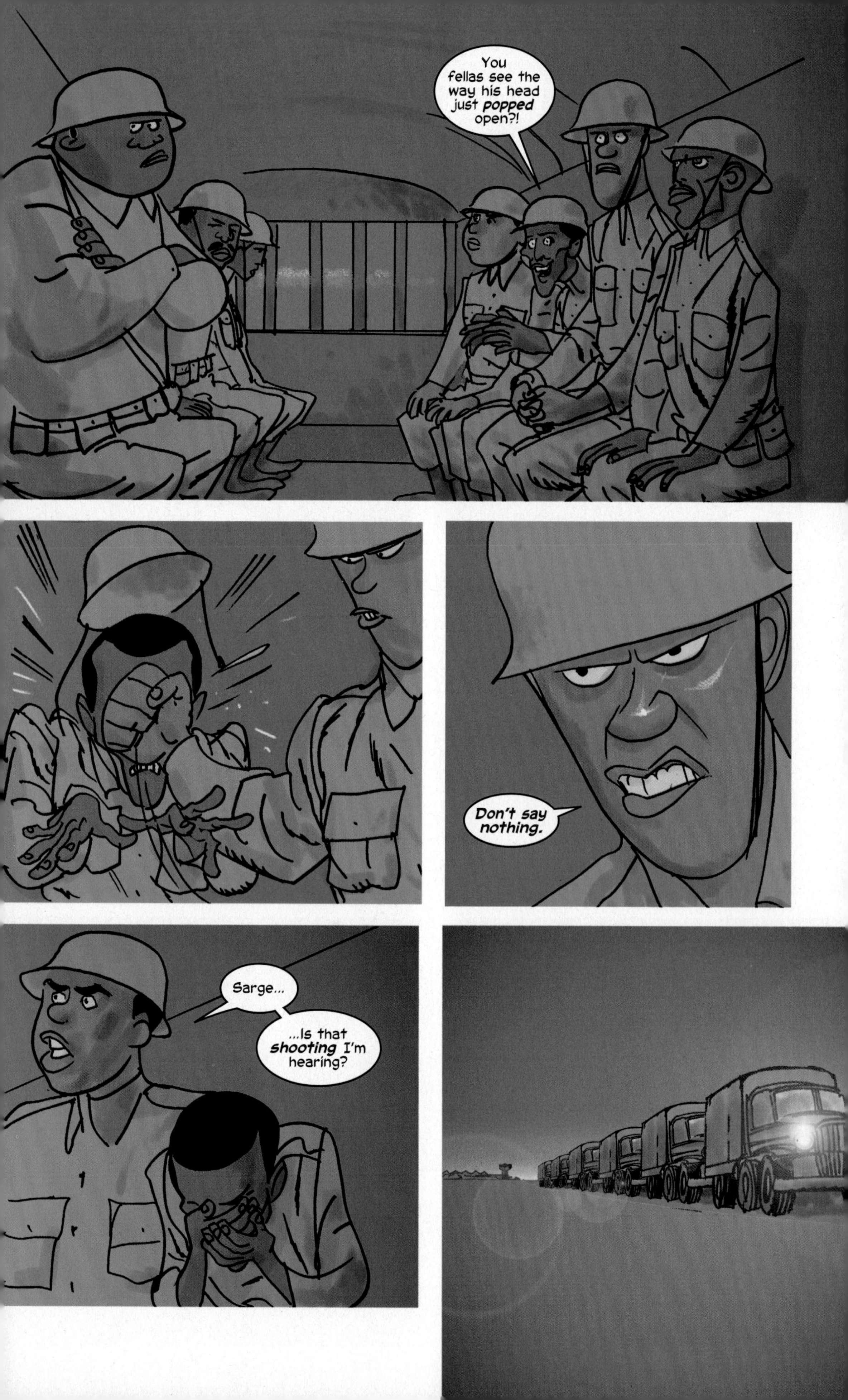
You fellas see the way his head just *popped* open?!
Don't say nothing.
Sarge...
...Is that *shooting* I'm hearing?

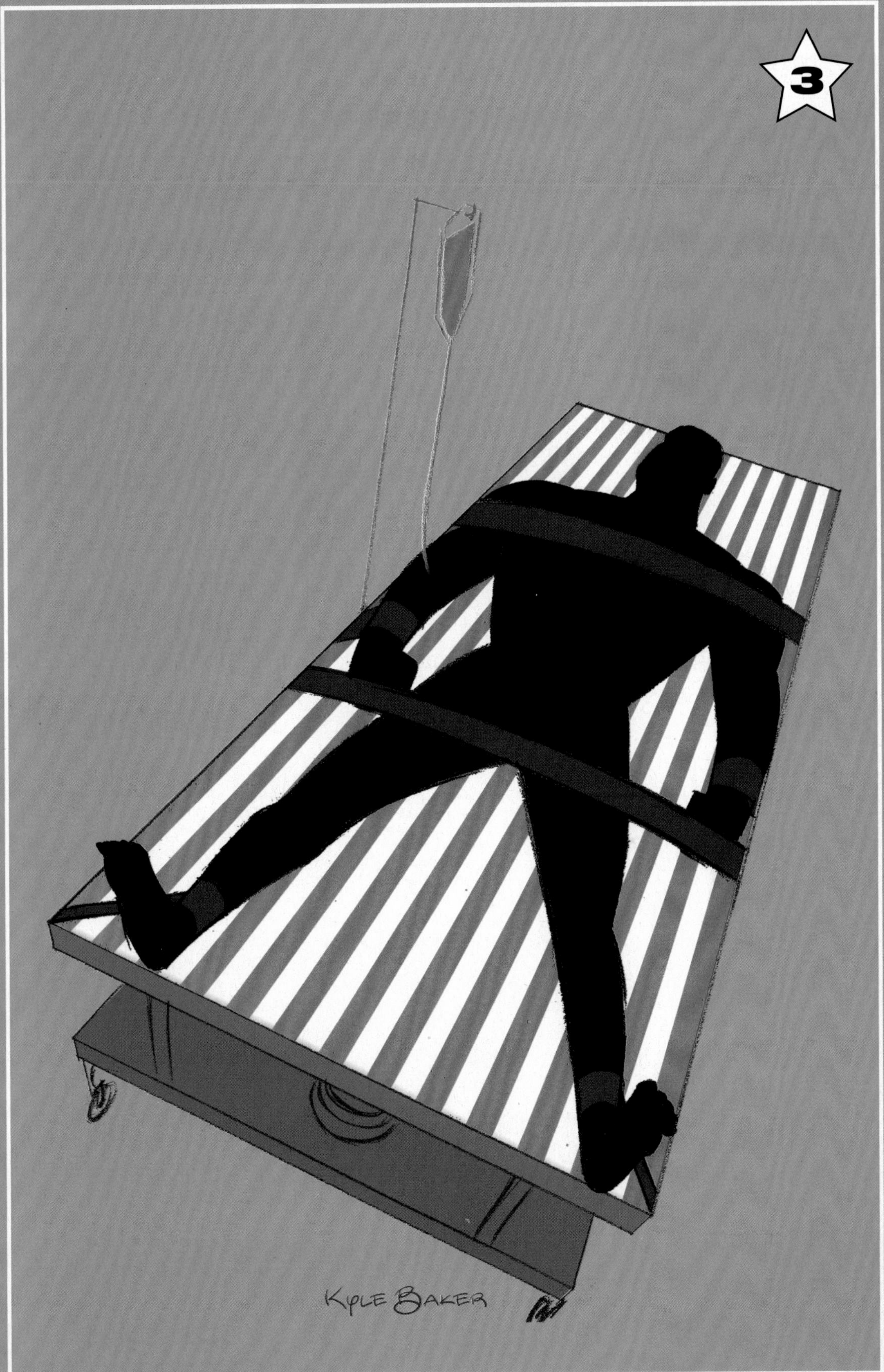
3
KYLE BAKER

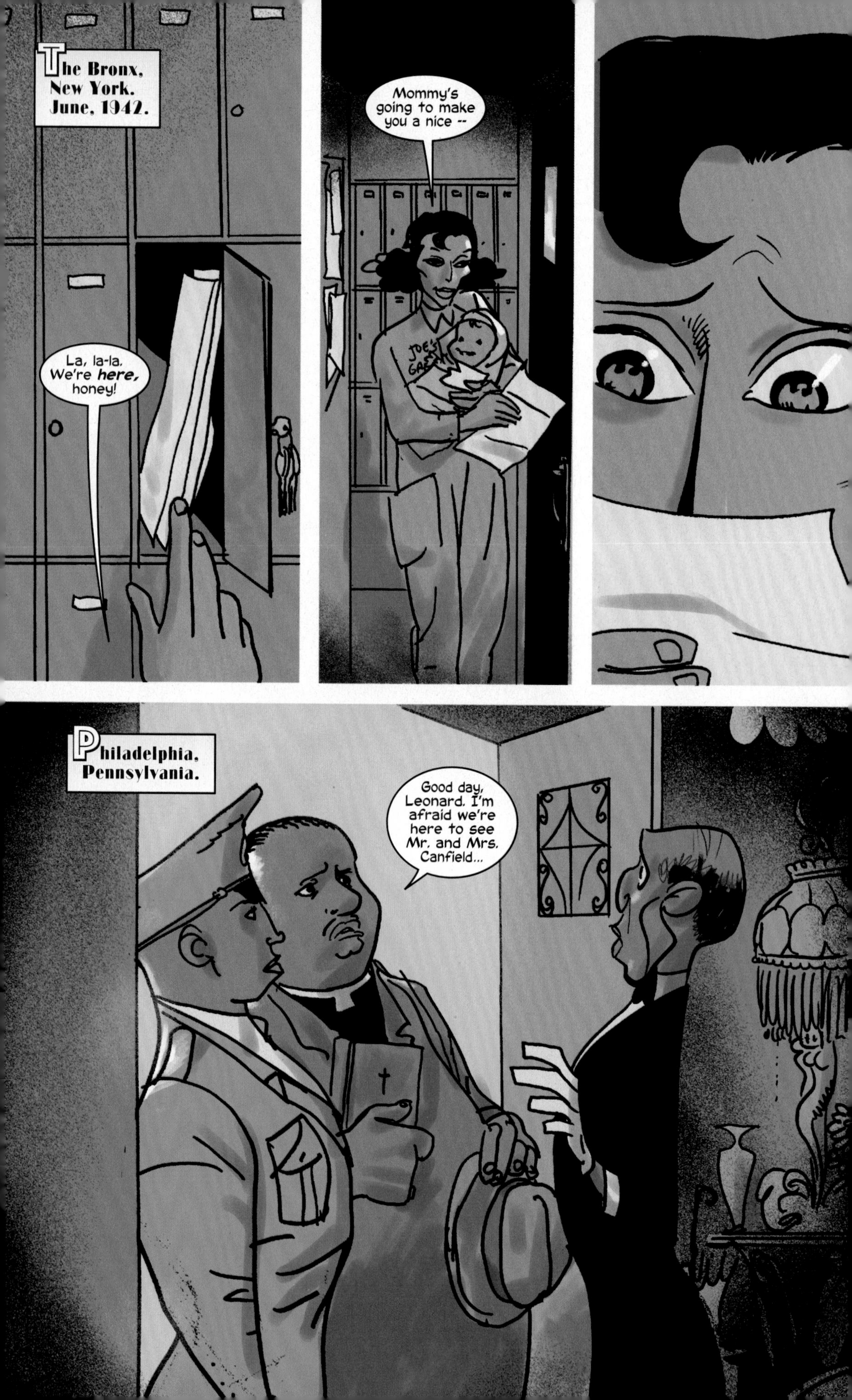
The Bronx, New York. June, 1942.
La, la-la. We're *here,* honey!
Mommy's going to make you a nice --
JOE'S GREASE
Philadelphia, Pennsylvania.
Good day, Leonard. I'm afraid we're here to see Mr. and Mrs. Canfield...

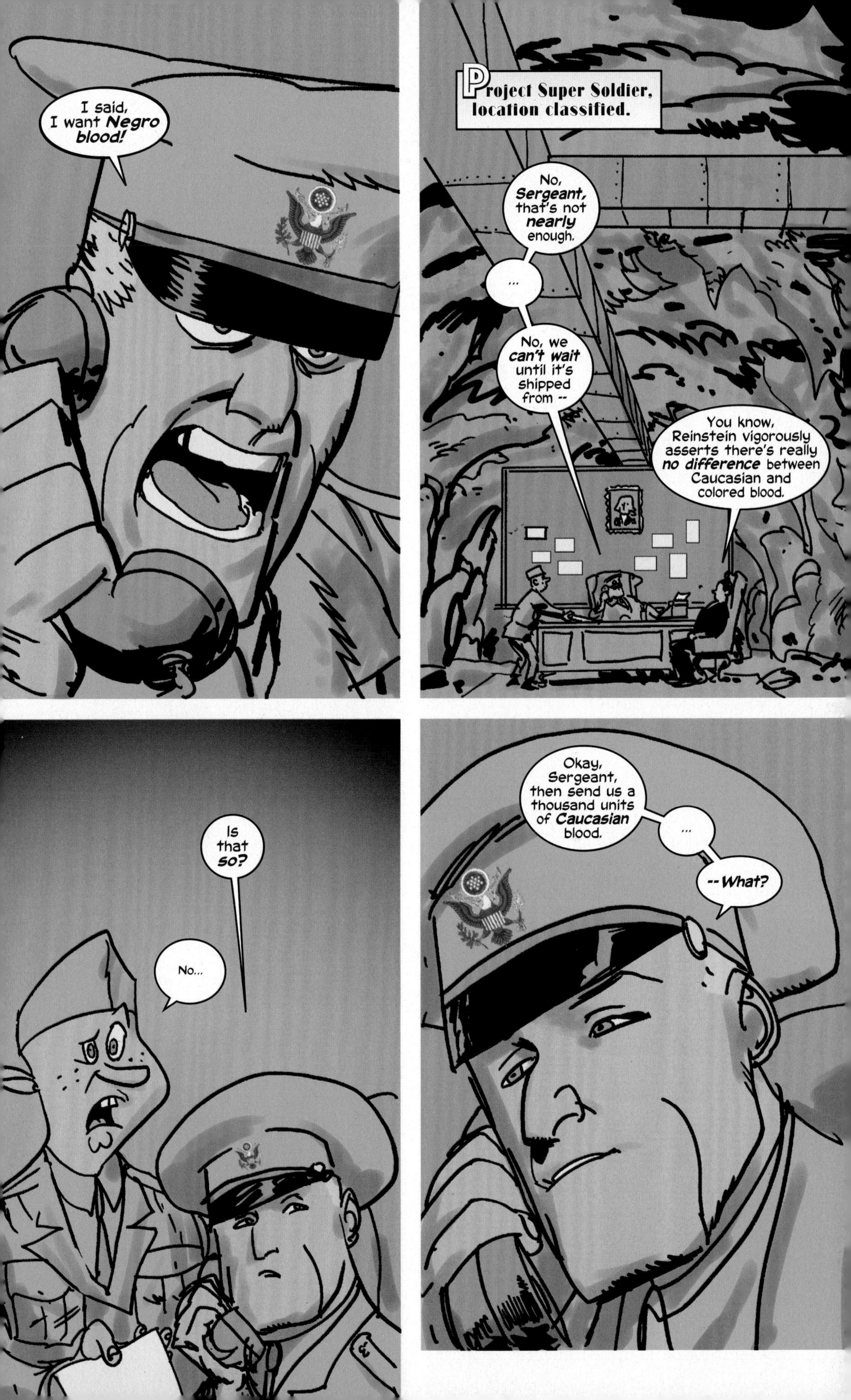
I said, I want Negro blood!
Project Super Soldier, location classified.
No, Sergeant, that's not nearly enough.
...
No, we can't wait until it's shipped from --
You know, Reinstein vigorously asserts there's really no difference between Caucasian and colored blood.
Is that so?
No...
Okay, Sergeant, then send us a thousand units of Caucasian blood.
...
--What?

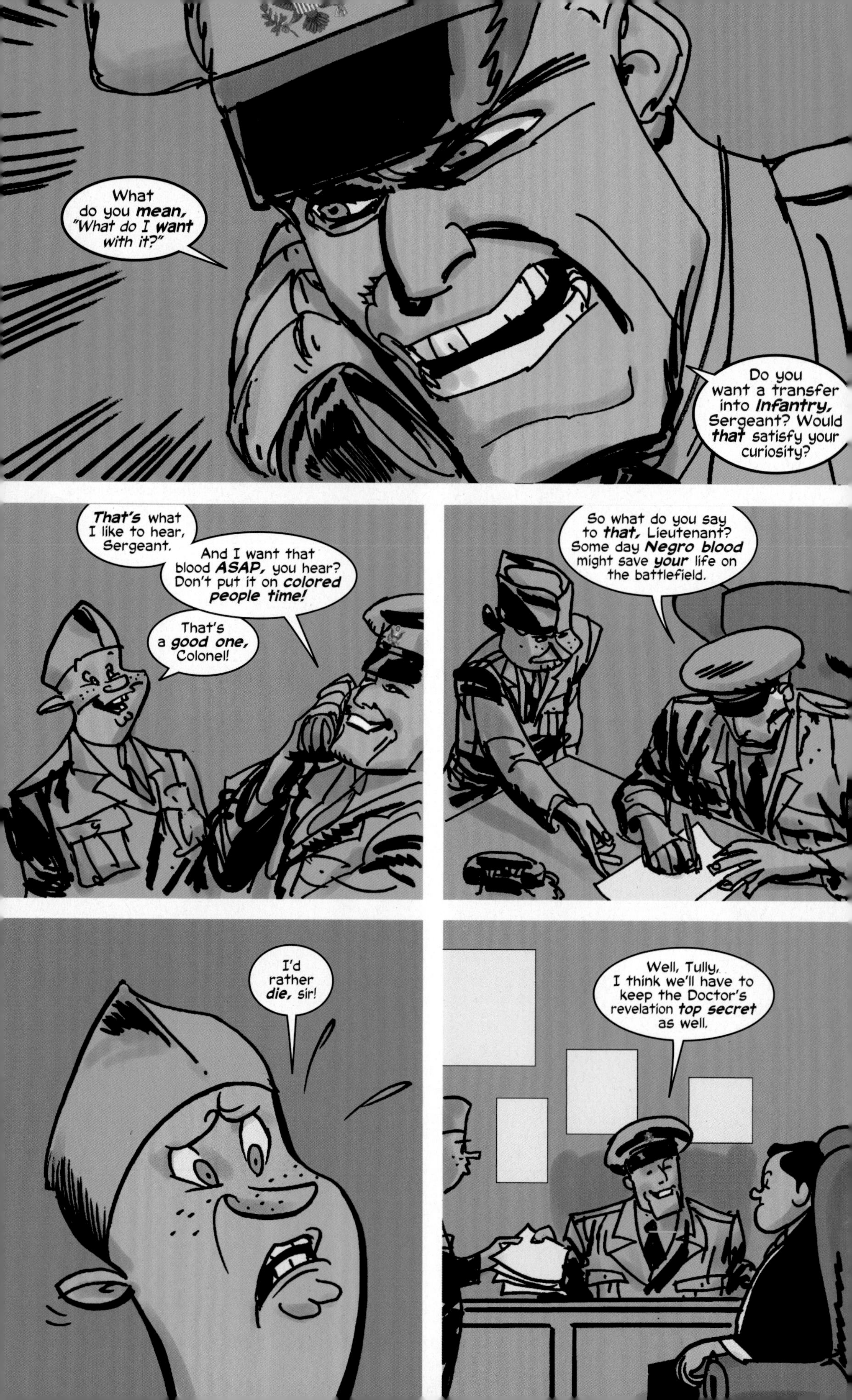
What do you mean, "What do I want with it?"
Do you want a transfer into Infantry, Sergeant? Would that satisfy your curiosity?
That's what I like to hear, Sergeant.
And I want that blood ASAP, you hear? Don't put it on colored people time!
That's a good one, Colonel!
So what do you say to that, Lieutenant? Some day Negro blood might save your life on the battlefield.
I'd rather die, sir!
Well, Tully, I think we'll have to keep the Doctor's revelation top secret as well.

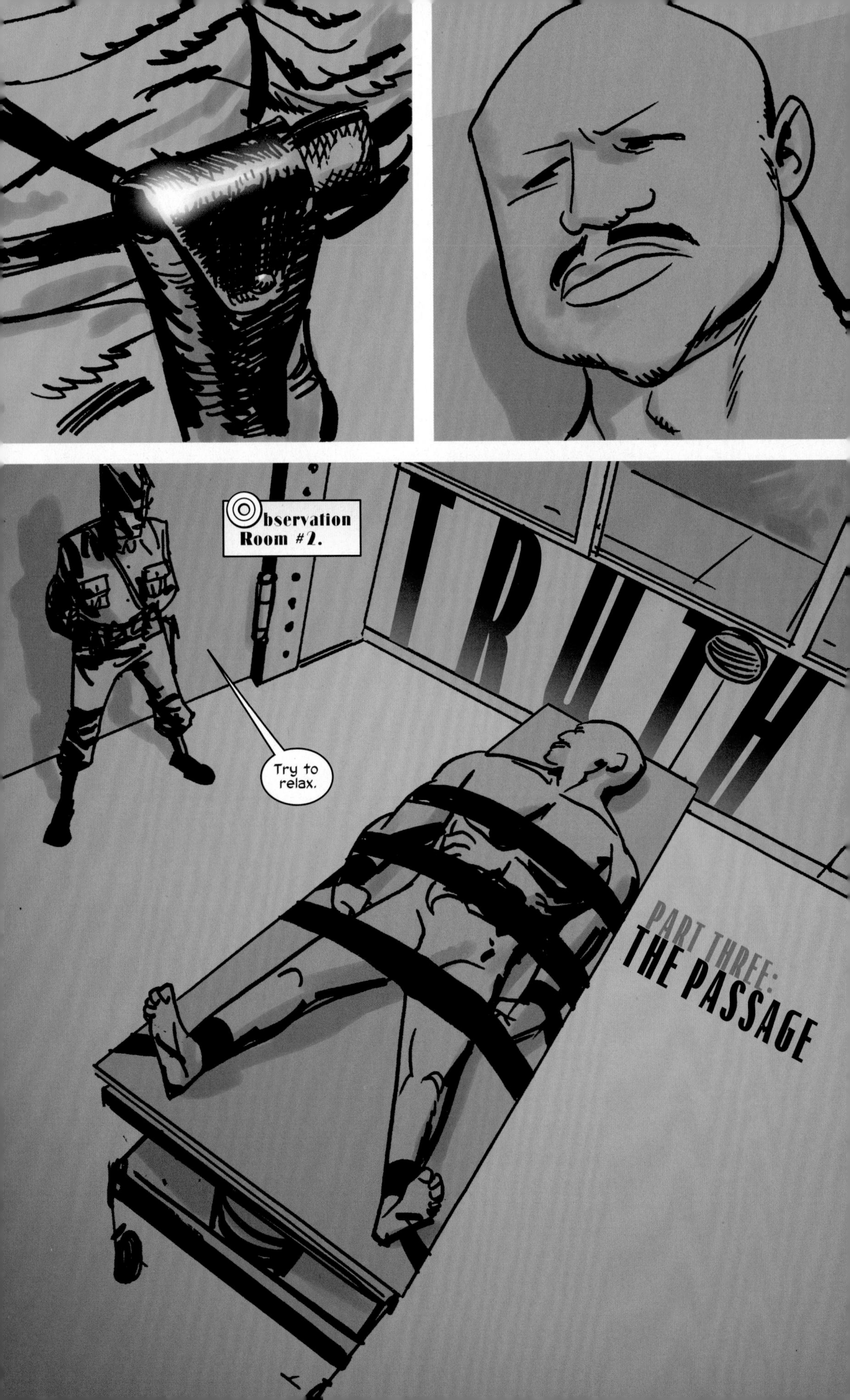
Observation Room #2.
Try to relax.
TRUTH
PART THREE:
THE PASSAGE

Very well, it is 1700 hours. Again we administer 5 cc's of the serum now to subject A-23.

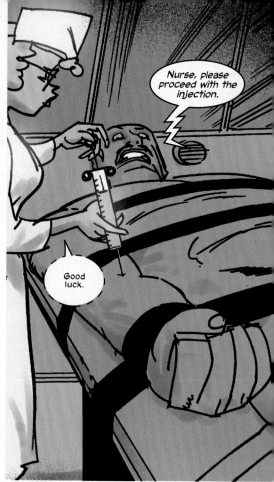

Nurse, please proceed with the injection.

Good luck.

The serum has been administered. Please evacuate the observation room.

CLANK

CLUNK

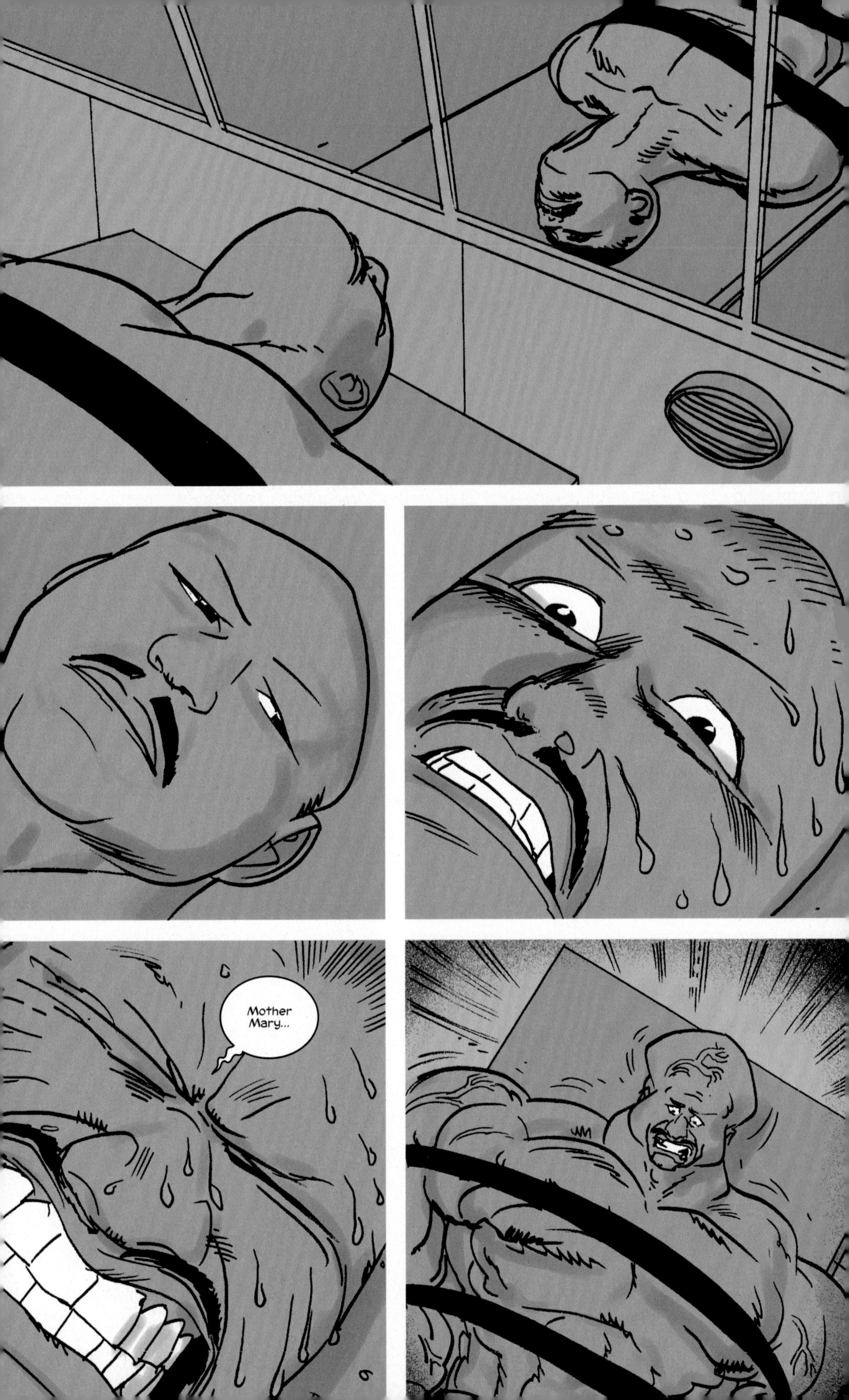
Mother
Mary...

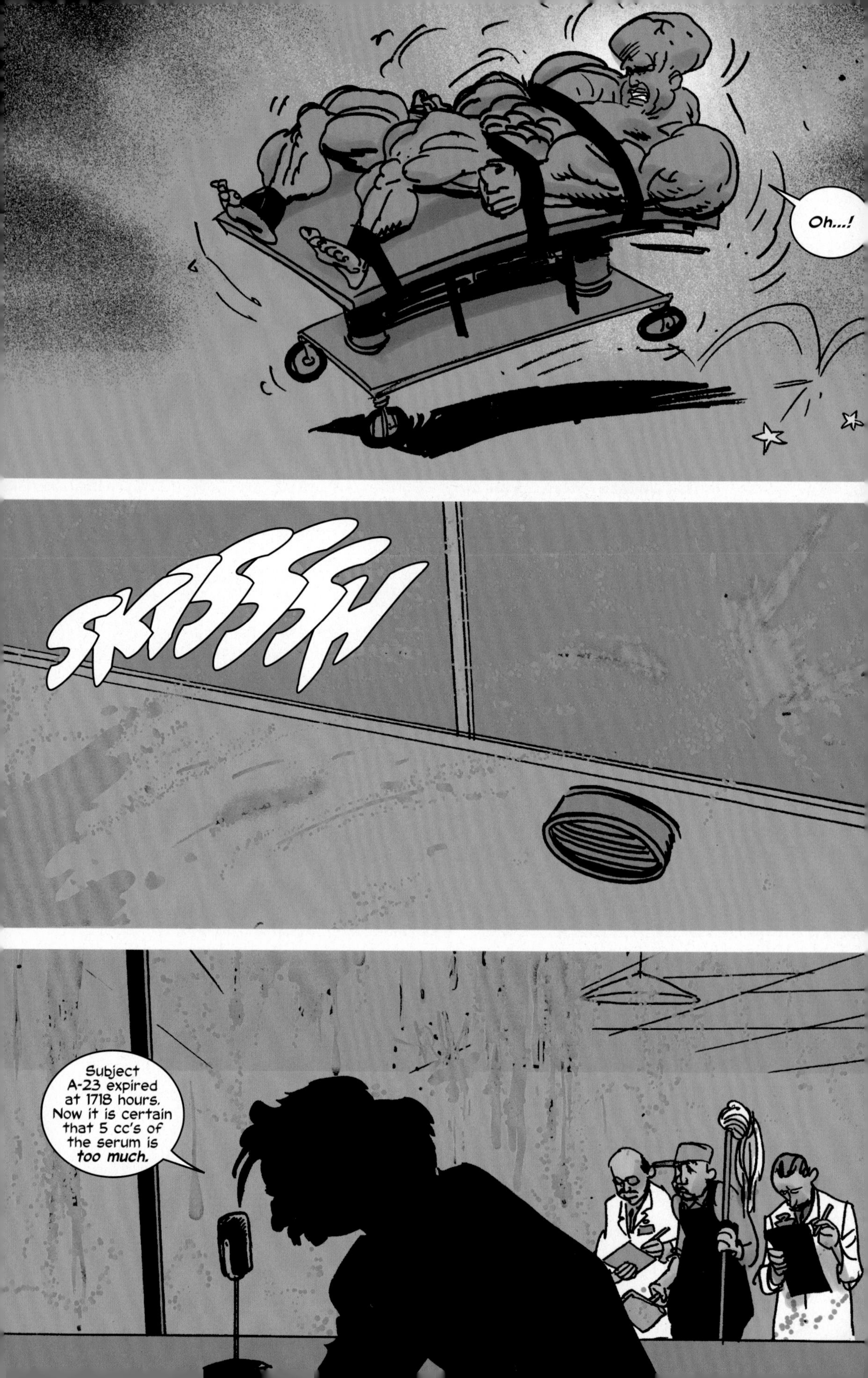
Oh...!
SKISSSH
Subject A-23 expired at 1718 hours. Now it is certain that 5 cc's of the serum is *too much.*

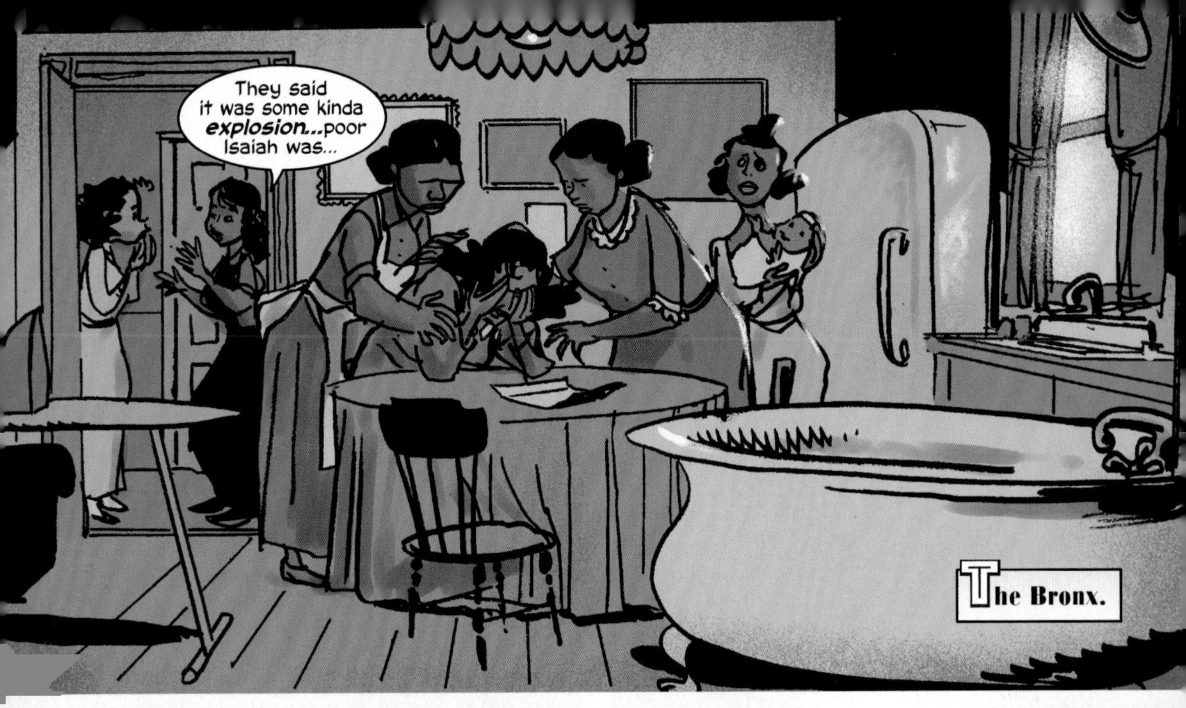
They said it was some kinda explosion...poor Isaiah was...
The Bronx.

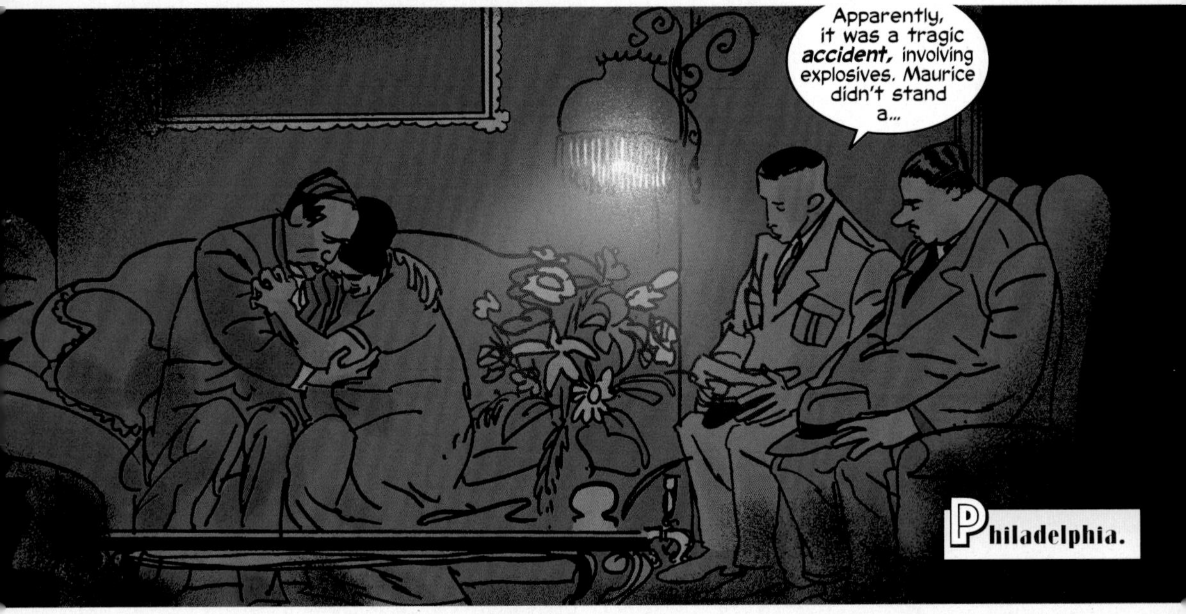
Apparently, it was a tragic accident, involving explosives. Maurice didn't stand a...
Philadelphia.

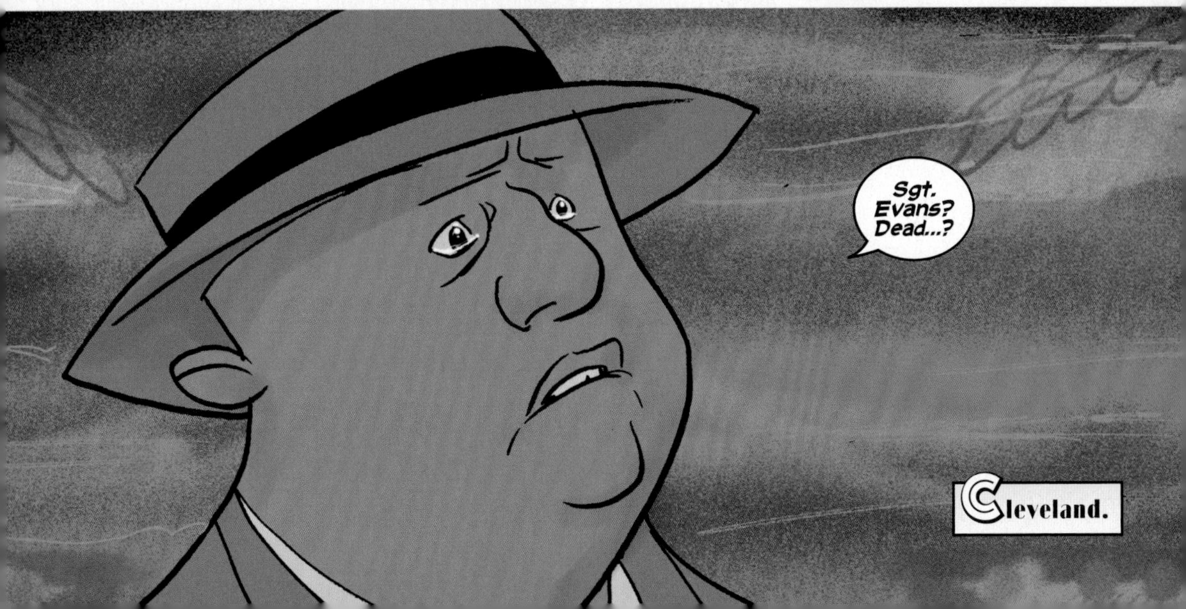
Sgt. Evans? Dead...?
Cleveland.

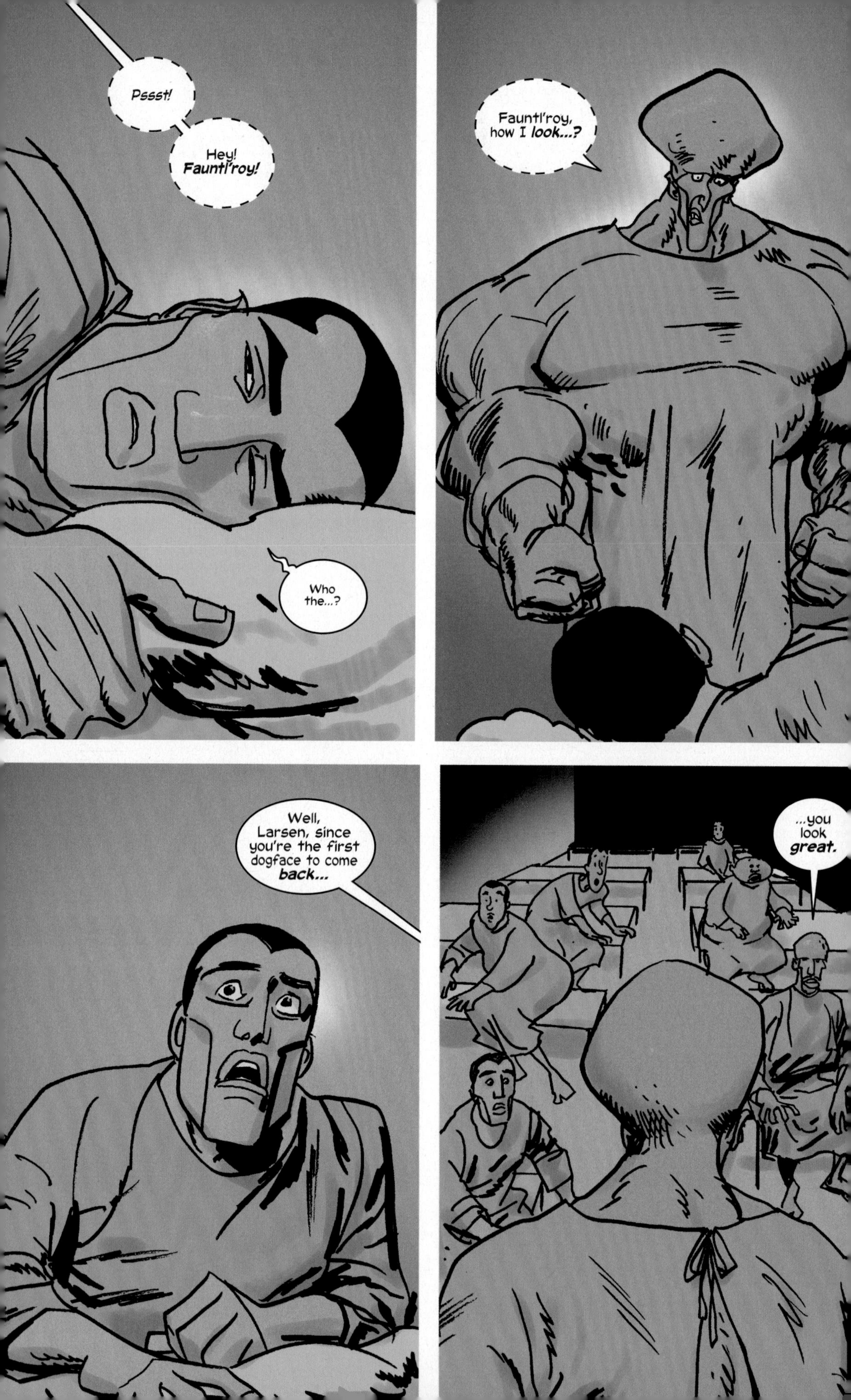

Pssst!
Hey! Fauntl'roy!
Who the...?
Fauntl'roy, how I look...?
Well, Larsen, since you're the first dogface to come back...
...you look great.

Three days later. Philadelphia.

...Dust to dust...

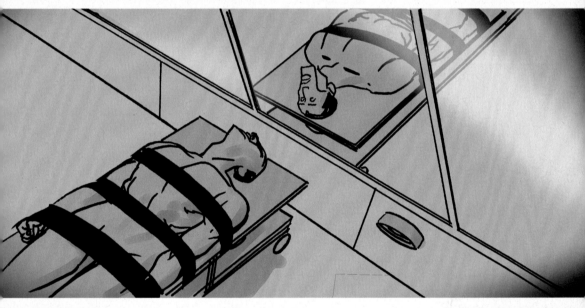

Cleveland.

H-h-here's to the Sarge!

To Lucas Evans!

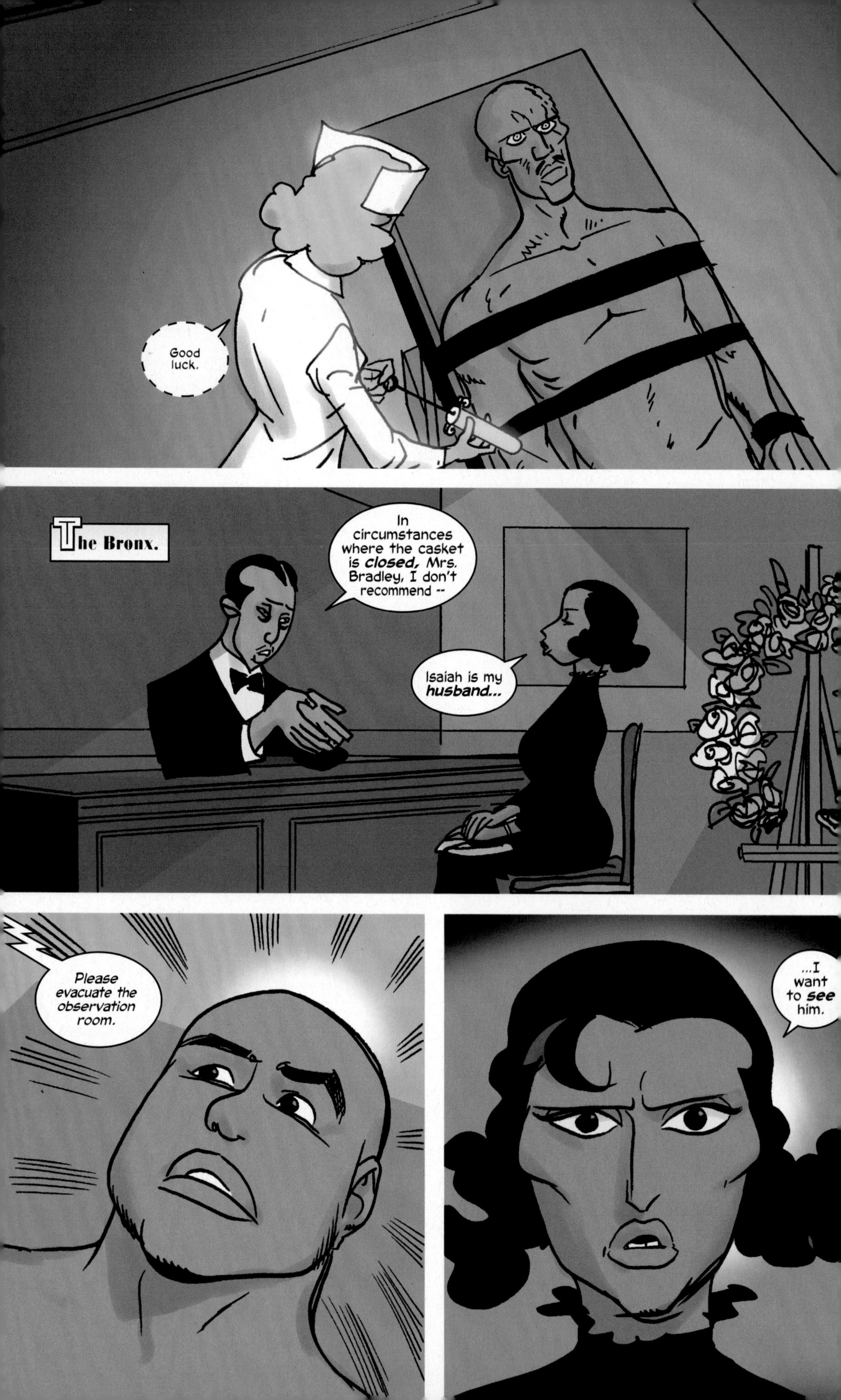
Good luck.
The Bronx.
In circumstances where the casket is closed, Mrs. Bradley, I don't recommend --
Isaiah is my husband...
Please evacuate the observation room.
...I want to see him.

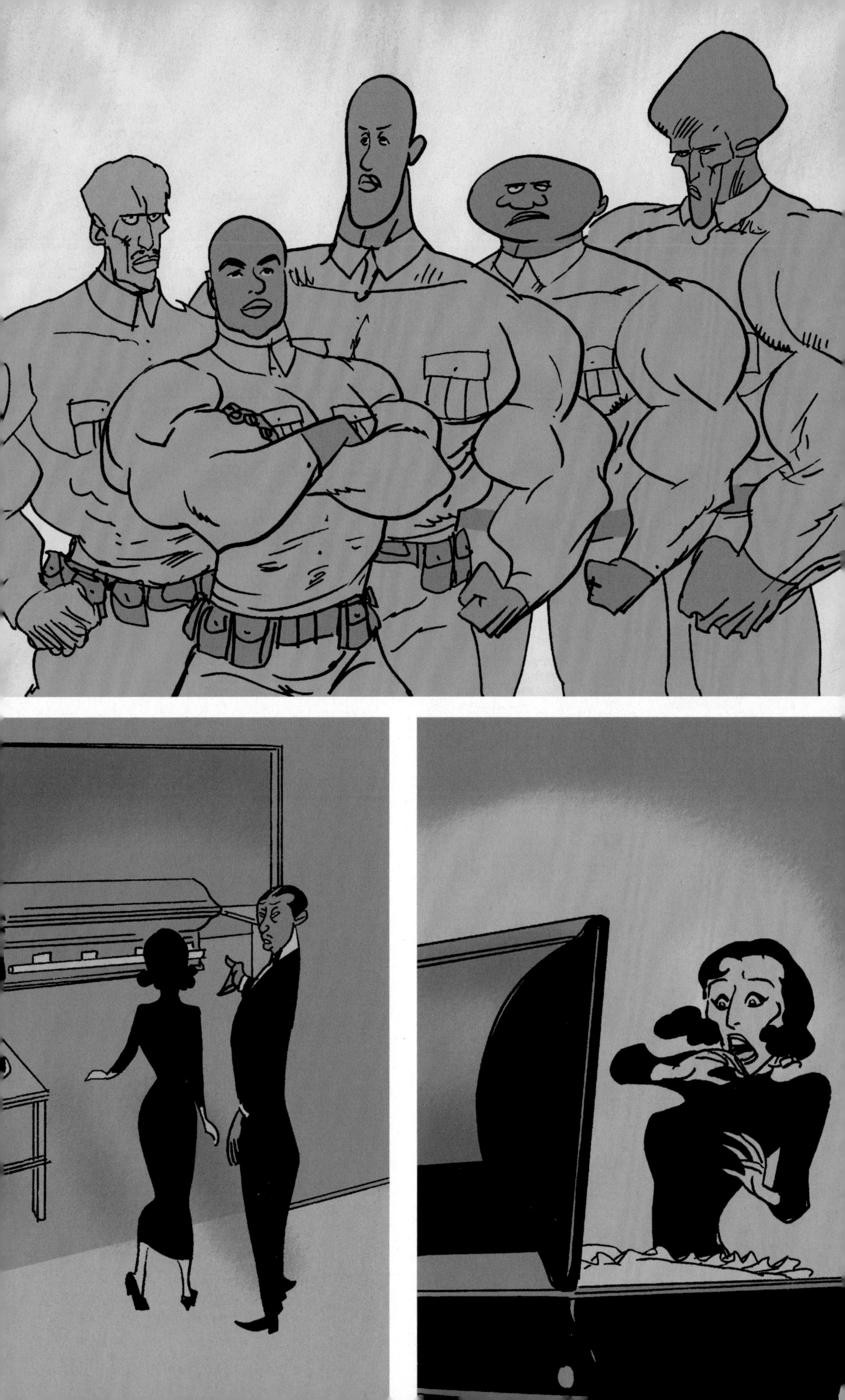

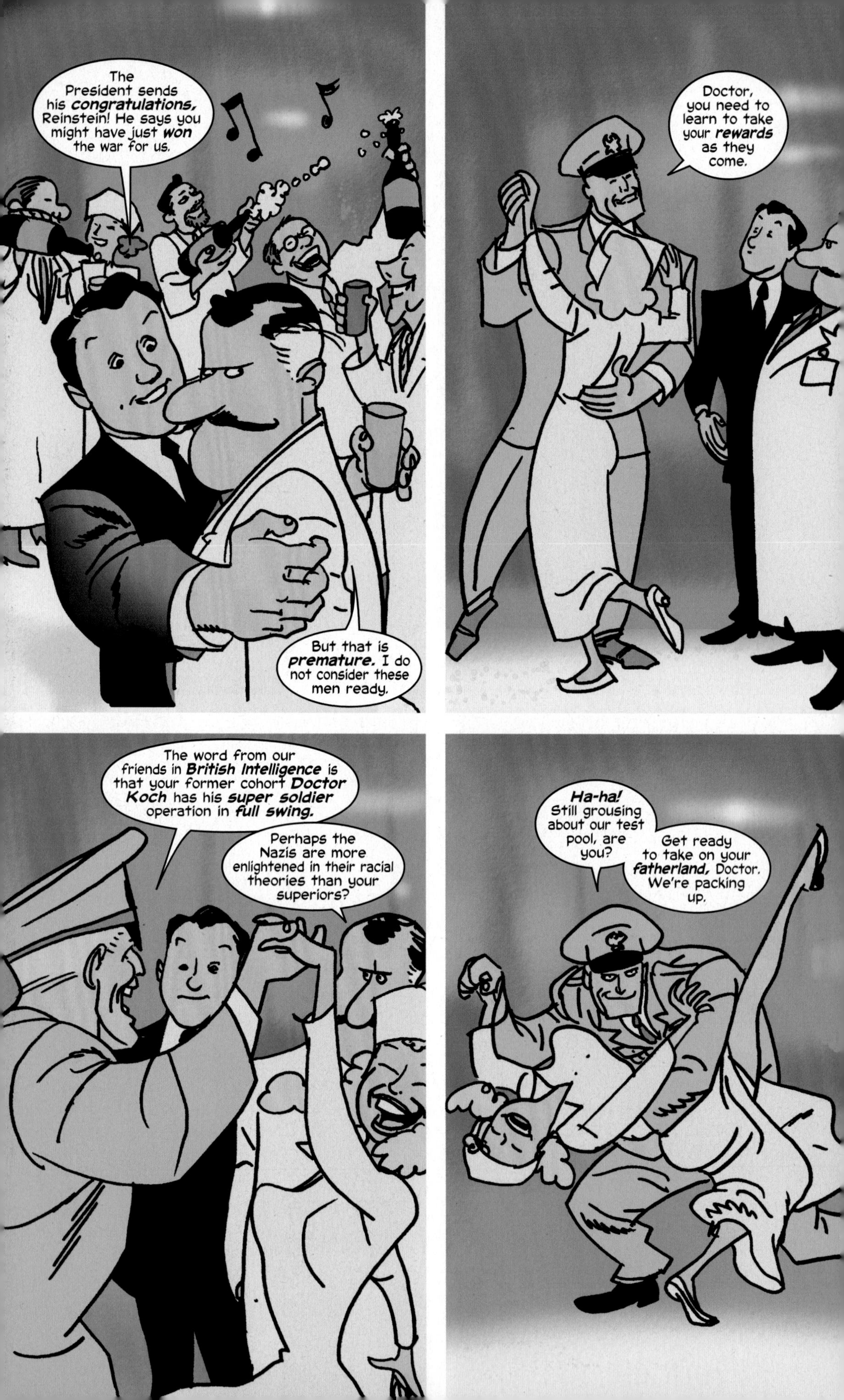
The President sends his **congratulations,** Reinstein! He says you might have just **won** the war for us.
But that is **premature.** I do not consider these men ready.
Doctor, you need to learn to take your **rewards** as they come.
The word from our friends in **British Intelligence** is that your former cohort **Doctor Koch** has his **super soldier** operation in **full swing.**
Perhaps the Nazis are more enlightened in their racial theories than your superiors?
Ha-ha! Still grousing about our test pool, are you?
Get ready to take on your **fatherland,** Doctor. We're packing up.

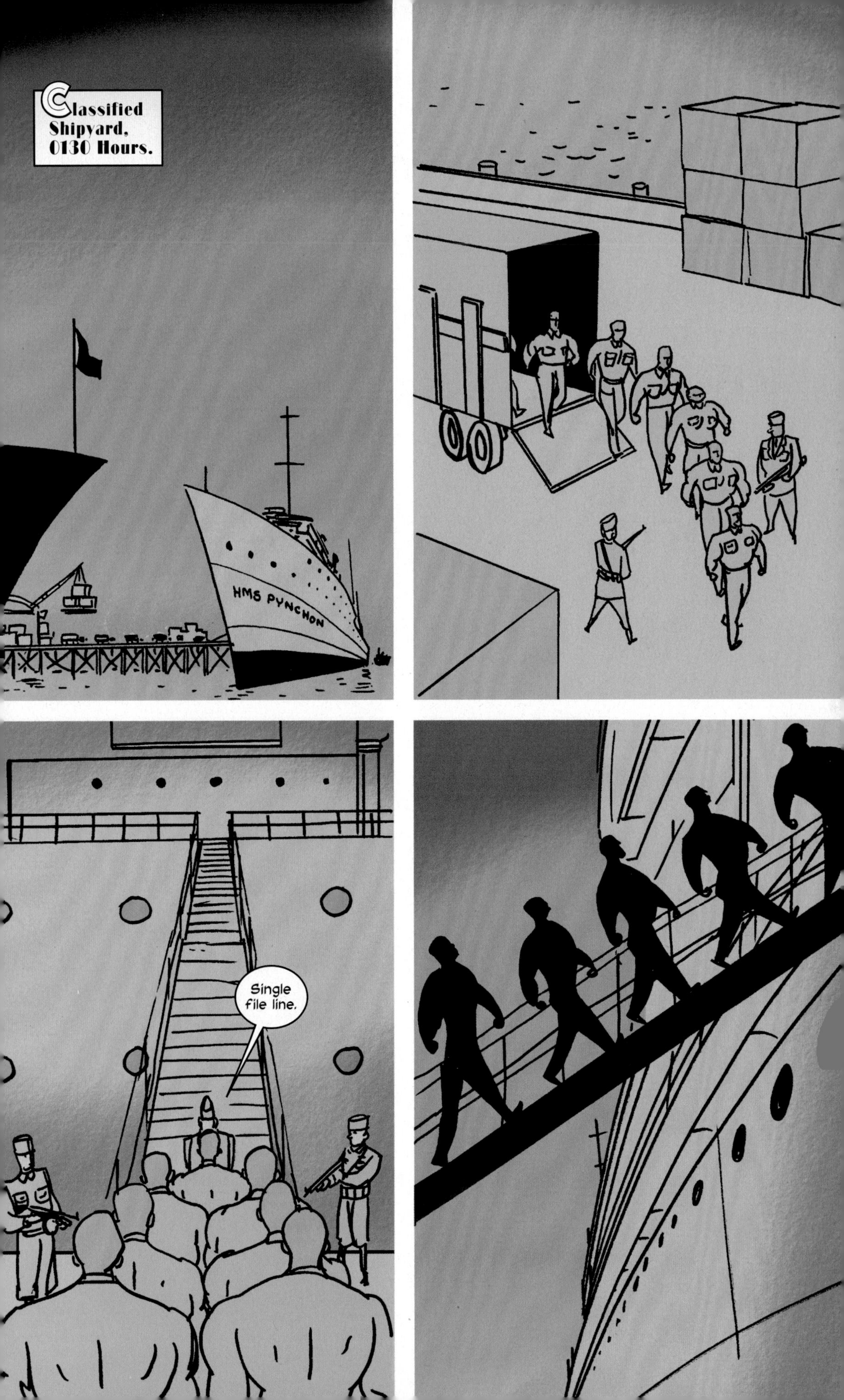
Classified Shipyard, 0130 Hours.
HMS PYNCHON
Single file line.

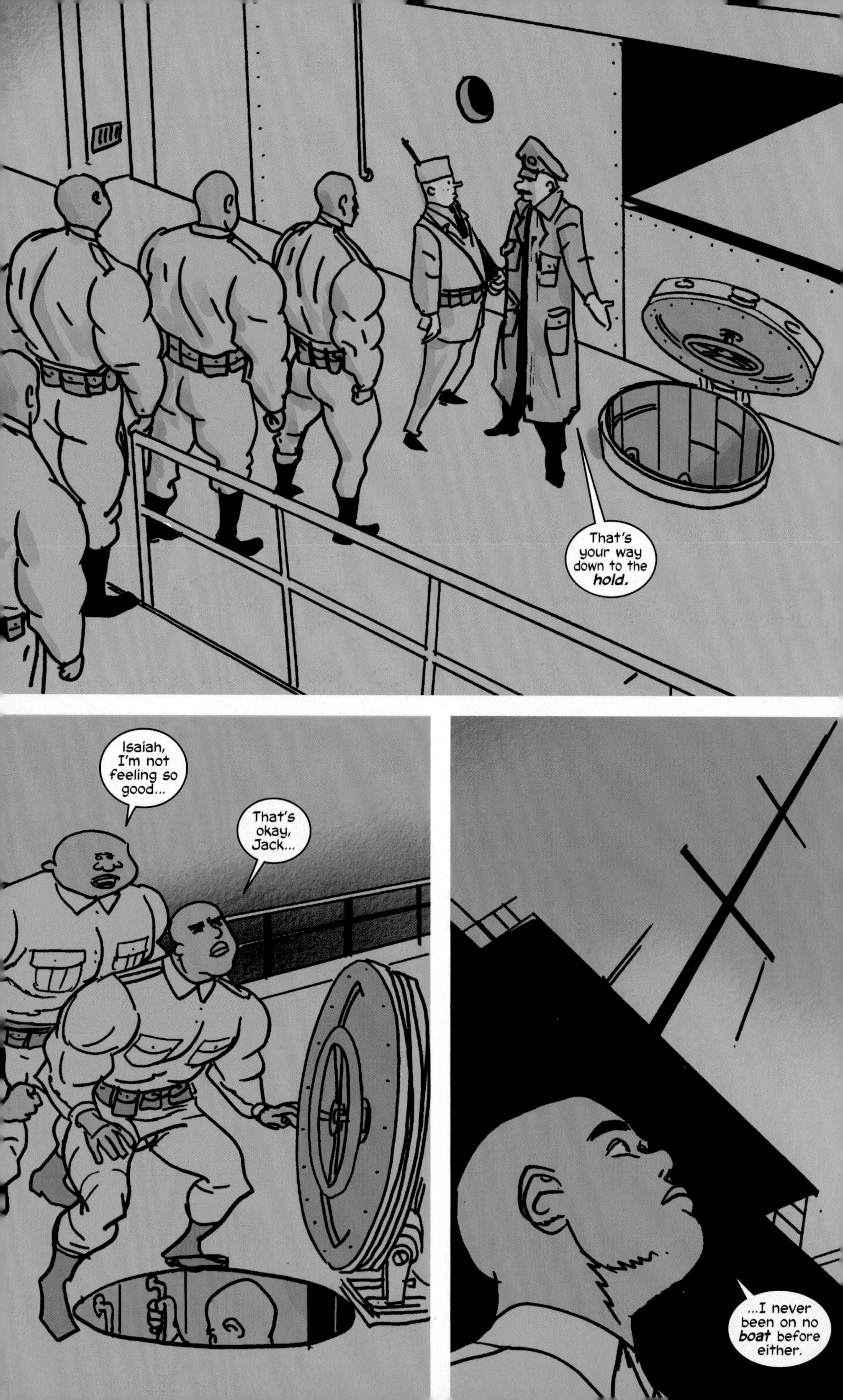
That's your way down to the **hold.**
Isaiah, I'm not feeling so good...
That's okay, Jack...
...I never been on no **boat** before either.

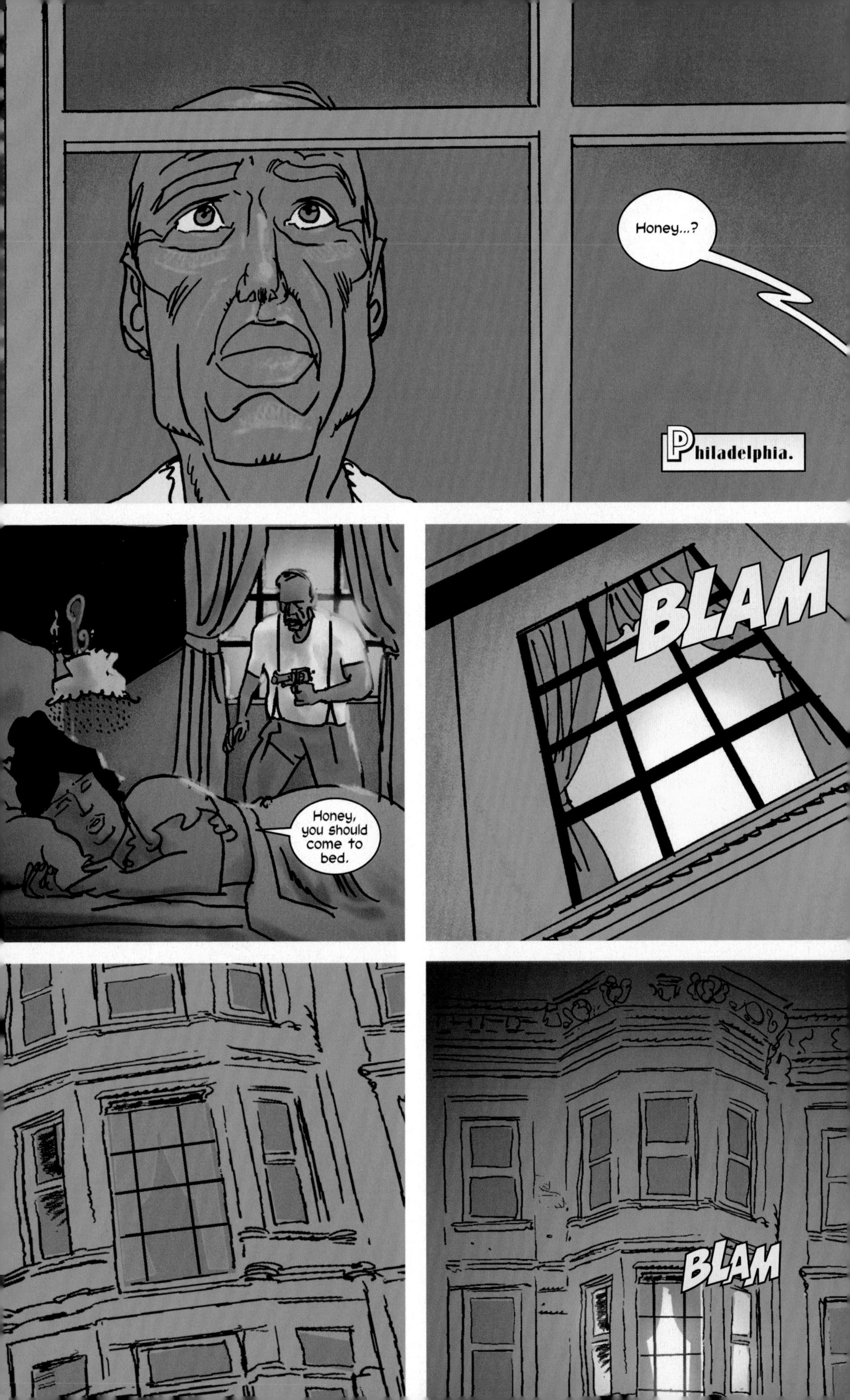
Honey...?
Philadelphia.
Honey, you should come to bed.
BLAM
BLAM

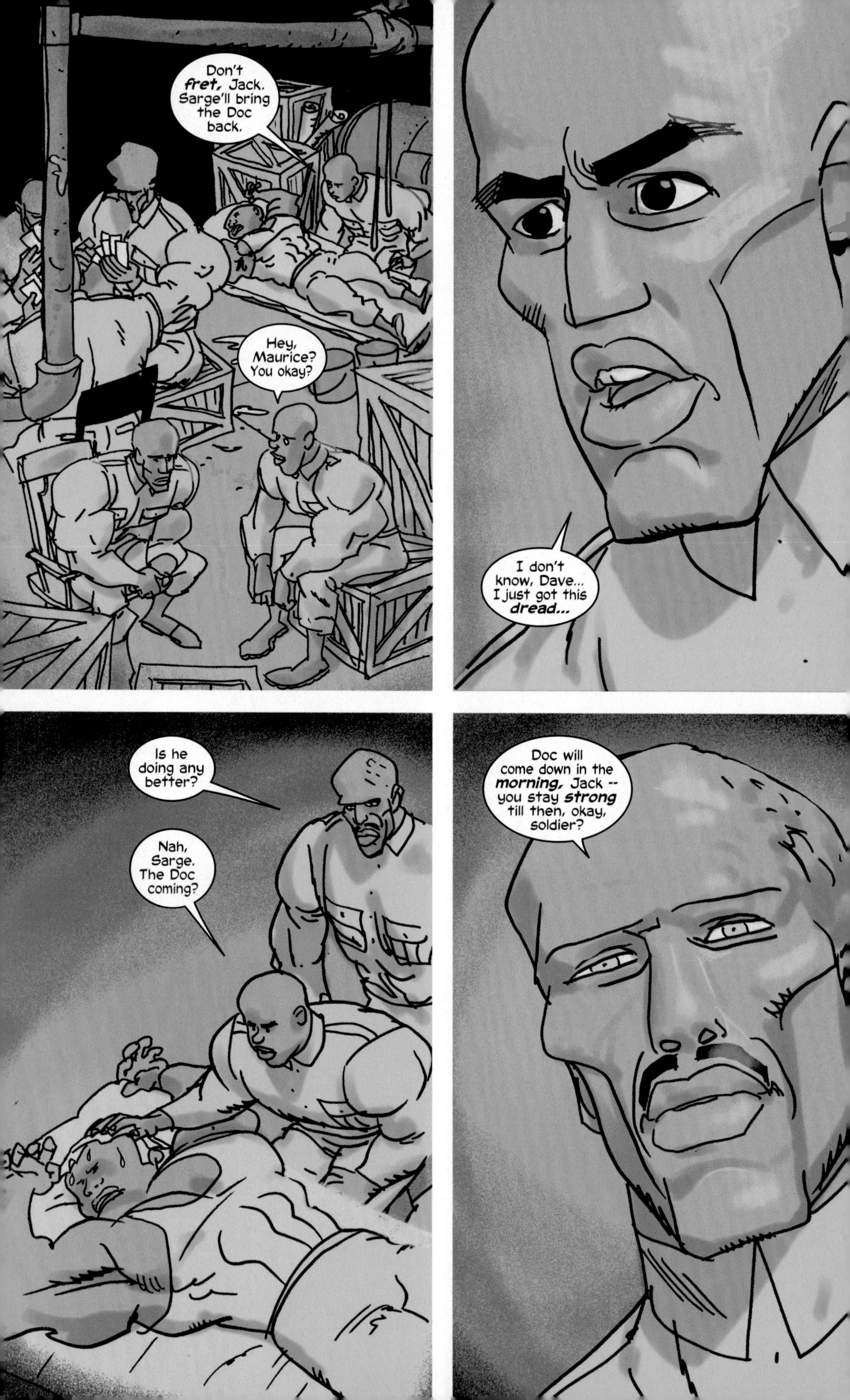
Don't *fret,* Jack. Sarge'll bring the Doc back.
Hey, Maurice? You okay?
I don't know, Dave... I just got this *dread...*
Is he doing any better?
Nah, Sarge. The Doc coming?
Doc will come down in the *morning,* Jack -- you stay *strong* till then, okay, soldier?

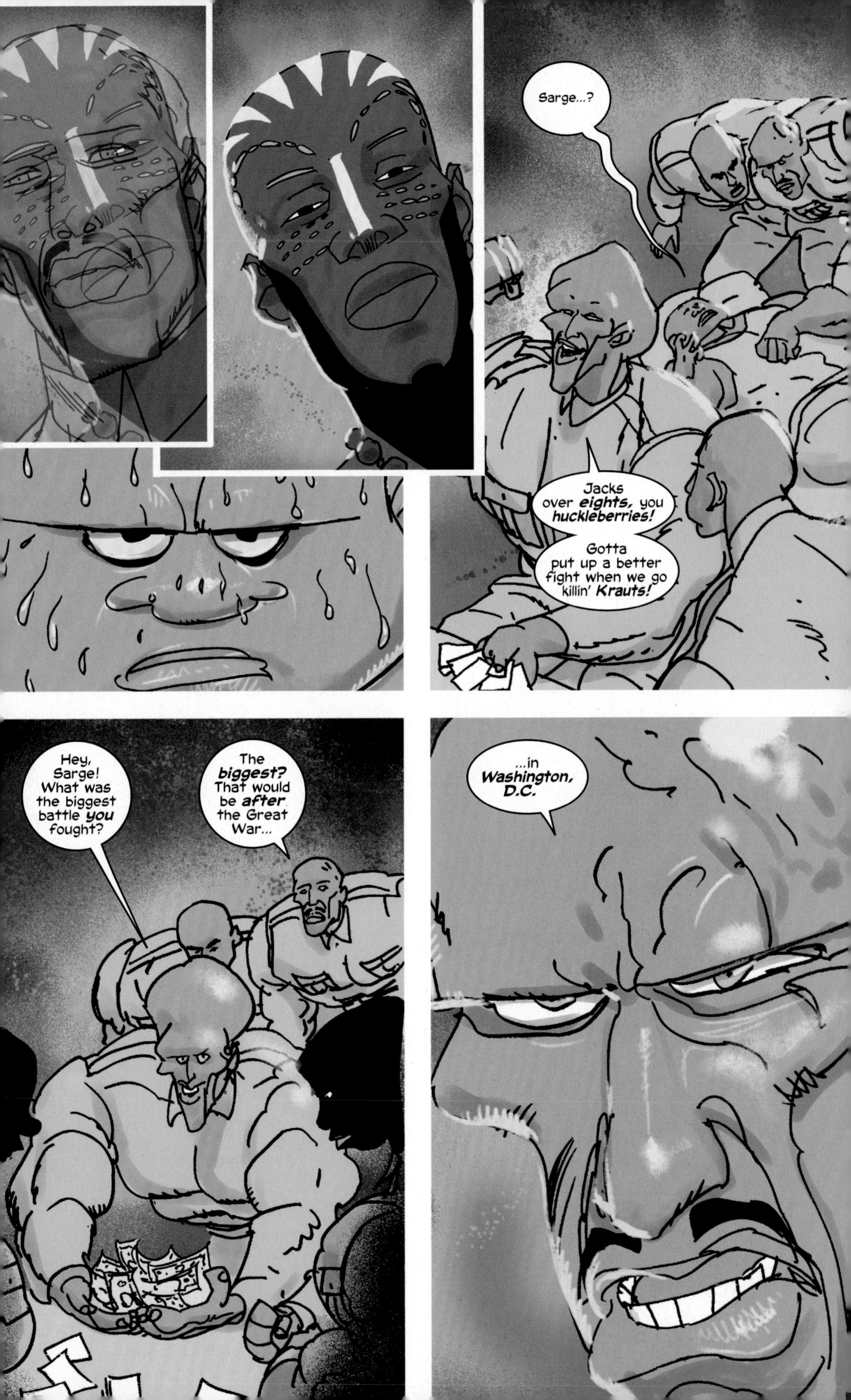
Sarge...?
Jacks over eights, you huckleberries!
Gotta put up a better fight when we go killin' Krauts!
Hey, Sarge! What was the biggest battle you fought?
The biggest? That would be after the Great War...
...in Washington, D.C.

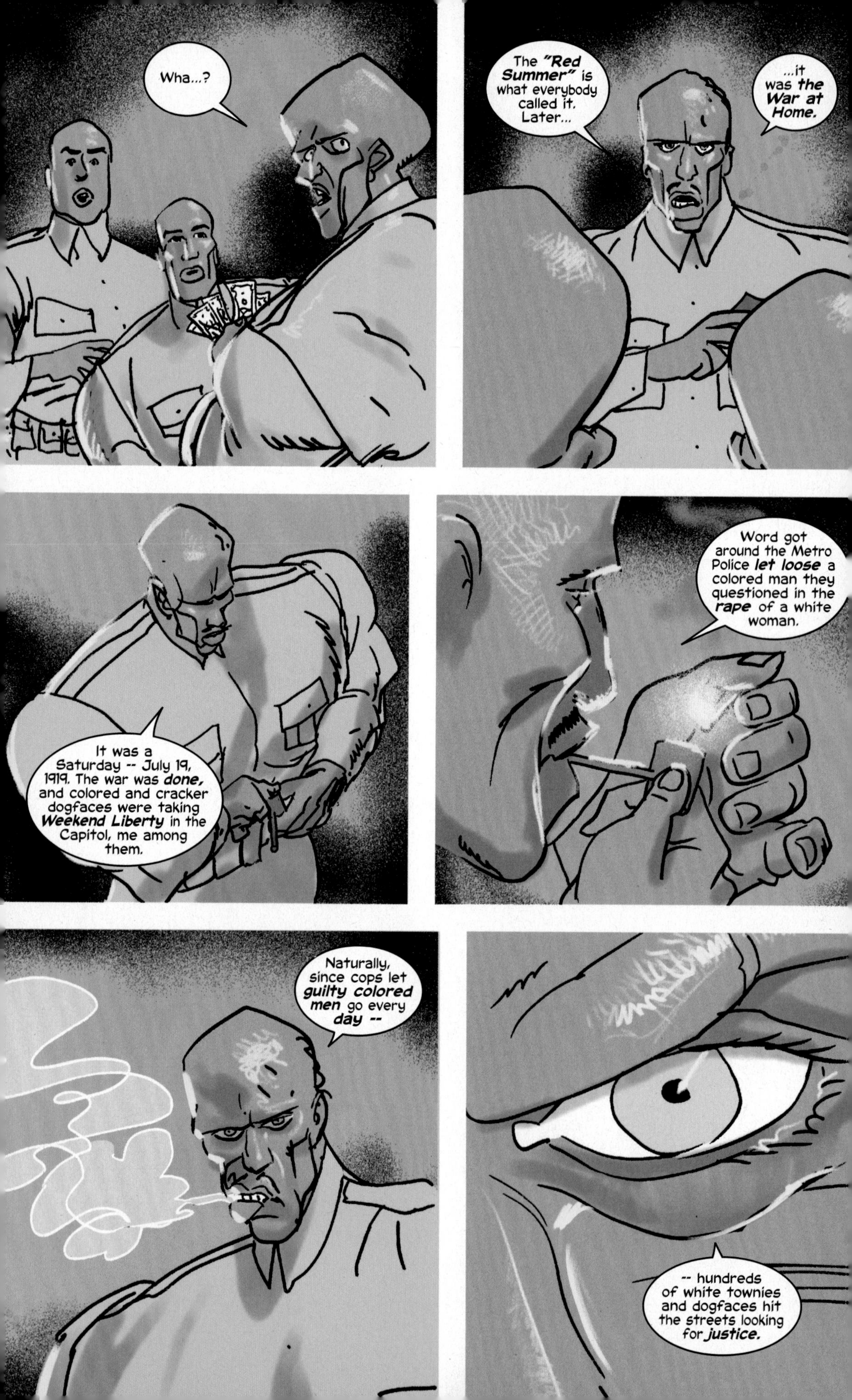
Wha...?
The "Red Summer" is what everybody called it. Later...
...it was the War at Home.
It was a Saturday -- July 19, 1919. The war was done, and colored and cracker dogfaces were taking Weekend Liberty in the Capitol, me among them.
Word got around the Metro Police let loose a colored man they questioned in the rape of a white woman.
Naturally, since cops let guilty colored men go every day --
-- hundreds of white townies and dogfaces hit the streets looking for justice.

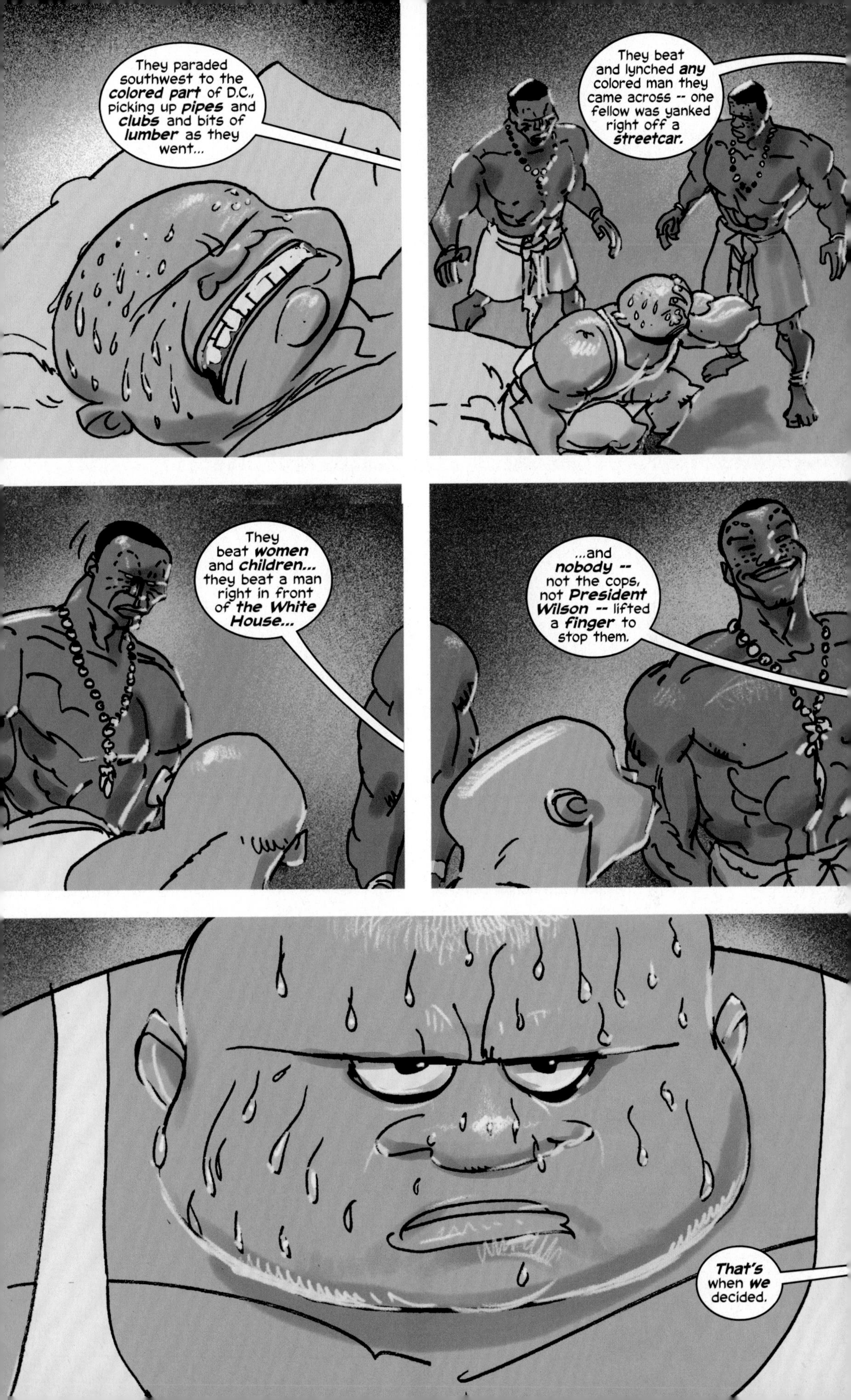
They paraded southwest to the **colored part** of D.C., picking up **pipes** and **clubs** and bits of **lumber** as they went...
They beat and lynched **any** colored man they came across -- one fellow was yanked right off a **streetcar.**
They beat **women** and **children...** they beat a man right in front of **the White House...**
...and **nobody --** not the cops, not **President Wilson --** lifted a **finger** to stop them.
That's when **we** decided.

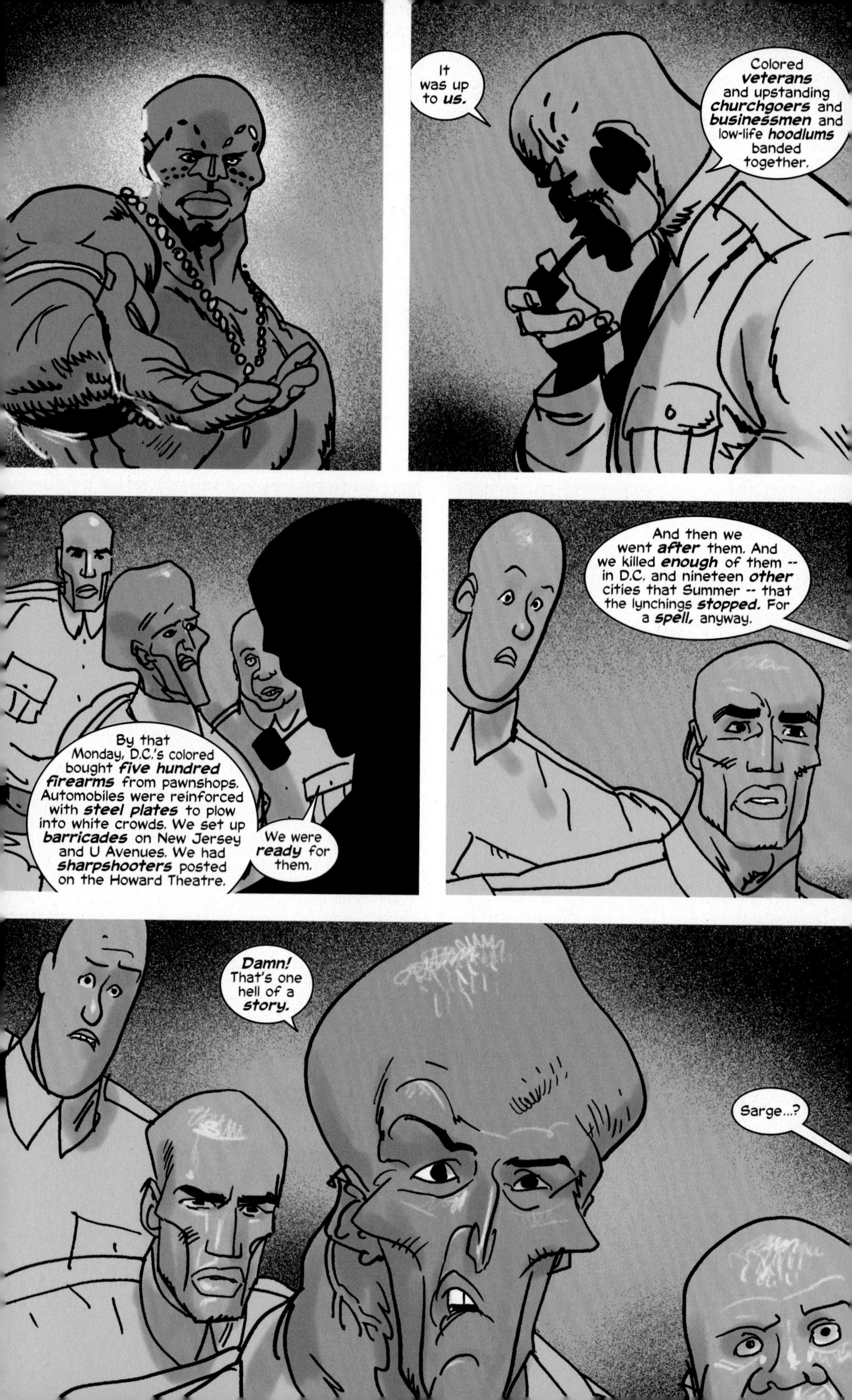
It was up to **us.**
Colored **veterans** and upstanding **churchgoers** and **businessmen** and low-life **hoodlums** banded together.
By that Monday, D.C.'s colored bought **five hundred firearms** from pawnshops. Automobiles were reinforced with **steel plates** to plow into white crowds. We set up **barricades** on New Jersey and U Avenues. We had **sharpshooters** posted on the Howard Theatre.
We were **ready** for them.
And then we went **after** them. And we killed **enough** of them -- in D.C. and nineteen **other** cities that Summer -- that the lynchings **stopped.** For a **spell,** anyway.
Damn! That's one hell of a **story.**
Sarge...?

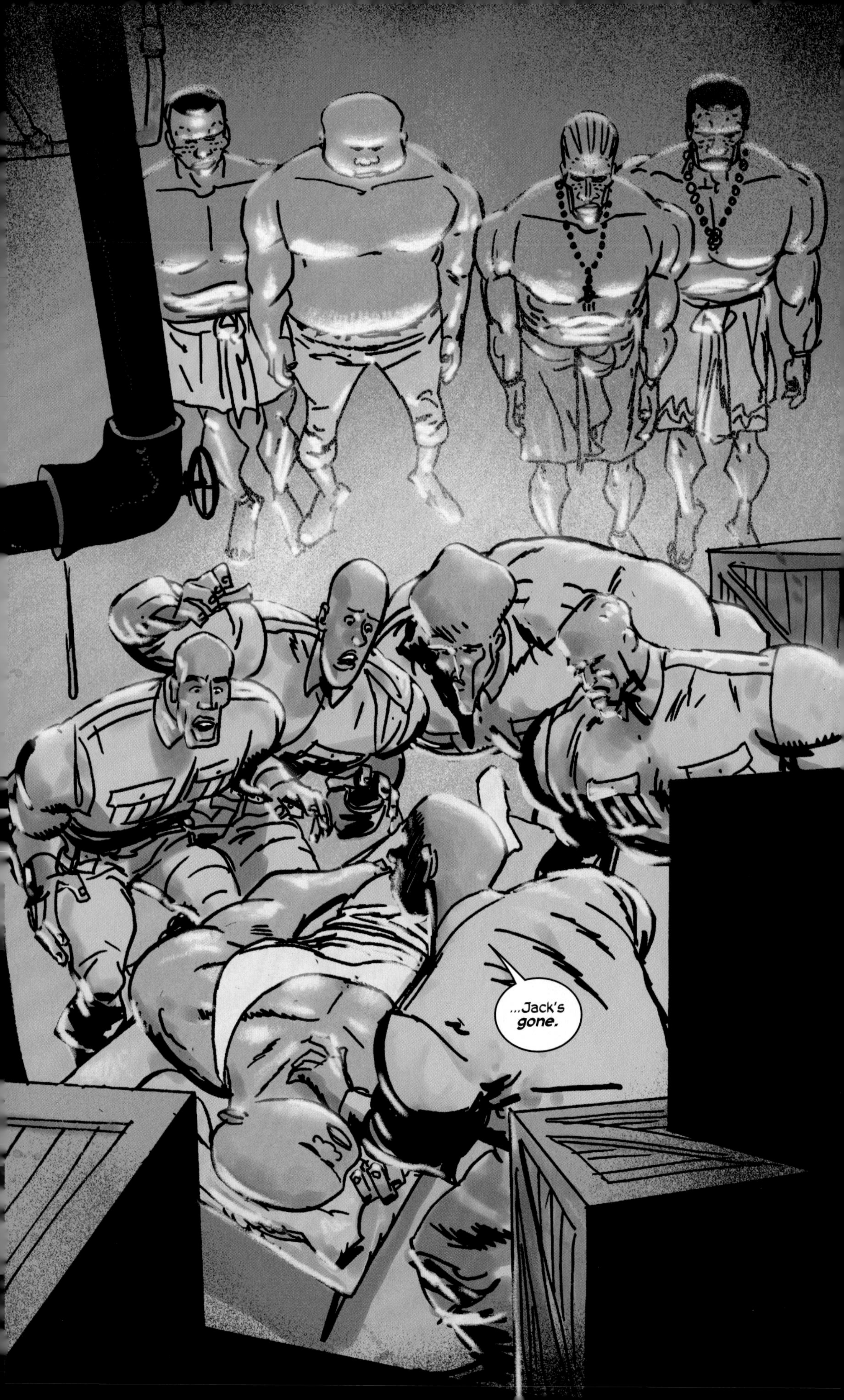
...Jack's gone.

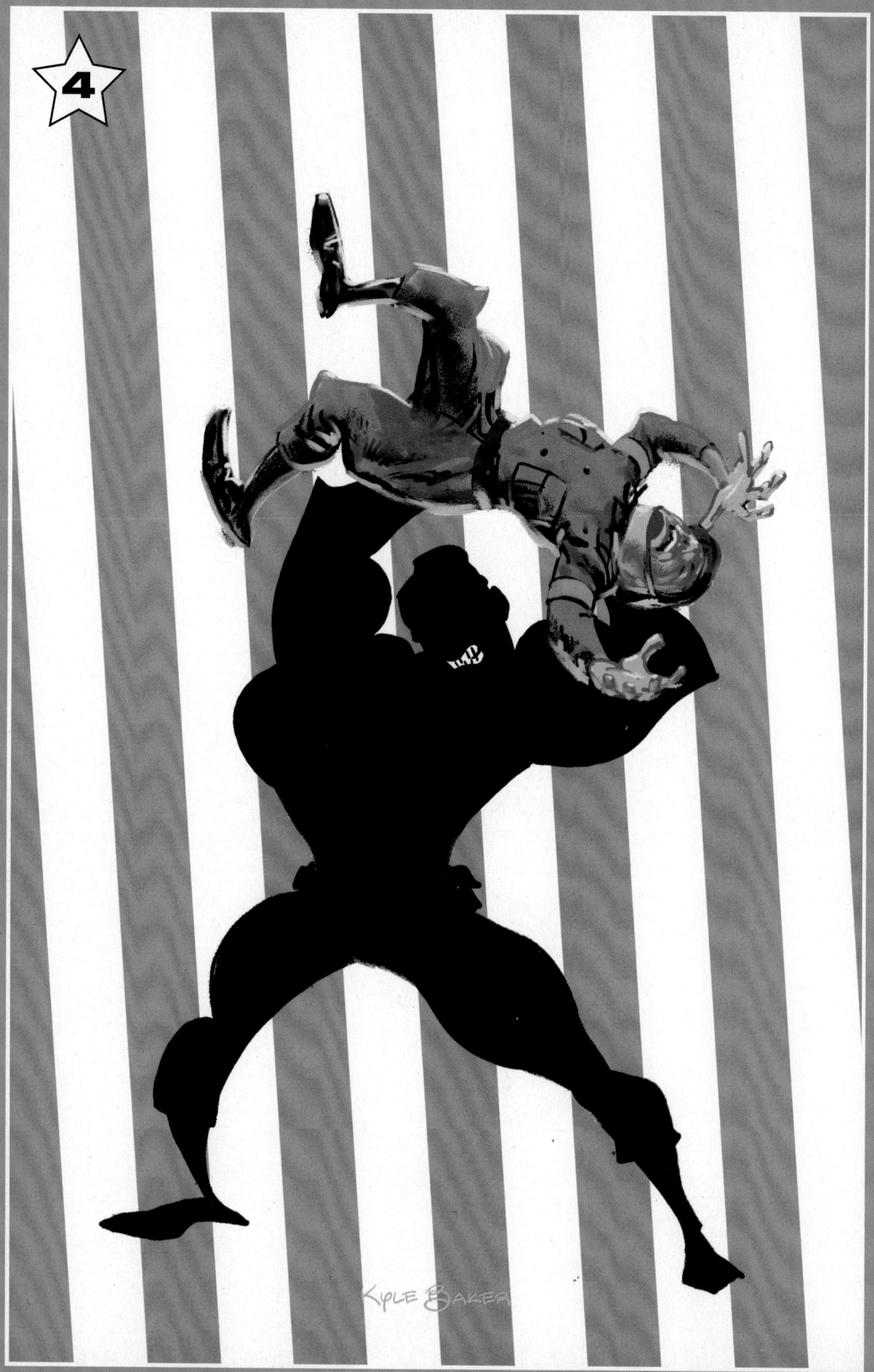
4
KYLE BAKER

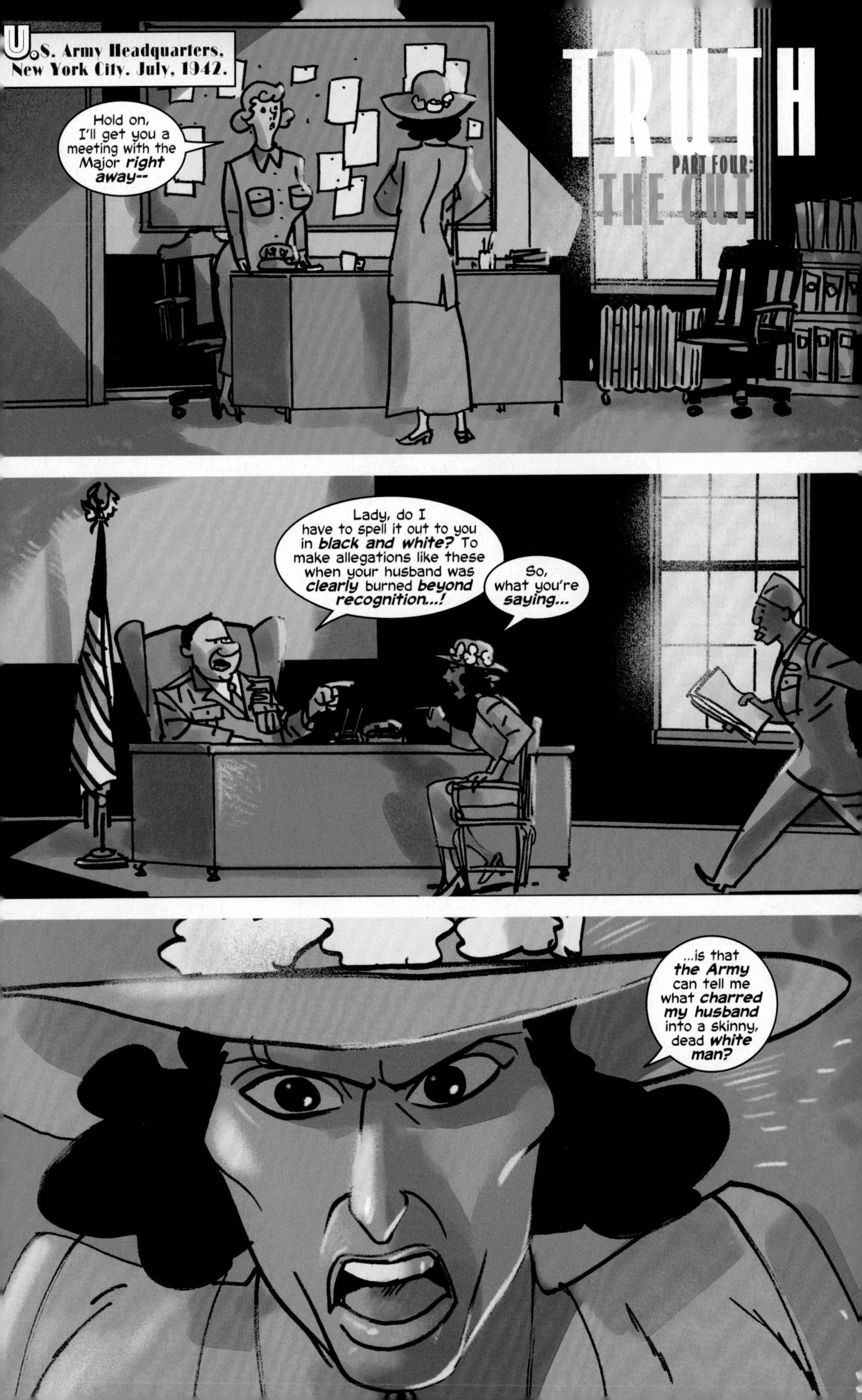

U.S. Army Headquarters, New York City. July, 1942.
TRUTH
PART FOUR: THE CUT
Hold on, I'll get you a meeting with the Major right away--
Lady, do I have to spell it out to you in black and white? To make allegations like these when your husband was clearly burned beyond recognition...!
So, what you're saying...
...is that the Army can tell me what charred my husband into a skinny, dead white man?

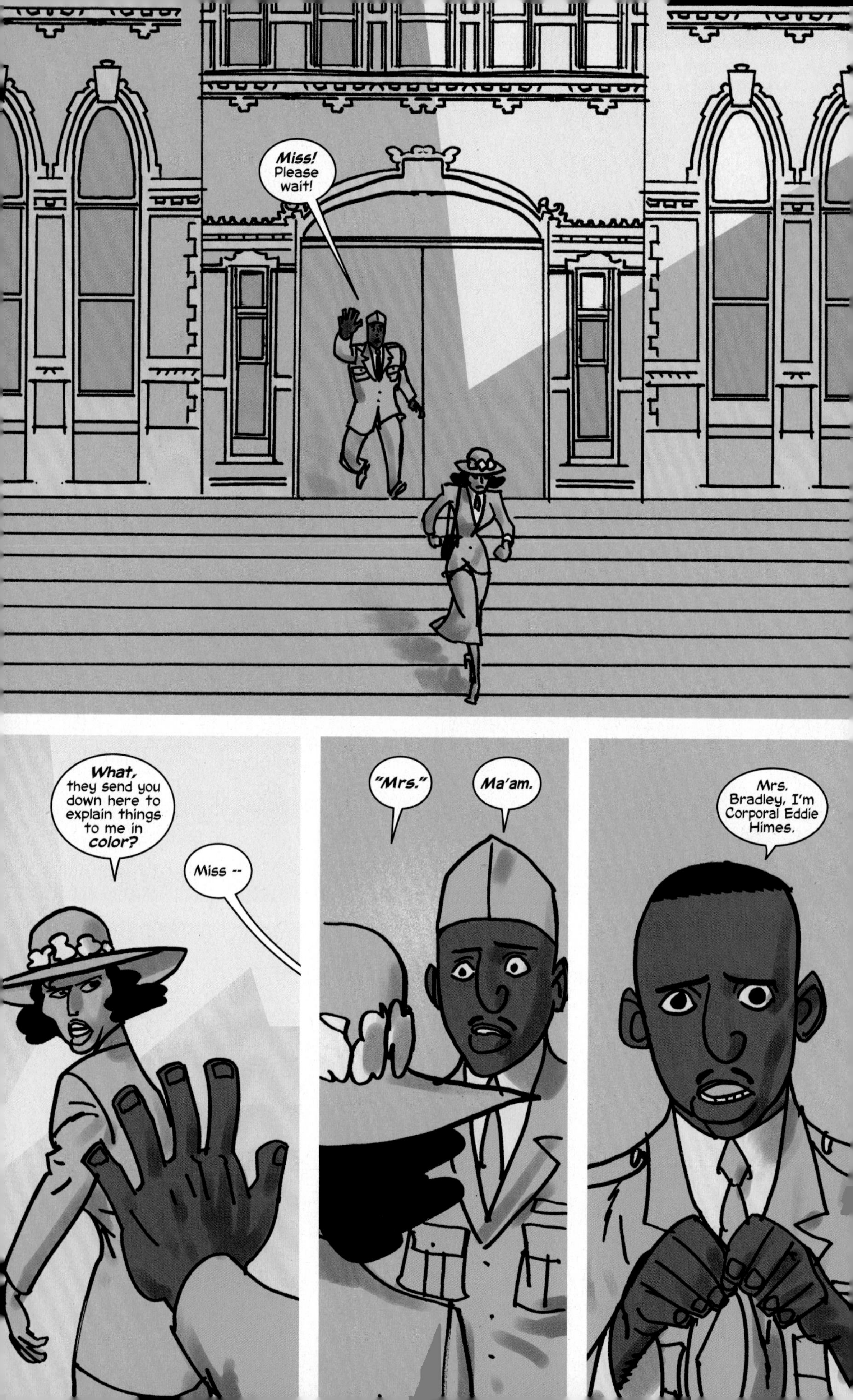
Miss! Please wait!
What, they send you down here to explain things to me in color?
Miss --
"Mrs."
Ma'am.
Mrs. Bradley, I'm Corporal Eddie Himes.

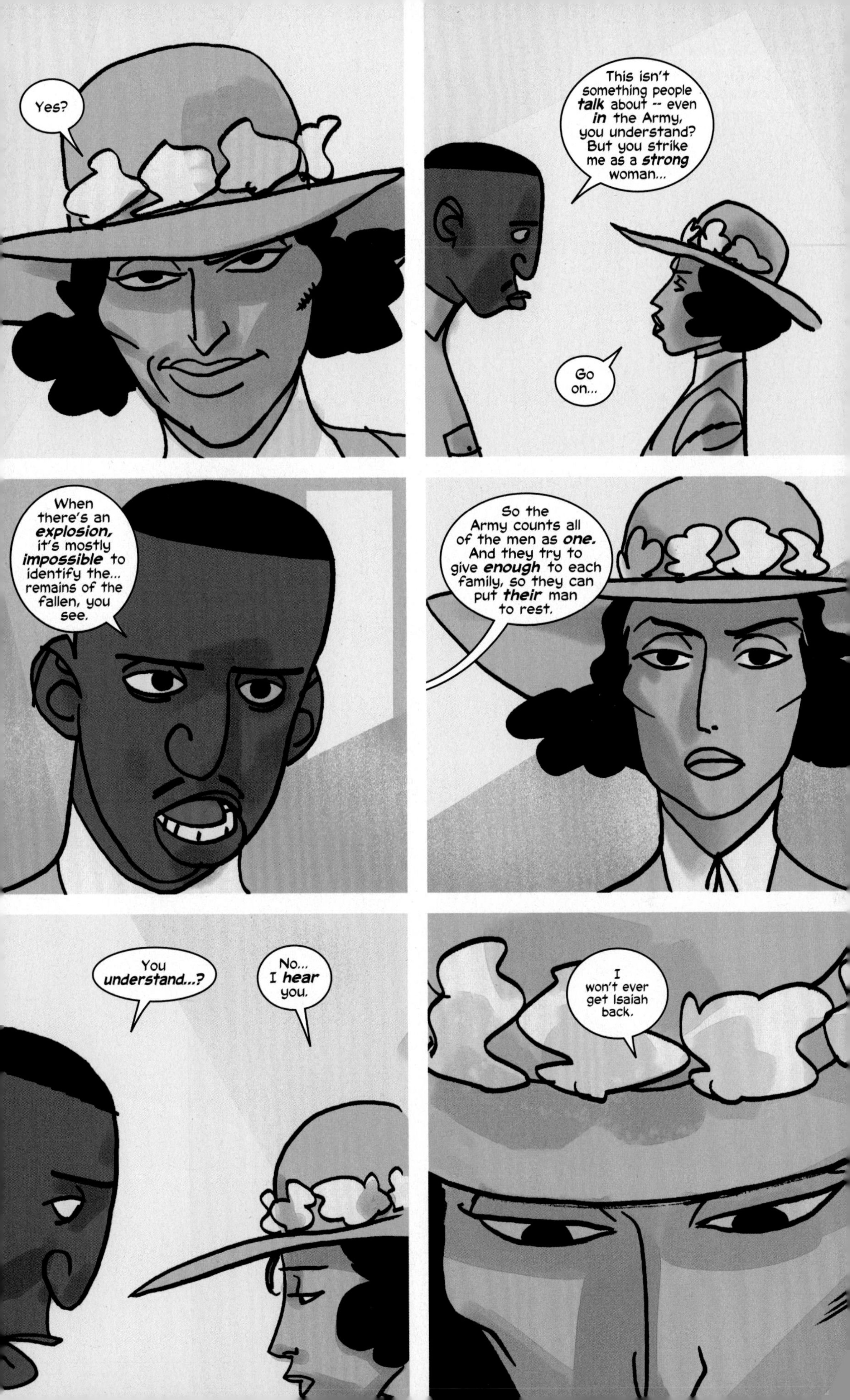
Yes?
This isn't something people talk about -- even in the Army, you understand? But you strike me as a strong woman...
Go on...
When there's an explosion, it's mostly impossible to identify the... remains of the fallen, you see.
So the Army counts all of the men as one. And they try to give enough to each family, so they can put their man to rest.
You understand...?
No... I hear you.
I won't ever get Isaiah back.

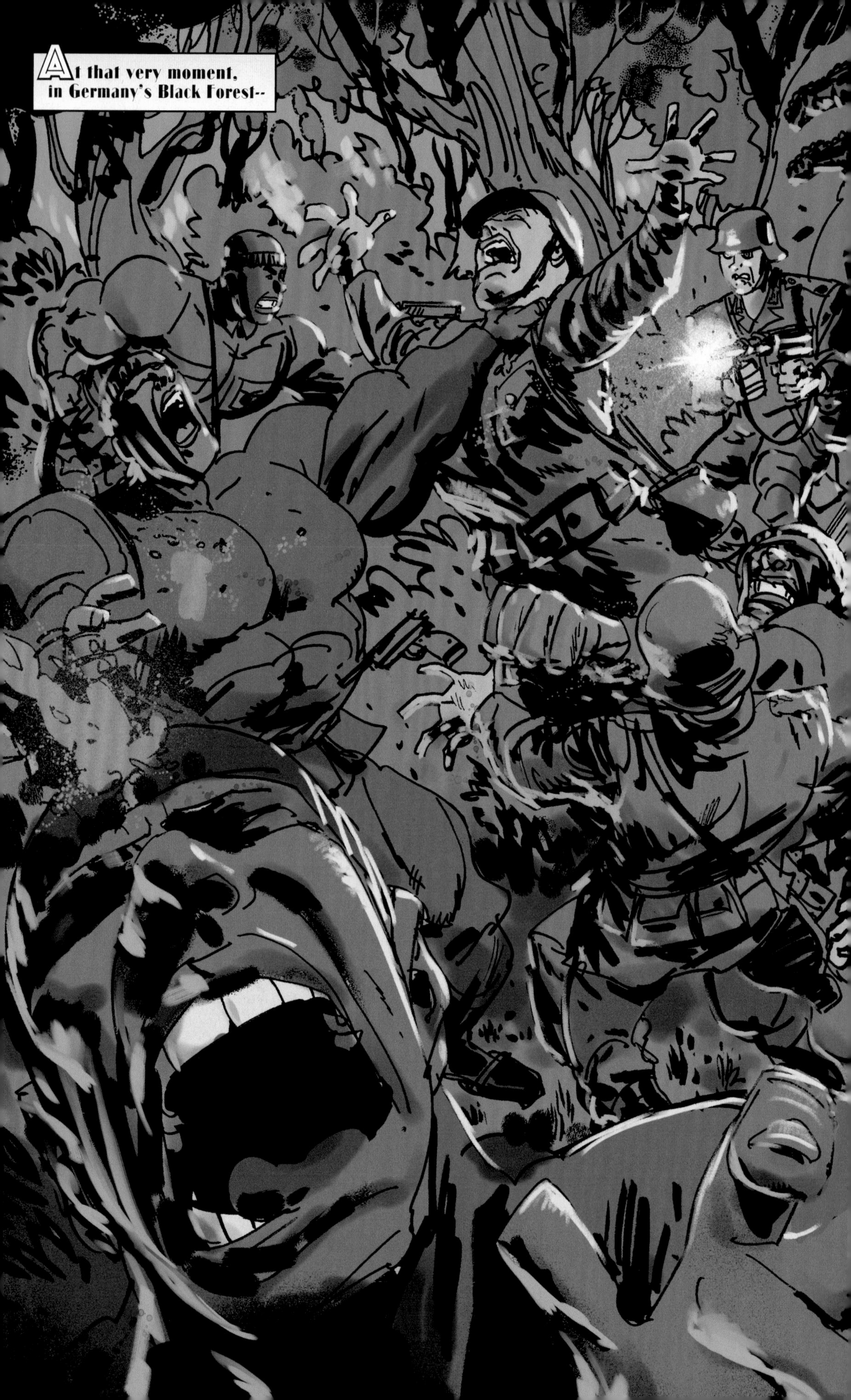
At that very moment, in Germany's Black Forest--

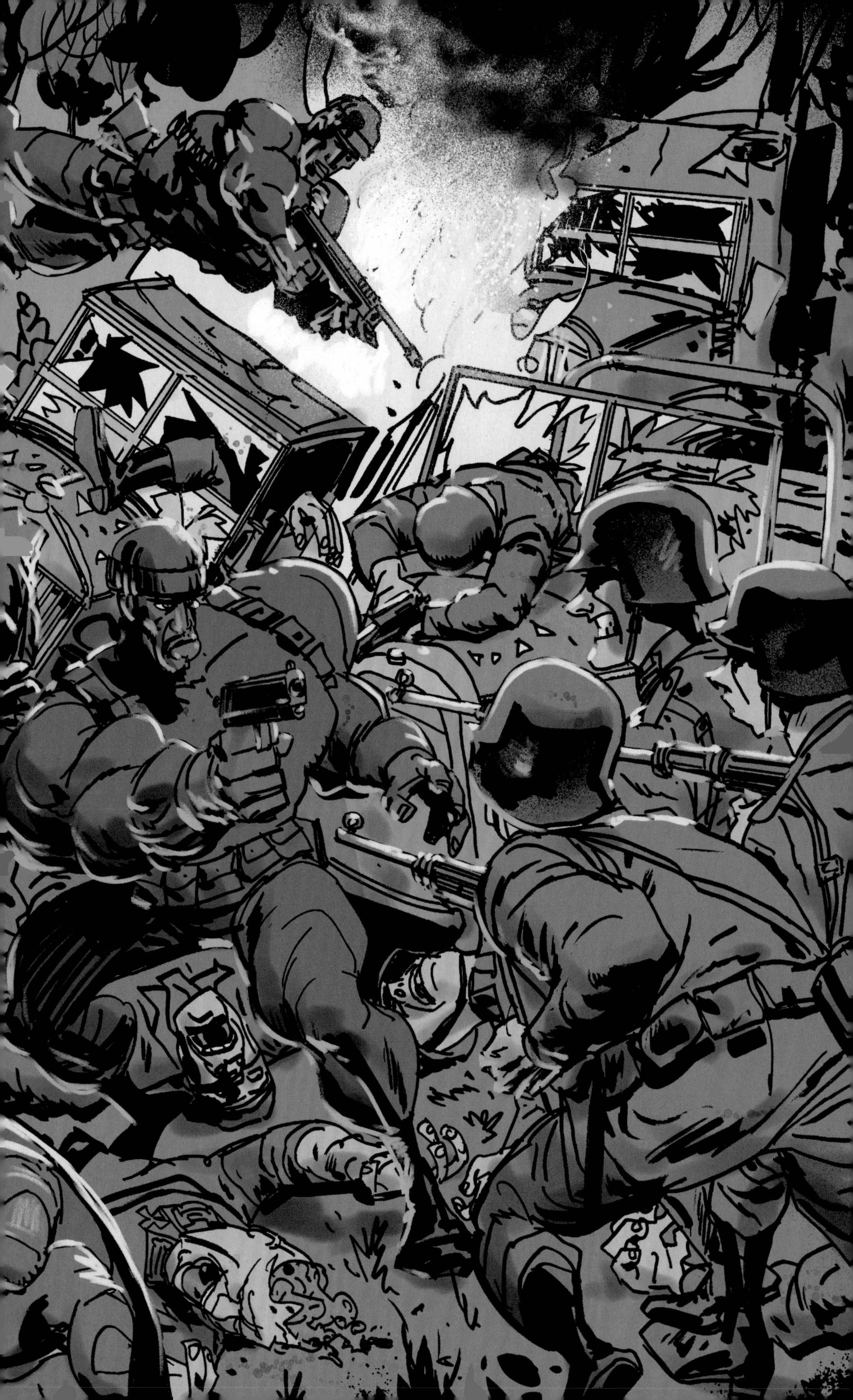

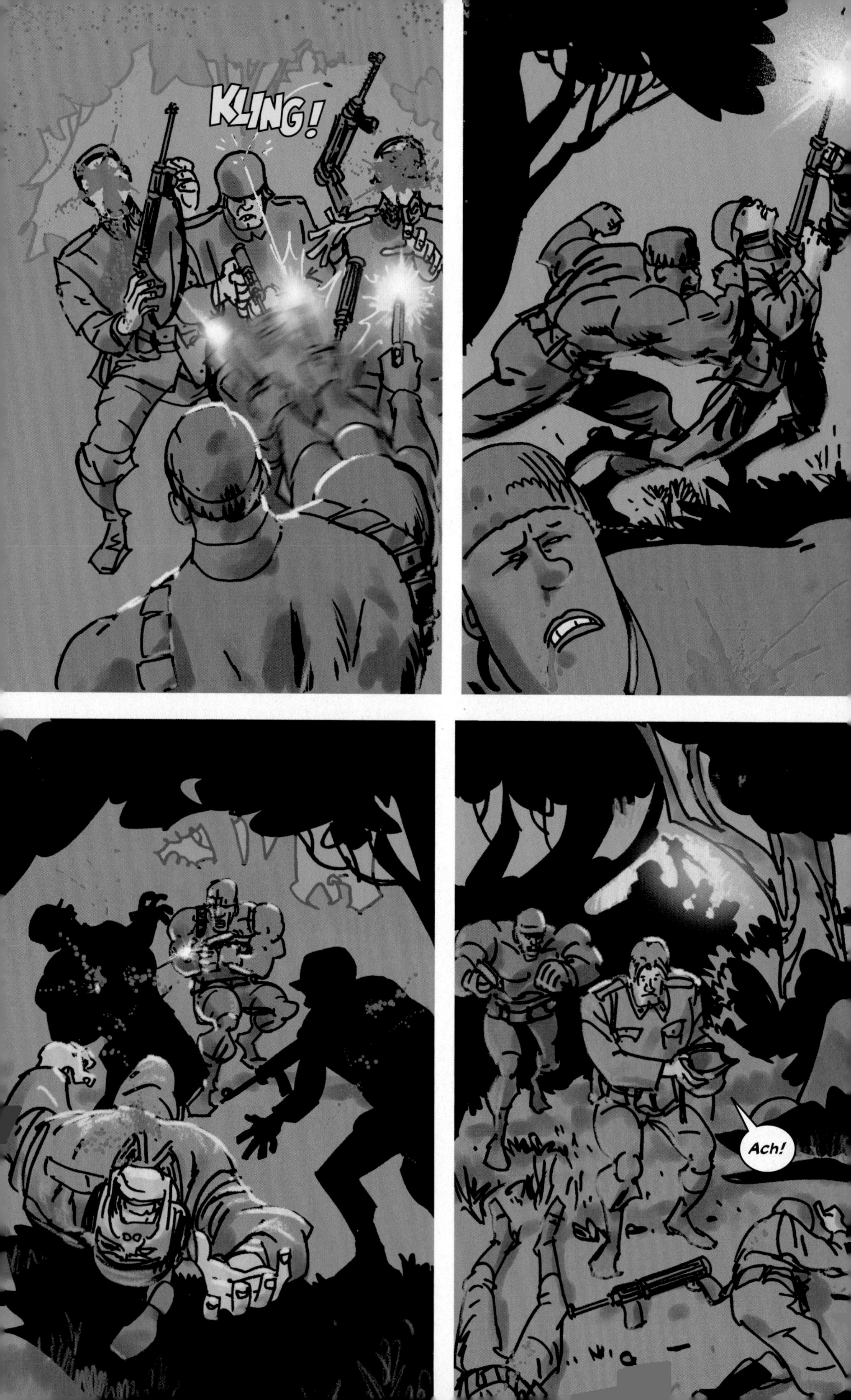
KLING!
Ach!

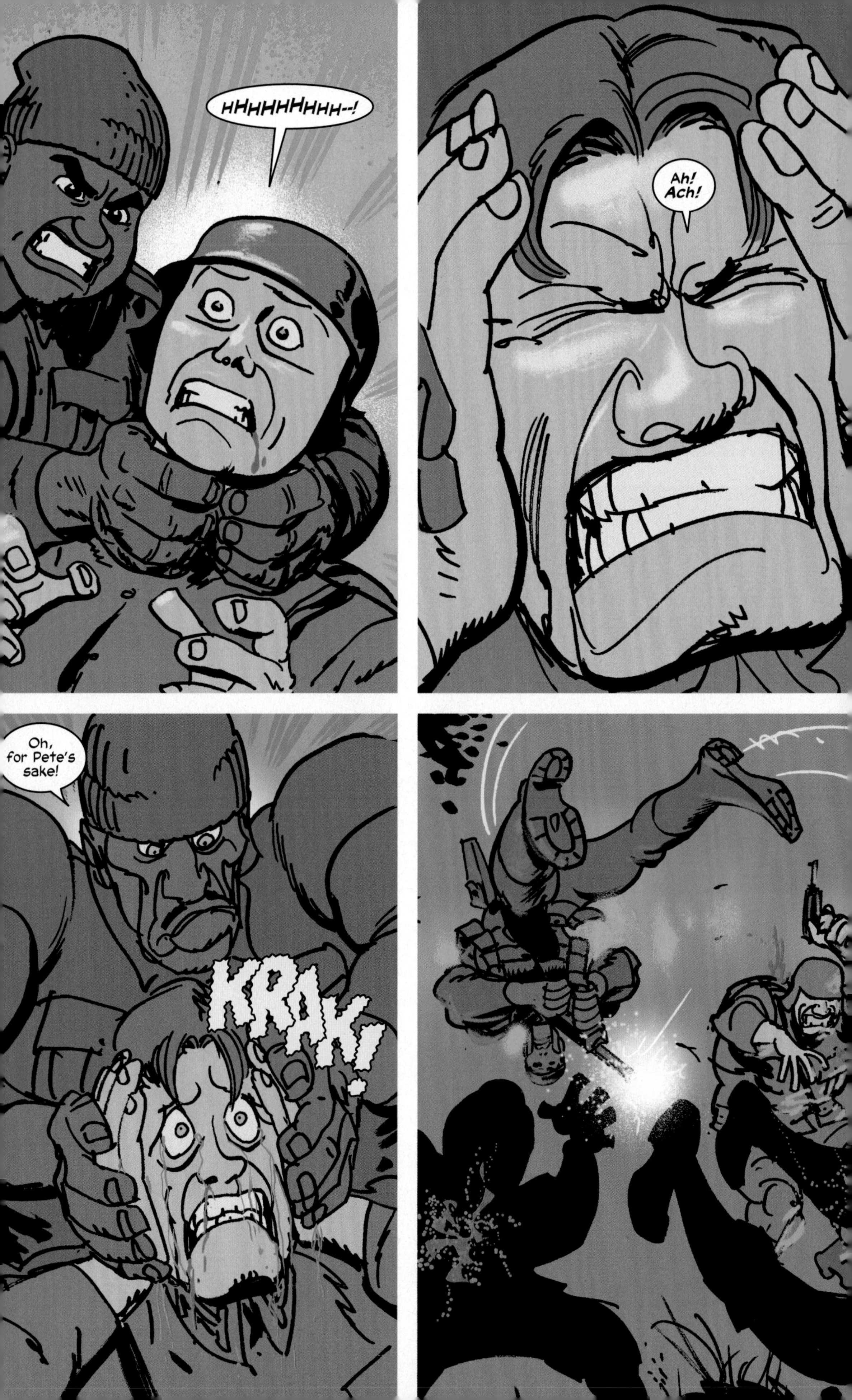
HHHHHHHHH--!
Ah! Ach!
Oh, for Pete's sake!
KRAK!

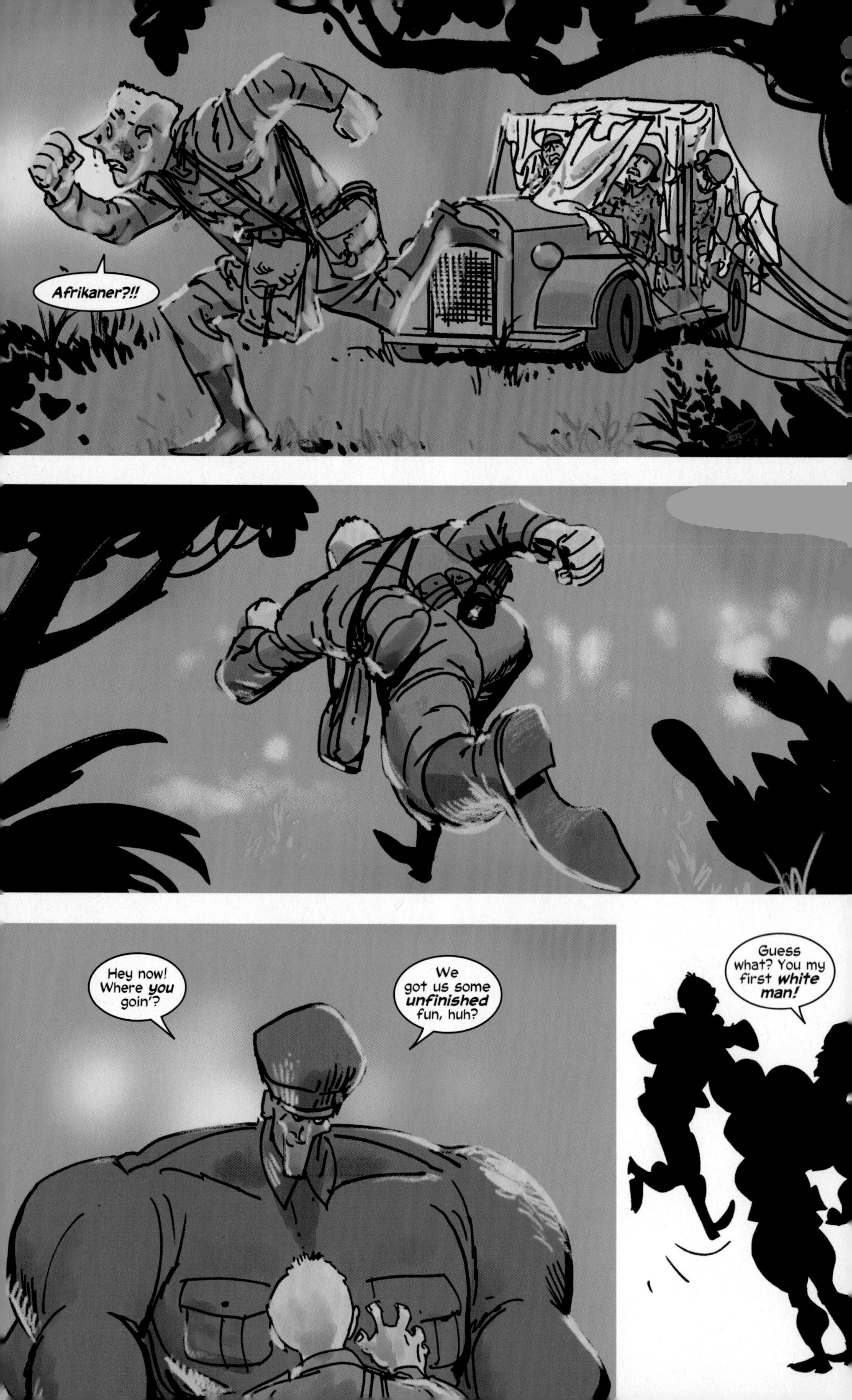
Afrikaner?!!
Hey now! Where you goin'?
We got us some unfinished fun, huh?
Guess what? You my first white man!

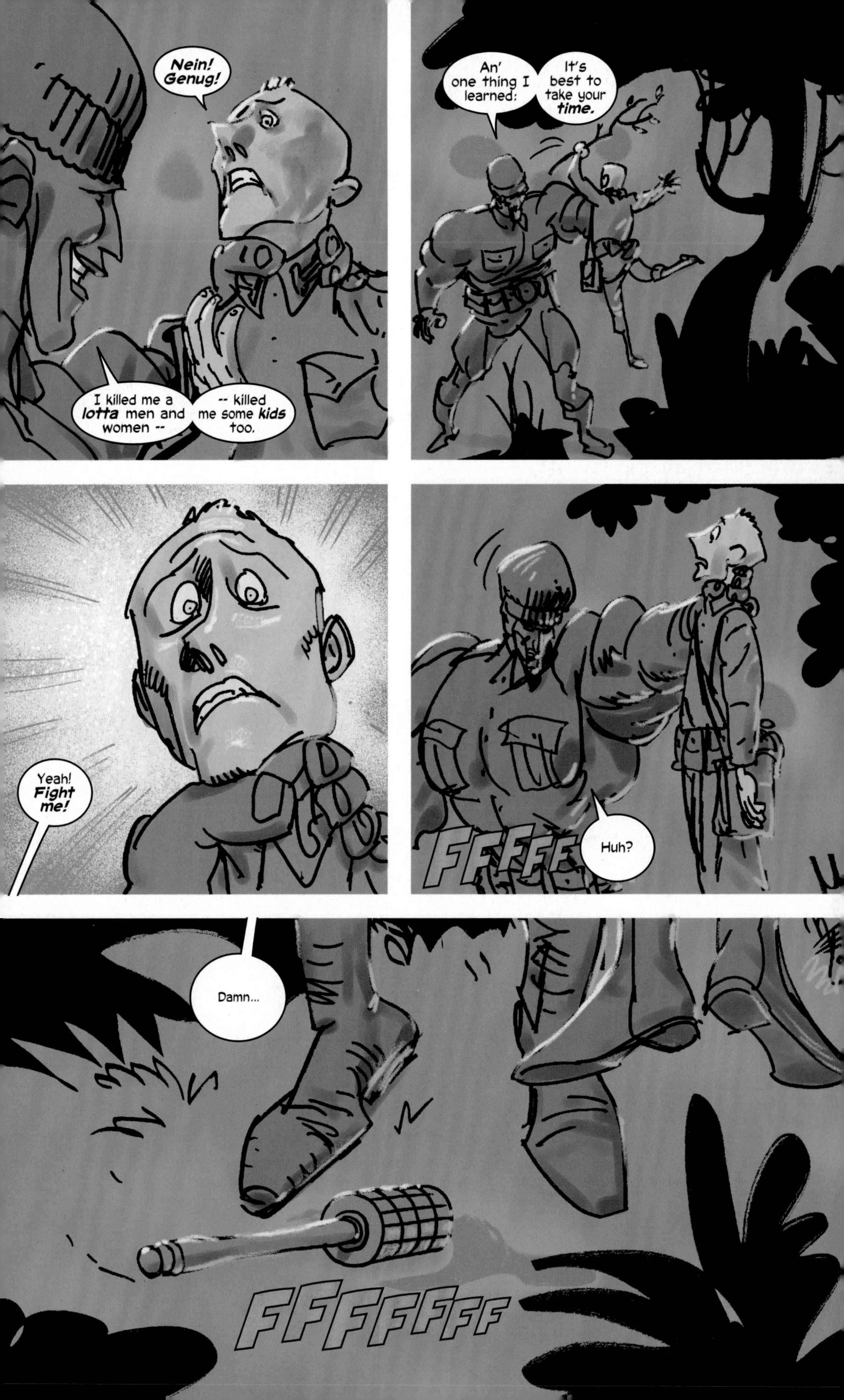

Nein! Genug!
I killed me a lotta men and women --
-- killed me some kids too.
An' one thing I learned:
It's best to take your time.
Yeah! Fight me!
FFFFF
Huh?
Damn...
FFFFFFF

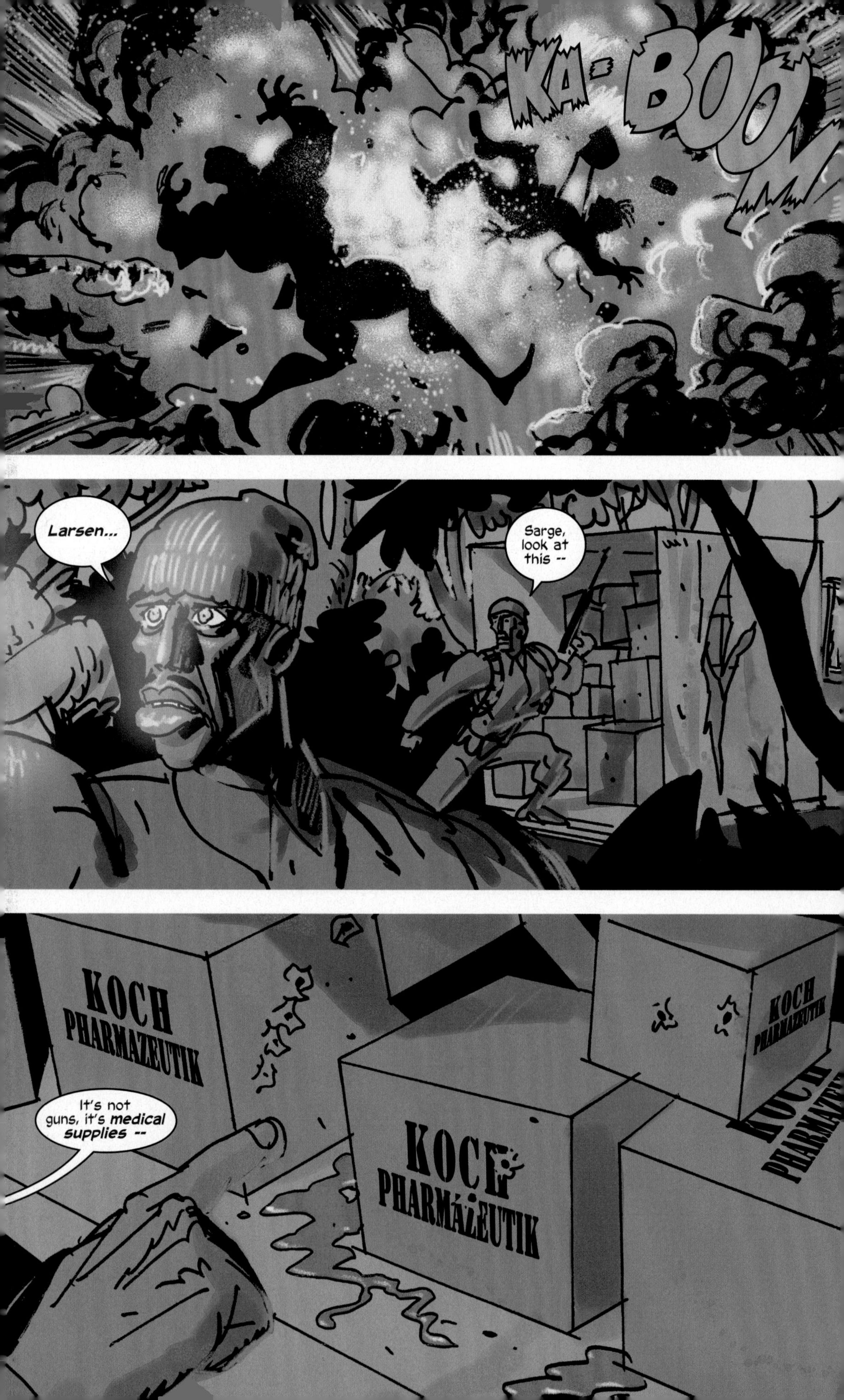
KA-BOOM
Larsen...
Sarge, look at this --
KOCH PHARMAZEUTIK
It's not guns, it's *medical* *supplies* --
KOCH PHARMAZEUTIK
KOCH PHARMAZEUTIK

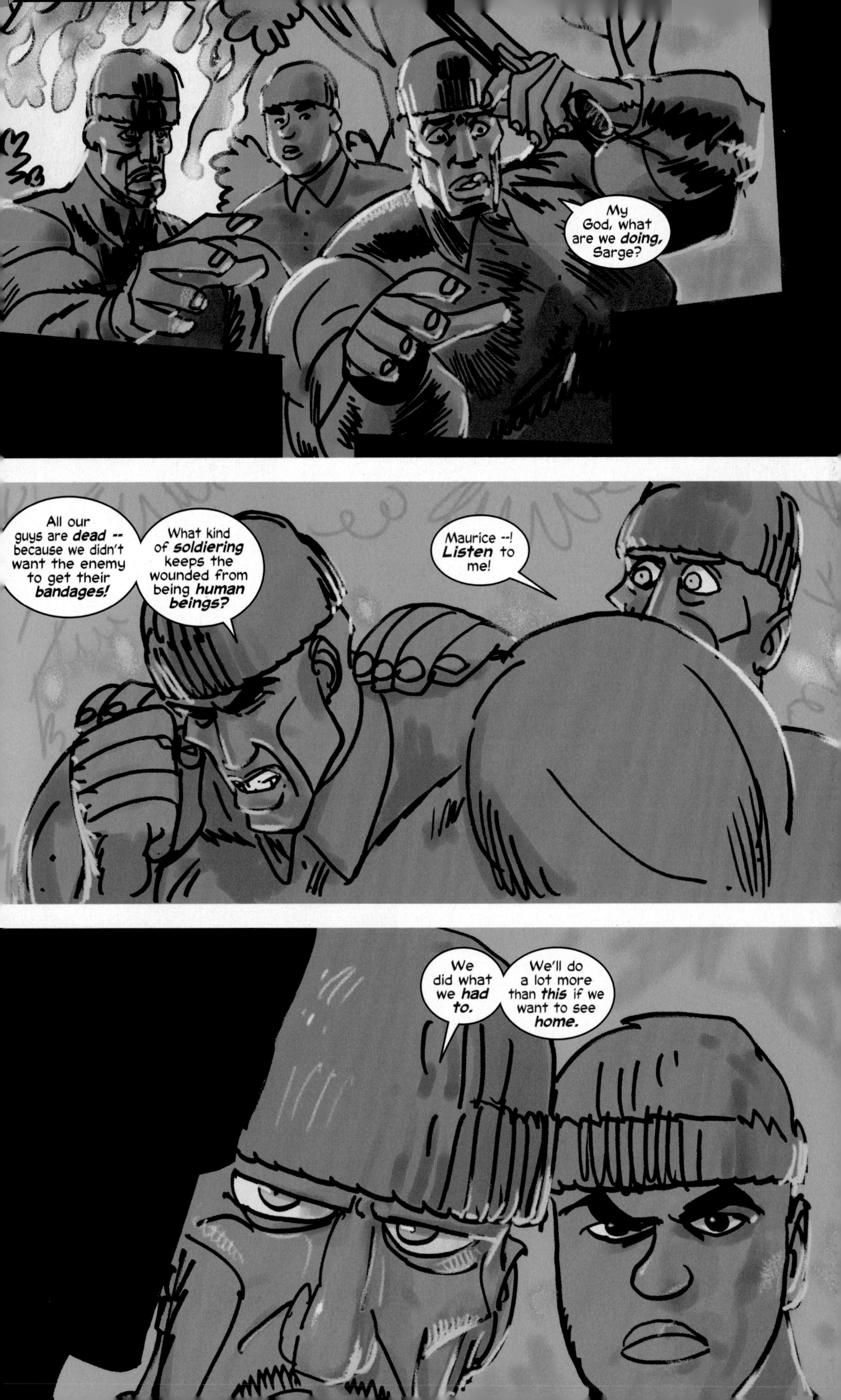

My God, what are we *doing,* Sarge?
All our guys are *dead --* because we didn't want the enemy to get their *bandages!*
What kind of *soldiering* keeps the wounded from being *human beings?*
Maurice --! *Listen* to me!
We did what we *had to.*
We'll do a lot more than *this* if we want to see *home.*

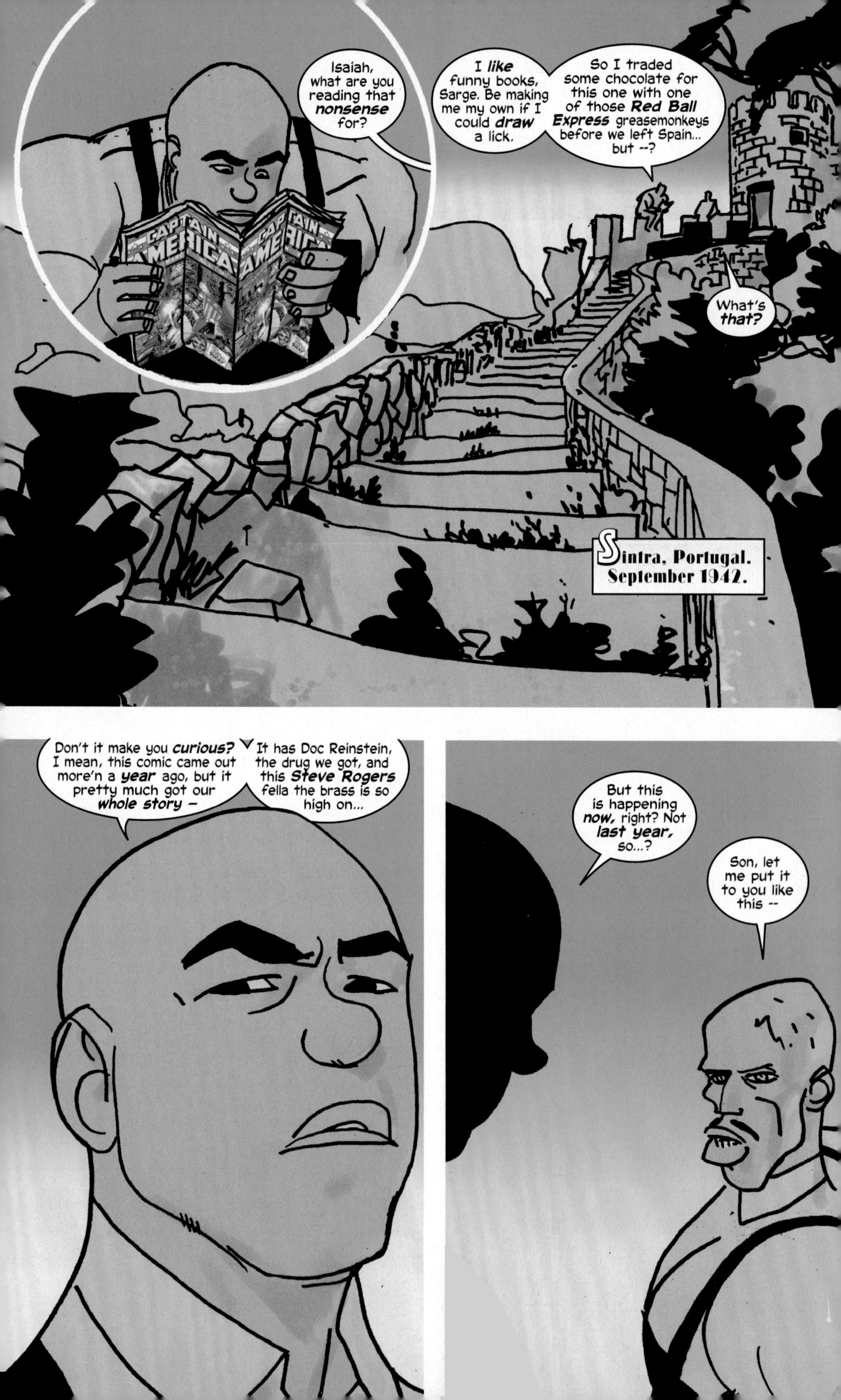
Isaiah, what are you reading that nonsense for?
I like funny books, Sarge. Be making me my own if I could draw a lick.
So I traded some chocolate for this one with one of those Red Ball Express greasemonkeys before we left Spain... but --?
What's that?
Sintra, Portugal. September 1942.
Don't it make you curious? I mean, this comic came out more'n a year ago, but it pretty much got our whole story –
It has Doc Reinstein, the drug we got, and this Steve Rogers fella the brass is so high on...
But this is happening now, right? Not last year, so...?
Son, let me put it to you like this --

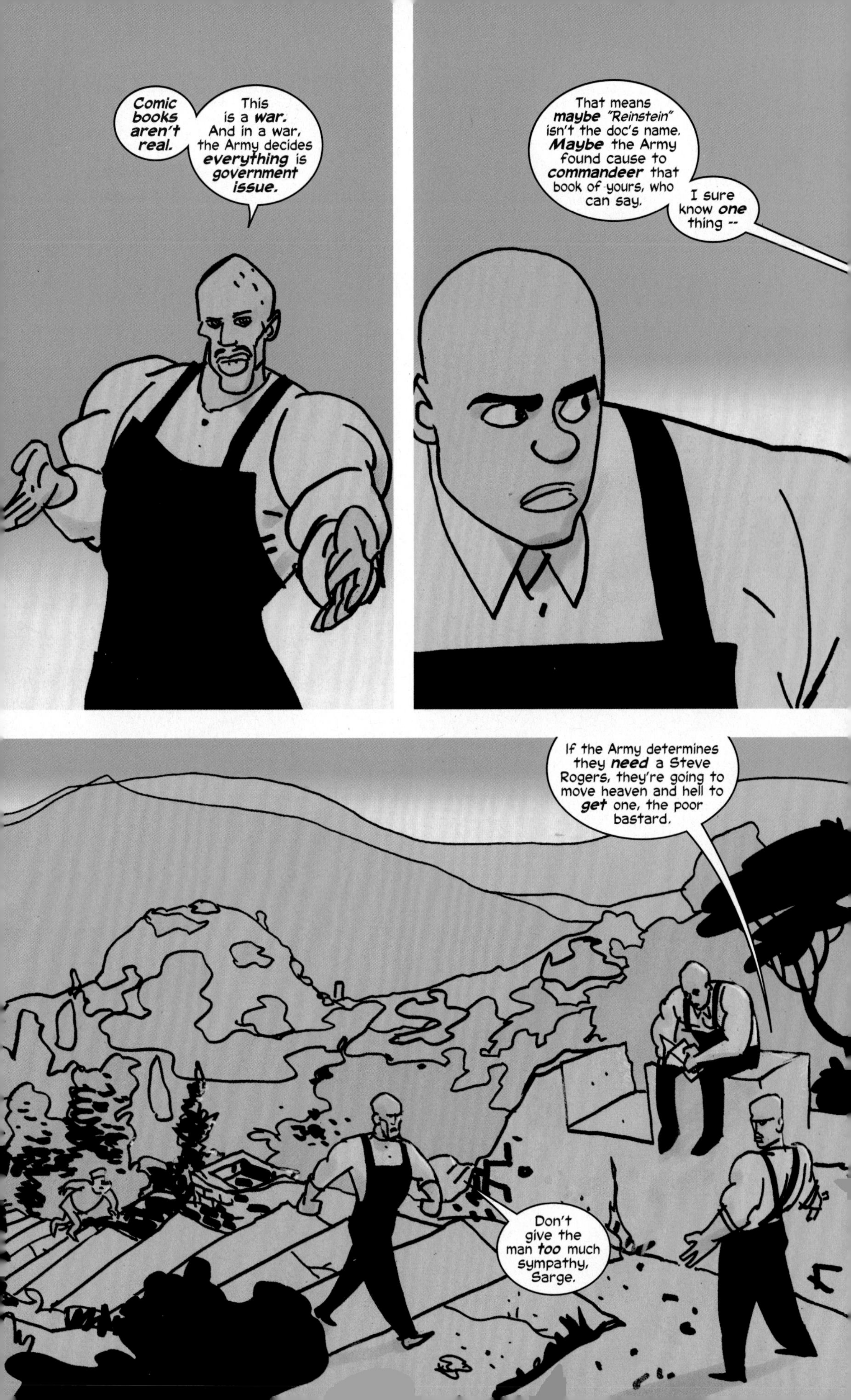

Comic books aren't real.
This is a war. And in a war, the Army decides everything is government issue.
That means maybe "Reinstein" isn't the doc's name. Maybe the Army found cause to commandeer that book of yours, who can say.
I sure know one thing --
If the Army determines they need a Steve Rogers, they're going to move heaven and hell to get one, the poor bastard.
Don't give the man too much sympathy, Sarge.

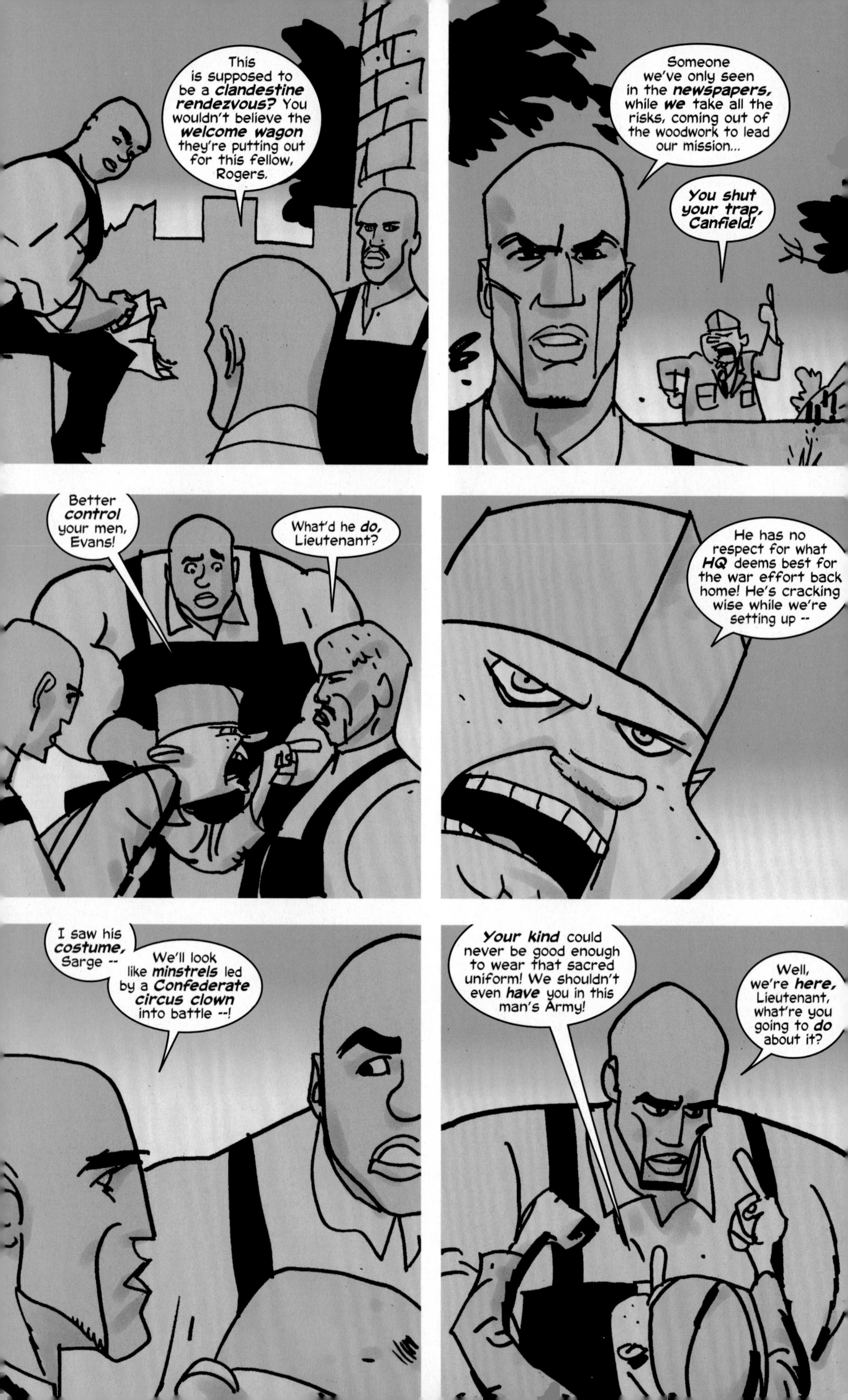
This is supposed to be a clandestine rendezvous? You wouldn't believe the welcome wagon they're putting out for this fellow, Rogers.
Someone we've only seen in the newspapers, while we take all the risks, coming out of the woodwork to lead our mission...
You shut your trap, Canfield!
Better control your men, Evans!
What'd he do, Lieutenant?
He has no respect for what HQ deems best for the war effort back home! He's cracking wise while we're setting up --
I saw his costume, Sarge --
We'll look like minstrels led by a Confederate circus clown into battle --!
Your kind could never be good enough to wear that sacred uniform! We shouldn't even have you in this man's Army!
Well, we're here, Lieutenant, what're you going to do about it?

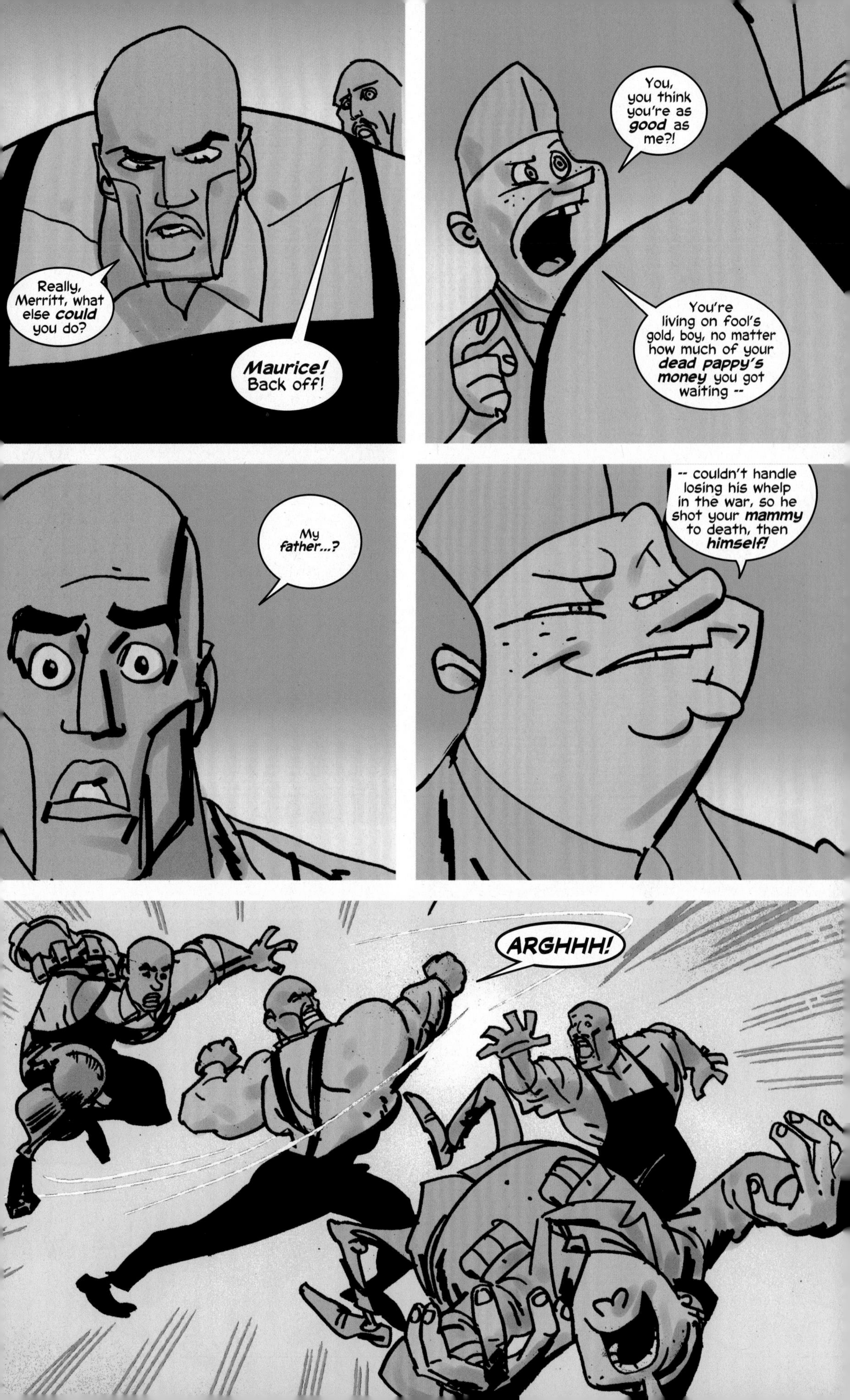

Really, Merritt, what else could you do?
Maurice! Back off!
You, you think you're as good as me?!
You're living on fool's gold, boy, no matter how much of your dead pappy's money you got waiting --
My father...?
-- couldn't handle losing his whelp in the war, so he shot your mammy to death, then himself!
ARGHHH!

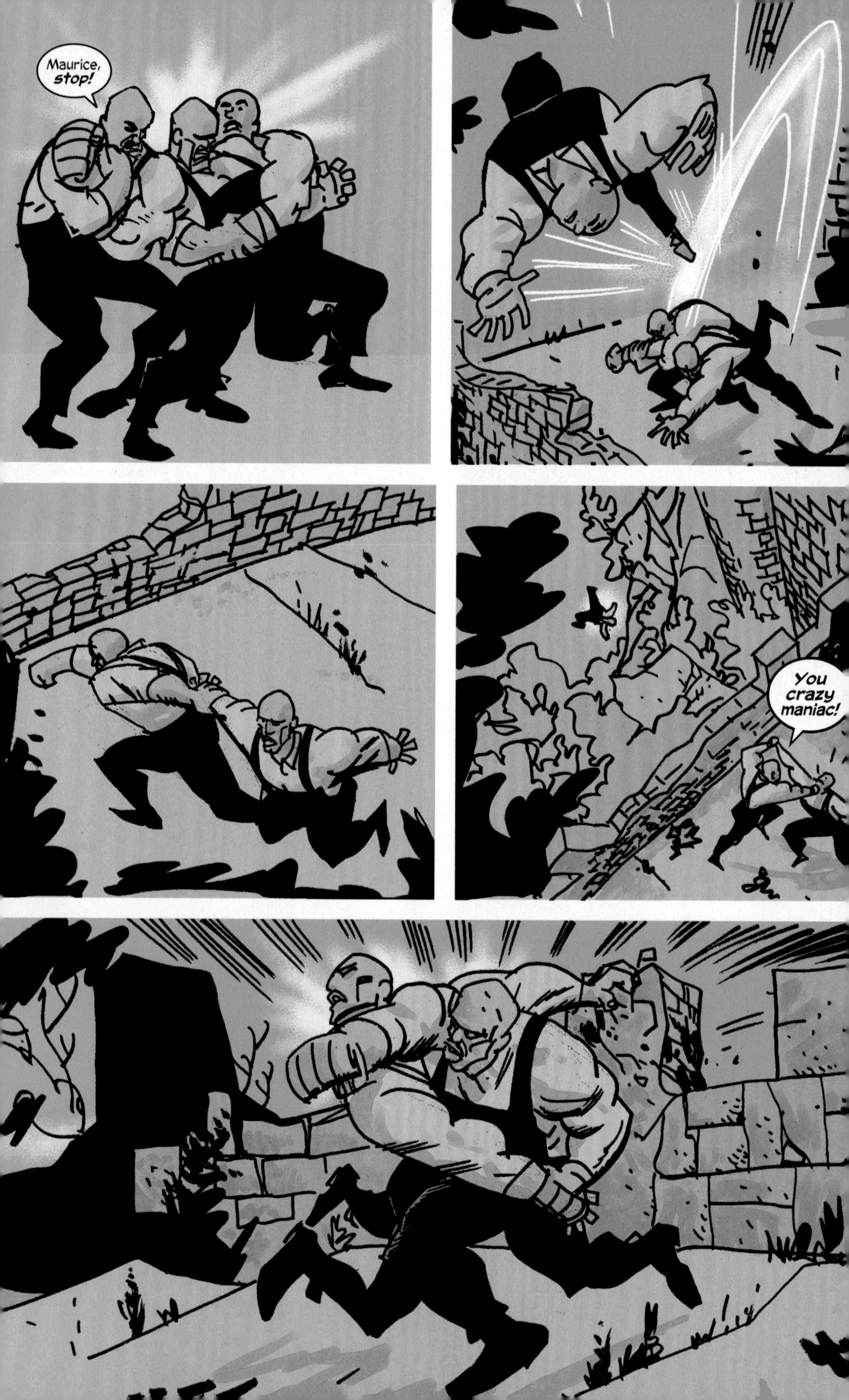

Maurice, stop!
You crazy maniac!

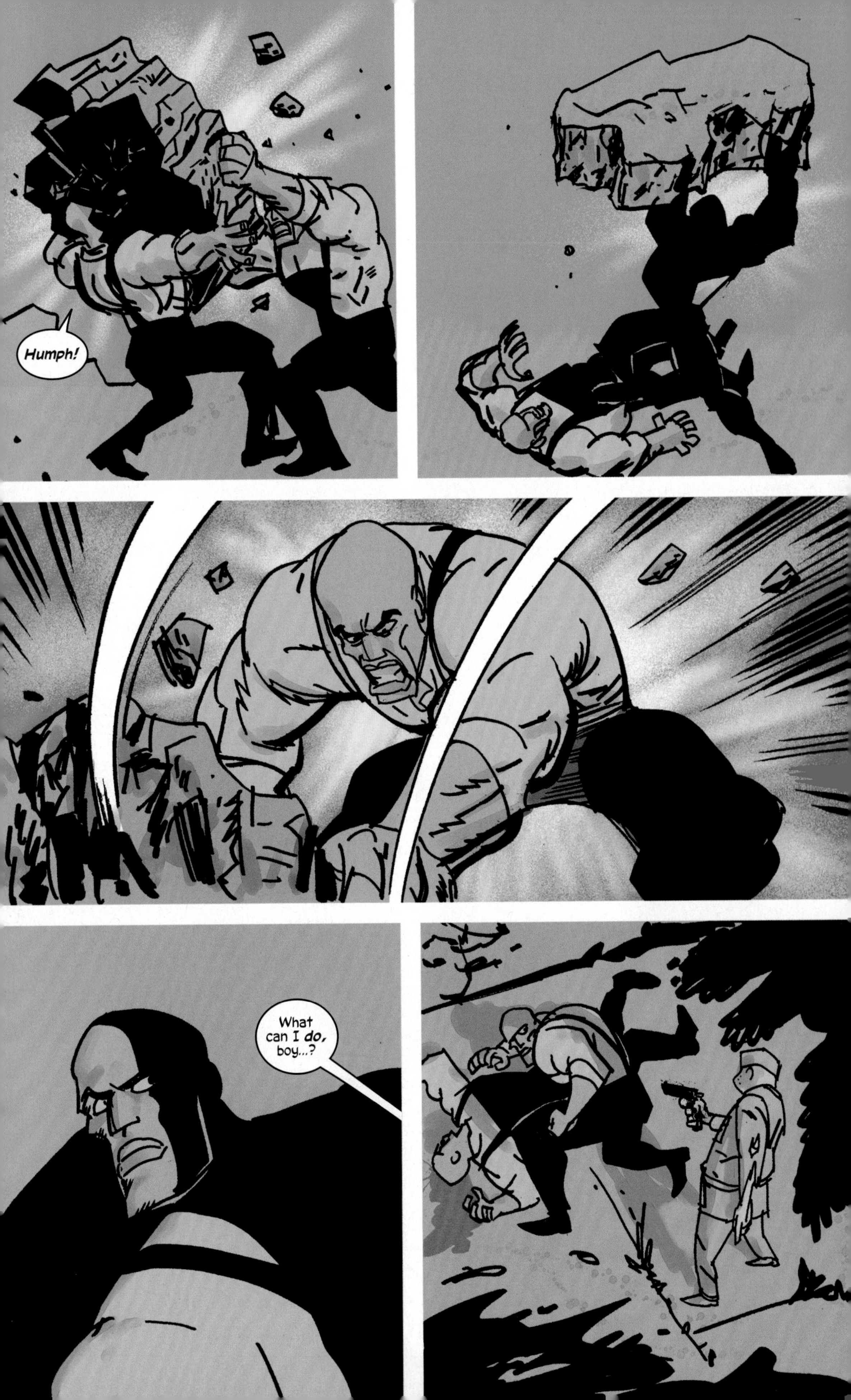

Humph!
What can I *do*, boy...?

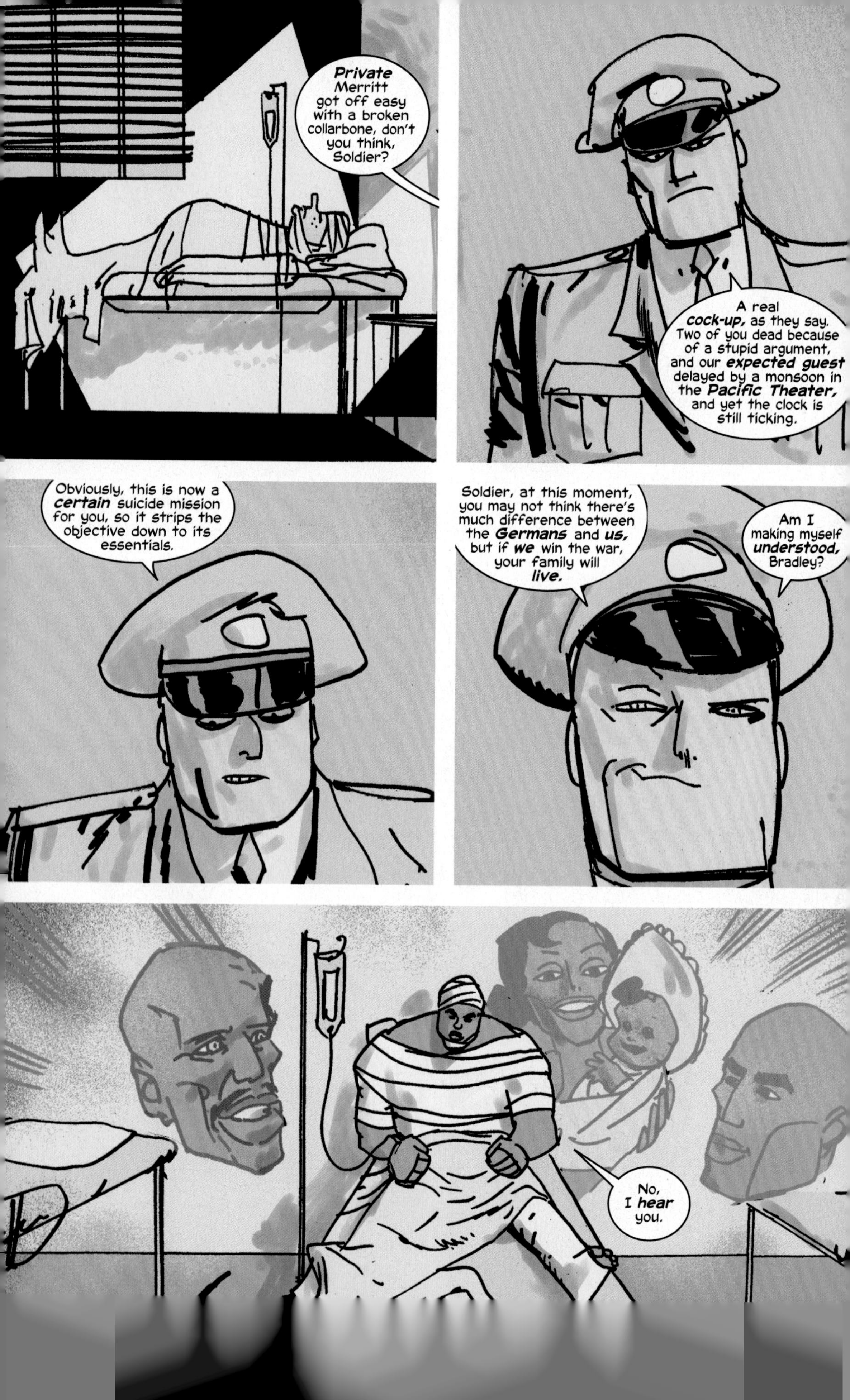
Private Merritt got off easy with a broken collarbone, don't you think, Soldier?
A real cock-up, as they say. Two of you dead because of a stupid argument, and our expected guest delayed by a monsoon in the Pacific Theater, and yet the clock is still ticking.
Obviously, this is now a certain suicide mission for you, so it strips the objective down to its essentials.
Soldier, at this moment, you may not think there's much difference between the Germans and us, but if we win the war, your family will live.
Am I making myself understood, Bradley?
No, I hear you.

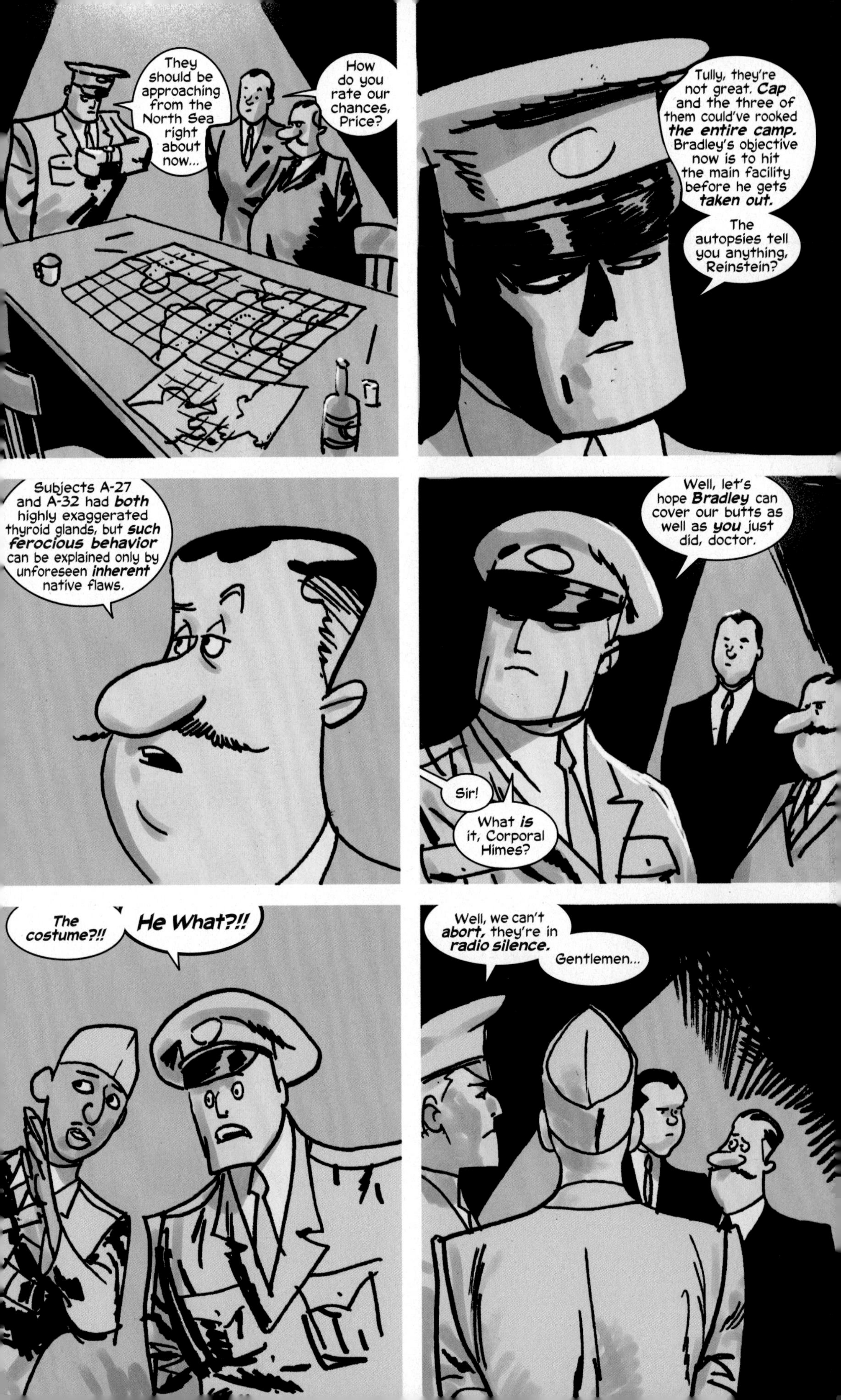
They should be approaching from the North Sea right about now...
How do you rate our chances, Price?
Tully, they're not great. Cap and the three of them could've rooked the entire camp. Bradley's objective now is to hit the main facility before he gets taken out.
The autopsies tell you anything, Reinstein?
Subjects A-27 and A-32 had both highly exaggerated thyroid glands, but such ferocious behavior can be explained only by unforeseen inherent native flaws.
Well, let's hope Bradley can cover our butts as well as you just did, doctor.
Sir!
What is it, Corporal Himes?
The costume?!!
He What?!!
Well, we can't abort, they're in radio silence.
Gentlemen...

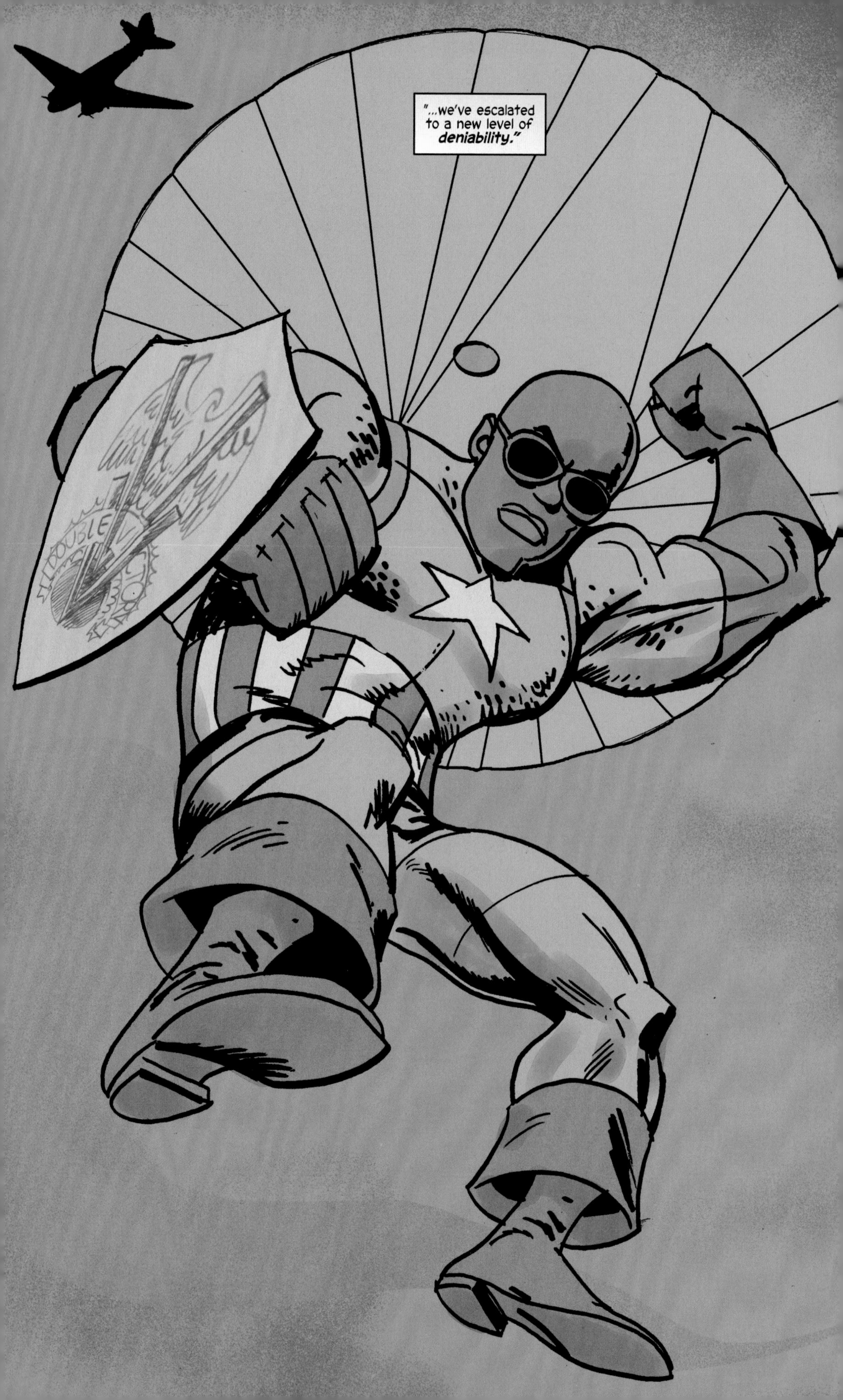
"...we've escalated to a new level of *deniability.*"

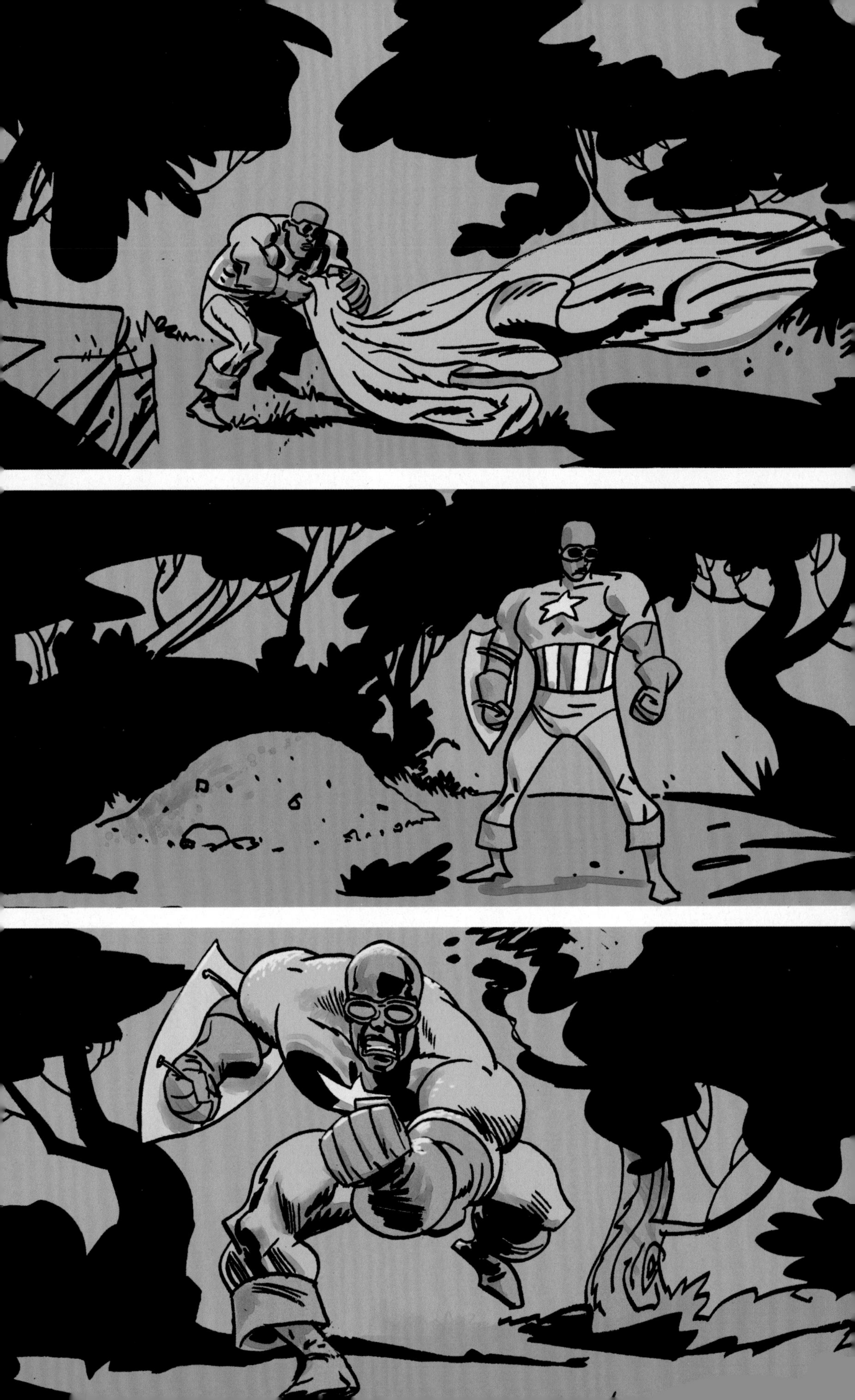

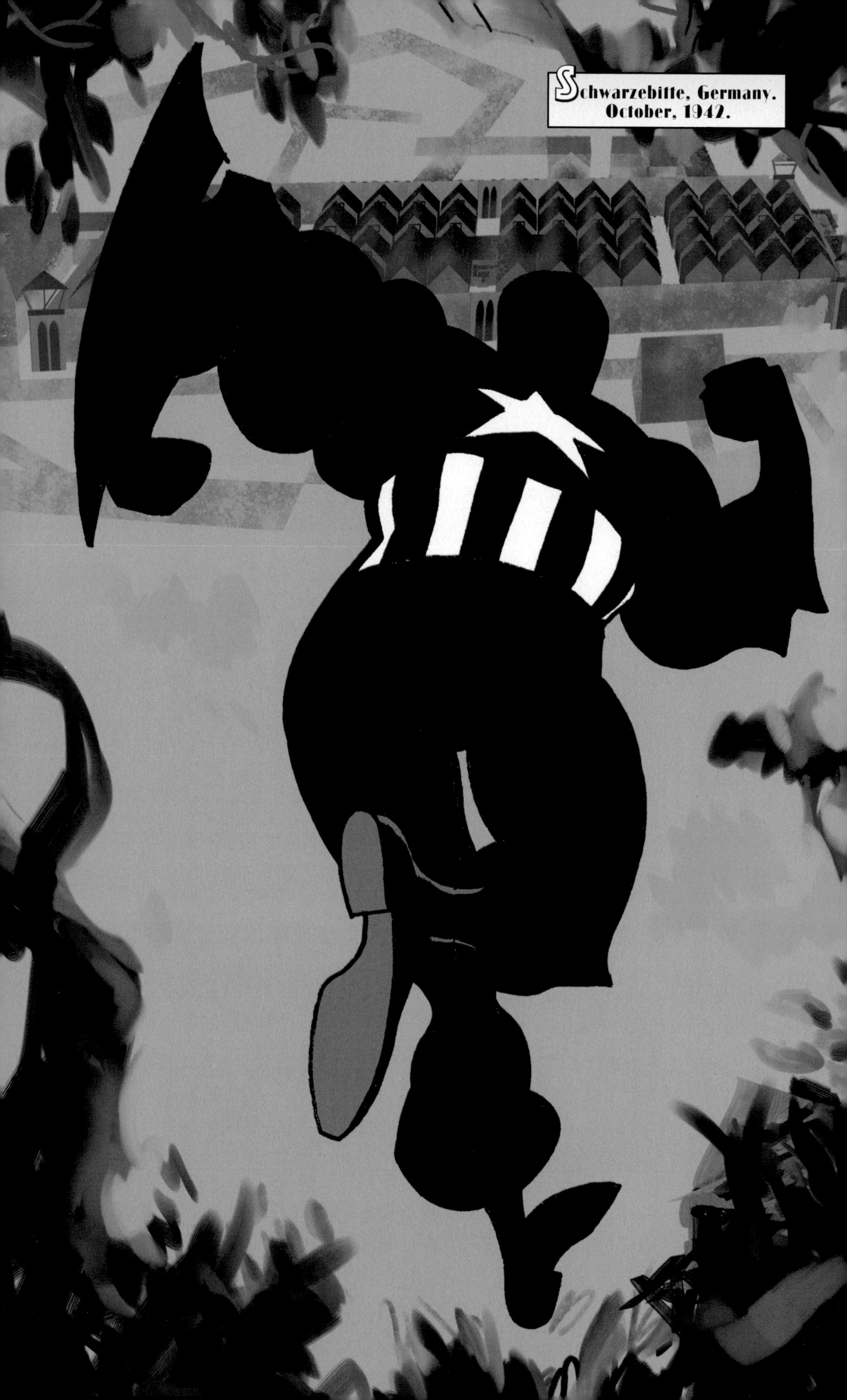
Schwarzebitte, Germany.
October, 1942.

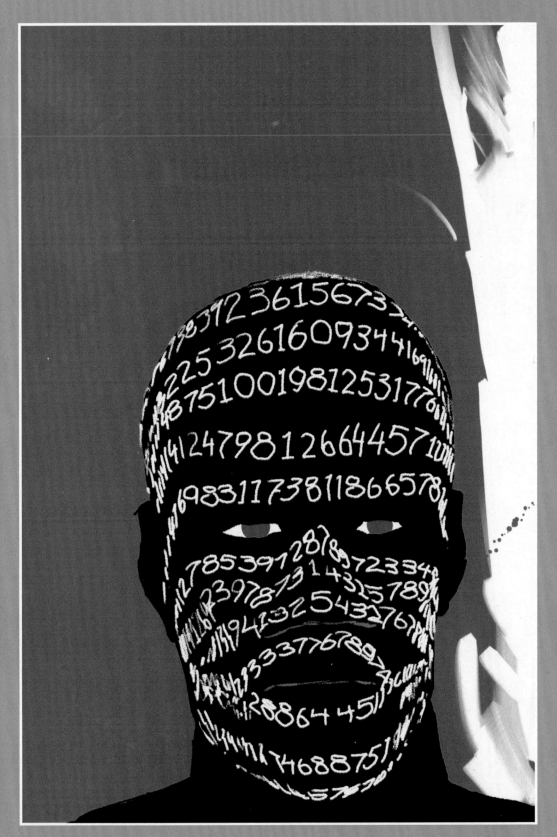

UNUSED TREATMENT, #5 COVER

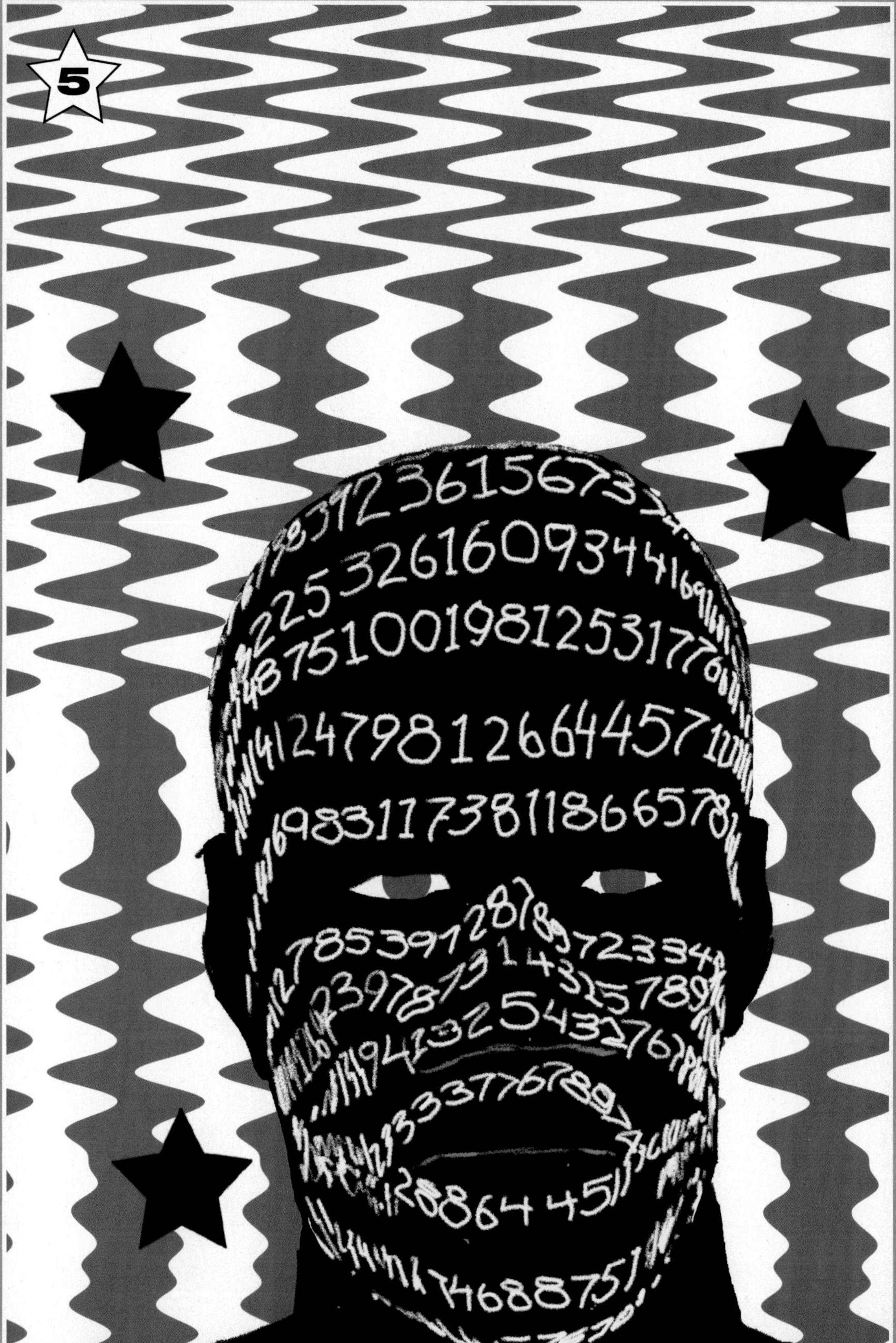
5

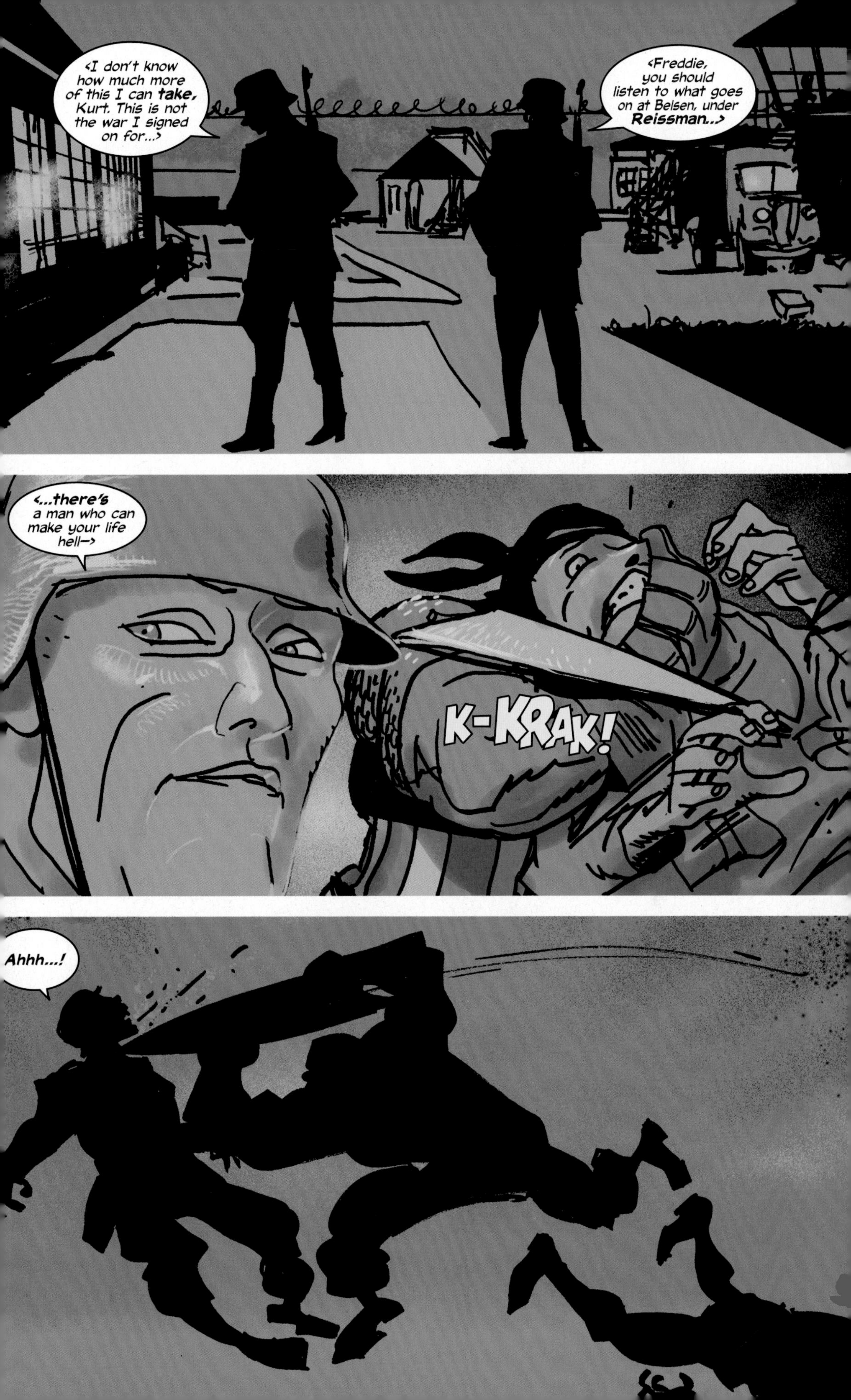

<I don't know how much more of this I can take, Kurt. This is not the war I signed on for...>
<Freddie, you should listen to what goes on at Belsen, under Reissman...>
<...there's a man who can make your life hell—>
K-KRAK!
Ahhh...!

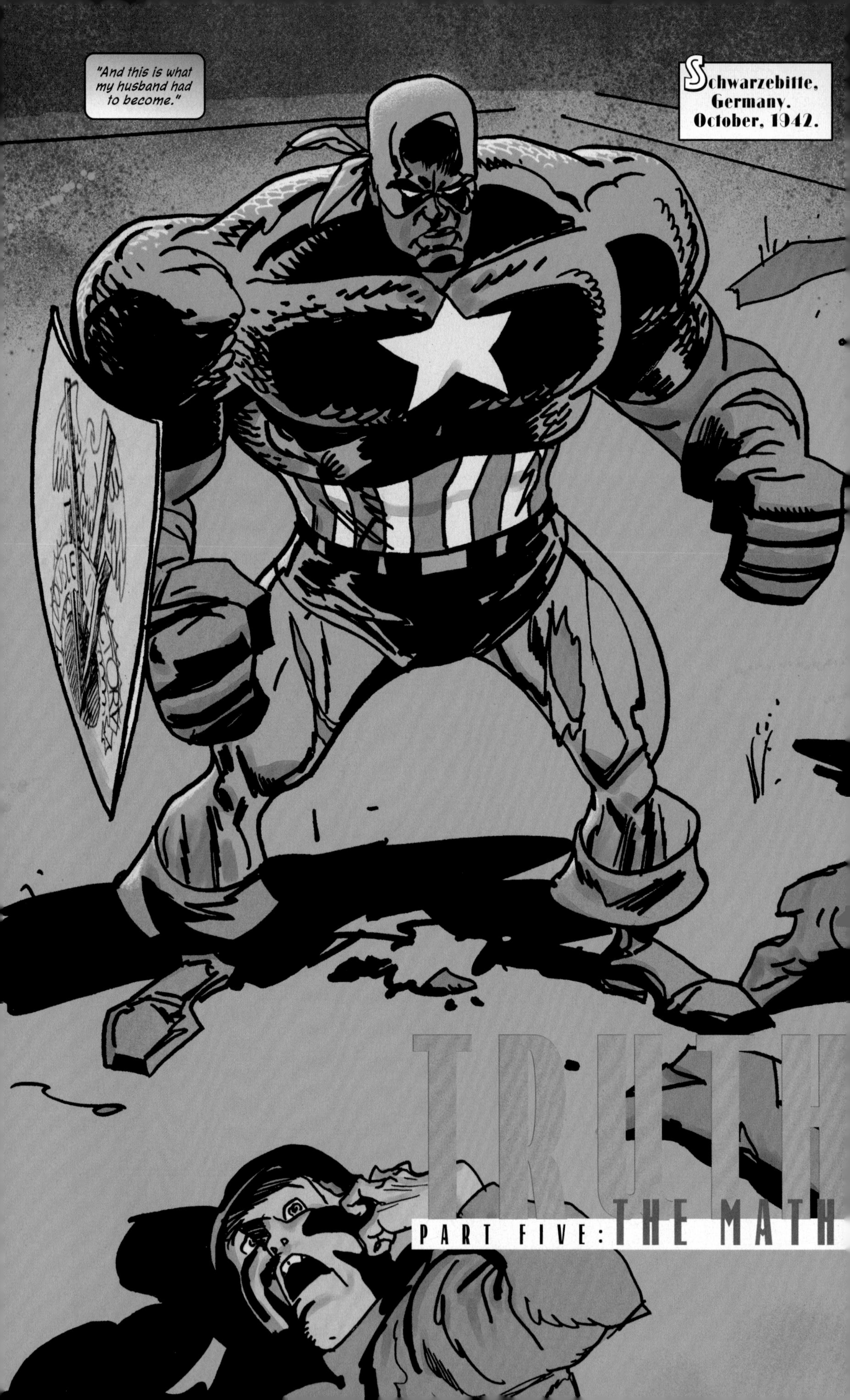
"And this is what my husband had to become."
Schwarzebitte, Germany. October, 1942.
TRUTH
PART FIVE: THE MATH

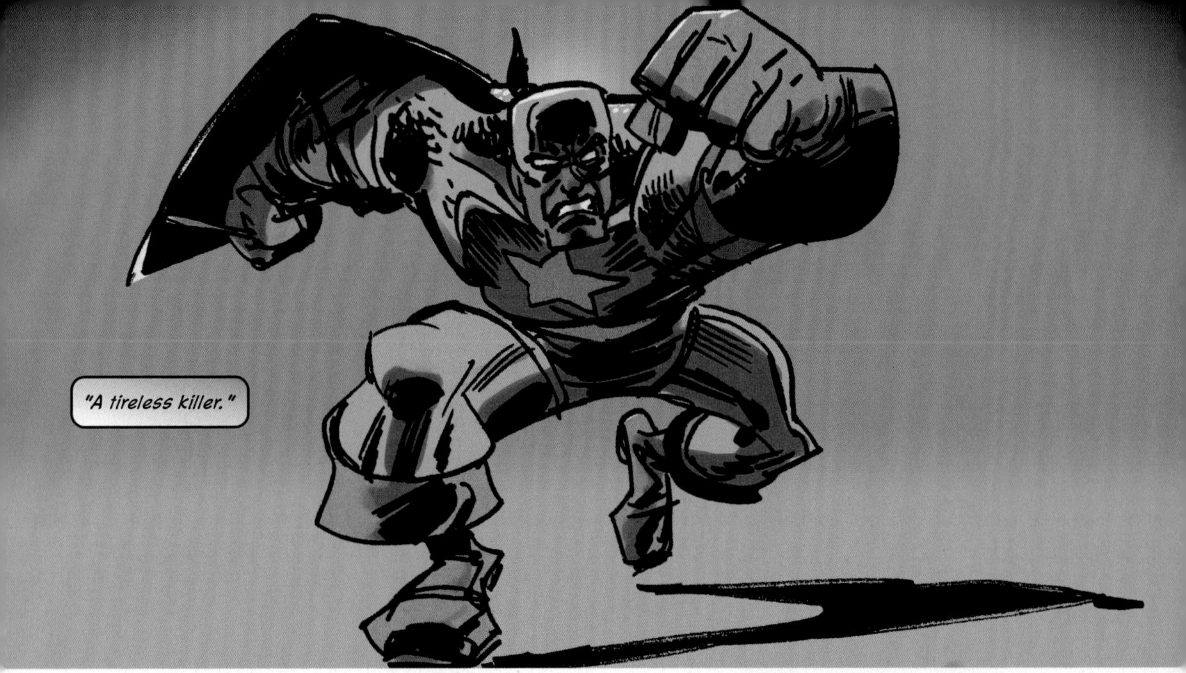
"A tireless killer."

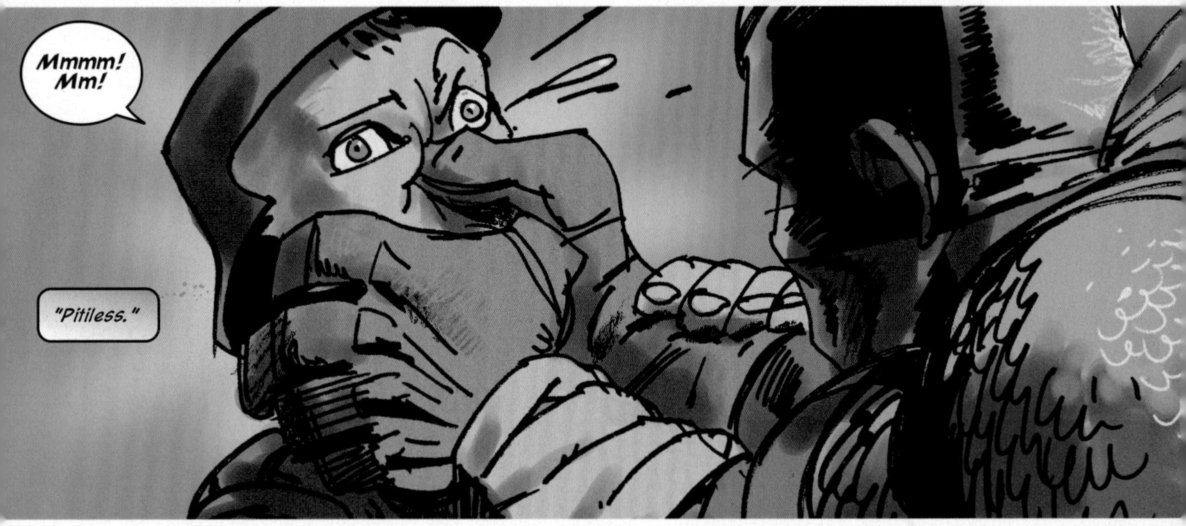
Mmmm! Mm!
"Pitiless."

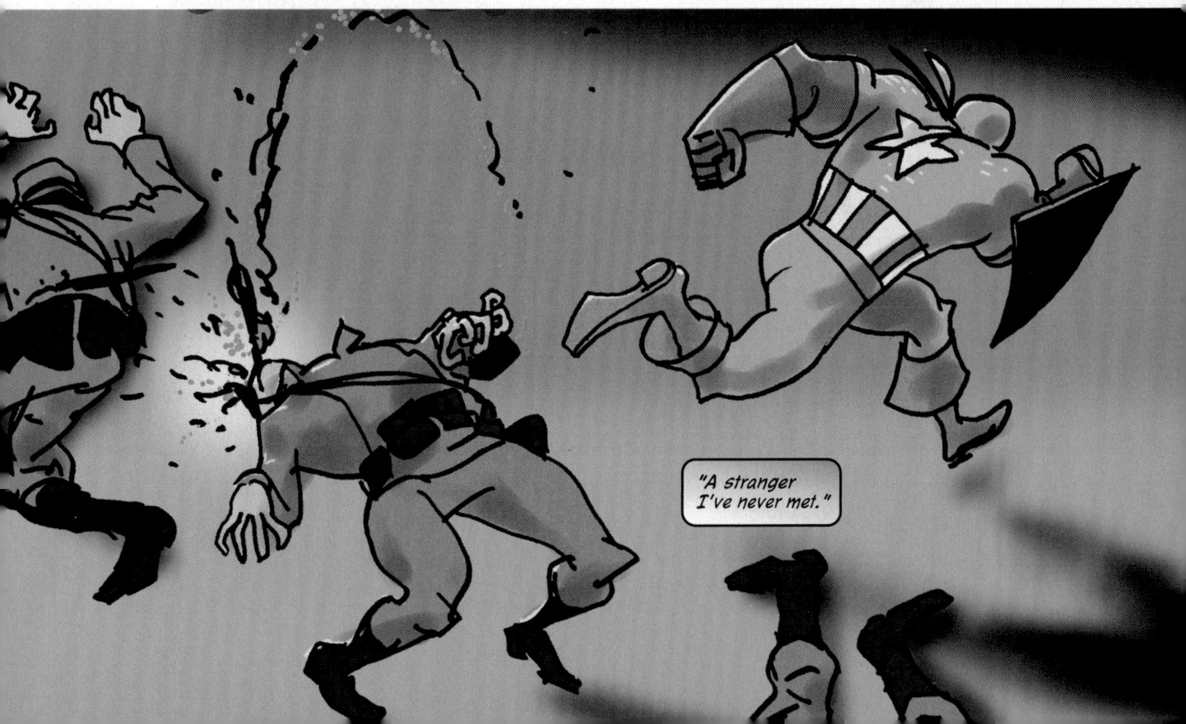
"A stranger I've never met."

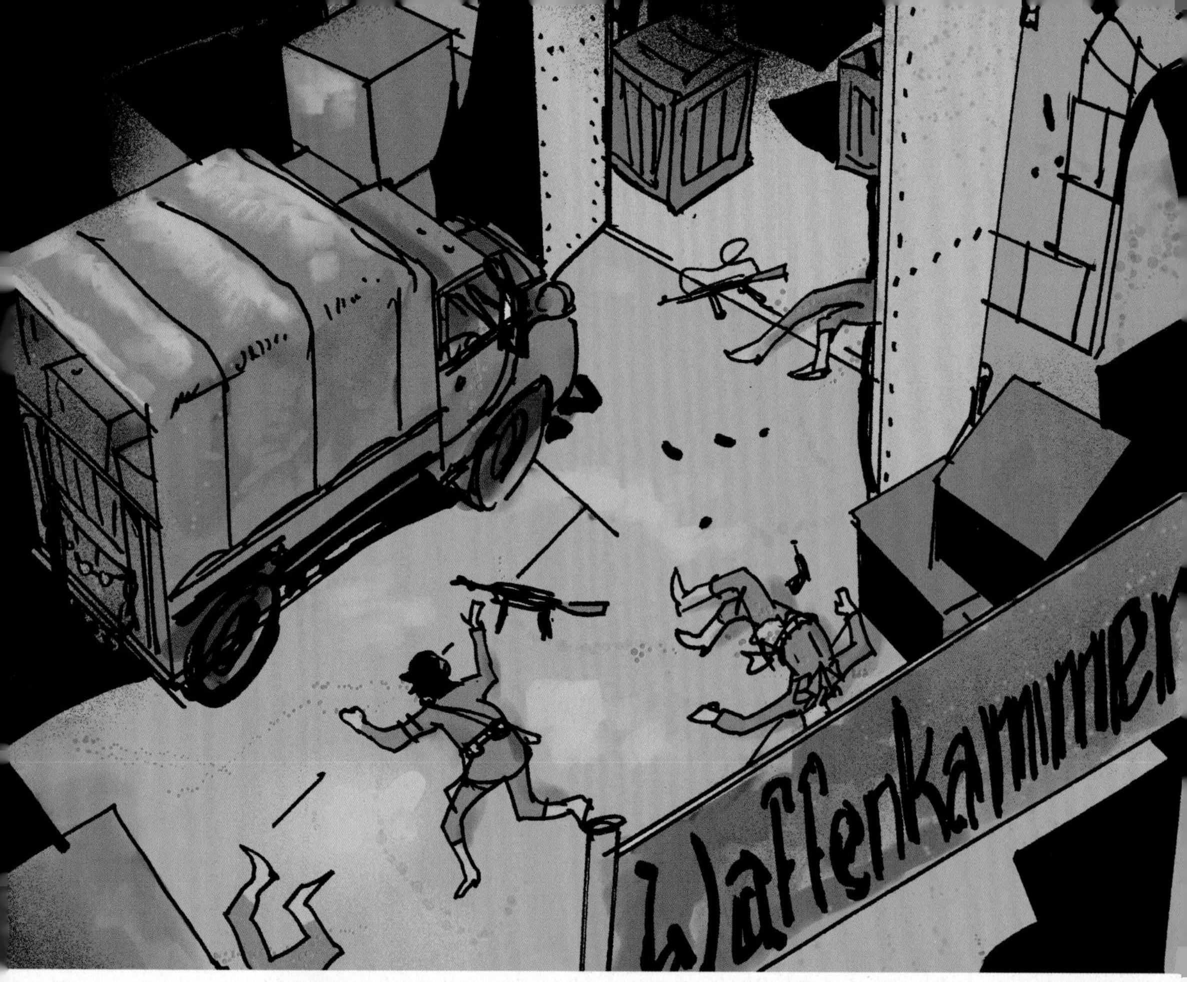
Waffenkammer
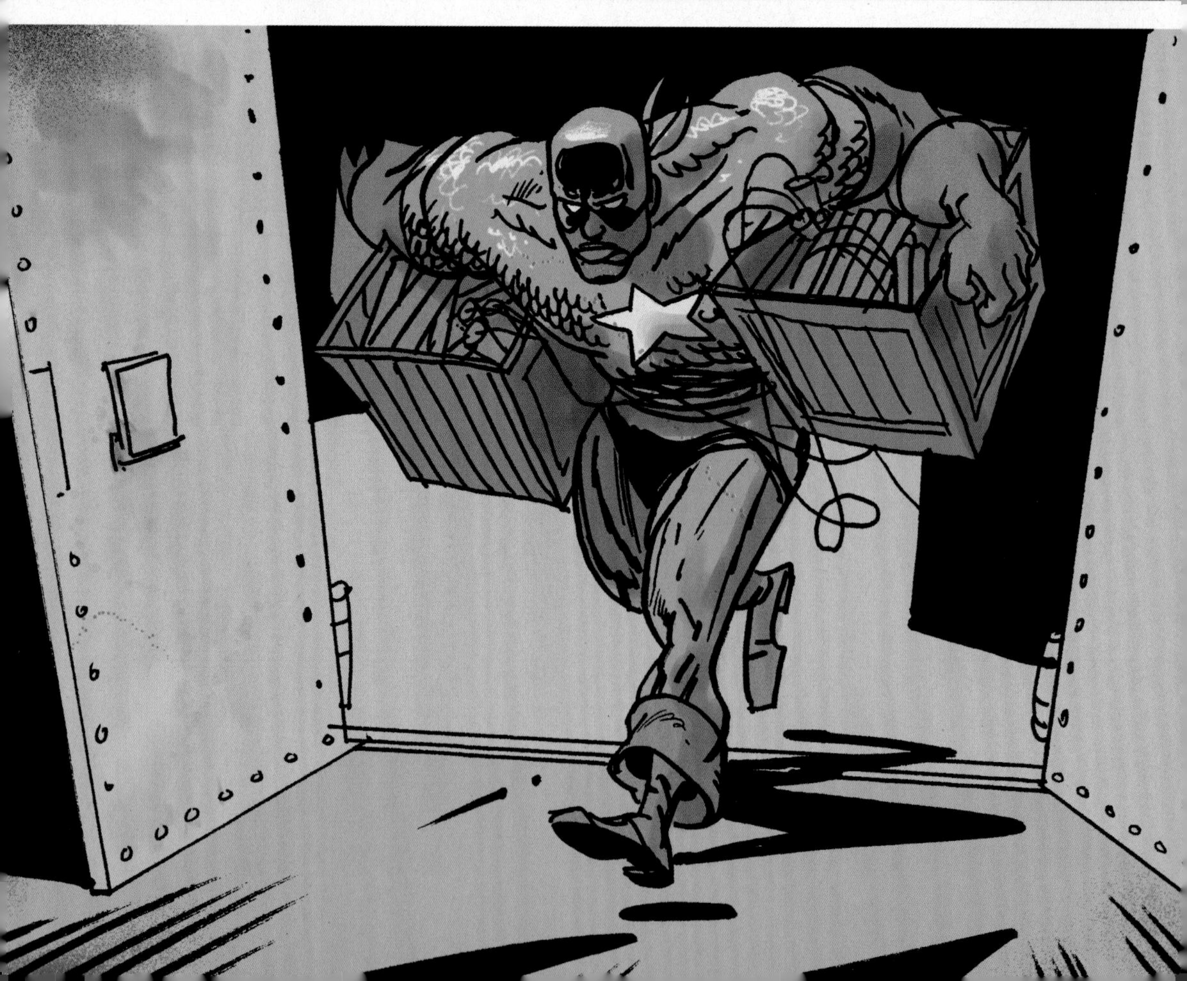

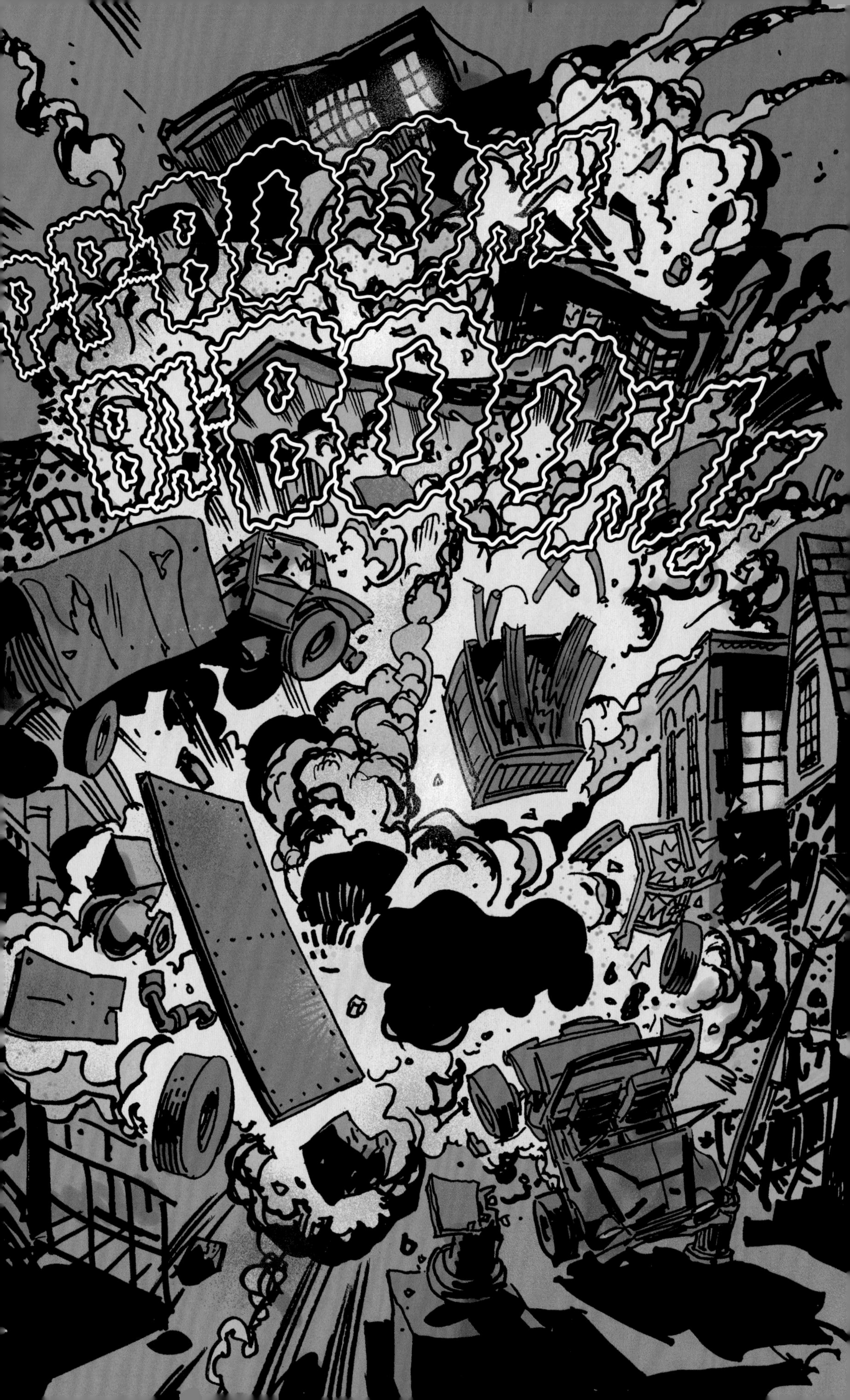
PRROOM!
BHOOM!!

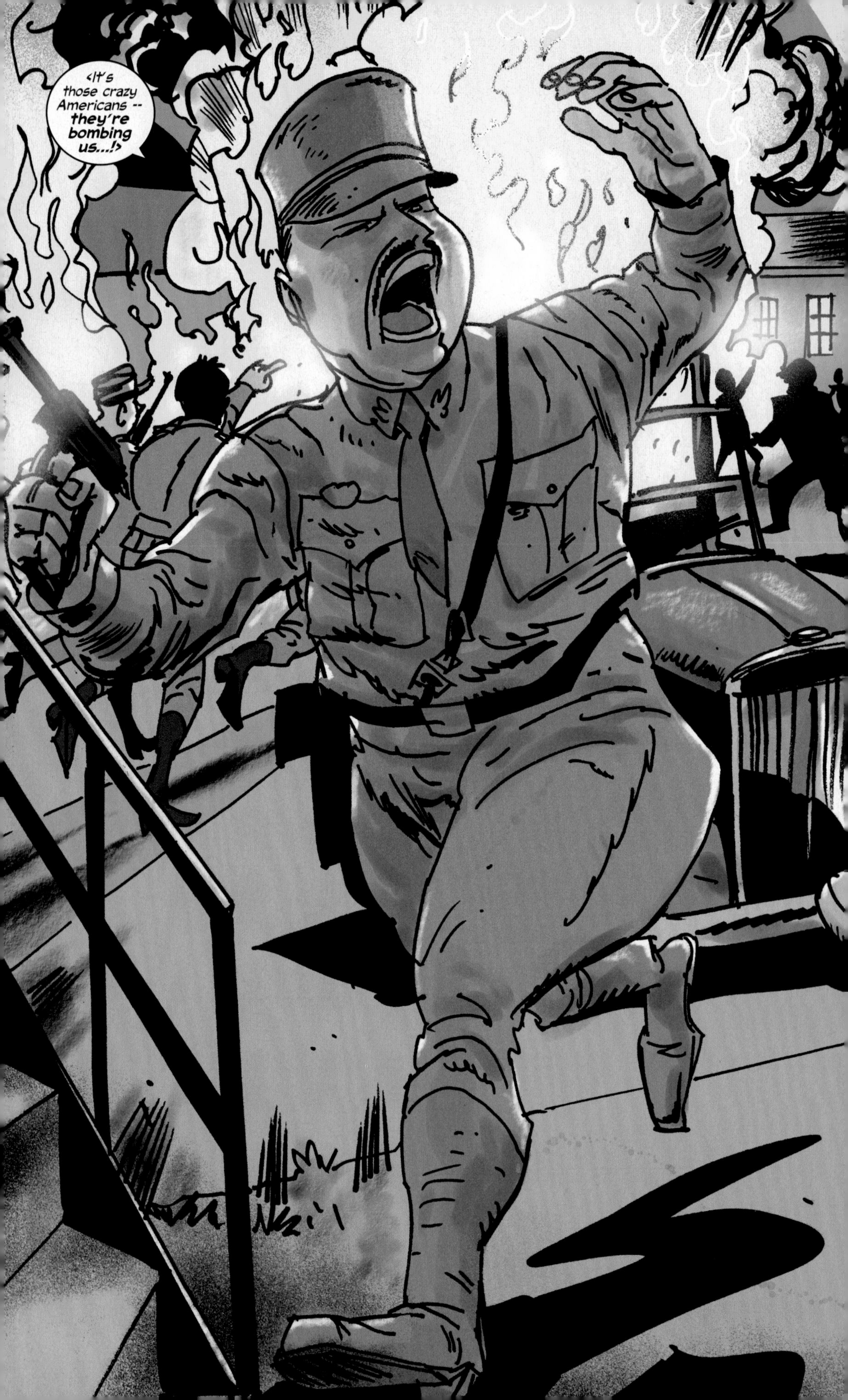
<It's those crazy Americans -- they're bombing us...!>

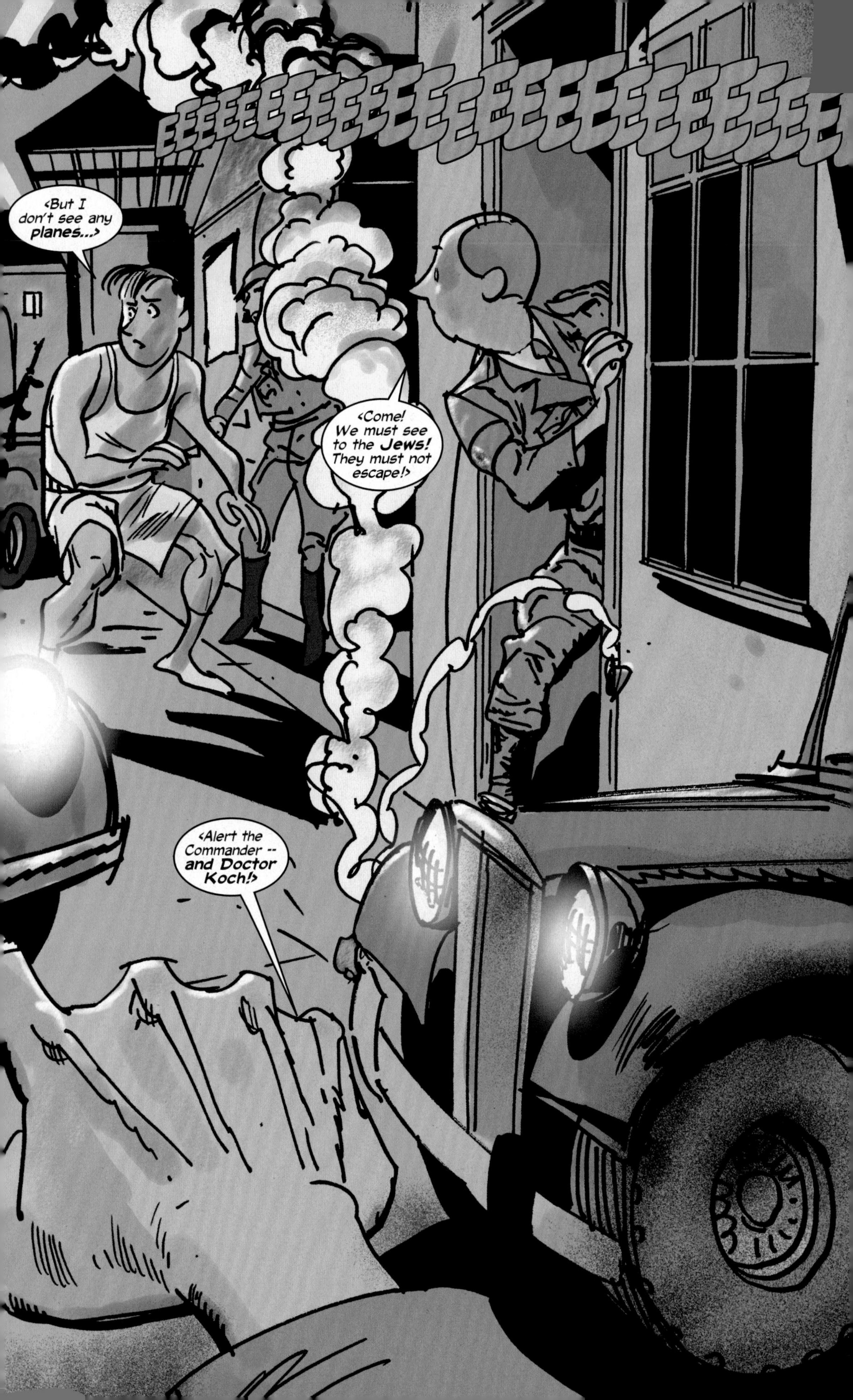
EEEEEEEEEEEEEEEEEEEEEEEEE
‹But I don't see any planes...›
‹Come! We must see to the Jews! They must not escape!›
‹Alert the Commander -- and Doctor Koch!›

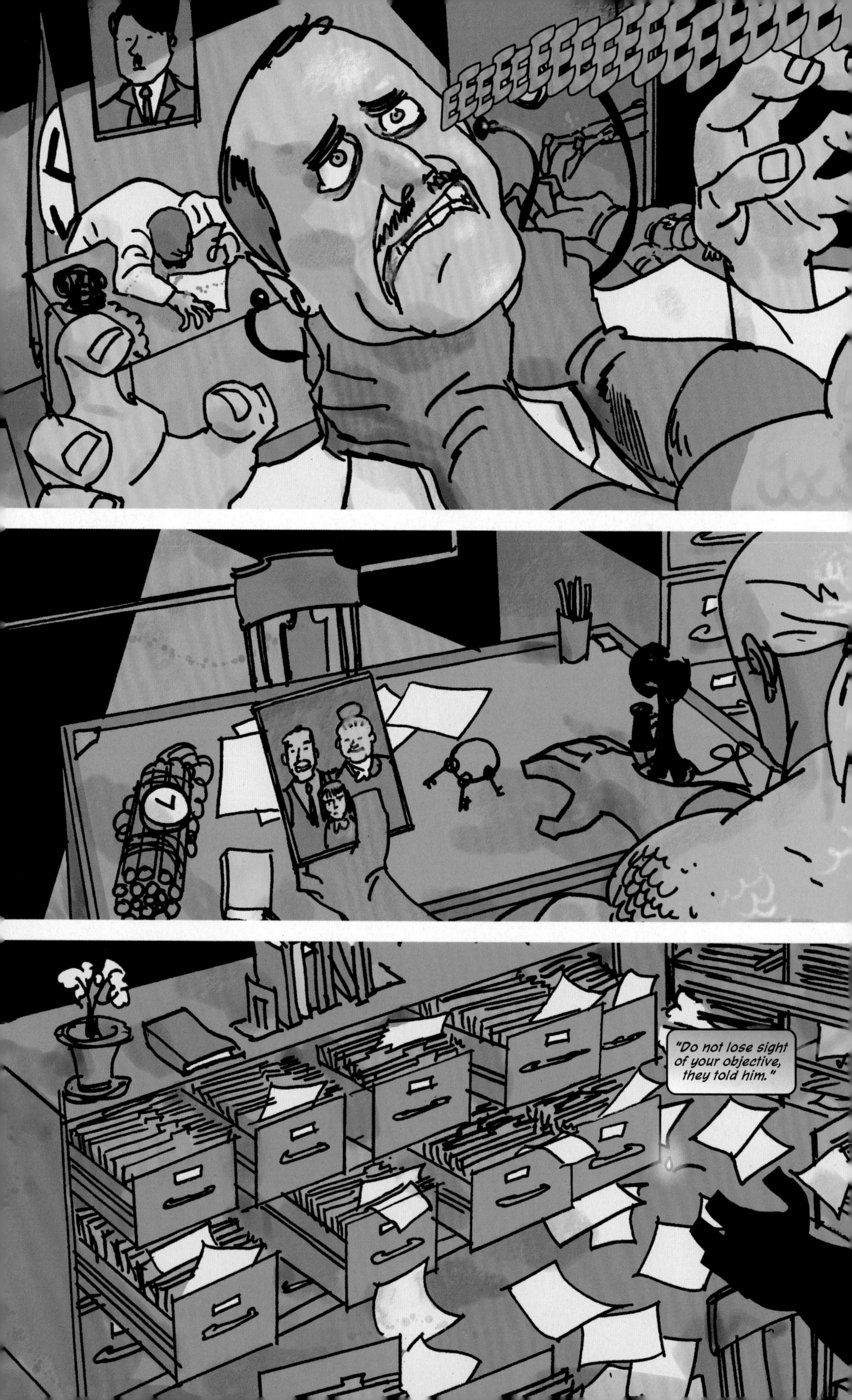
EEEEEEEEEEEEEEEE
"Do not lose sight of your objective, they told him."

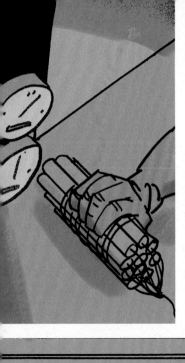
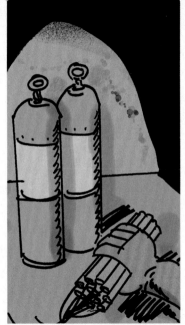

"Do not allow yourself to be distracted by whatever you may see, they warned him."

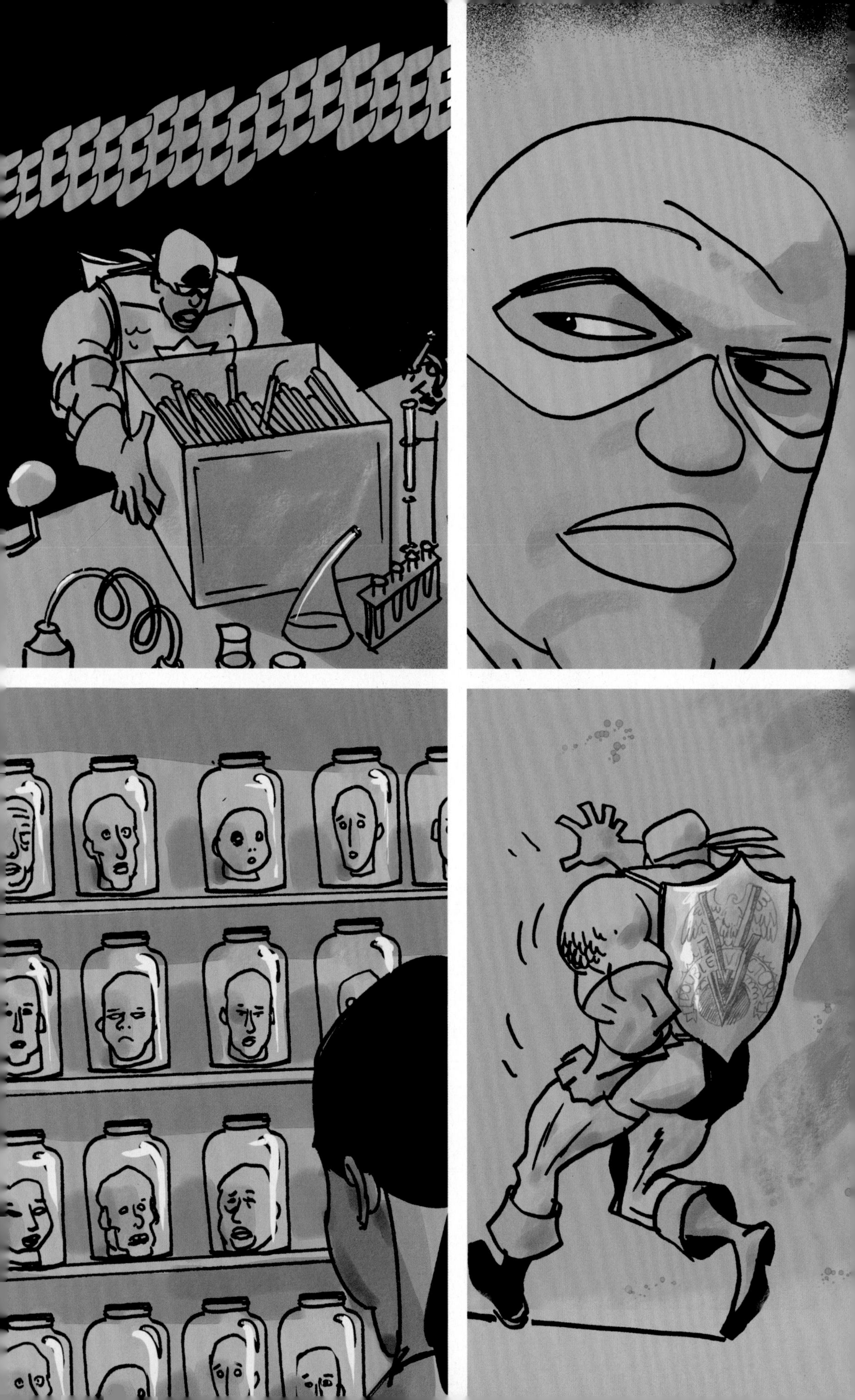

EEEEEEEEEEEEEEEEEEEEE
DOUBLE VICTORY

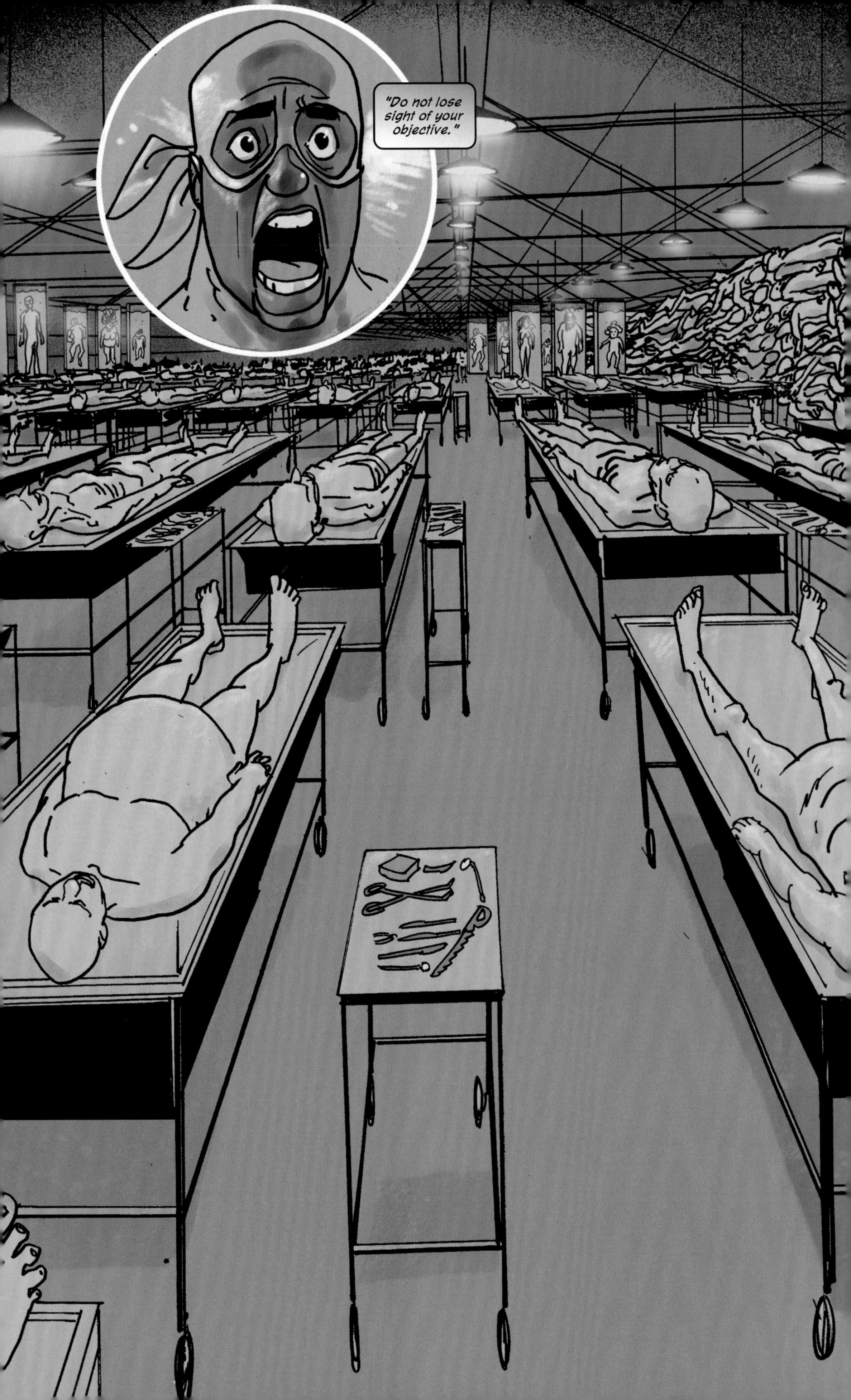
"Do not lose sight of your objective."

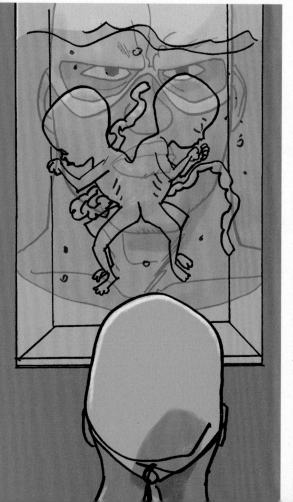

"Do not consider what we did to you, is what they didn't say."

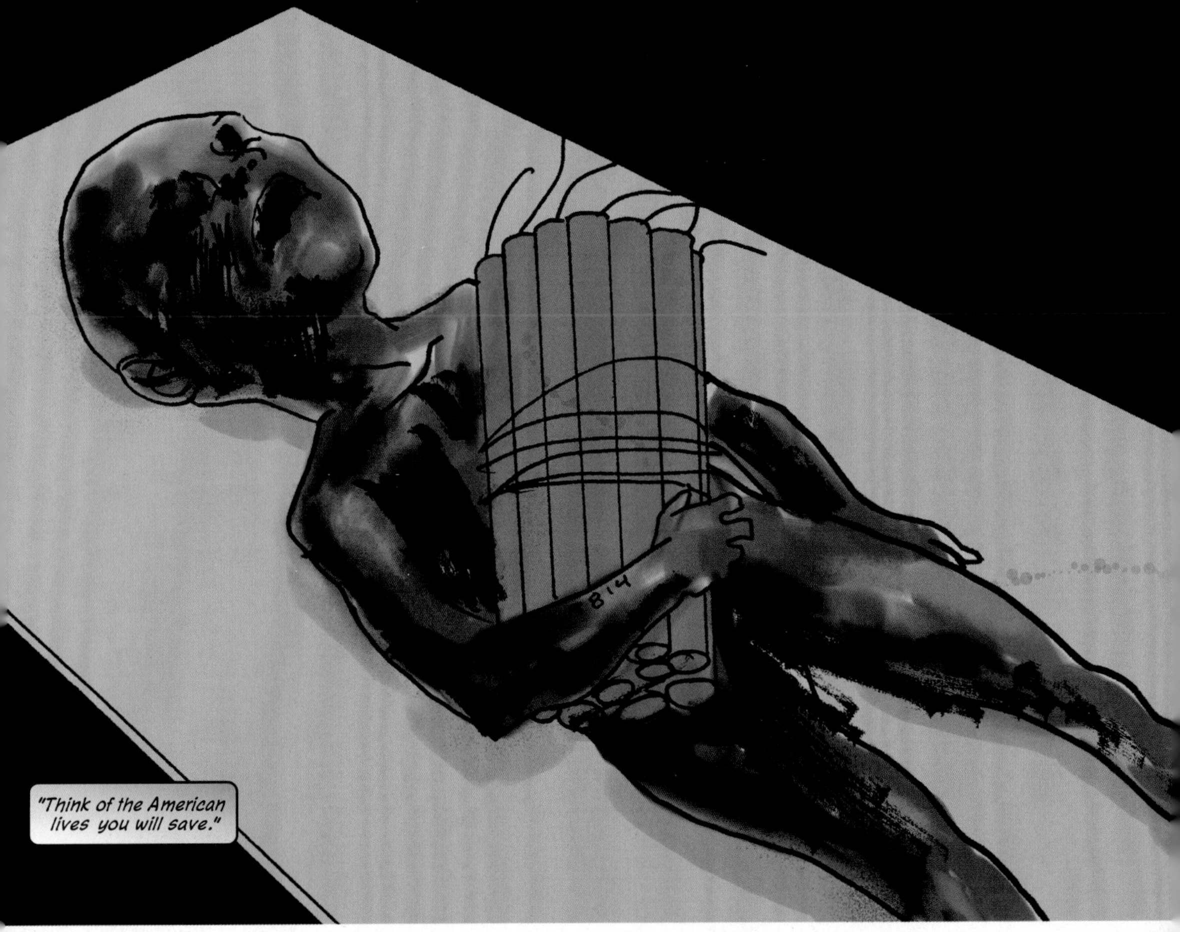
"Think of the American lives you will save."
814

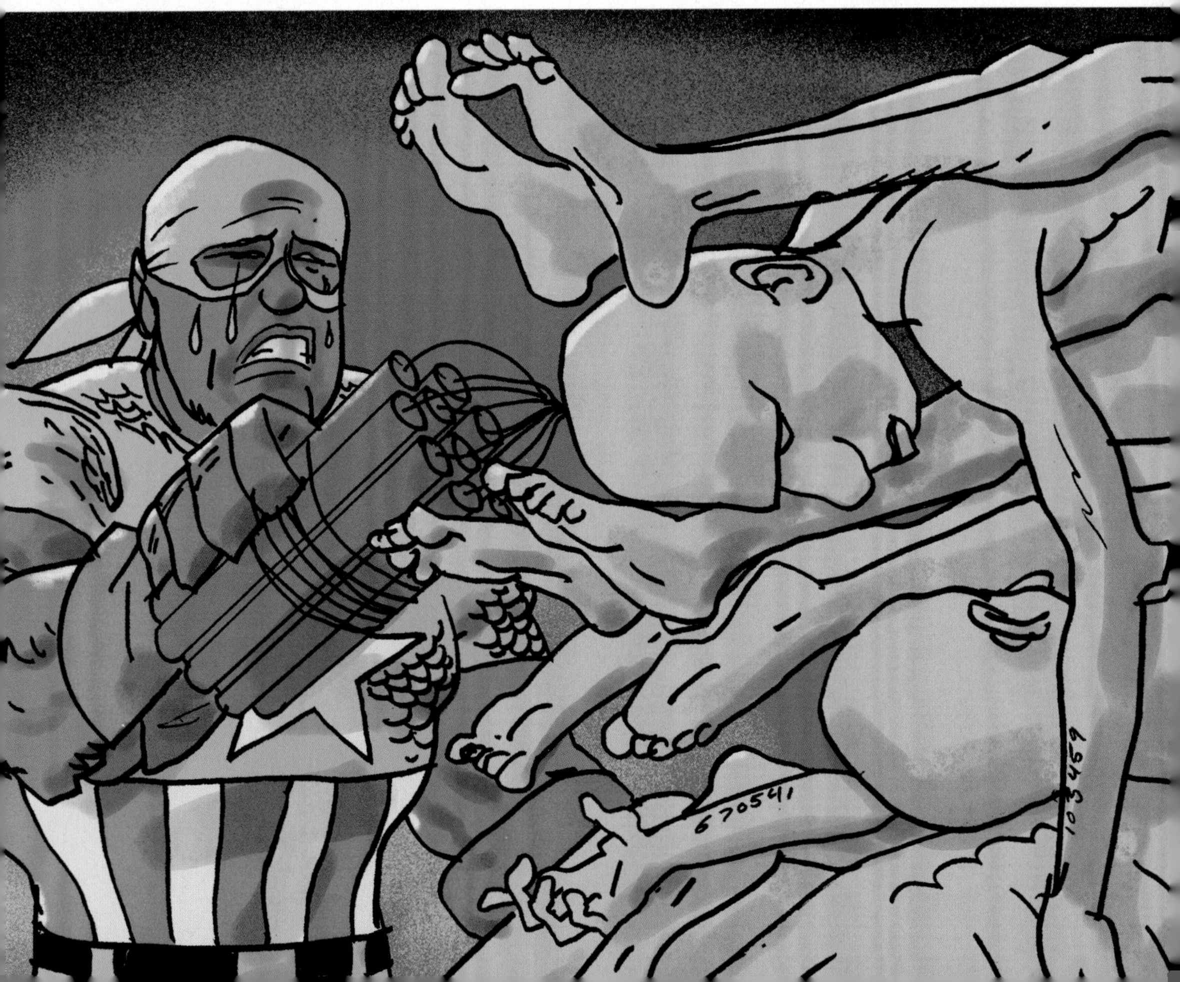
670541
103469

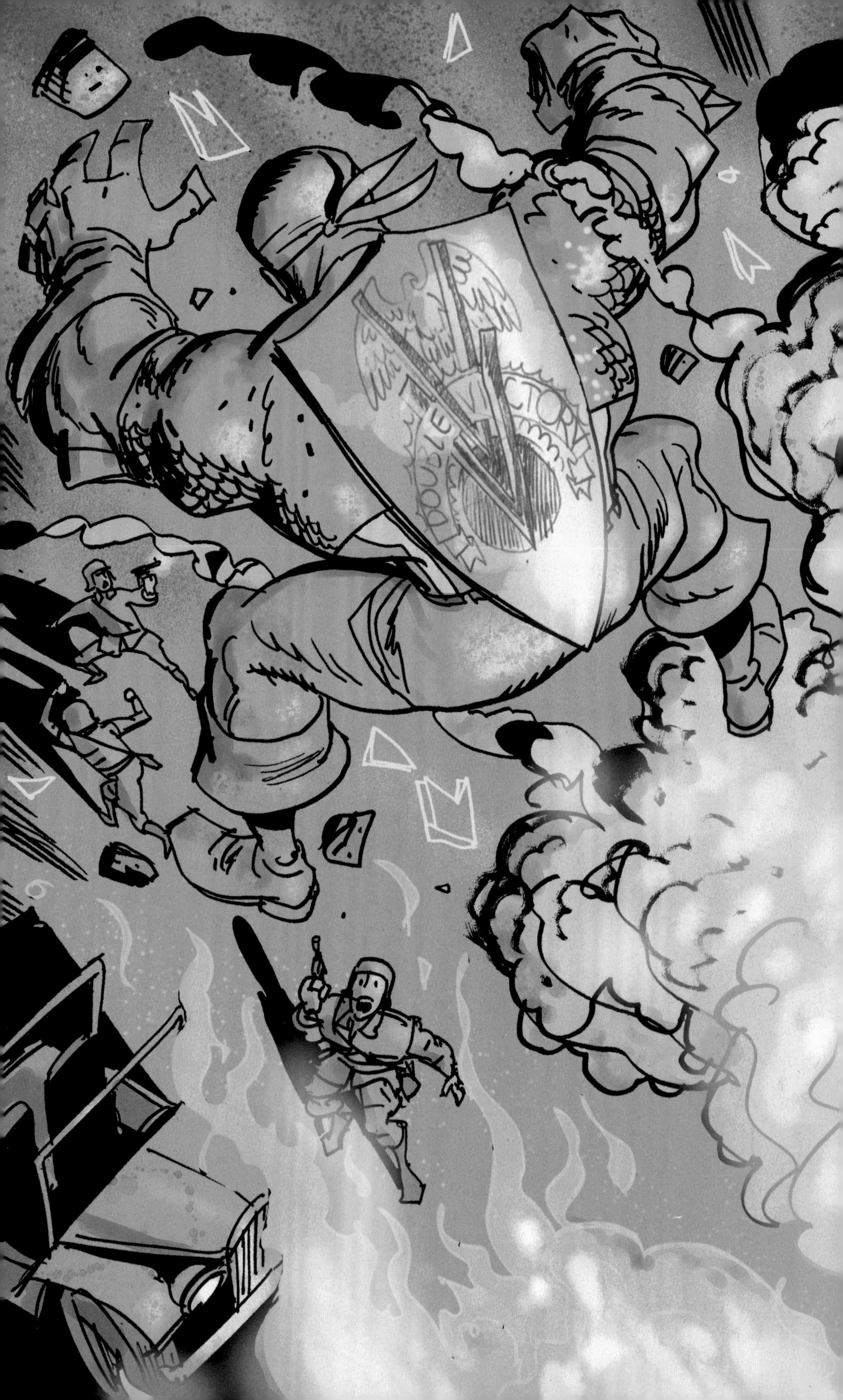
DOUBLE VICTORY

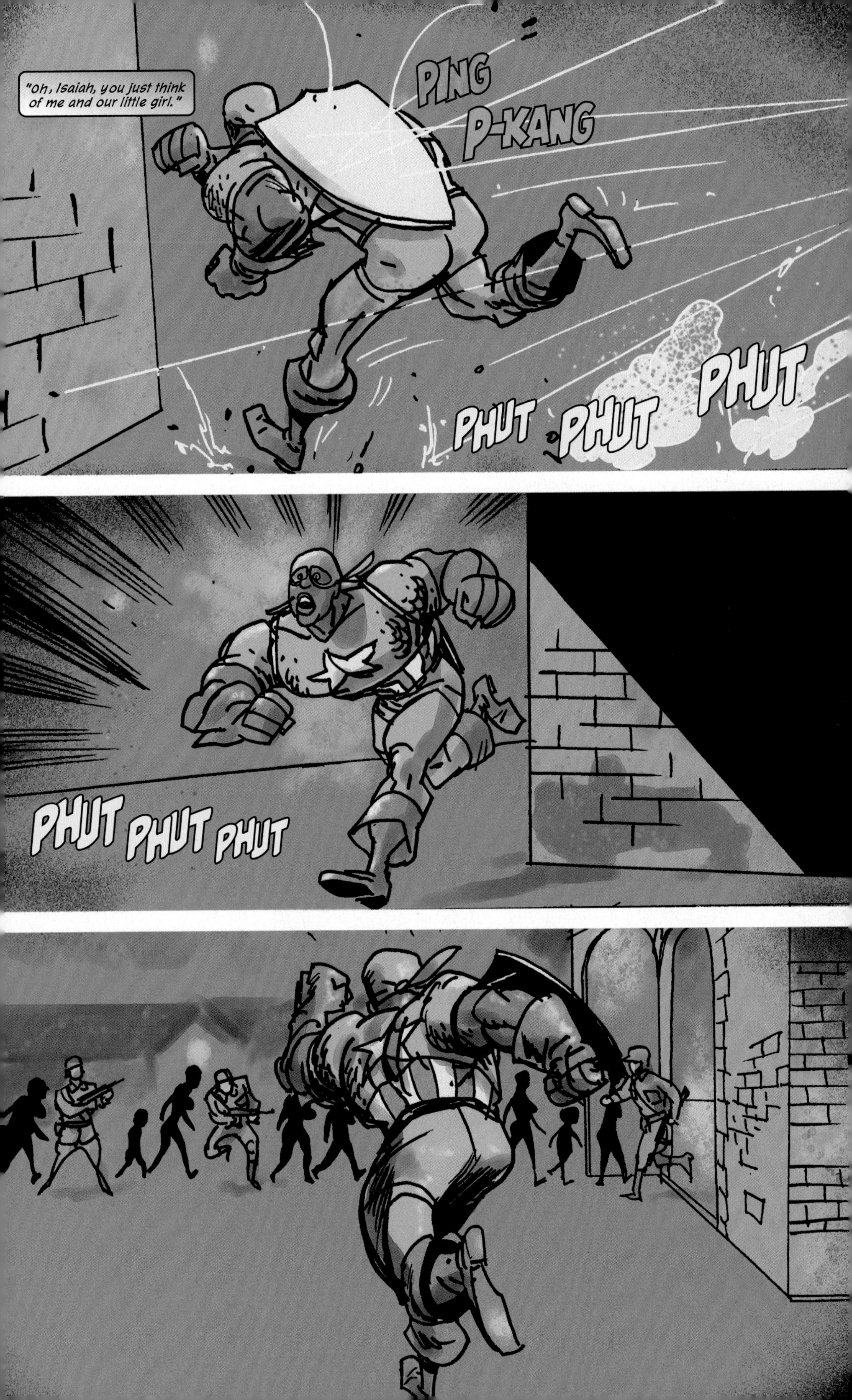
"Oh, Isaiah, you just think of me and our little girl."
PING
P-KANG
PHUT PHUT PHUT
PHUT PHUT PHUT

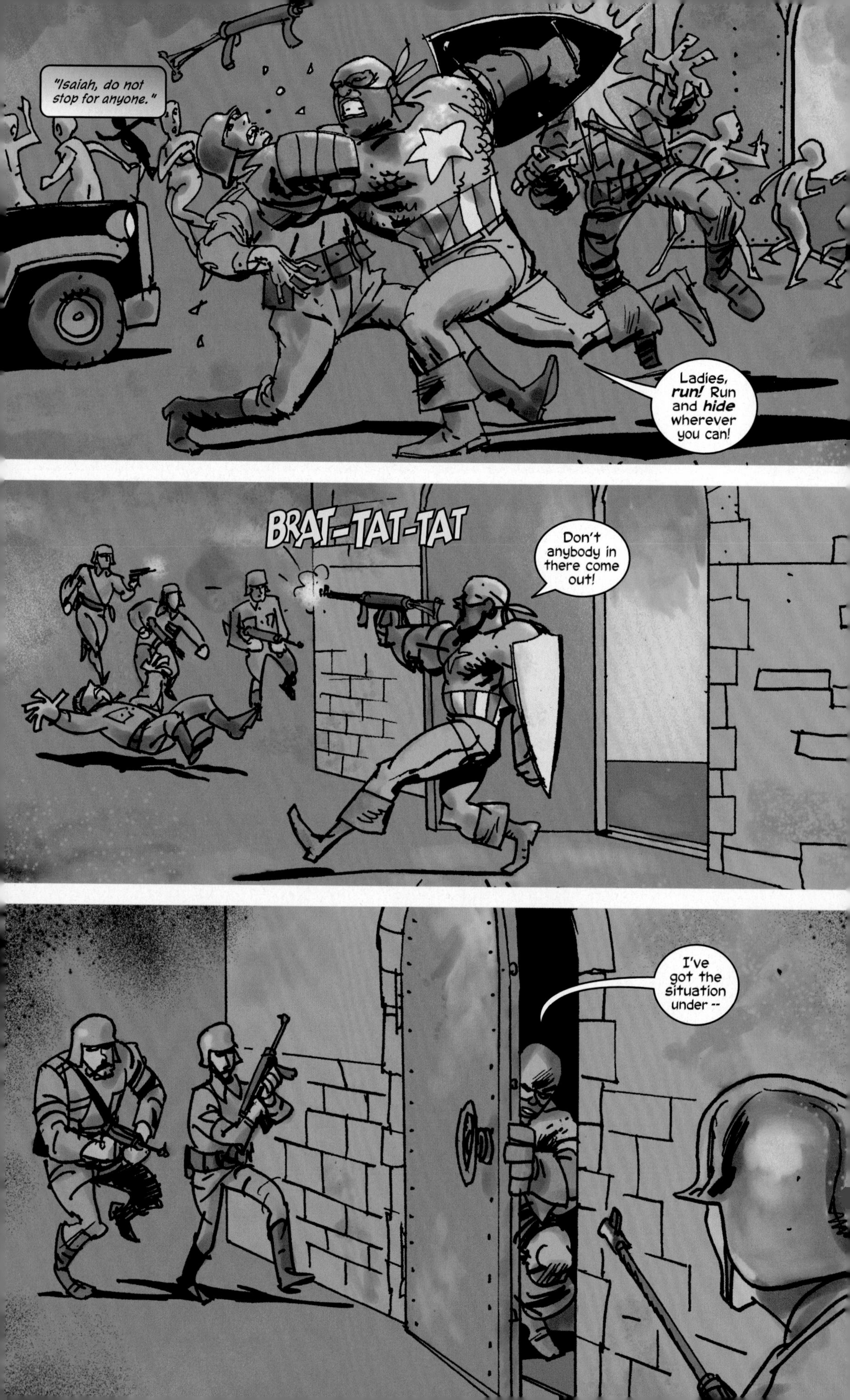
"Isaiah, do not stop for anyone."
Ladies, run! Run and hide wherever you can!
BRAT-TAT-TAT
Don't anybody in there come out!
I've got the situation under --

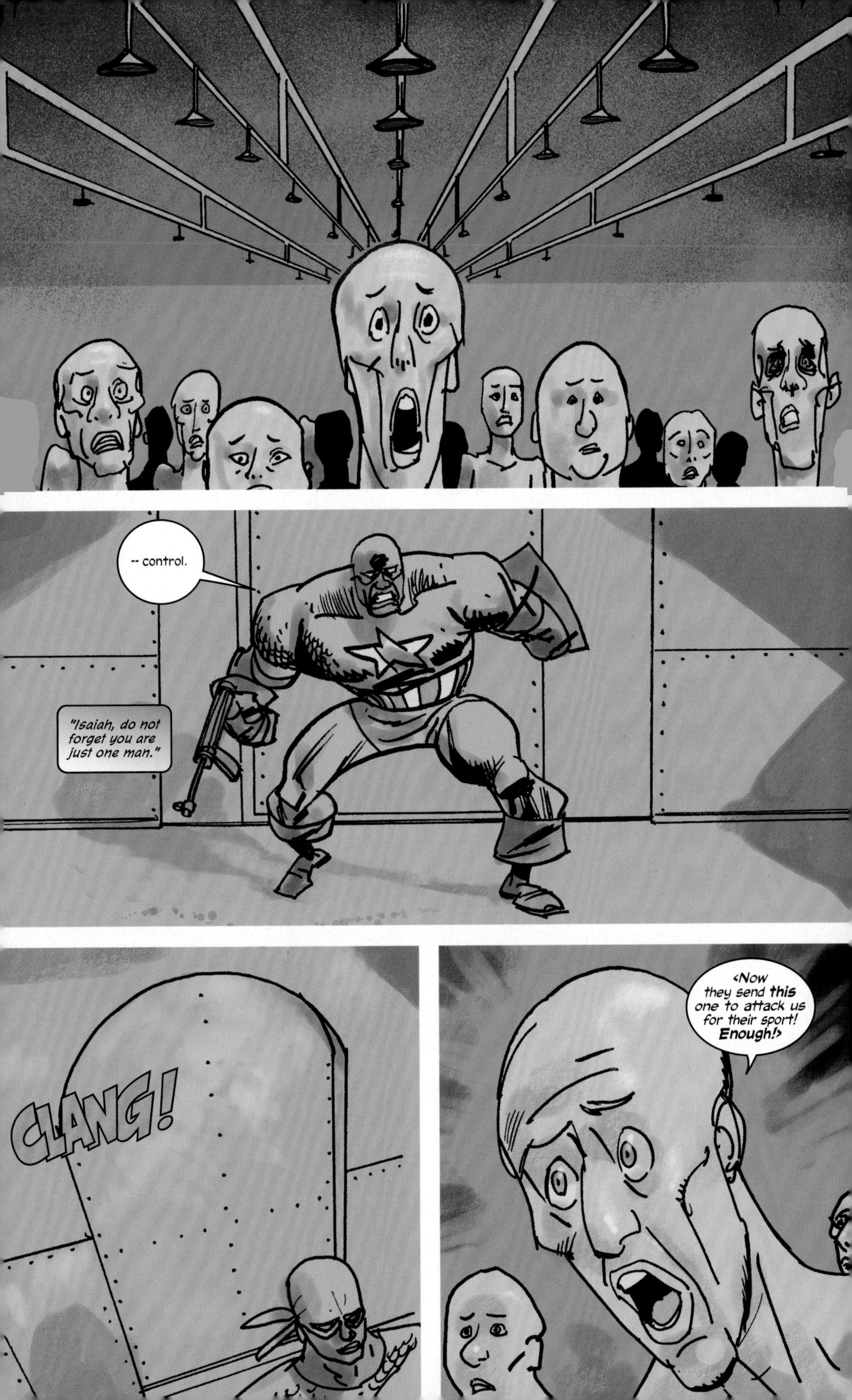
-- control.
"Isaiah, do not forget you are just one man."
CLANG!
<Now they send this one to attack us for their sport! Enough!>

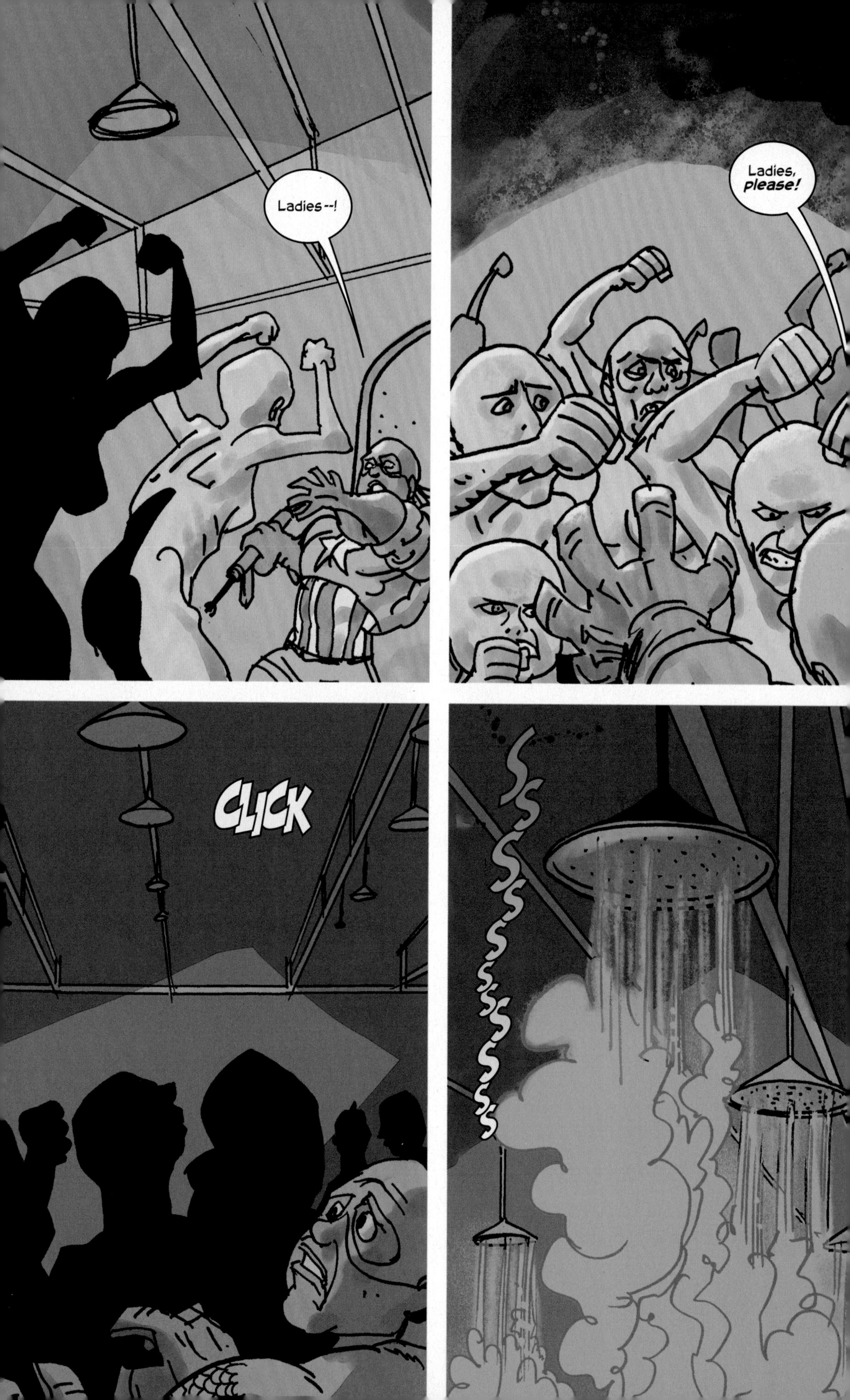
Ladies--!
Ladies, *please!*
CLICK
SSSSSSSSSSSSSSS

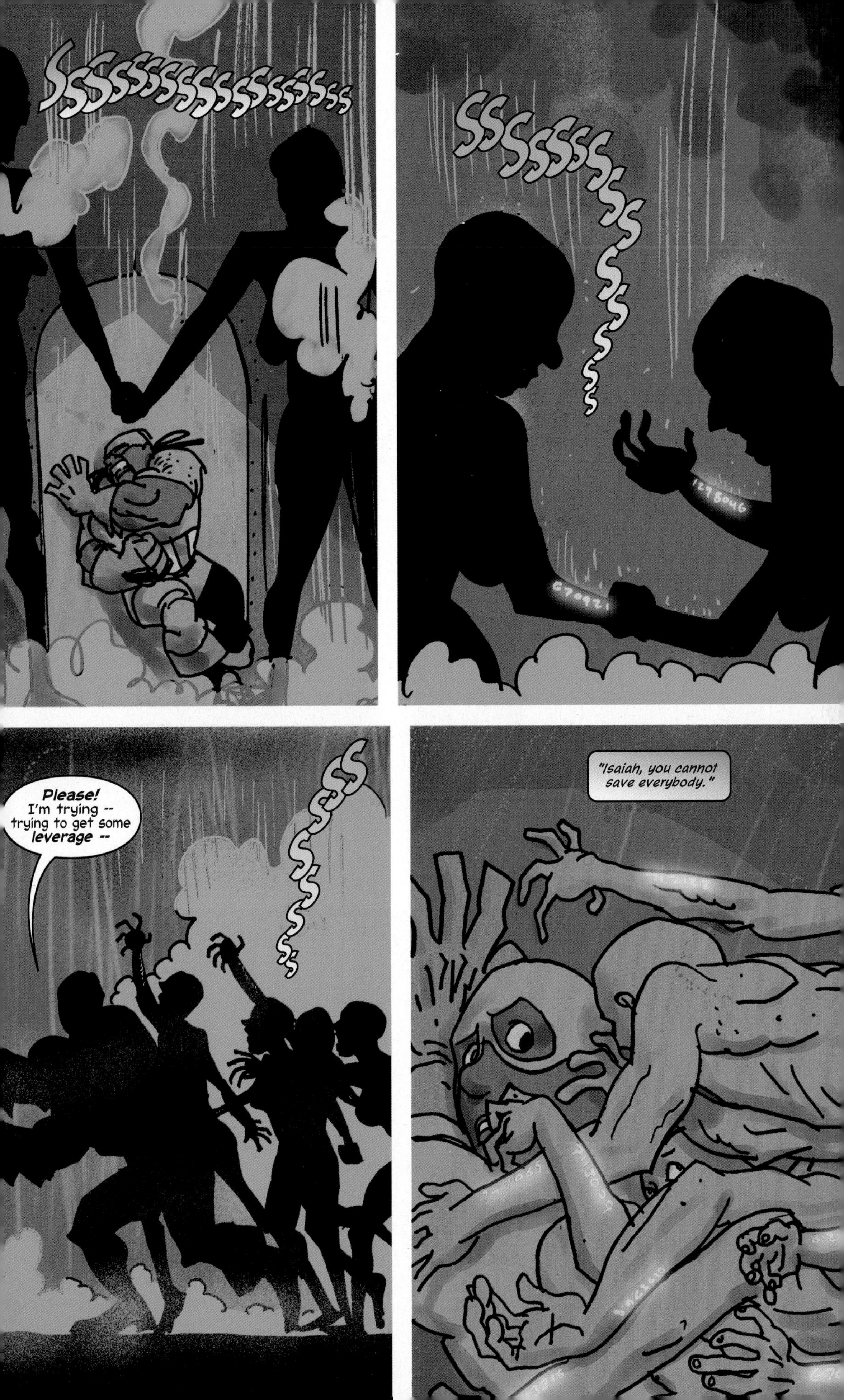
SSSSSSSSSSSSSSSSSss
SSSSSSSSSSSSSSSS
SSSSSSSS
Please!
I'm trying --
trying to get some
leverage --
"Isaiah, you cannot
save everybody."

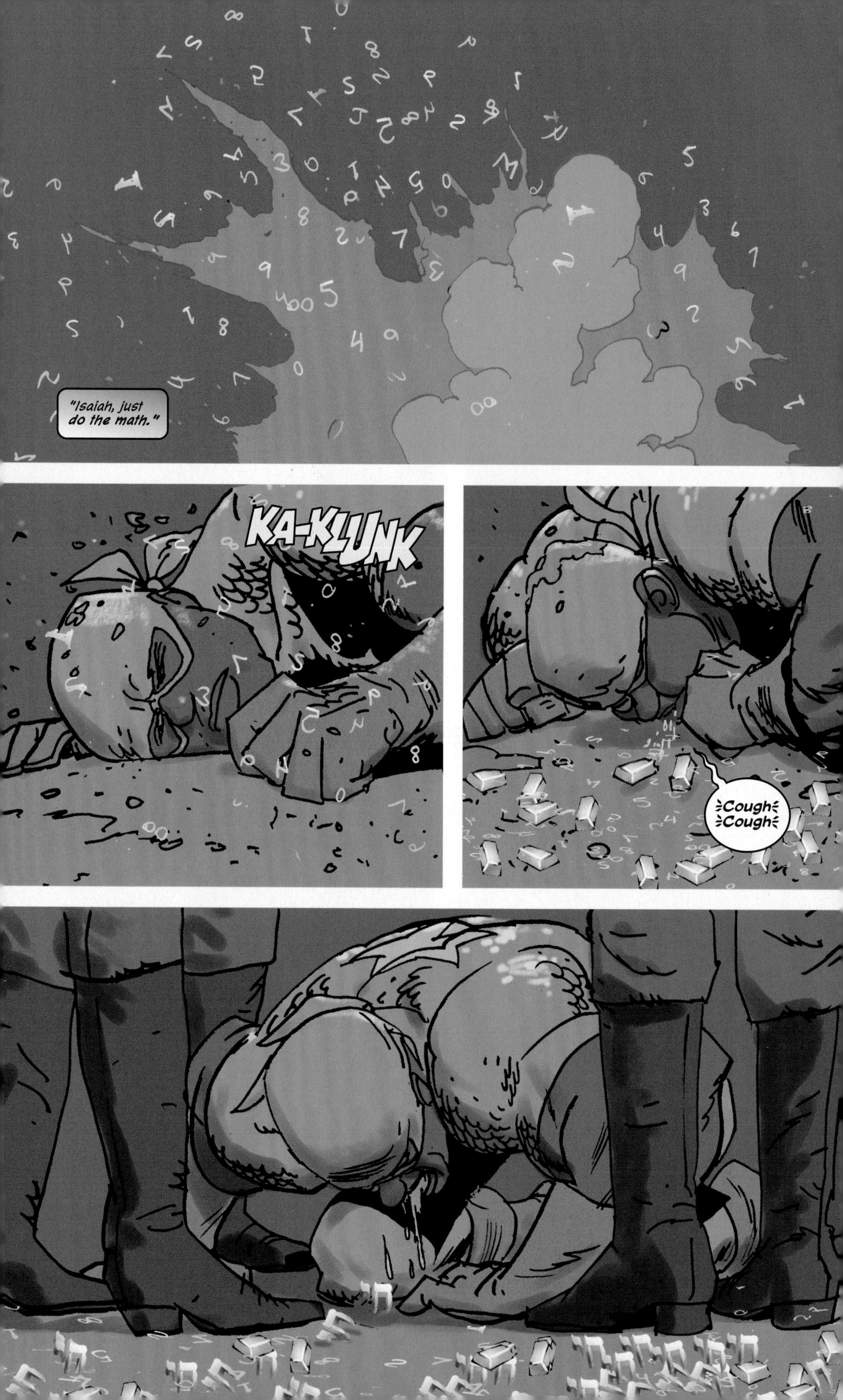
"Isaiah, just do the math."
KA-KLUNK
Cough
Cough

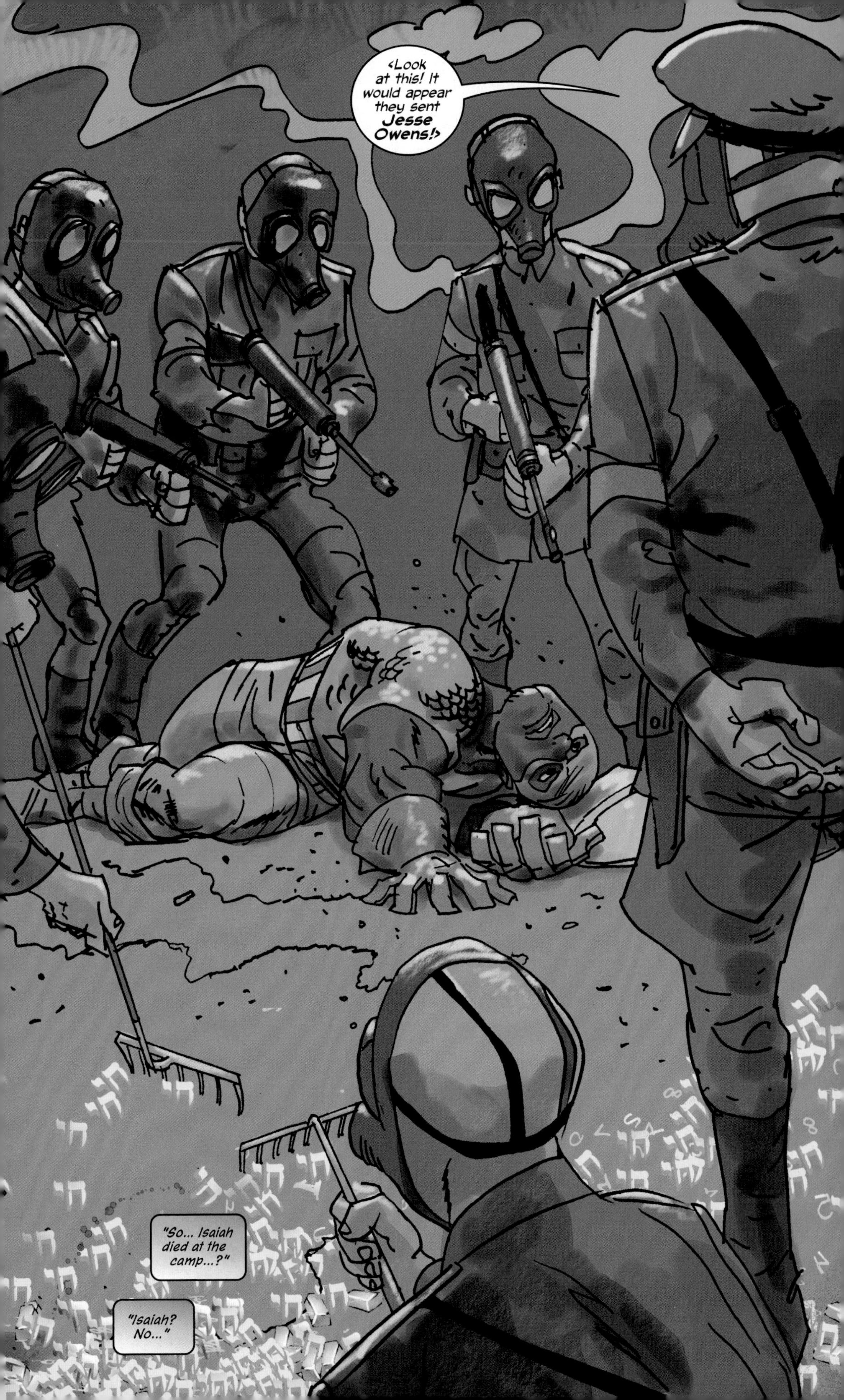

‹Look at this! It would appear they sent Jesse Owens!›
"So... Isaiah died at the camp...?"
"Isaiah? No..."

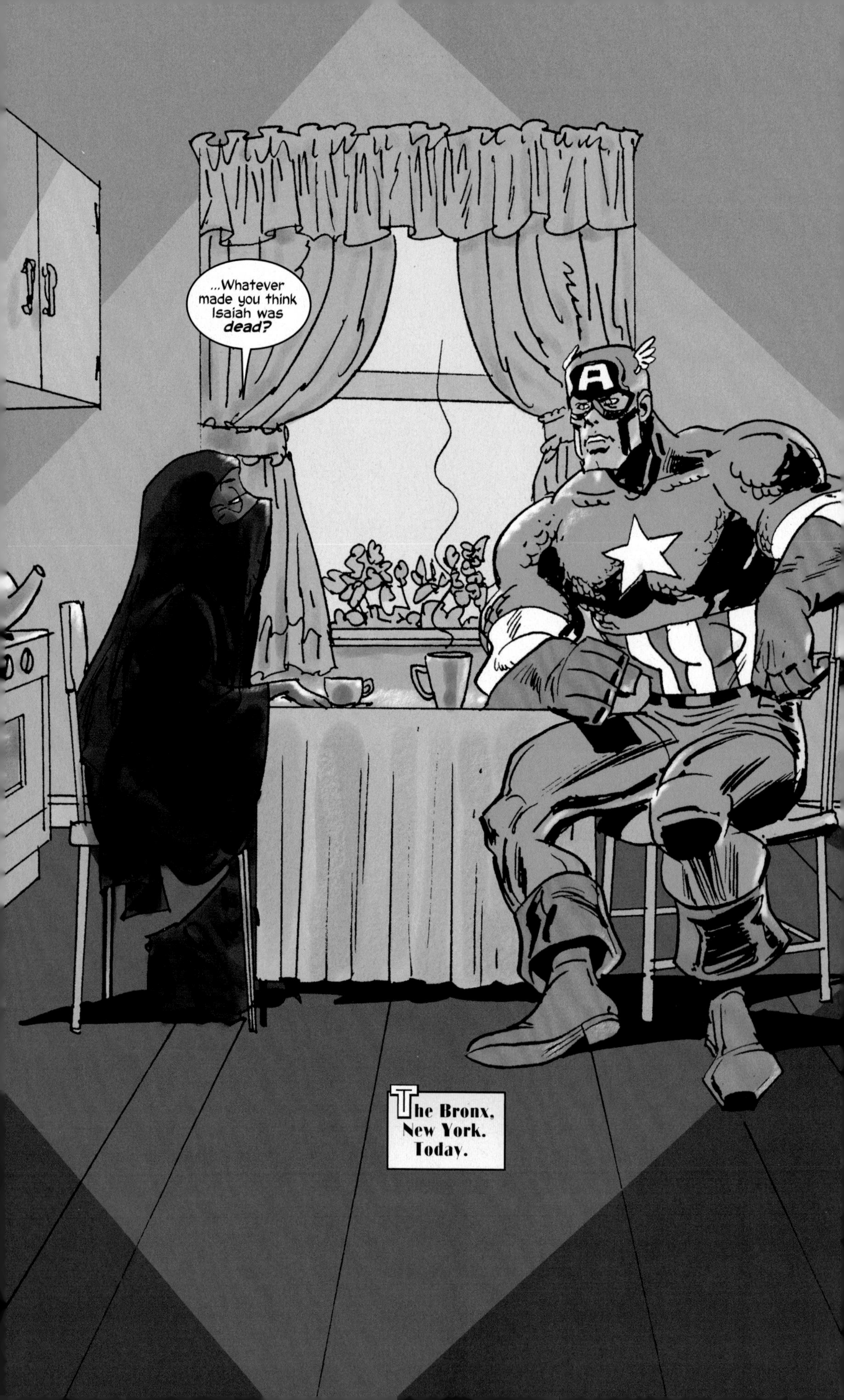

...Whatever made you think Isaiah was dead?
The Bronx, New York. Today.

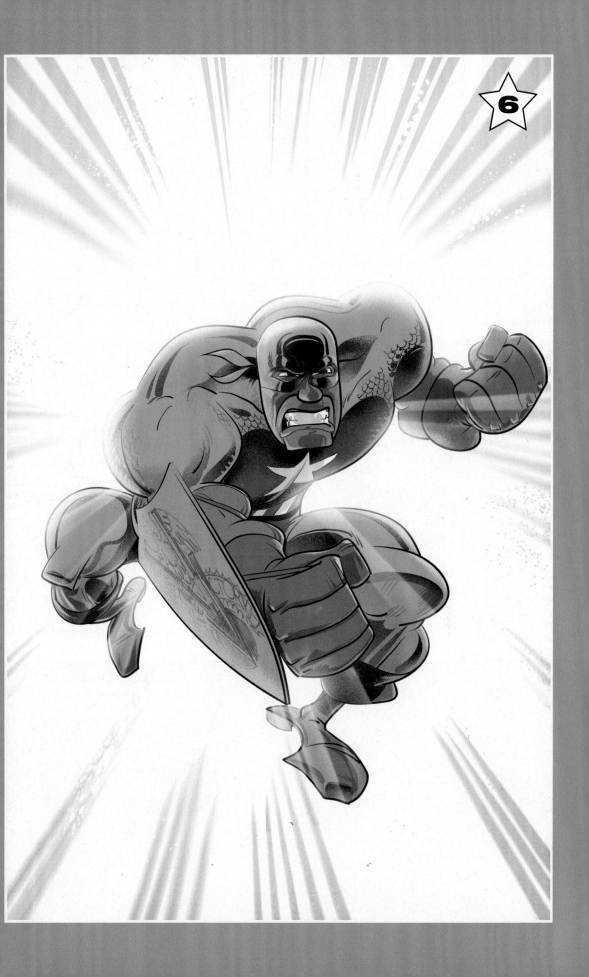

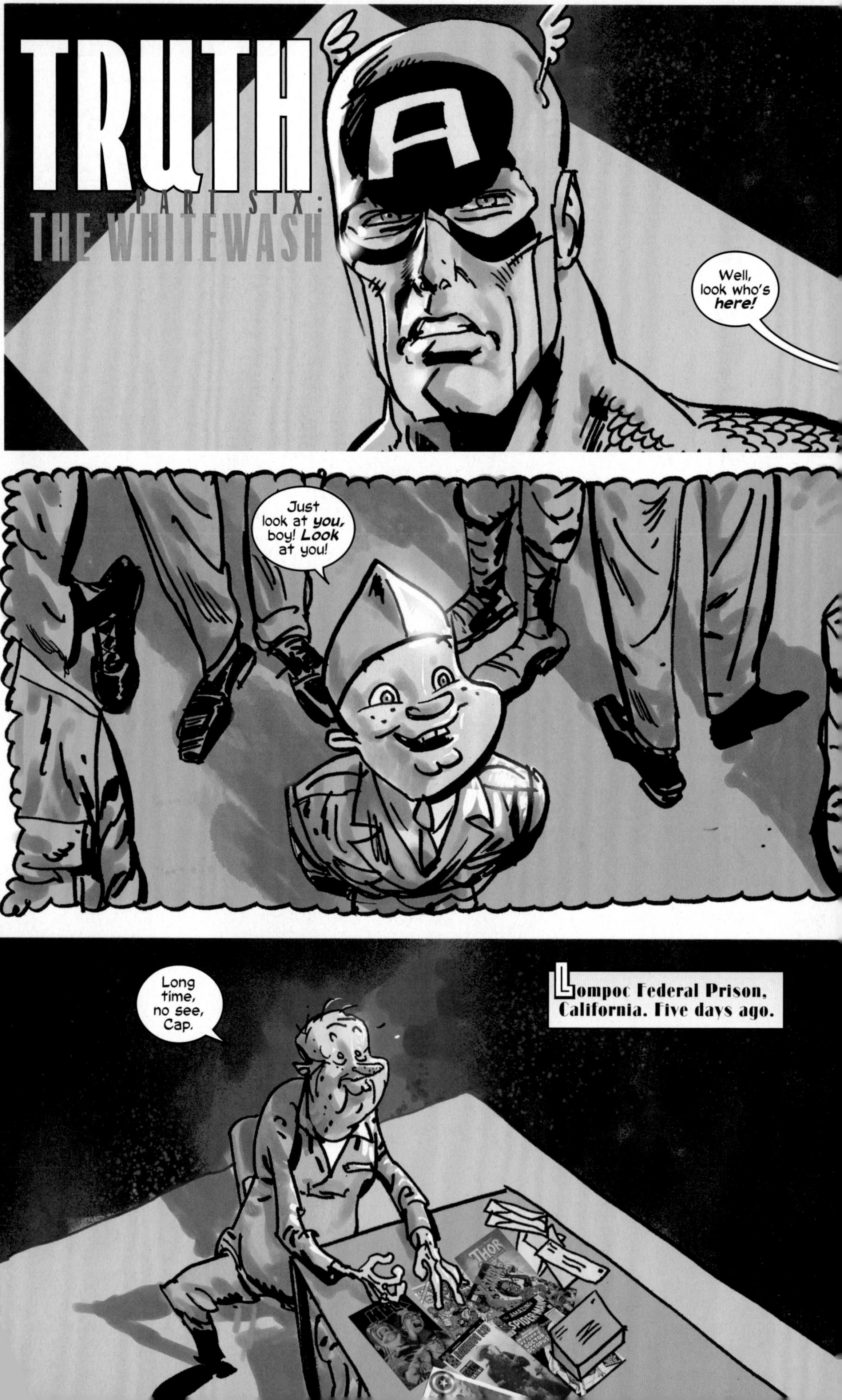
TRUTH
PART SIX:
THE WHITEWASH
Well, look who's here!
Just look at you, boy! Look at you!
Long time, no see, Cap.
Lompoc Federal Prison, California. Five days ago.
THOR
THE AMAZING SPIDER-MAN

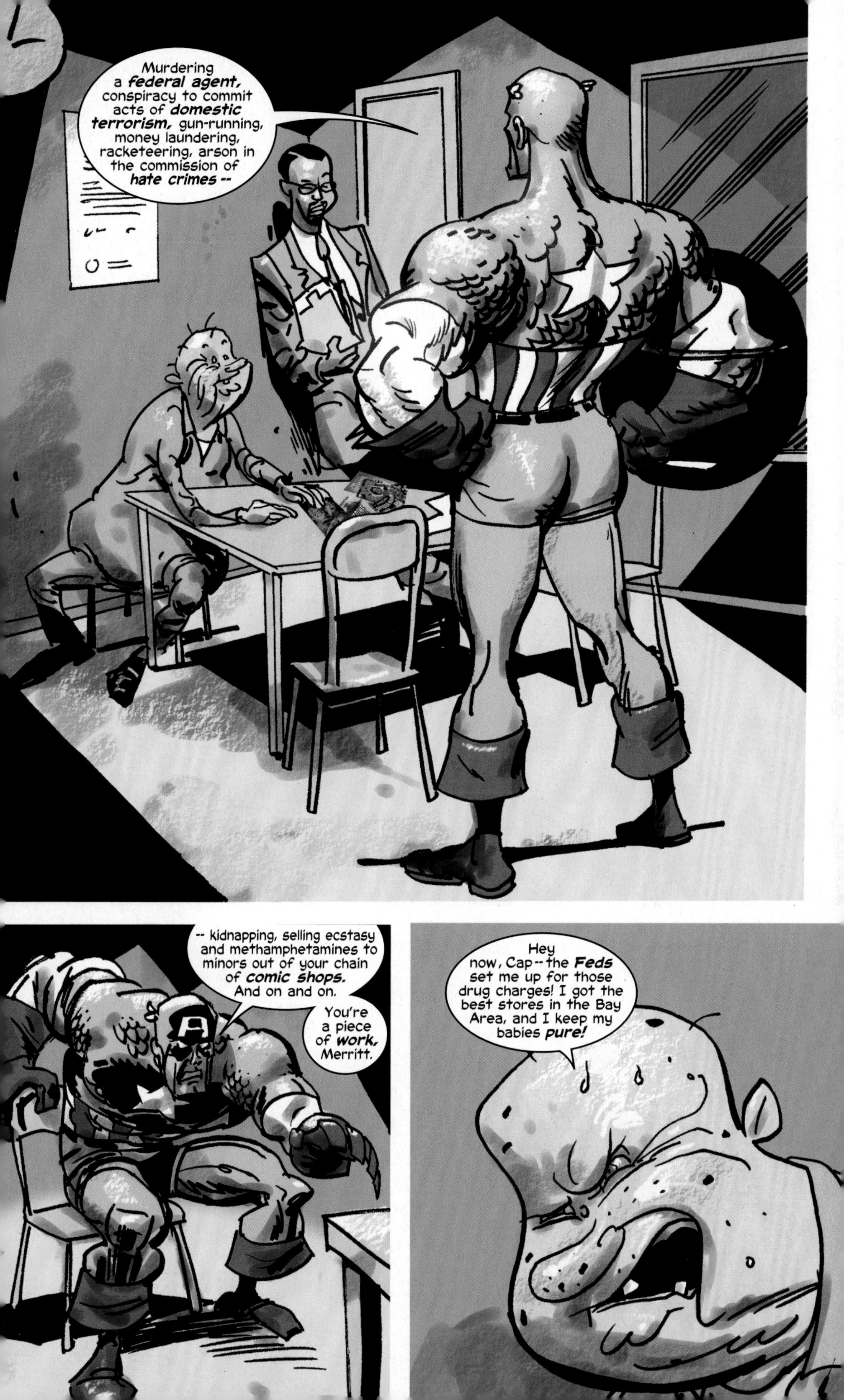
Murdering a federal agent, conspiracy to commit acts of domestic terrorism, gun-running, money laundering, racketeering, arson in the commission of hate crimes --
-- kidnapping, selling ecstasy and methamphetamines to minors out of your chain of comic shops. And on and on.
You're a piece of work, Merritt.
Hey now, Cap -- the Feds set me up for those drug charges! I got the best stores in the Bay Area, and I keep my babies pure!

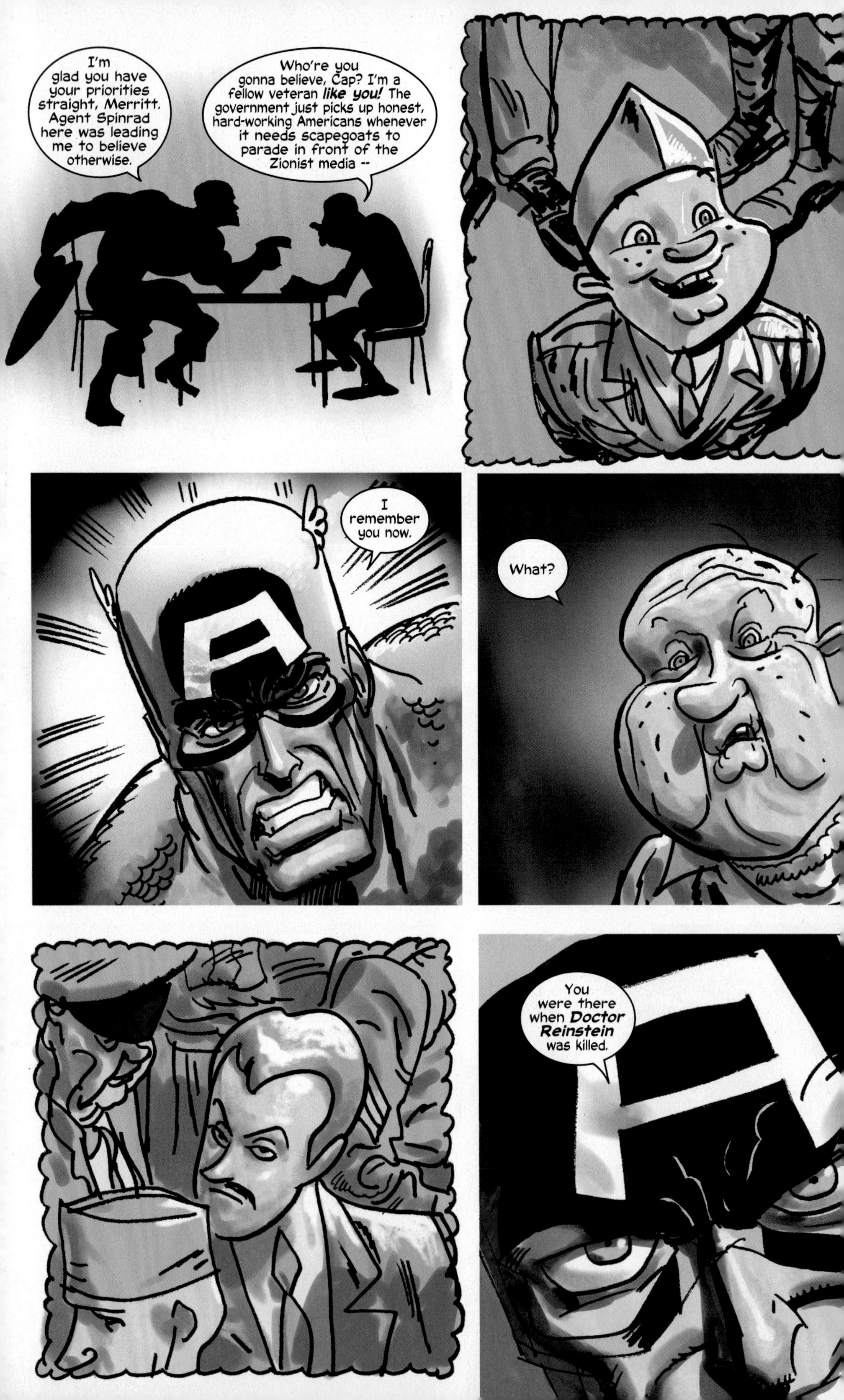
I'm glad you have your priorities straight, Merritt. Agent Spinrad here was leading me to believe otherwise.
Who're you gonna believe, Cap? I'm a fellow veteran like you! The government just picks up honest, hard-working Americans whenever it needs scapegoats to parade in front of the Zionist media --
I remember you now.
What?
You were there when Doctor Reinstein was killed.

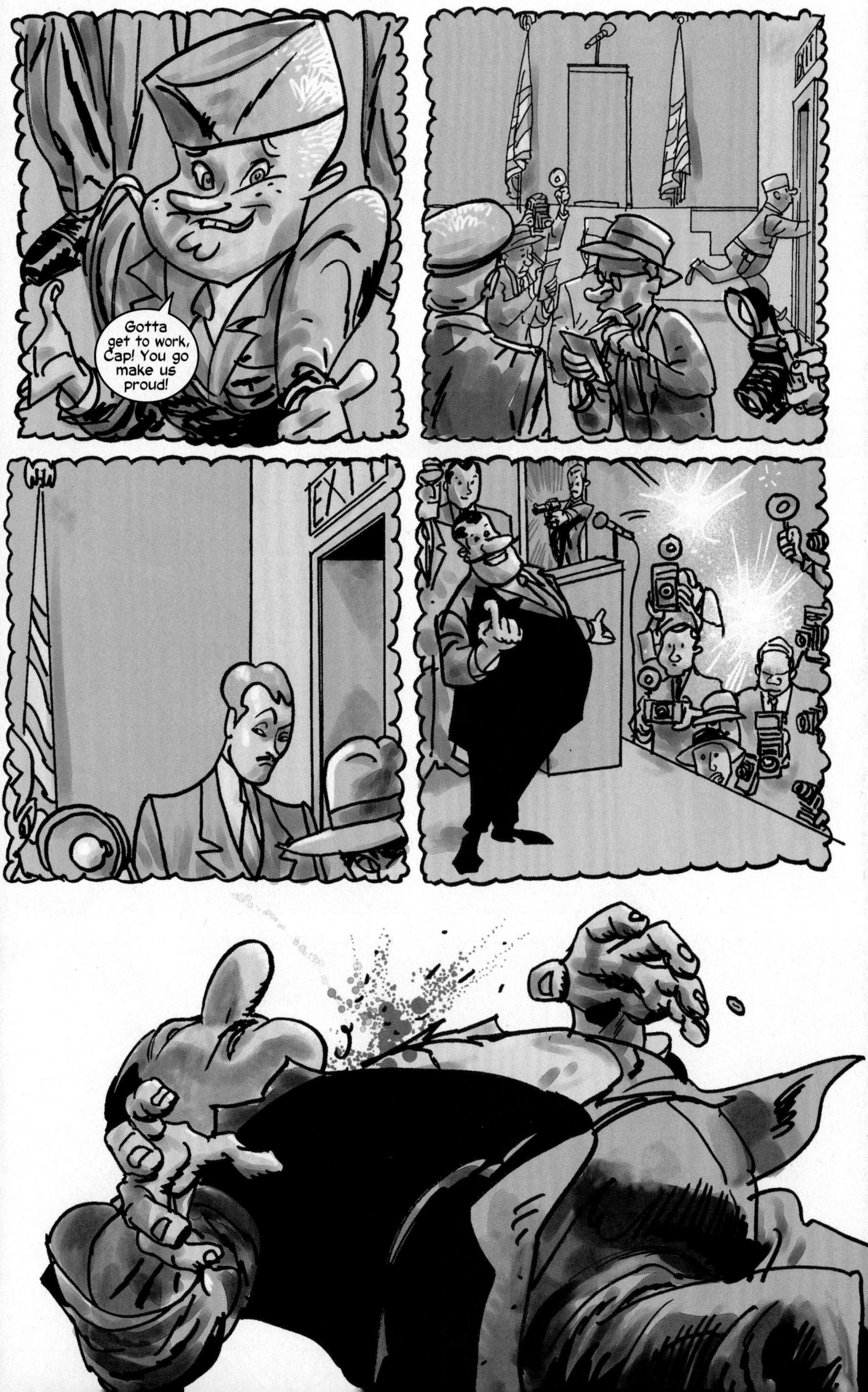
Gotta get to work, Cap! You go make us proud!
EXIT

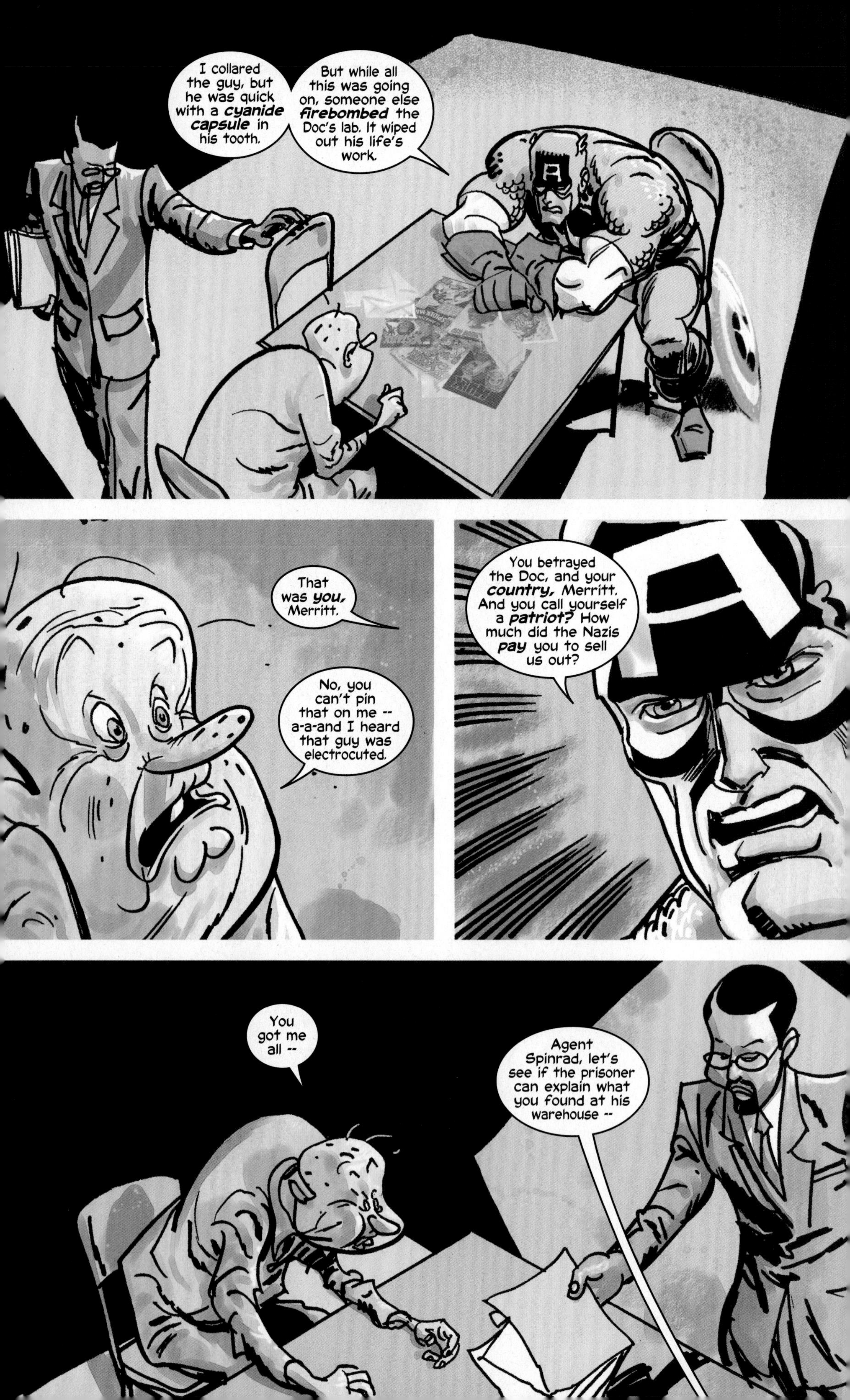
I collared the guy, but he was quick with a *cyanide capsule* in his tooth.
But while all this was going on, someone else *firebombed* the Doc's lab. It wiped out his life's work.
That was *you,* Merritt.
No, you can't pin that on me -- a-a-and I heard that guy was electrocuted.
You betrayed the Doc, and your *country,* Merritt. And you call yourself a *patriot?* How much did the Nazis *pay* you to sell us out?
You got me all --
Agent Spinrad, let's see if the prisoner can explain what you found at his warehouse --

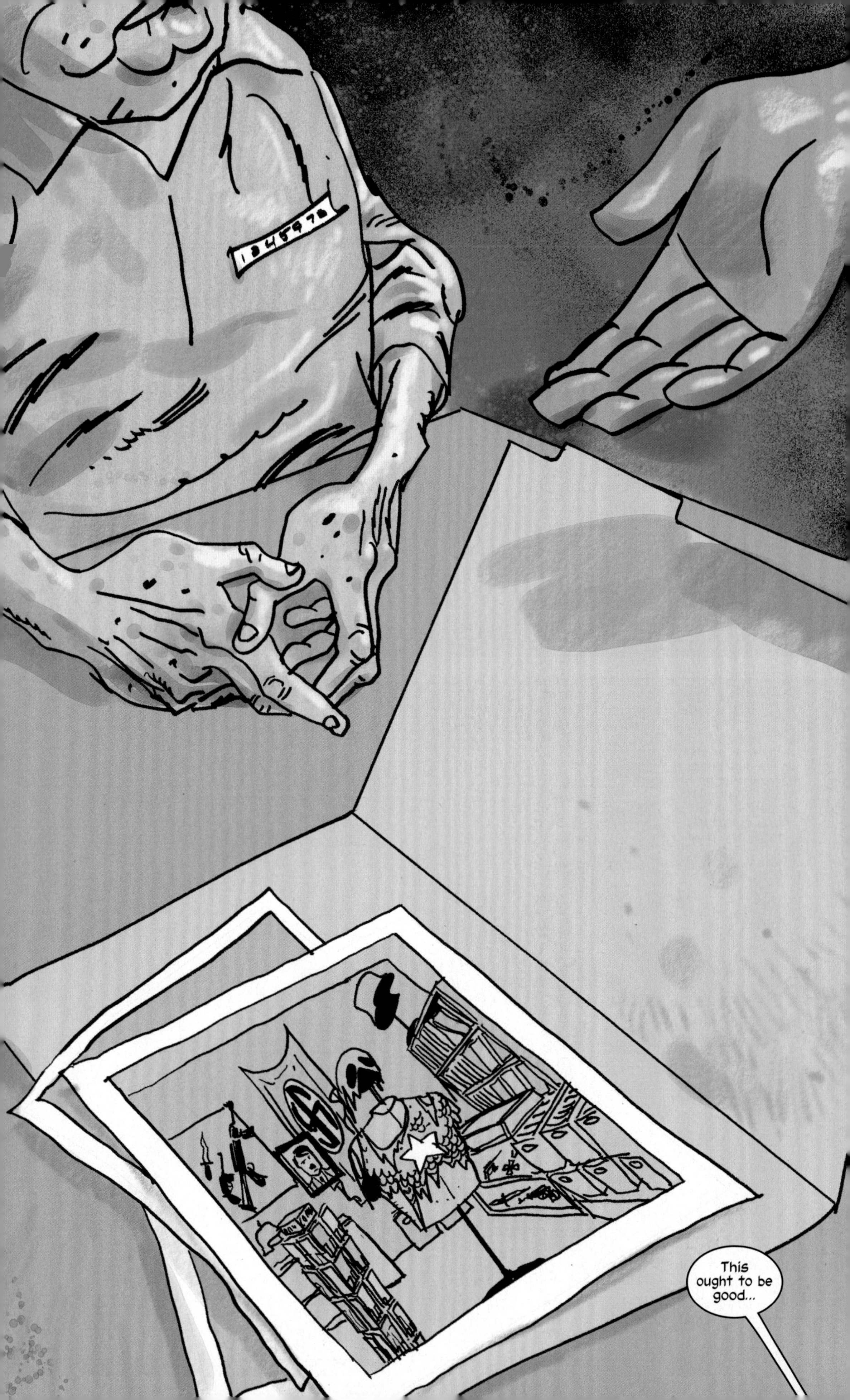
This ought to be good...

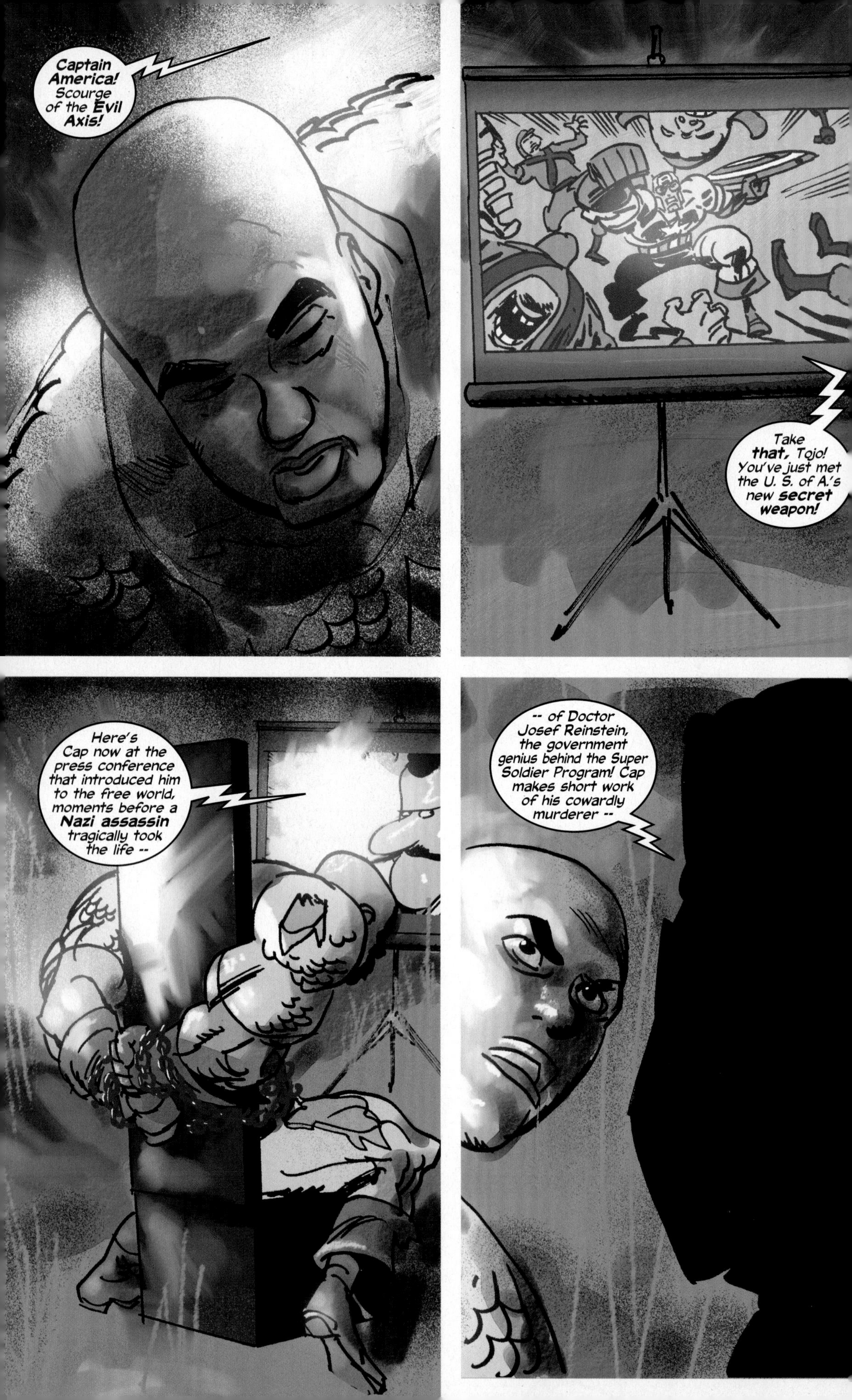
Captain America! Scourge of the Evil Axis!
Take that, Tojo! You've just met the U. S. of A.'s new secret weapon!
Here's Cap now at the press conference that introduced him to the free world, moments before a Nazi assassin tragically took the life --
-- of Doctor Josef Reinstein, the government genius behind the Super Soldier Program! Cap makes short work of his cowardly murderer --

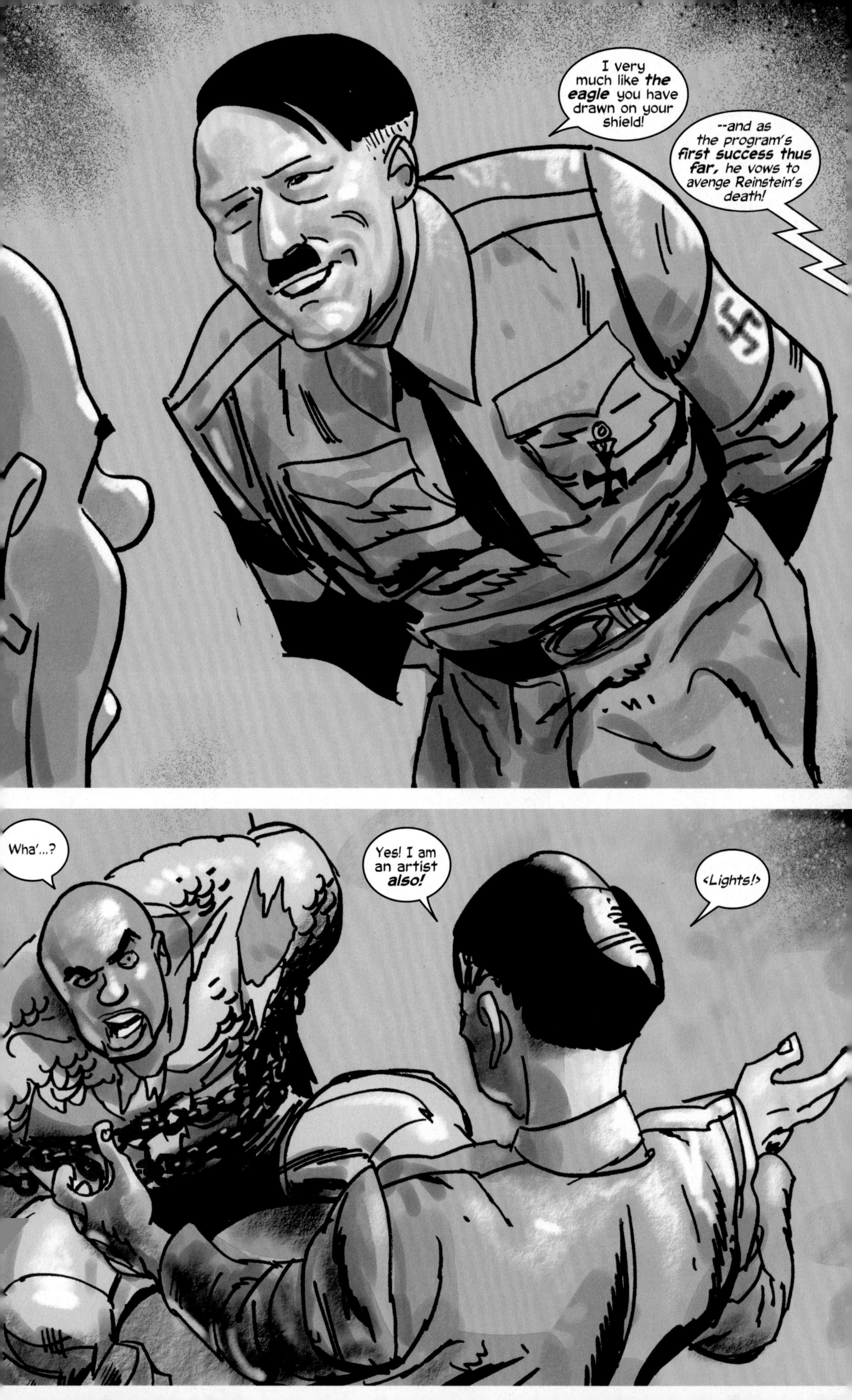
I very much like the eagle you have drawn on your shield!
--and as the program's first success thus far, he vows to avenge Reinstein's death!
Wha'...?
Yes! I am an artist also!
<Lights!>

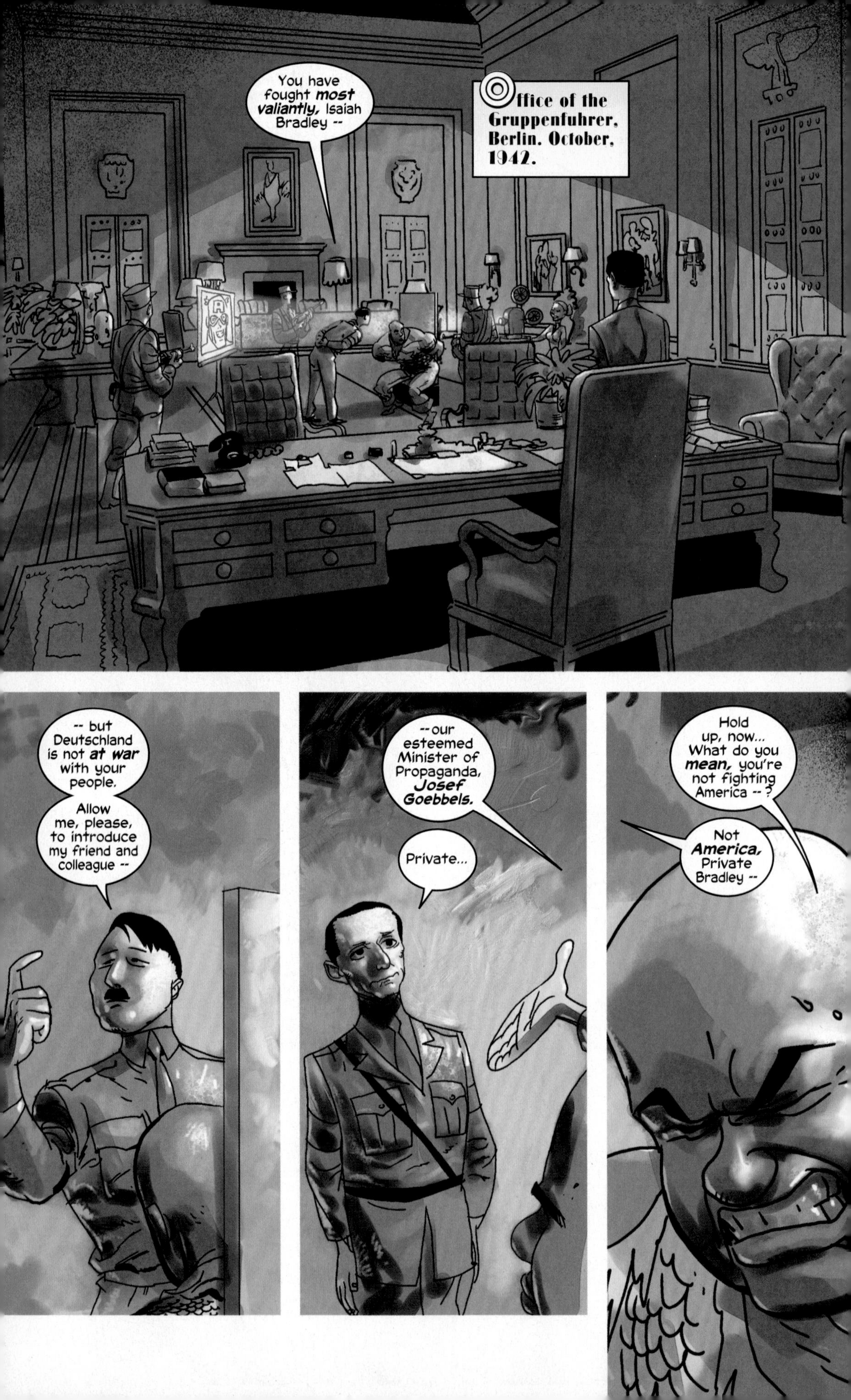

Office of the Gruppenfuhrer, Berlin. October, 1942.
You have fought most valiantly, Isaiah Bradley --
-- but Deutschland is not at war with your people.
Allow me, please, to introduce my friend and colleague --
--our esteemed Minister of Propaganda, Josef Goebbels.
Private...
Hold up, now... What do you mean, you're not fighting America -- ?
Not America, Private Bradley --

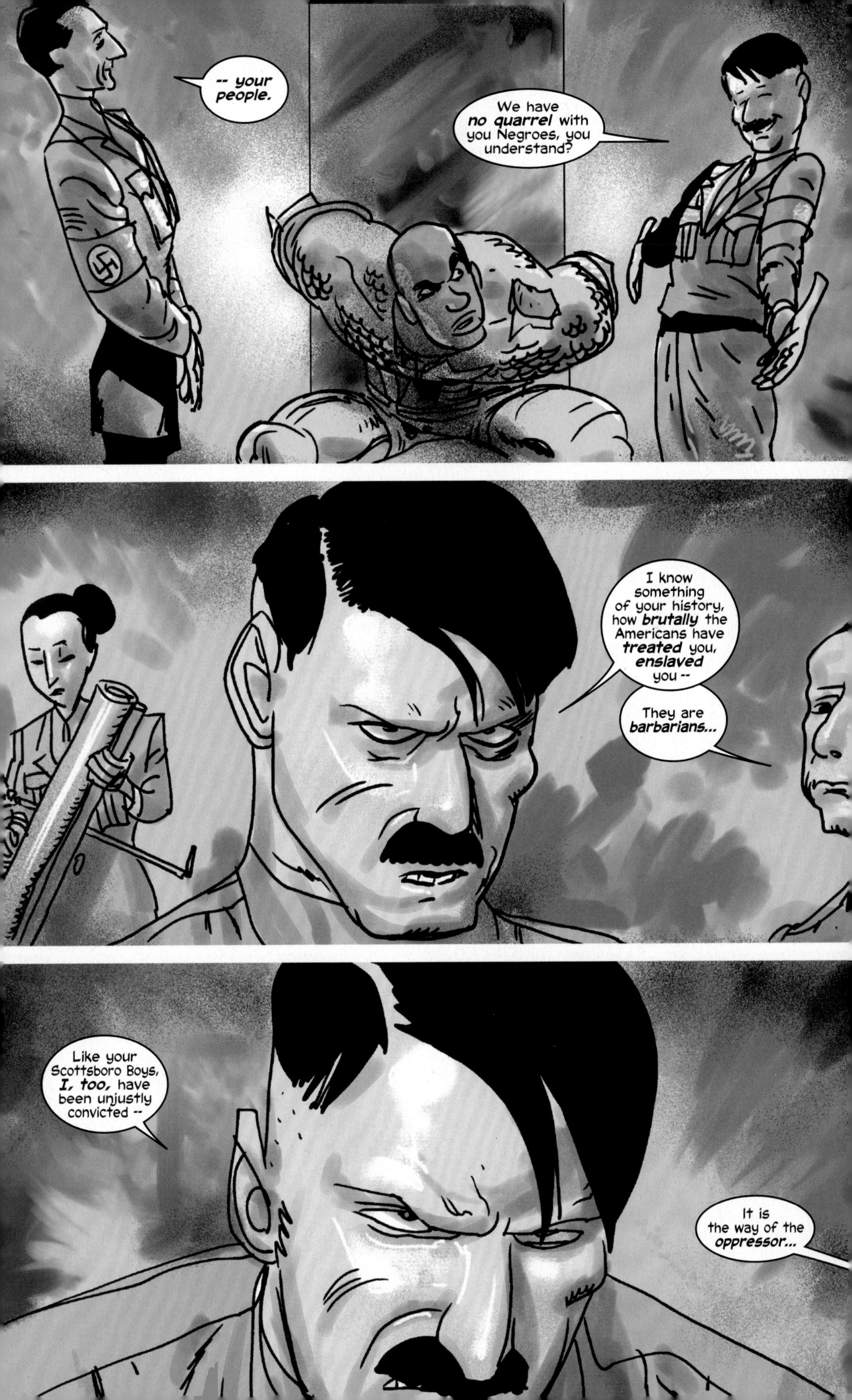
We have no quarrel with you Negroes, you understand?
-- your people.
I know something of your history, how brutally the Americans have treated you, enslaved you --
They are barbarians...
Like your Scottsboro Boys, I, too, have been unjustly convicted --
It is the way of the oppressor...

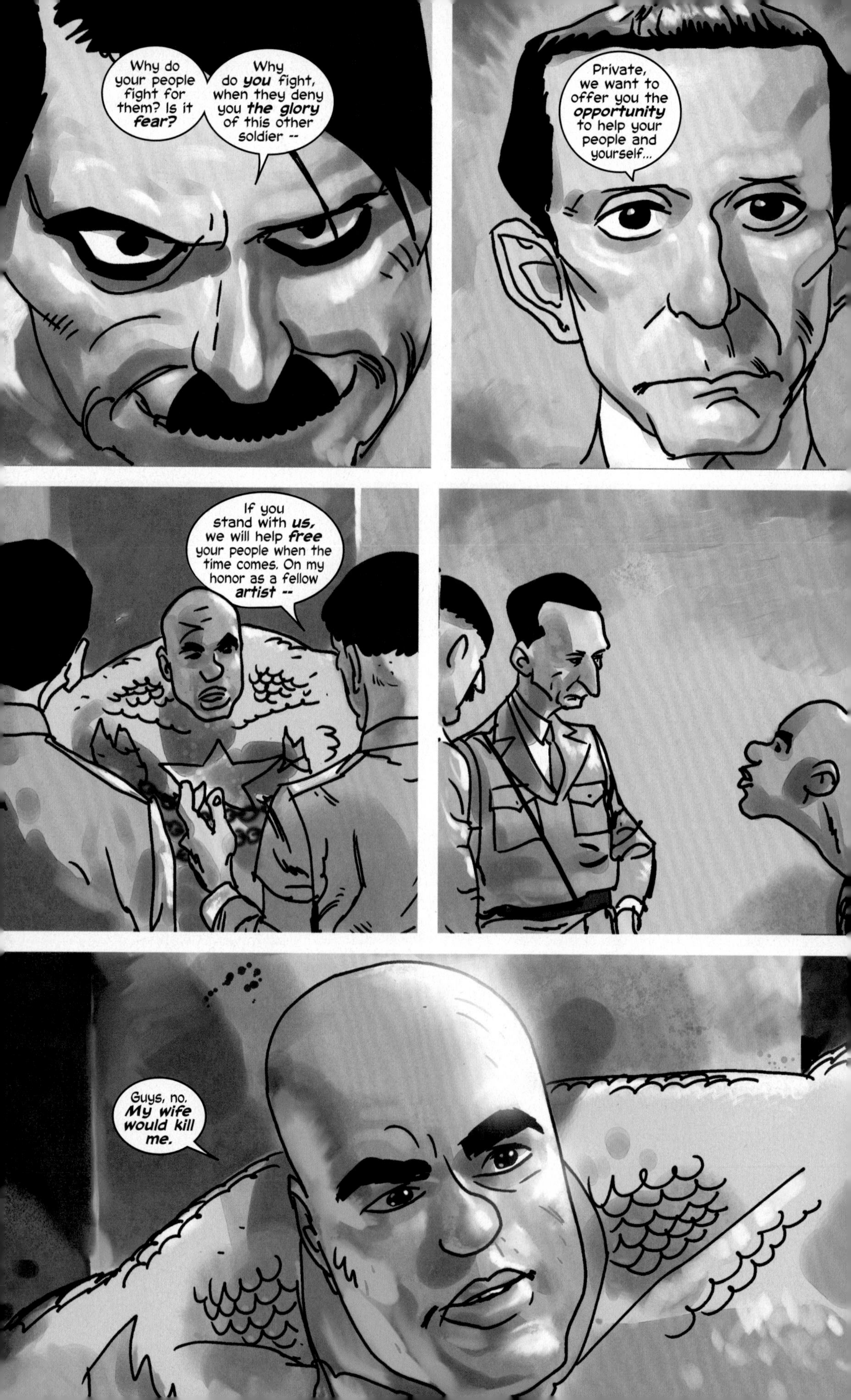
Why do your people fight for them? Is it fear?
Why do you fight, when they deny you the glory of this other soldier --
Private, we want to offer you the opportunity to help your people and yourself...
If you stand with us, we will help free your people when the time comes. On my honor as a fellow artist --
Guys, no. My wife would kill me.

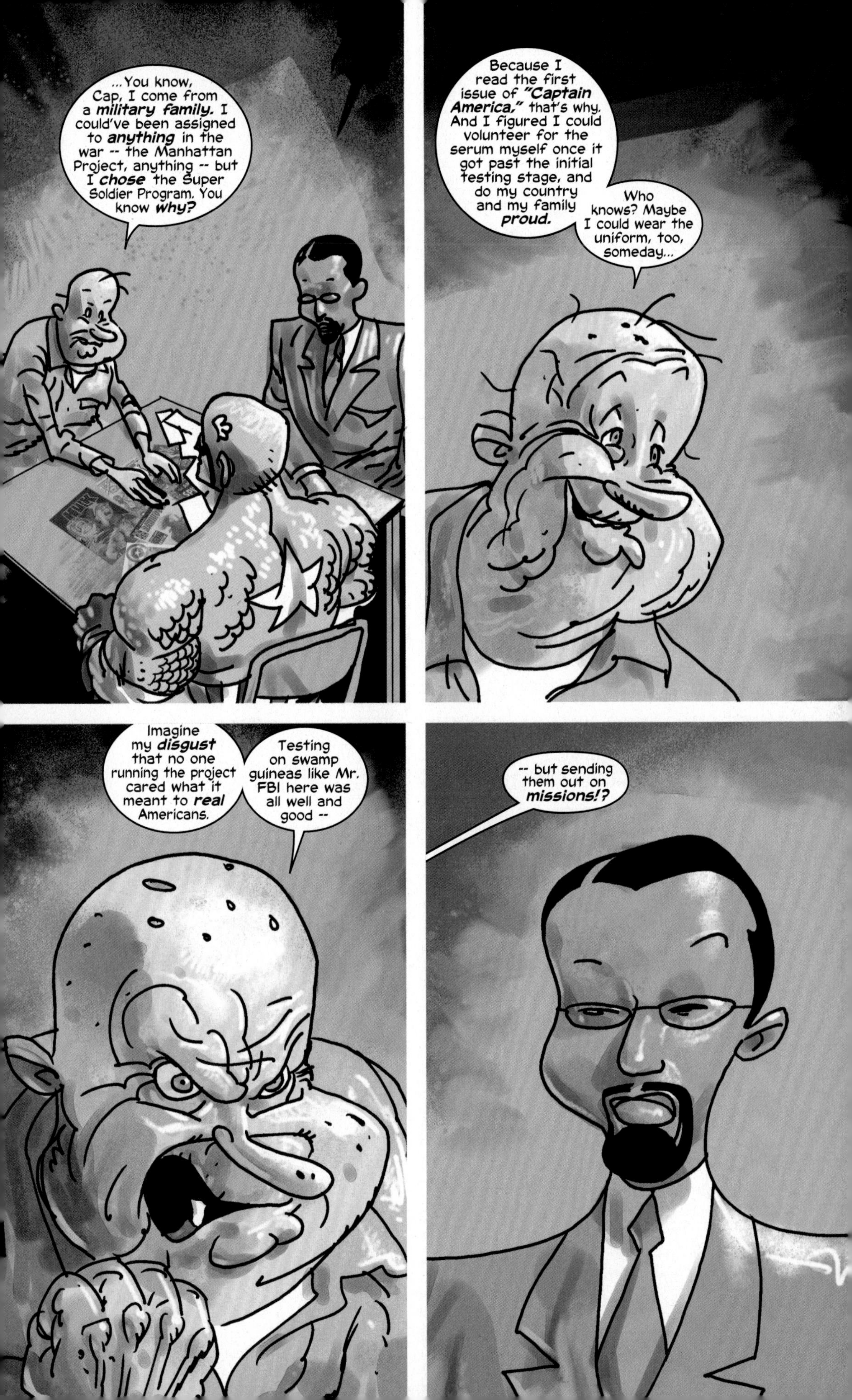
...You know, Cap, I come from a military family. I could've been assigned to anything in the war -- the Manhattan Project, anything -- but I chose the Super Soldier Program. You know why?
Because I read the first issue of "Captain America," that's why. And I figured I could volunteer for the serum myself once it got past the initial testing stage, and do my country and my family proud.
Who knows? Maybe I could wear the uniform, too, someday...
Imagine my disgust that no one running the project cared what it meant to real Americans.
Testing on swamp guineas like Mr. FBI here was all well and good --
-- but sending them out on missions!?

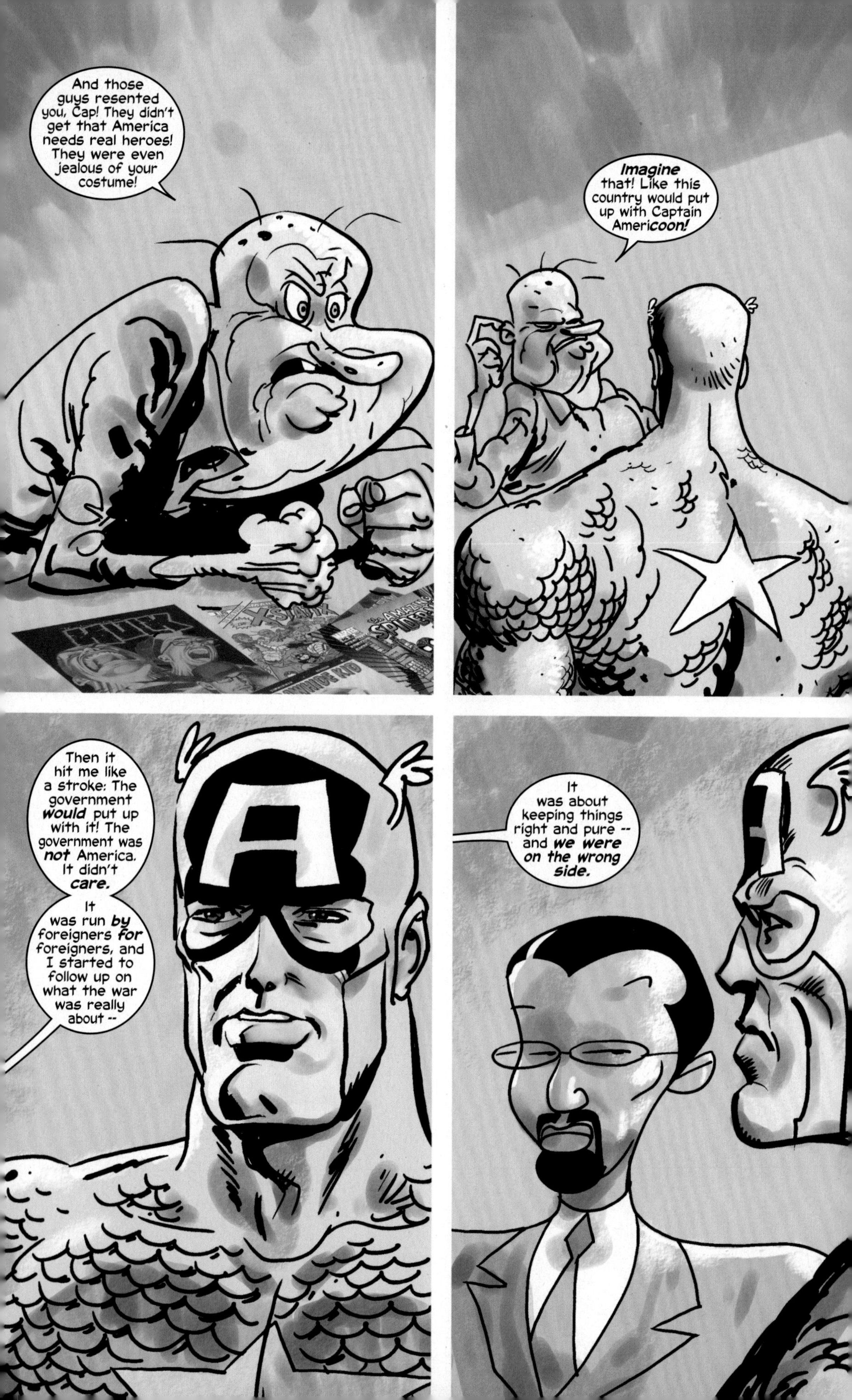
And those guys resented you, Cap! They didn't get that America needs real heroes! They were even jealous of your costume!
Imagine that! Like this country would put up with Captain Ameri*coon!*
Then it hit me like a stroke: The government *would* put up with it! The government was *not* America. It didn't *care.*
It was run *by* foreigners *for* foreigners, and I started to follow up on what the war was really about --
It was about keeping things right and pure -- and *we were on the wrong side.*

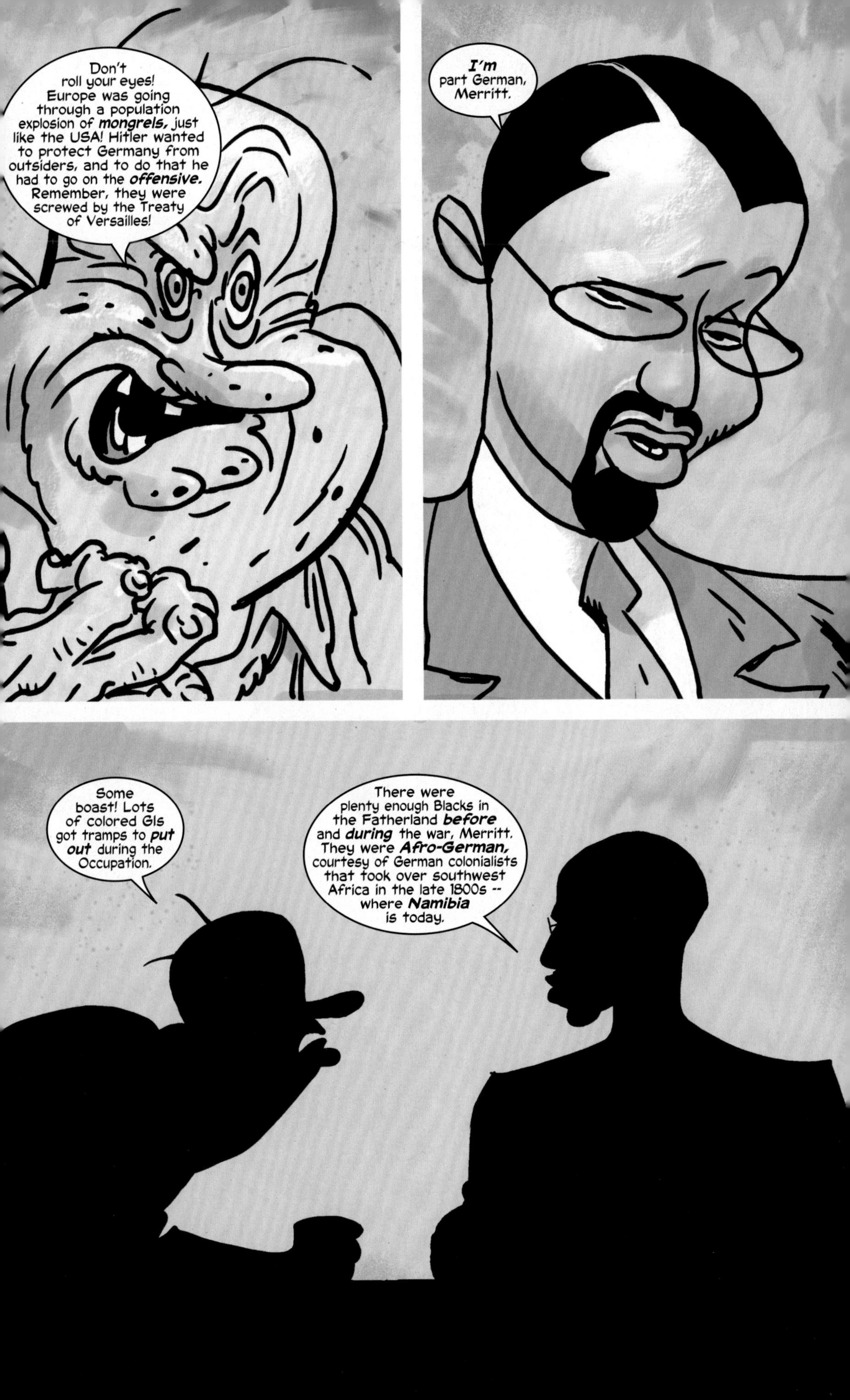

Don't roll your eyes! Europe was going through a population explosion of *mongrels,* just like the USA! Hitler wanted to protect Germany from outsiders, and to do that he had to go on the *offensive.* Remember, they were screwed by the Treaty of Versailles!
I'm part German, Merritt.
Some boast! Lots of colored GIs got tramps to *put out* during the Occupation.
There were plenty enough Blacks in the Fatherland *before* and *during* the war, Merritt. They were *Afro-German,* courtesy of German colonialists that took over southwest Africa in the late 1800s -- where *Namibia* is today.

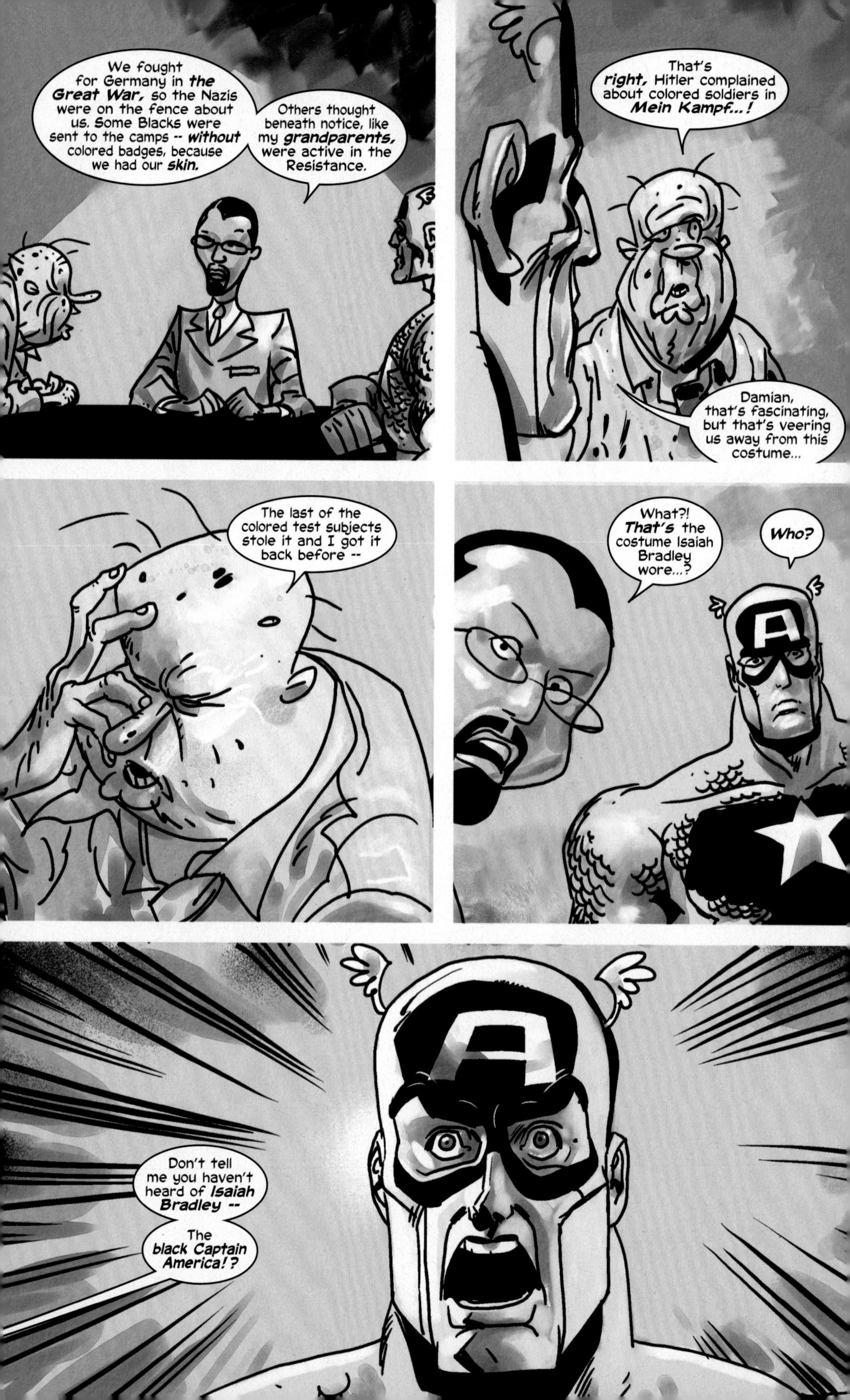
We fought for Germany in **the Great War,** so the Nazis were on the fence about us. Some Blacks were sent to the camps -- ***without*** colored badges, because we had our ***skin.***
Others thought beneath notice, like my ***grandparents,*** were active in the Resistance.
That's ***right,*** Hitler complained about colored soldiers in ***Mein Kampf...!***
Damian, that's fascinating, but that's veering us away from this costume...
The last of the colored test subjects stole it and I got it back before --
What?! ***That's*** the costume Isaiah Bradley wore...?
Who?
Don't tell me you haven't heard of ***Isaiah Bradley --***
The ***black Captain America!?***

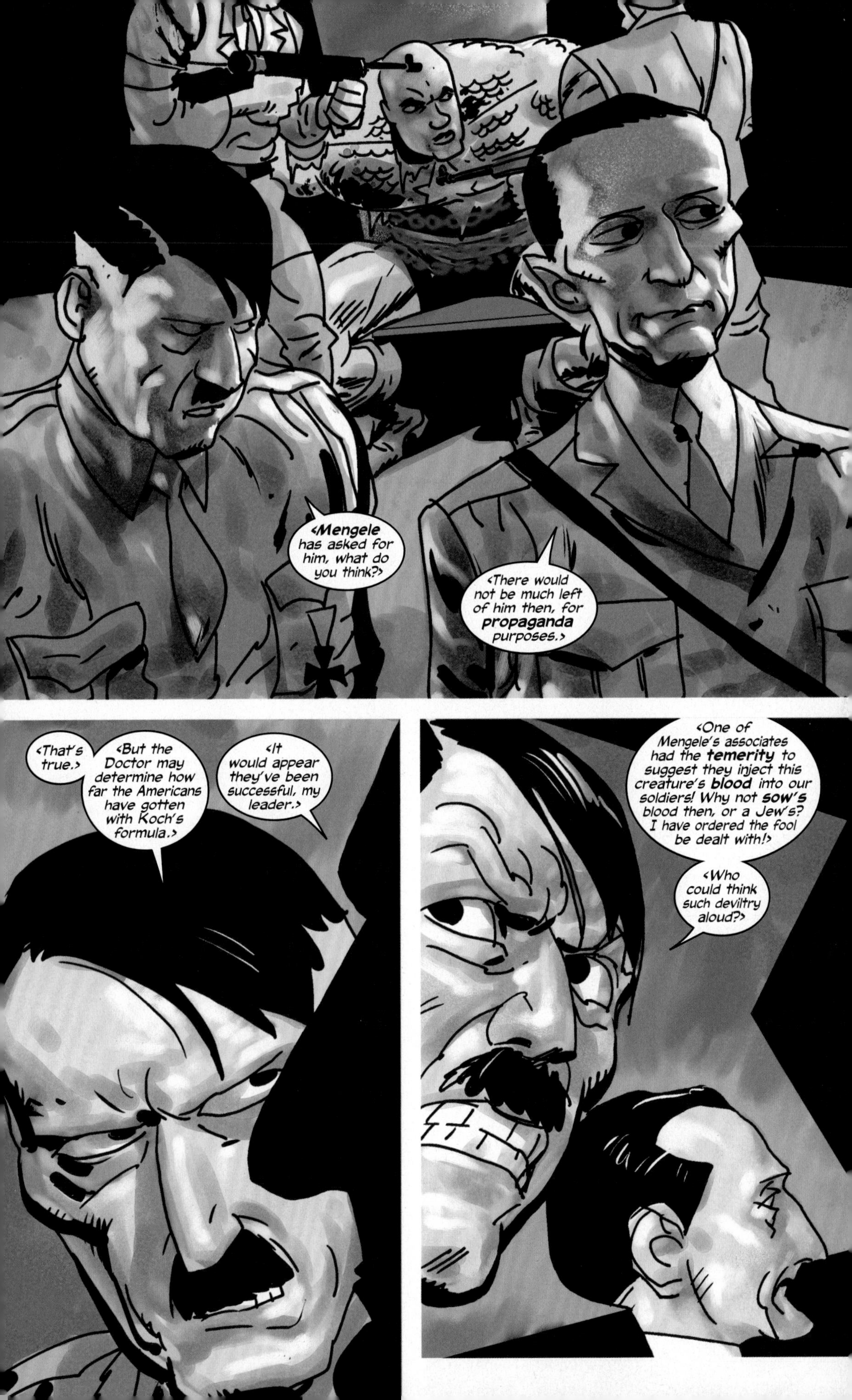
‹Mengele has asked for him, what do you think?›
‹There would not be much left of him then, for propaganda purposes.›
‹That's true.›
‹But the Doctor may determine how far the Americans have gotten with Koch's formula.›
‹It would appear they've been successful, my leader.›
‹One of Mengele's associates had the temerity to suggest they inject this creature's blood into our soldiers! Why not sow's blood then, or a Jew's? I have ordered the fool be dealt with!›
‹Who could think such deviltry aloud?›

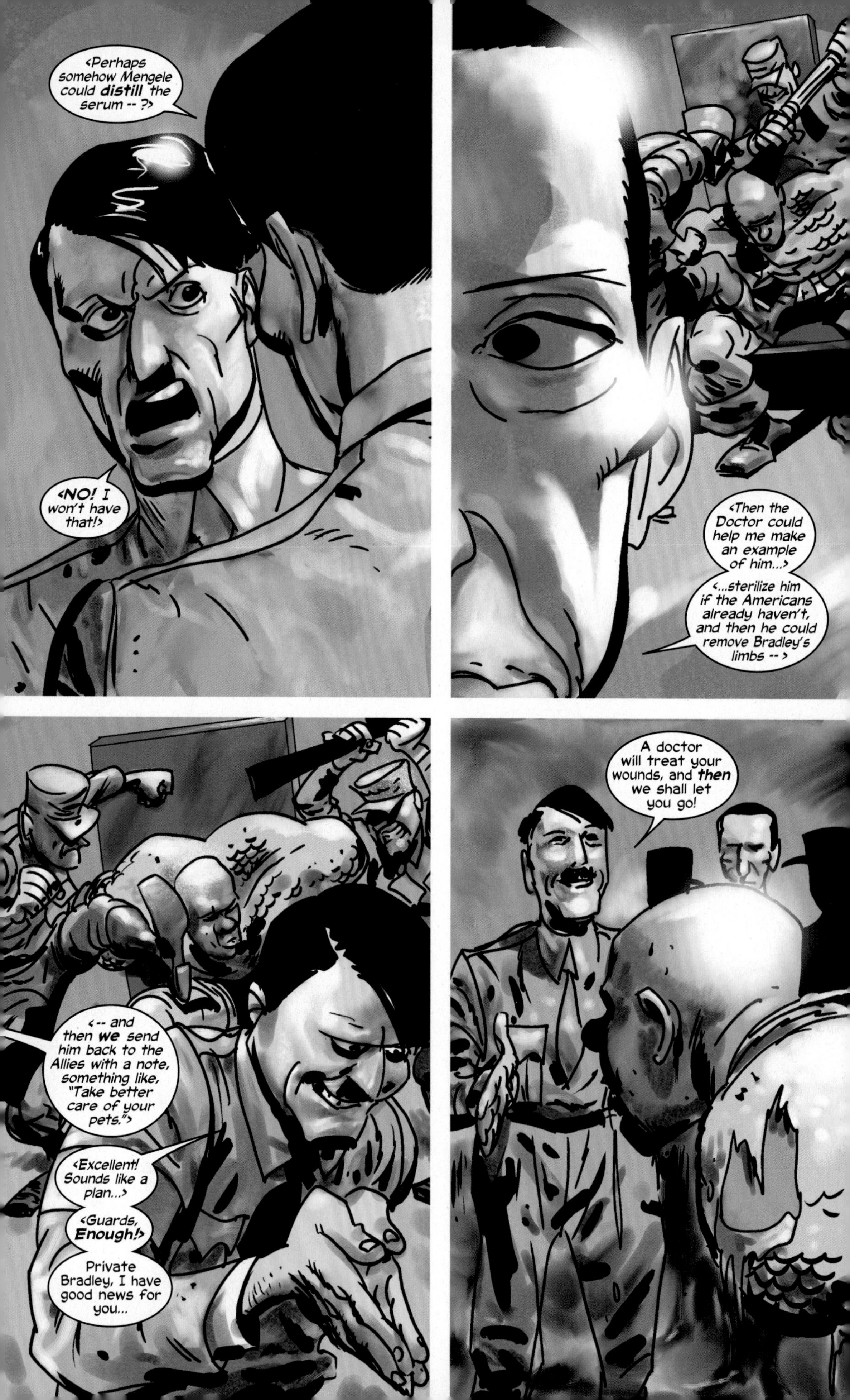

<Perhaps somehow Mengele could **distill** the serum -- ?>
<**NO!** I won't have that!>
<Then the Doctor could help me make an example of him...>
<...sterilize him if the Americans already haven't, and then he could remove Bradley's limbs -->
<-- and then **we** send him back to the Allies with a note, something like, "Take better care of your pets.">
<Excellent! Sounds like a plan...>
<Guards, **Enough!**>
Private Bradley, I have good news for you...
A doctor will treat your wounds, and **then** we shall let you go!

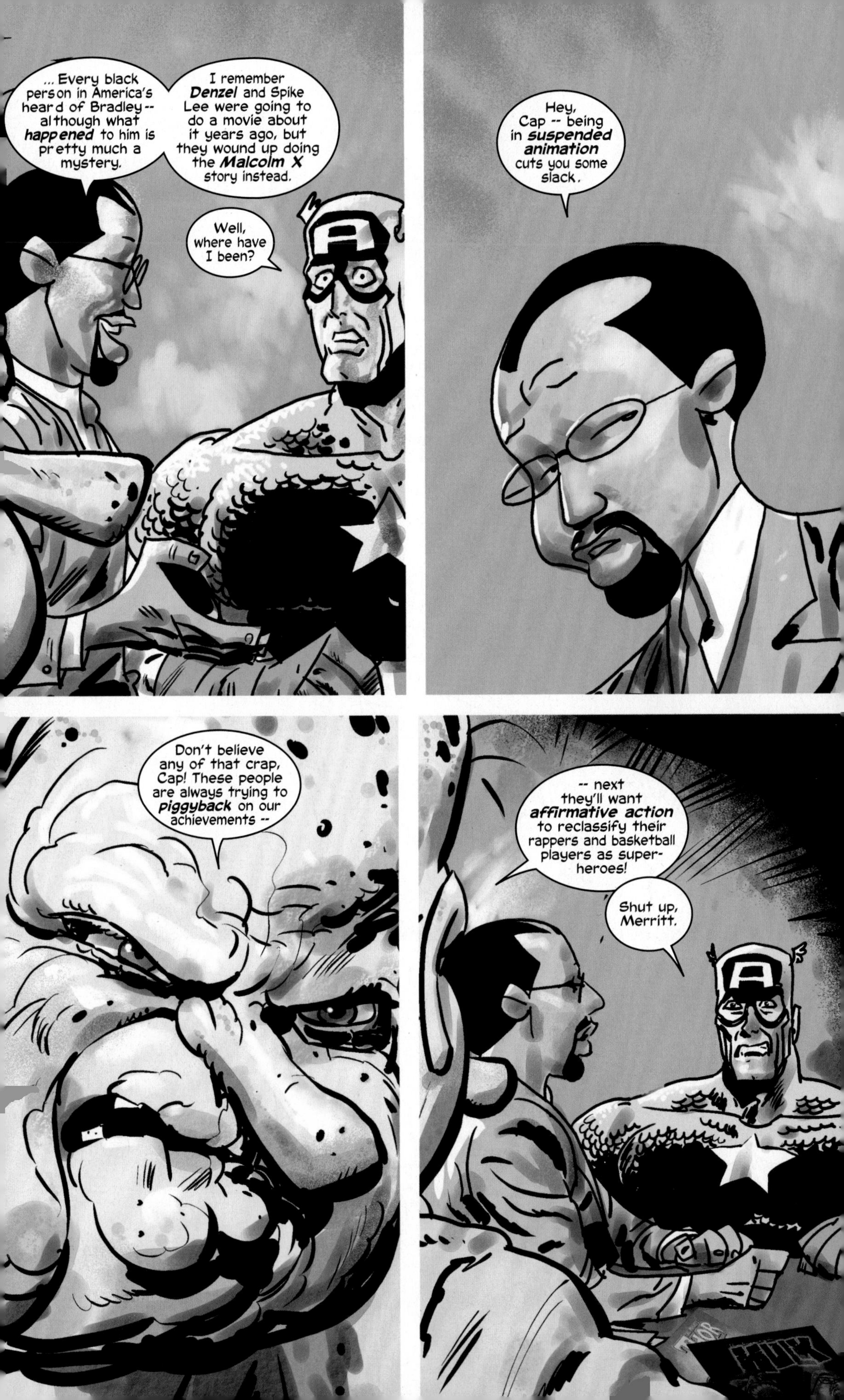
... Every black person in America's heard of Bradley -- although what happened to him is pretty much a mystery.
I remember Denzel and Spike Lee were going to do a movie about it years ago, but they wound up doing the Malcolm X story instead.
Well, where have I been?
Hey, Cap -- being in suspended animation cuts you some slack.
Don't believe any of that crap, Cap! These people are always trying to piggyback on our achievements --
-- next they'll want affirmative action to reclassify their rappers and basketball players as super-heroes!
Shut up, Merritt.

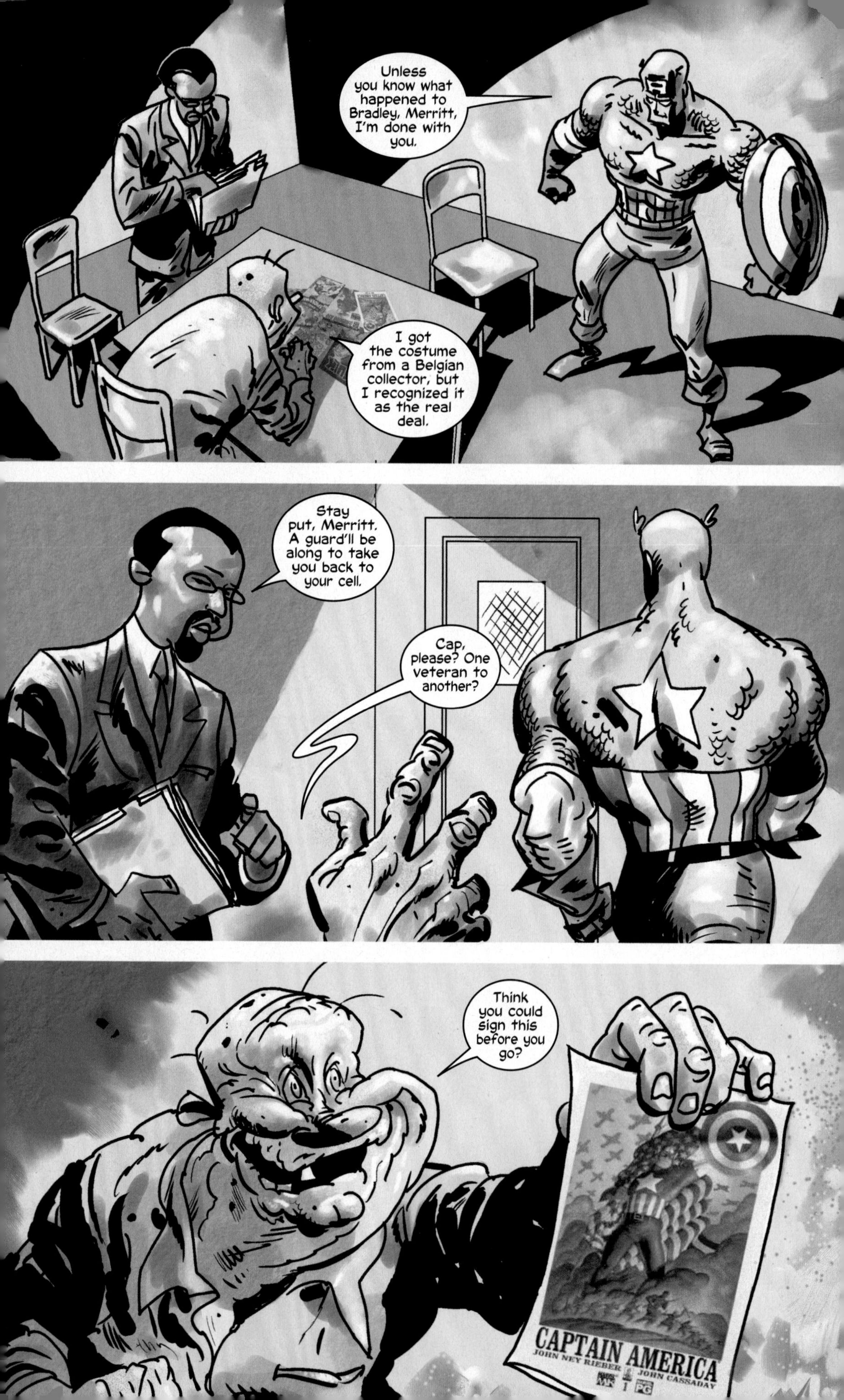
Unless you know what happened to Bradley, Merritt, I'm done with you.
I got the costume from a Belgian collector, but I recognized it as the real deal.
Stay put, Merritt. A guard'll be along to take you back to your cell.
Cap, please? One veteran to another?
Think you could sign this before you go?
CAPTAIN AMERICA
JOHN NEY RIEBER
JOHN CASSADAY

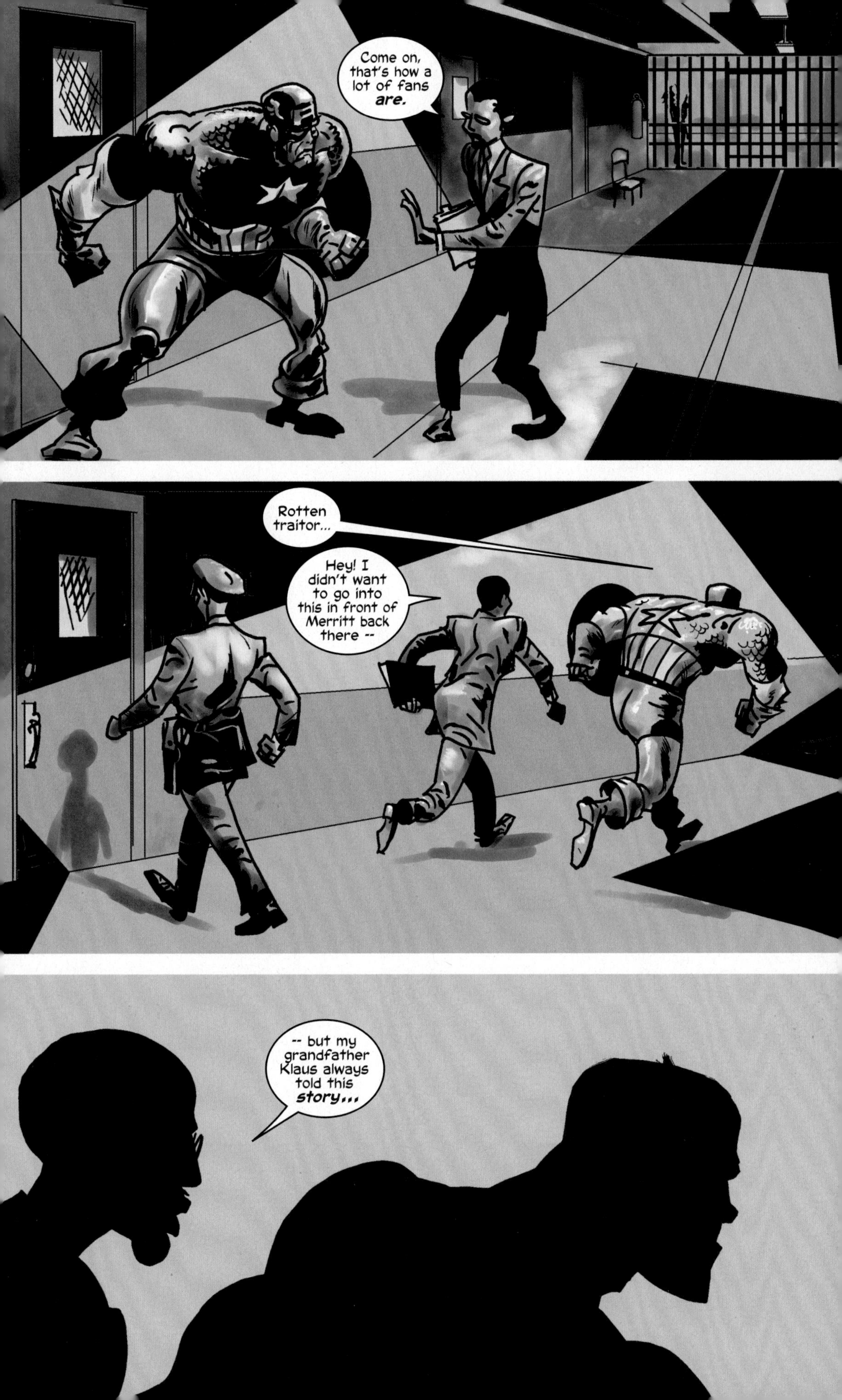
Come on, that's how a lot of fans **are.**
Rotten traitor...
Hey! I didn't want to go into this in front of Merritt back there --
-- but my grandfather Klaus always told this **story...**

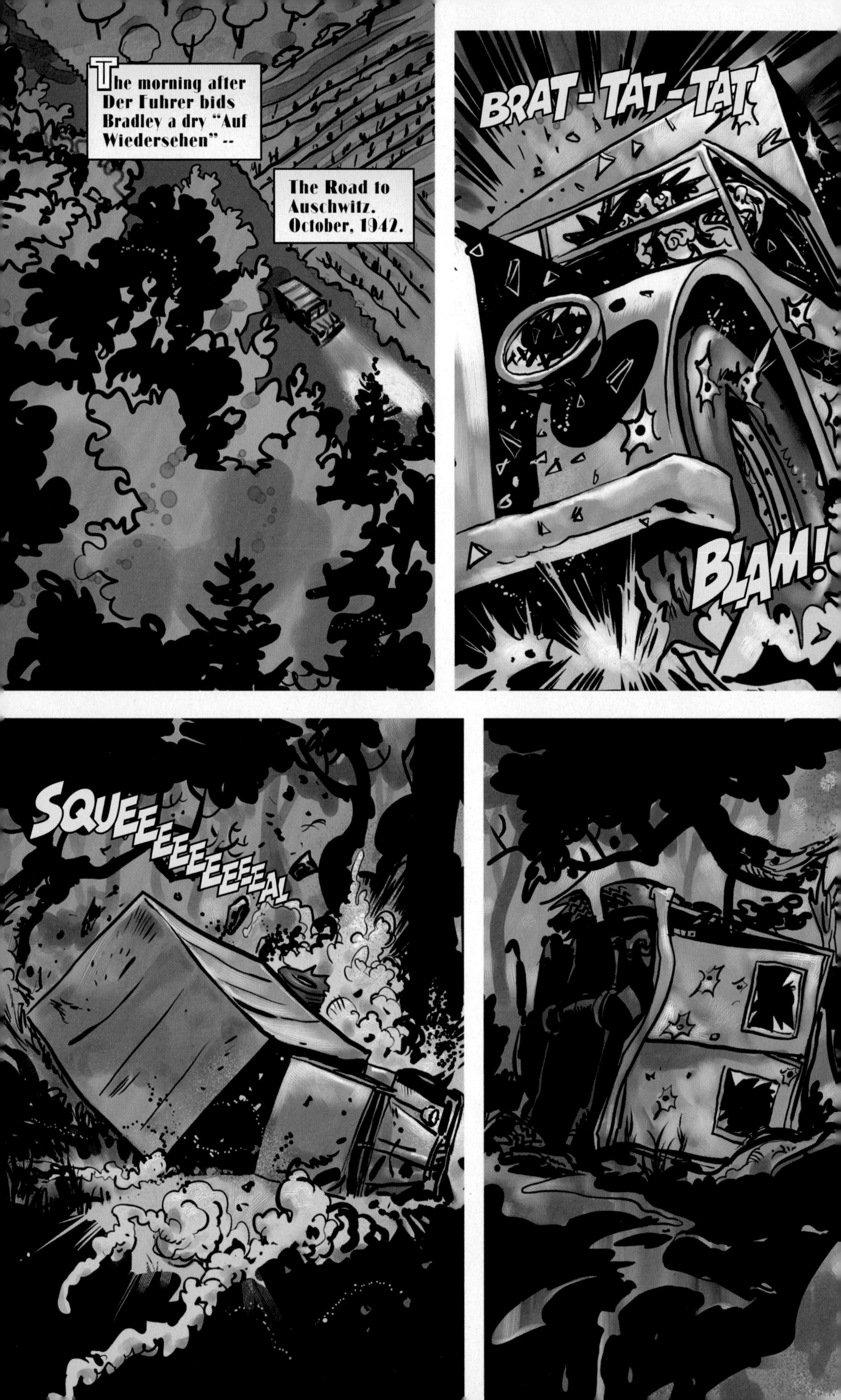
The morning after Der Fuhrer bids Bradley a dry "Auf Wiedersehen" --
The Road to Auschwitz. October, 1942.
BRAT-TAT-TAT
BLAM!
SQUEEEEEEEEEEEAL

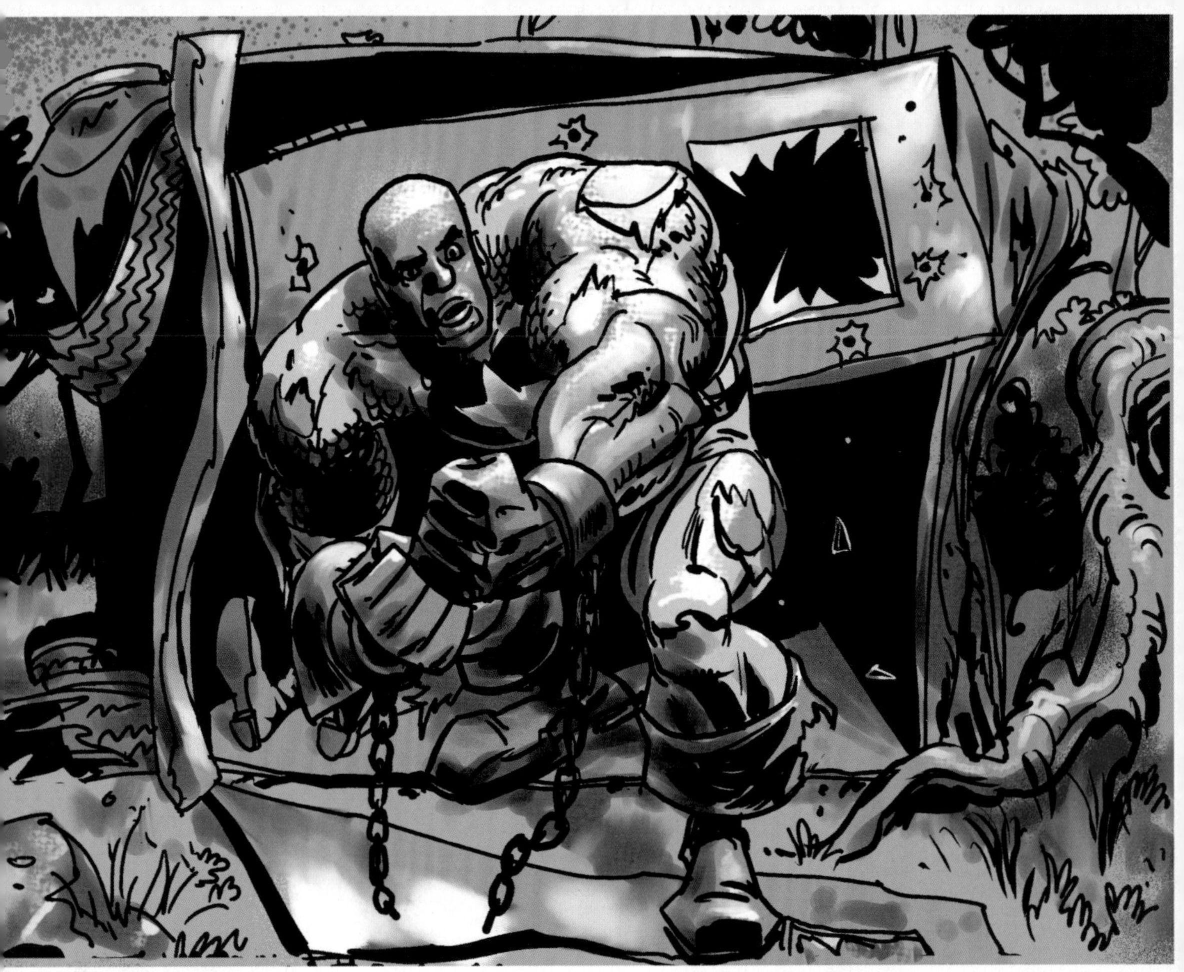

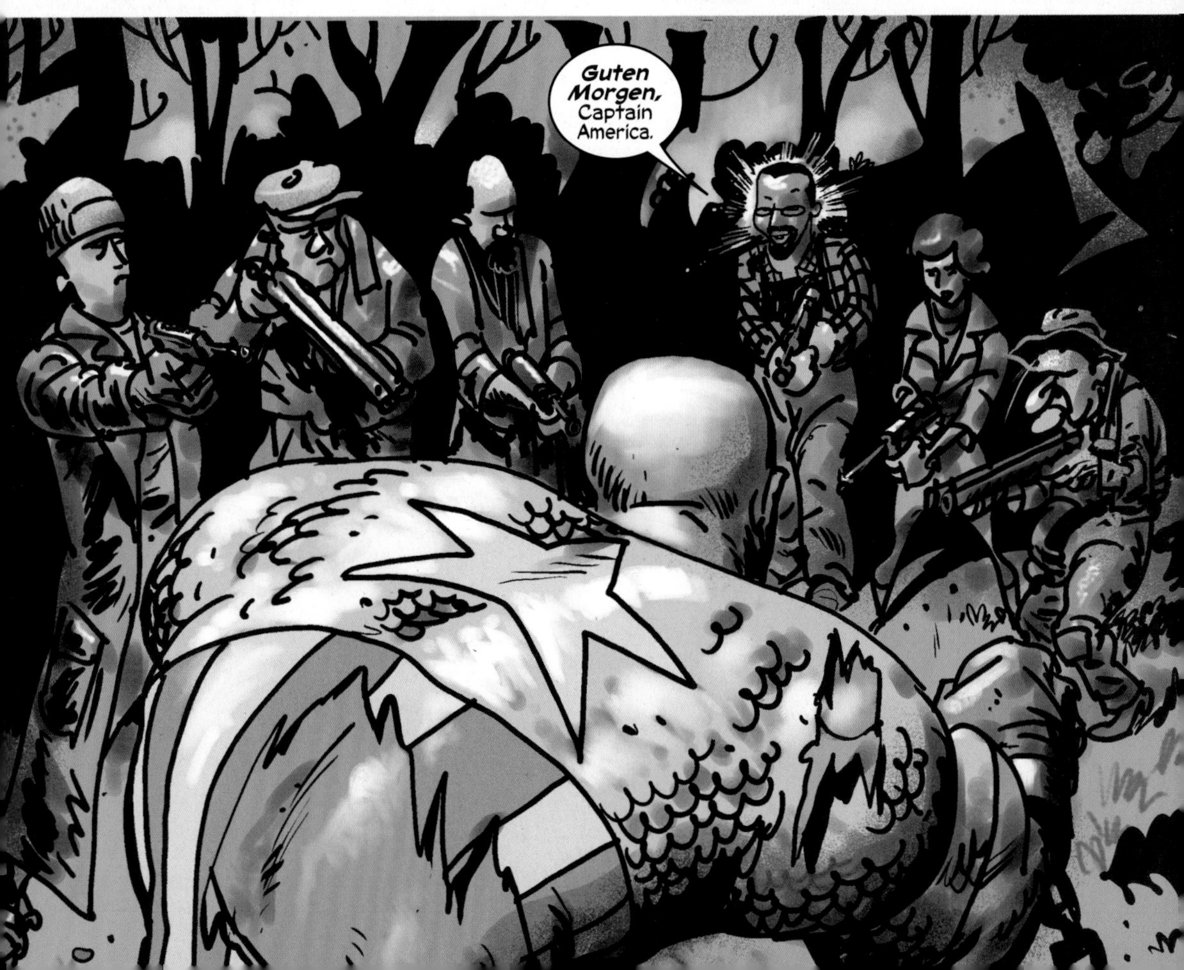
Guten Morgen, Captain America.

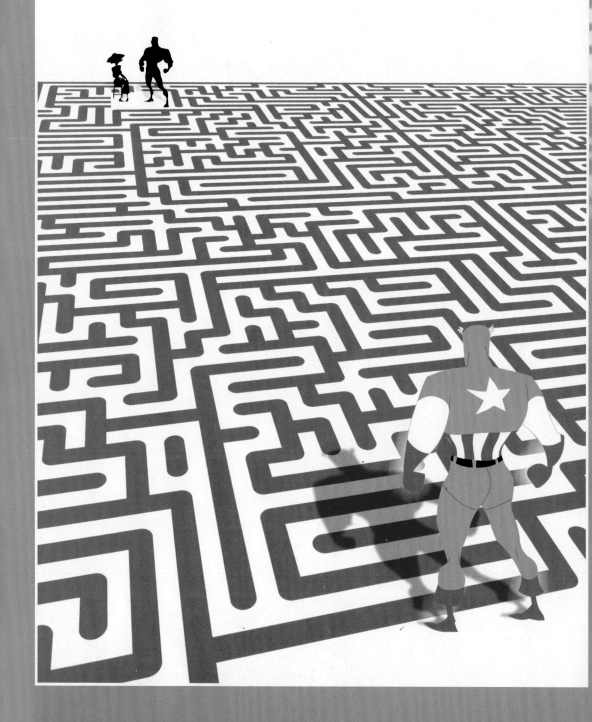

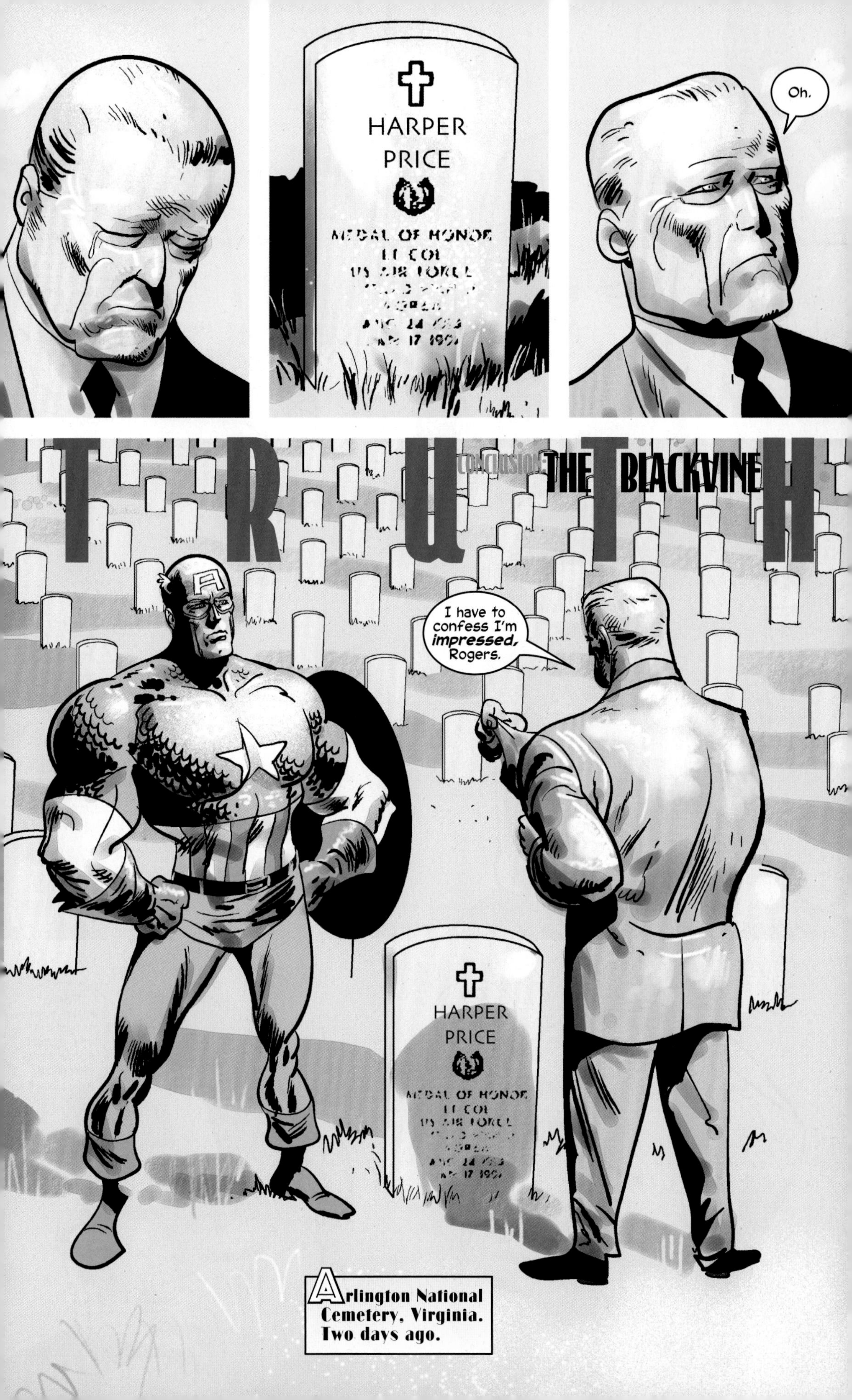
HARPER
PRICE
Oh.
TRUTH
CONCLUSION: THE BLACKVINE
I have to confess I'm *impressed,* Rogers.
HARPER
PRICE
Arlington National Cemetery, Virginia. Two days ago.

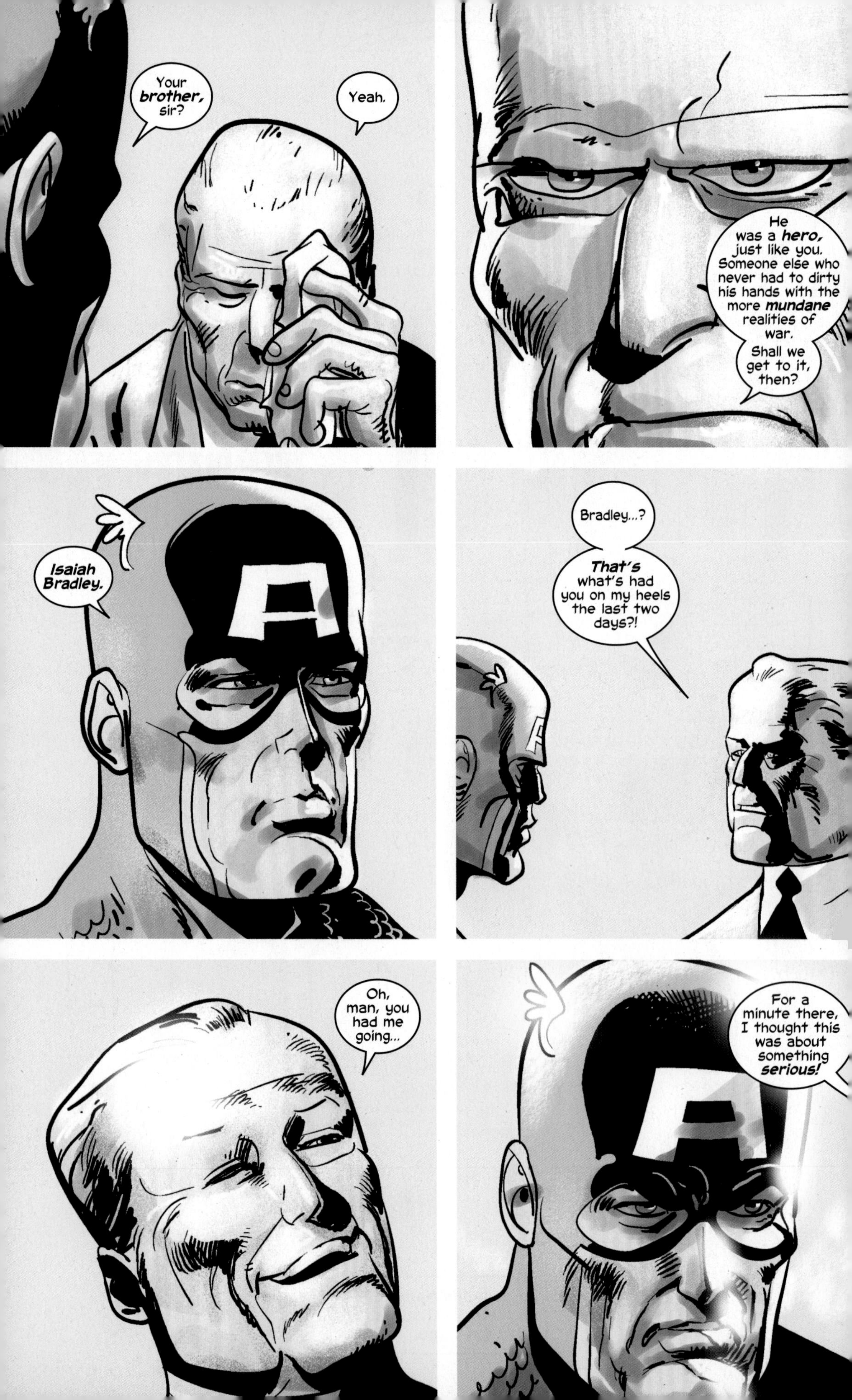
Your brother, sir?
Yeah.
He was a hero, just like you. Someone else who never had to dirty his hands with the more mundane realities of war.
Shall we get to it, then?
Isaiah Bradley.
Bradley...?
That's what's had you on my heels the last two days?!
Oh, man, you had me going...
For a minute there, I thought this was about something serious!

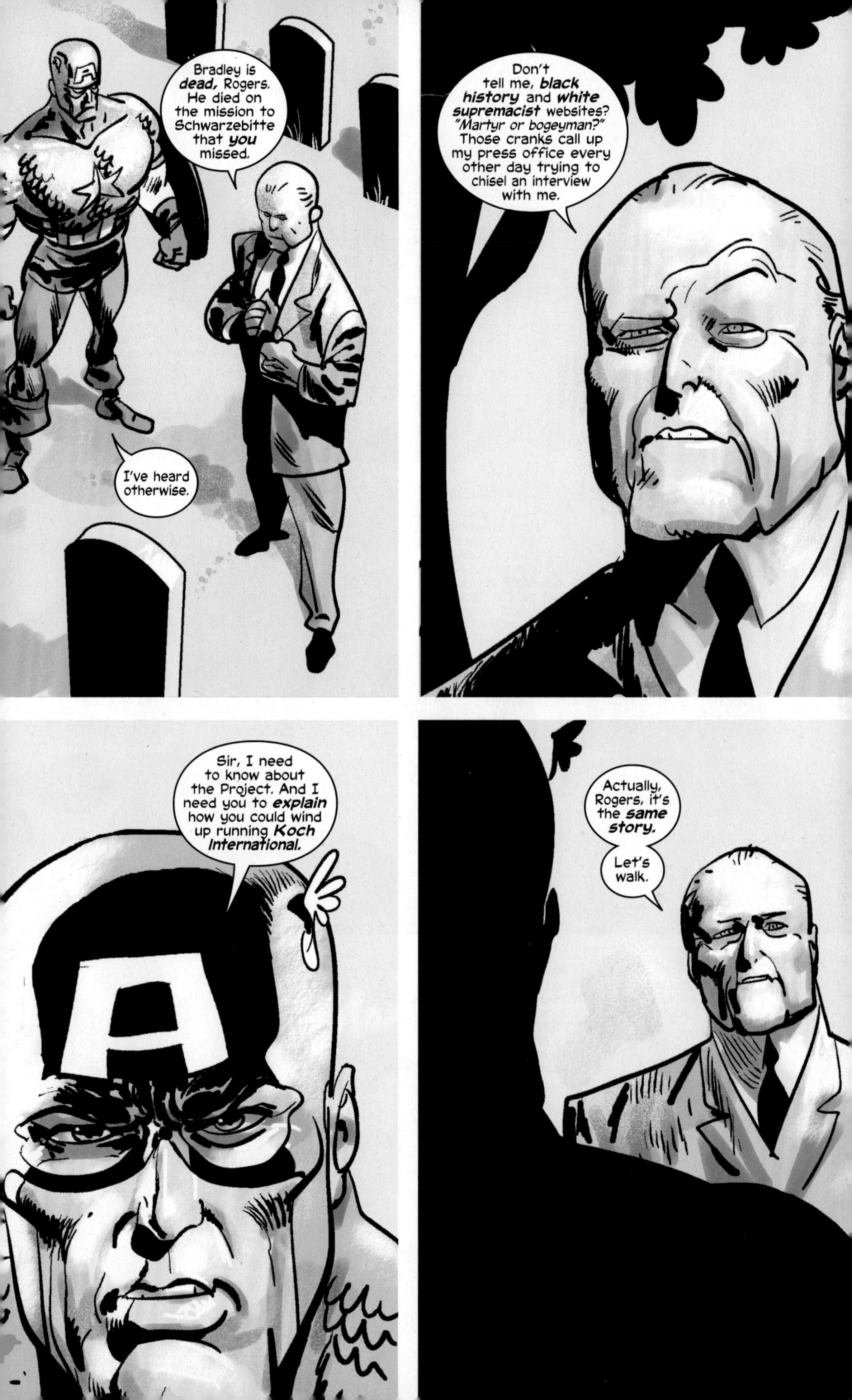

Bradley is dead, Rogers. He died on the mission to Schwarzebitte that you missed.
I've heard otherwise.
Don't tell me, black history and white supremacist websites? "Martyr or bogeyman?" Those cranks call up my press office every other day trying to chisel an interview with me.
Sir, I need to know about the Project. And I need you to explain how you could wind up running Koch International.
Actually, Rogers, it's the same story.
Let's walk.

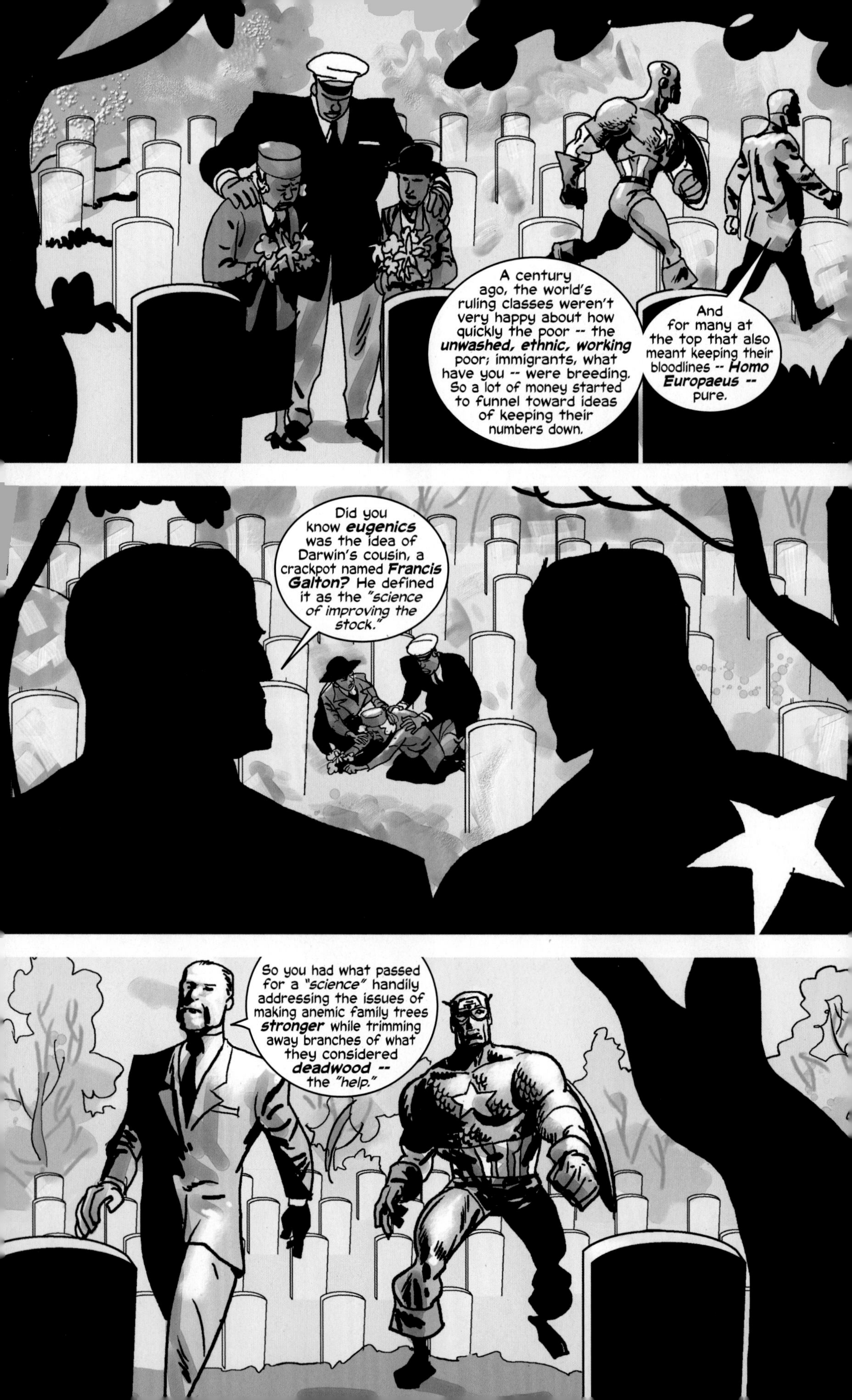
A century ago, the world's ruling classes weren't very happy about how quickly the poor -- the unwashed, ethnic, working poor; immigrants, what have you -- were breeding. So a lot of money started to funnel toward ideas of keeping their numbers down.
And for many at the top that also meant keeping their bloodlines -- Homo Europaeus -- pure.
Did you know eugenics was the idea of Darwin's cousin, a crackpot named Francis Galton? He defined it as the "science of improving the stock."
So you had what passed for a "science" handily addressing the issues of making anemic family trees stronger while trimming away branches of what they considered deadwood -- the "help."

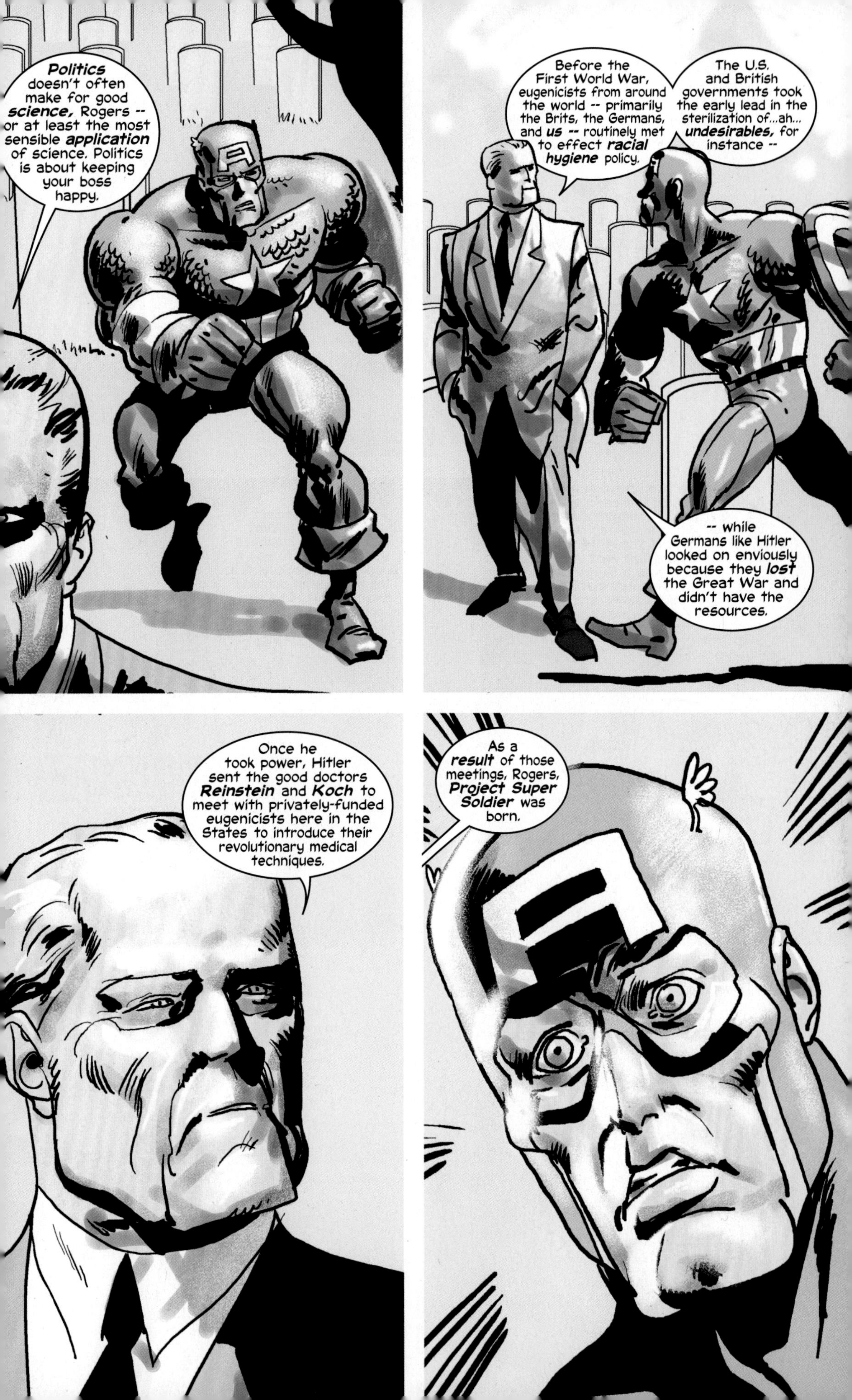
Politics doesn't often make for good science, Rogers -- or at least the most sensible application of science. Politics is about keeping your boss happy.
Before the First World War, eugenicists from around the world -- primarily the Brits, the Germans, and us -- routinely met to effect racial hygiene policy.
The U.S. and British governments took the early lead in the sterilization of...ah... undesirables, for instance --
-- while Germans like Hitler looked on enviously because they lost the Great War and didn't have the resources.
Once he took power, Hitler sent the good doctors Reinstein and Koch to meet with privately-funded eugenicists here in the States to introduce their revolutionary medical techniques.
As a result of those meetings, Rogers, Project Super Soldier was born.

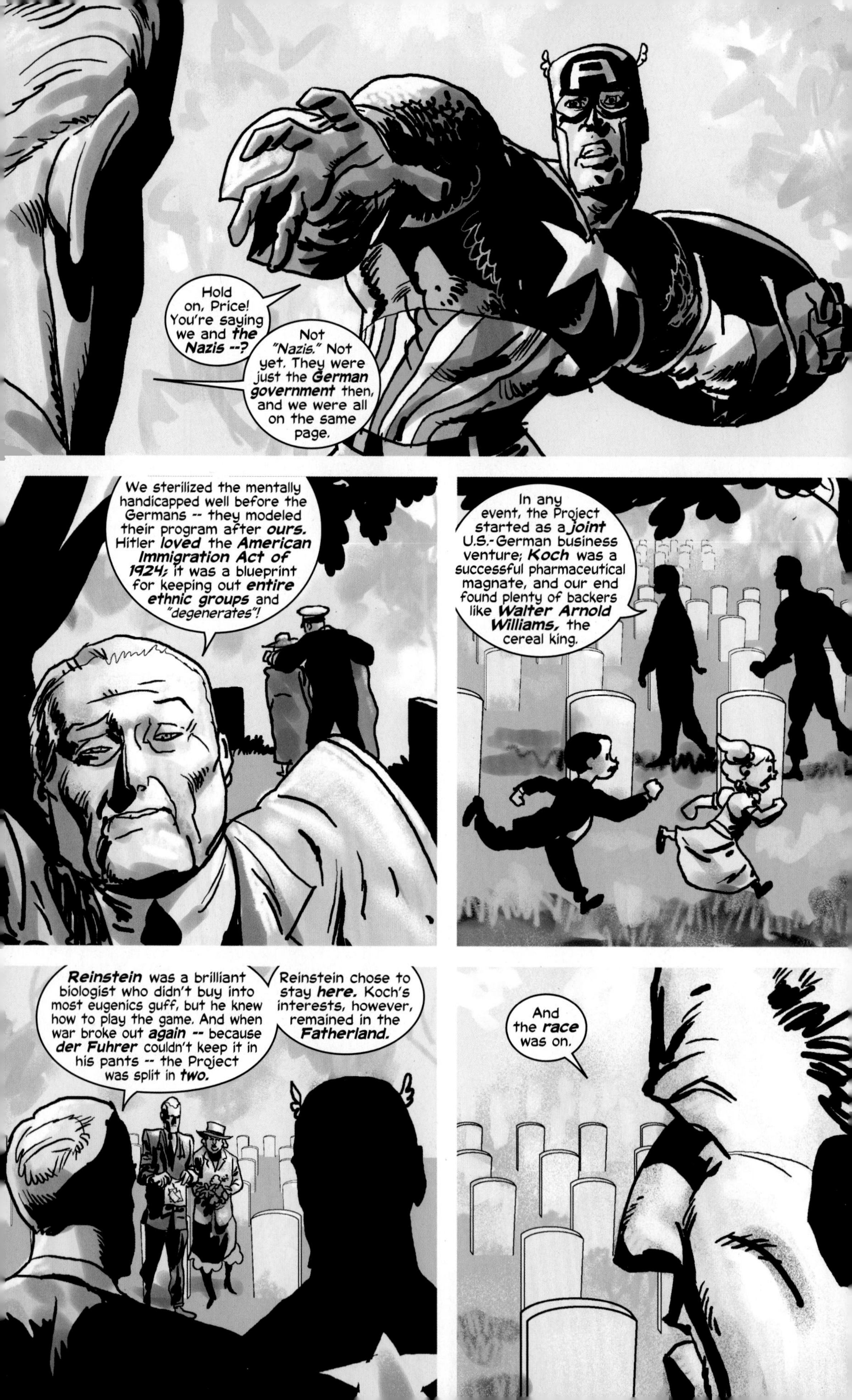
Hold on, Price! You're saying we and the Nazis --?
Not "Nazis." Not yet. They were just the German government then, and we were all on the same page.
We sterilized the mentally handicapped well before the Germans -- they modeled their program after ours. Hitler loved the American Immigration Act of 1924; it was a blueprint for keeping out entire ethnic groups and "degenerates"!
In any event, the Project started as a joint U.S.-German business venture; Koch was a successful pharmaceutical magnate, and our end found plenty of backers like Walter Arnold Williams, the cereal king.
Reinstein was a brilliant biologist who didn't buy into most eugenics guff, but he knew how to play the game. And when war broke out again -- because der Fuhrer couldn't keep it in his pants -- the Project was split in two.
Reinstein chose to stay here. Koch's interests, however, remained in the Fatherland.
And the race was on.

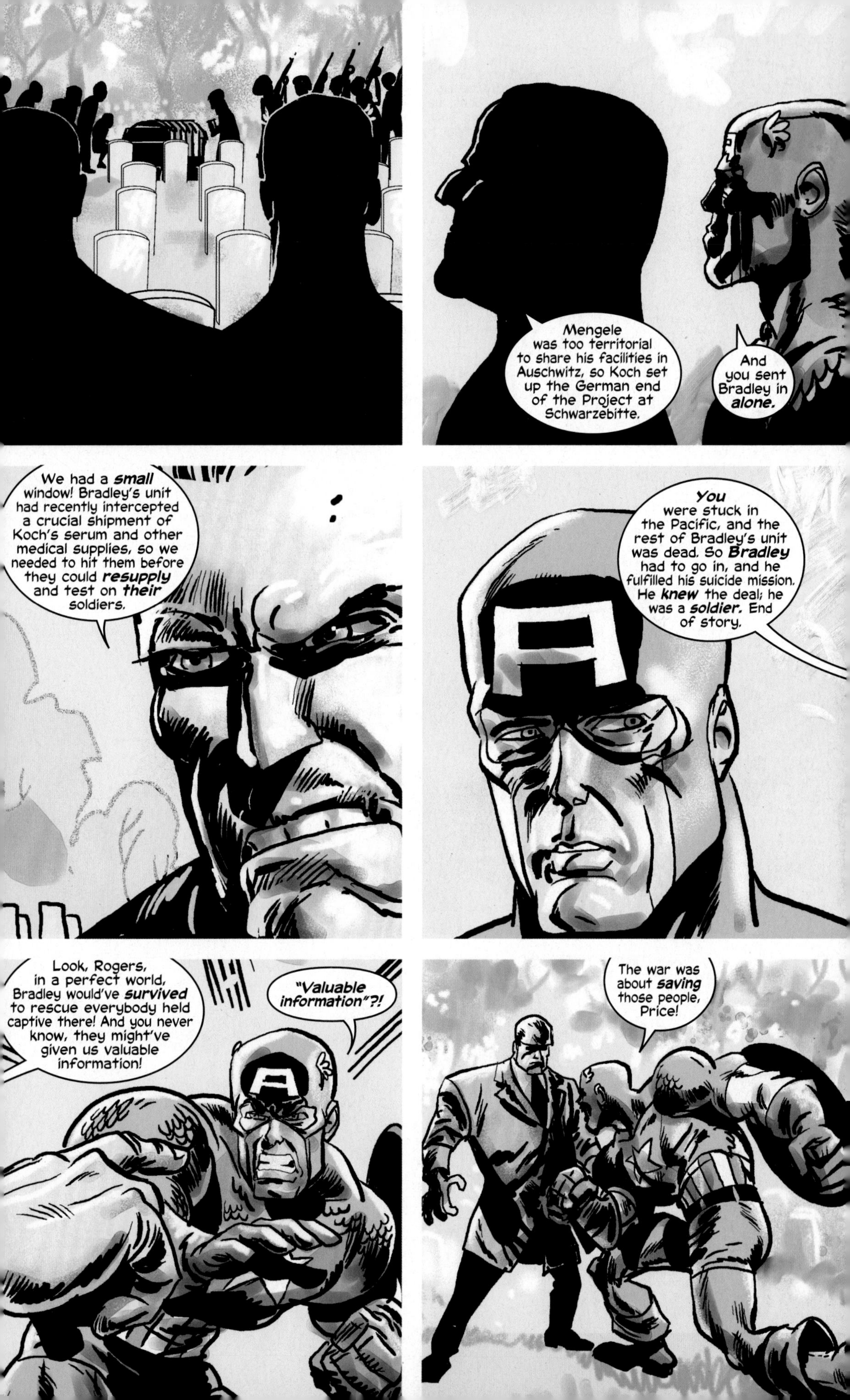
Mengele was too territorial to share his facilities in Auschwitz, so Koch set up the German end of the Project at Schwarzebitte.
And you sent Bradley in alone.
We had a small window! Bradley's unit had recently intercepted a crucial shipment of Koch's serum and other medical supplies, so we needed to hit them before they could resupply and test on their soldiers.
You were stuck in the Pacific, and the rest of Bradley's unit was dead. So Bradley had to go in, and he fulfilled his suicide mission. He knew the deal; he was a soldier. End of story.
Look, Rogers, in a perfect world, Bradley would've survived to rescue everybody held captive there! And you never know, they might've given us valuable information!
"Valuable information"?!
The war was about saving those people, Price!

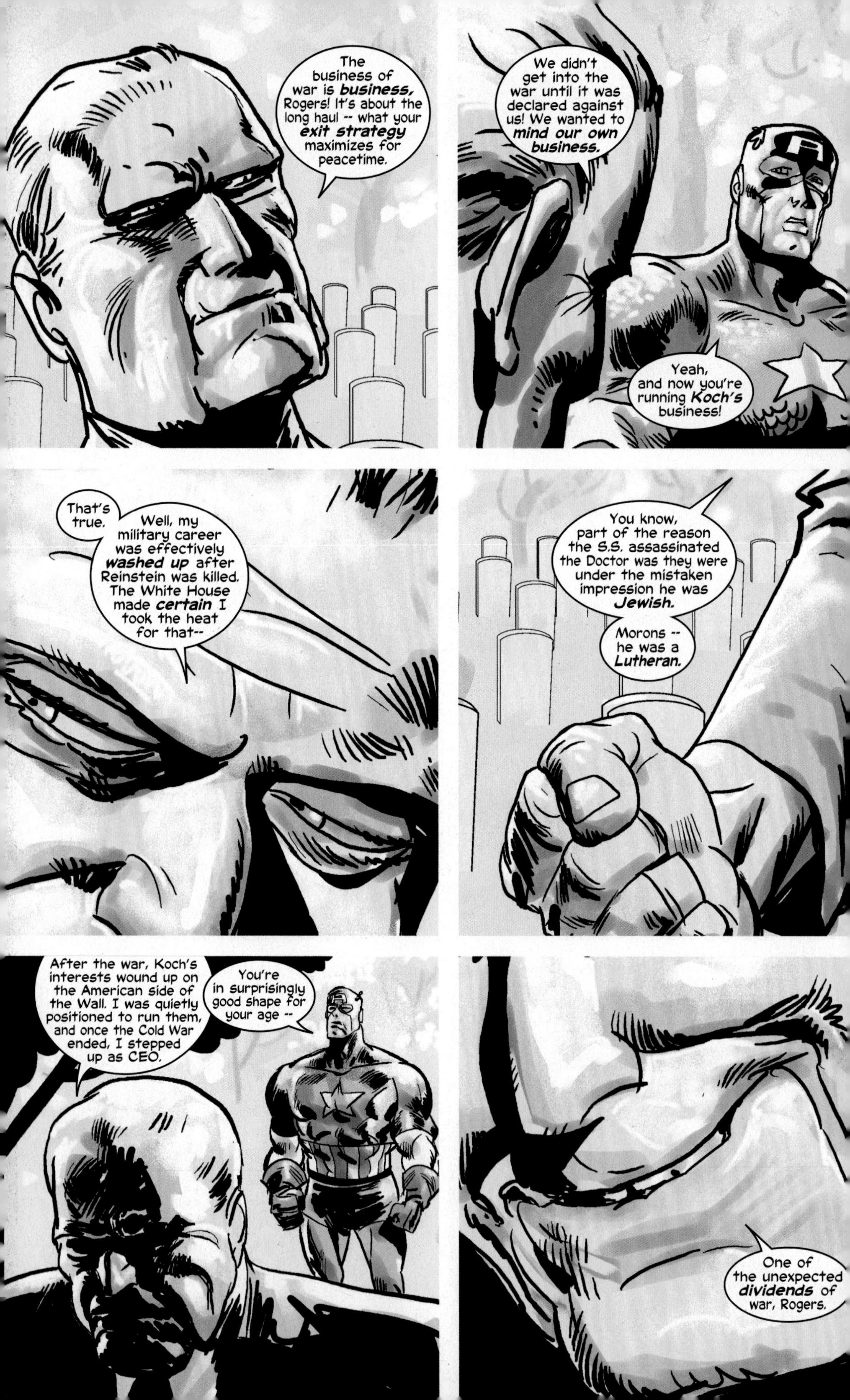
The business of war is **business,** Rogers! It's about the long haul -- what your ***exit strategy*** maximizes for peacetime.
We didn't get into the war until it was declared against us! We wanted to ***mind our own business.***
Yeah, and now you're running ***Koch's*** business!
That's true.
Well, my military career was effectively ***washed up*** after Reinstein was killed. The White House made ***certain*** I took the heat for that--
You know, part of the reason the S.S. assassinated the Doctor was they were under the mistaken impression he was ***Jewish.***
Morons -- he was a ***Lutheran.***
After the war, Koch's interests wound up on the American side of the Wall. I was quietly positioned to run them, and once the Cold War ended, I stepped up as CEO.
You're in surprisingly good shape for your age --
One of the unexpected ***dividends*** of war, Rogers.

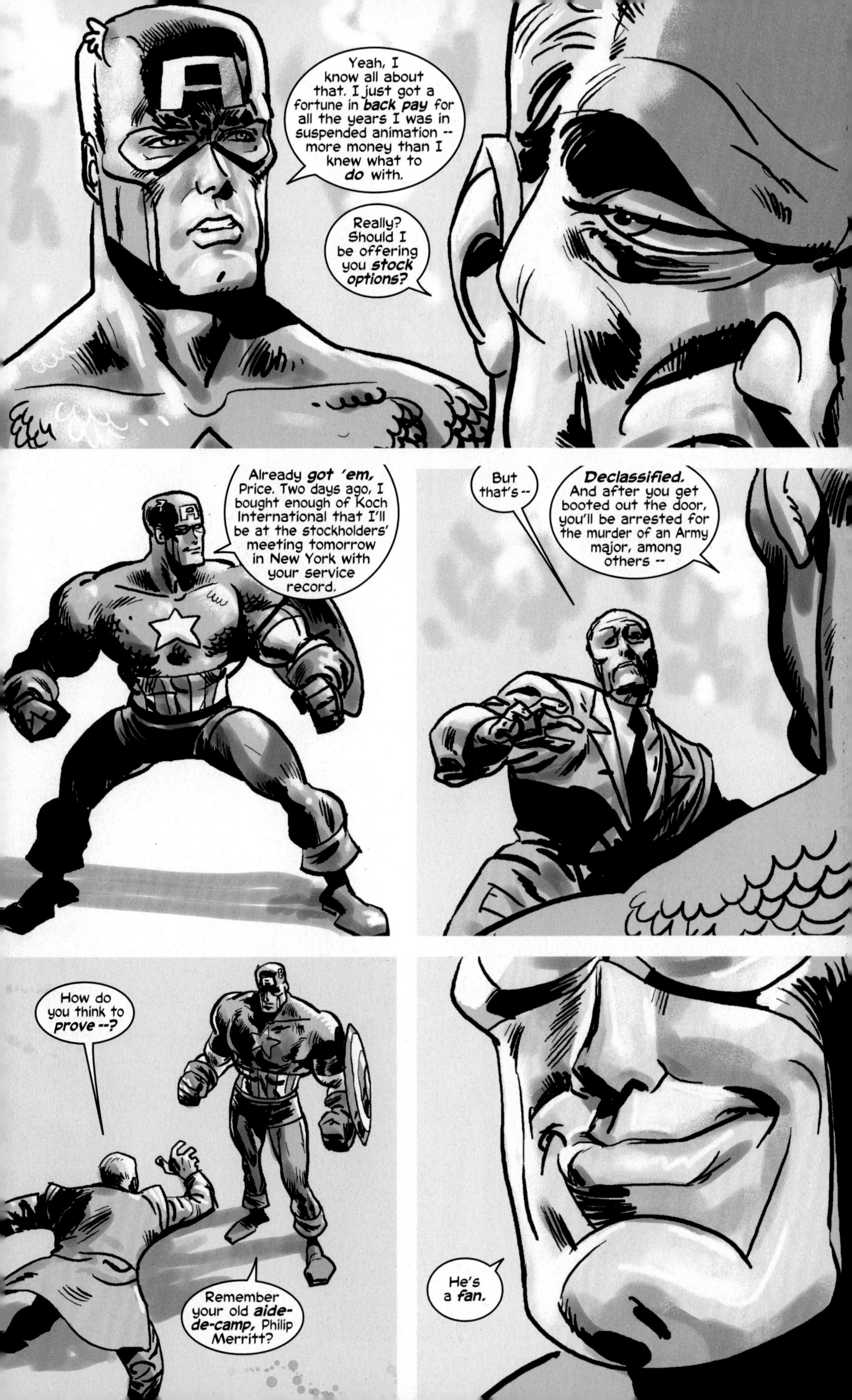
Yeah, I know all about that. I just got a fortune in **back pay** for all the years I was in suspended animation -- more money than I knew what to **do** with.
Really? Should I be offering you **stock options?**
Already **got 'em,** Price. Two days ago, I bought enough of Koch International that I'll be at the stockholders' meeting tomorrow in New York with your service record.
But that's --
Declassified. And after you get booted out the door, you'll be arrested for the murder of an Army major, among others --
How do you think to **prove --?**
Remember your old **aide-de-camp,** Philip Merritt?
He's a **fan.**

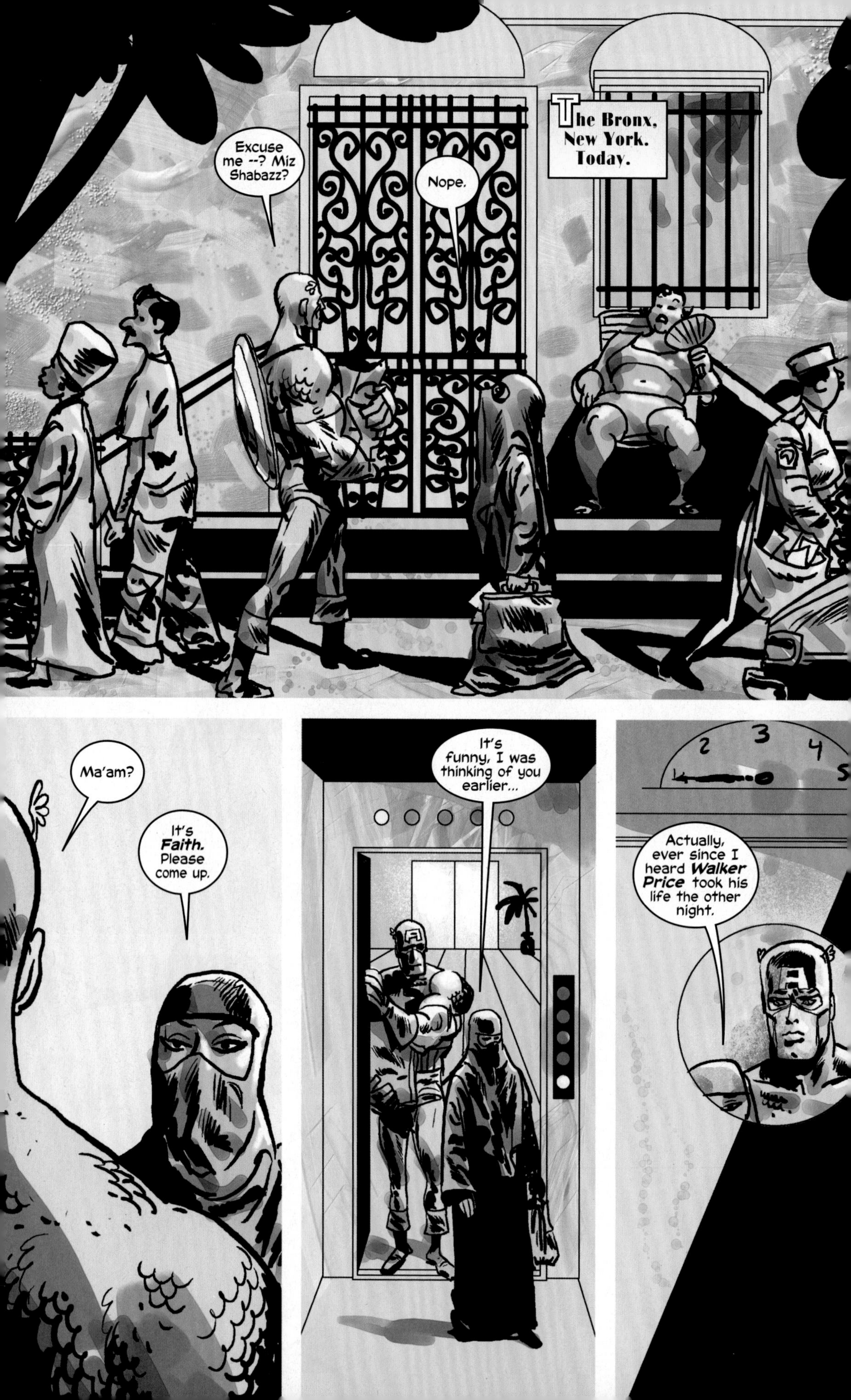
The Bronx, New York. Today.
Excuse me --? Miz Shabazz?
Nope.
Ma'am?
It's Faith. Please come up.
It's funny, I was thinking of you earlier...
Actually, ever since I heard Walker Price took his life the other night.

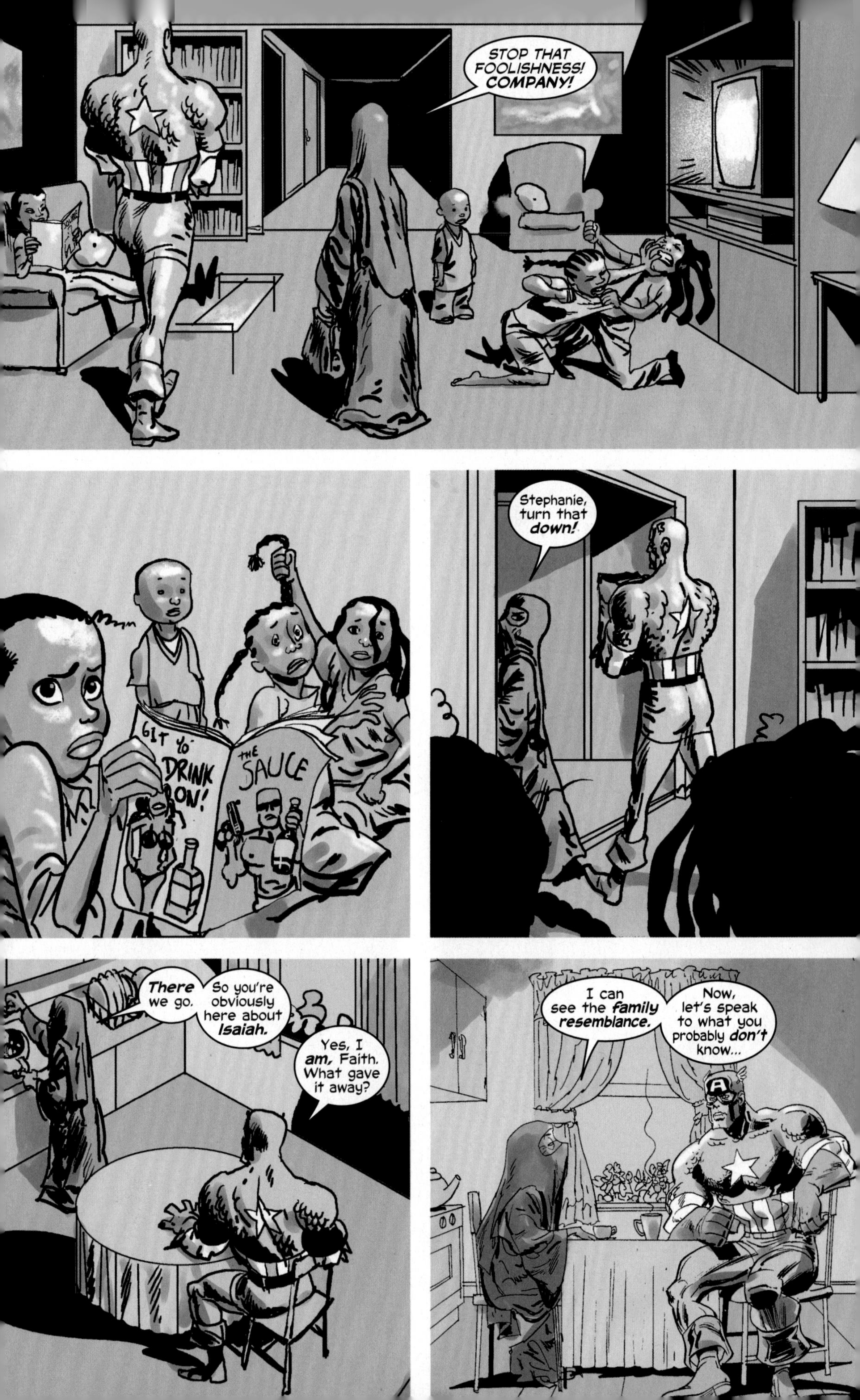

STOP THAT FOOLISHNESS! COMPANY!
GIT YO' DRINK ON!
THE SAUCE
Stephanie, turn that down!
There we go.
So you're obviously here about Isaiah.
Yes, I am, Faith. What gave it away?
I can see the family resemblance.
Now, let's speak to what you probably don't know...

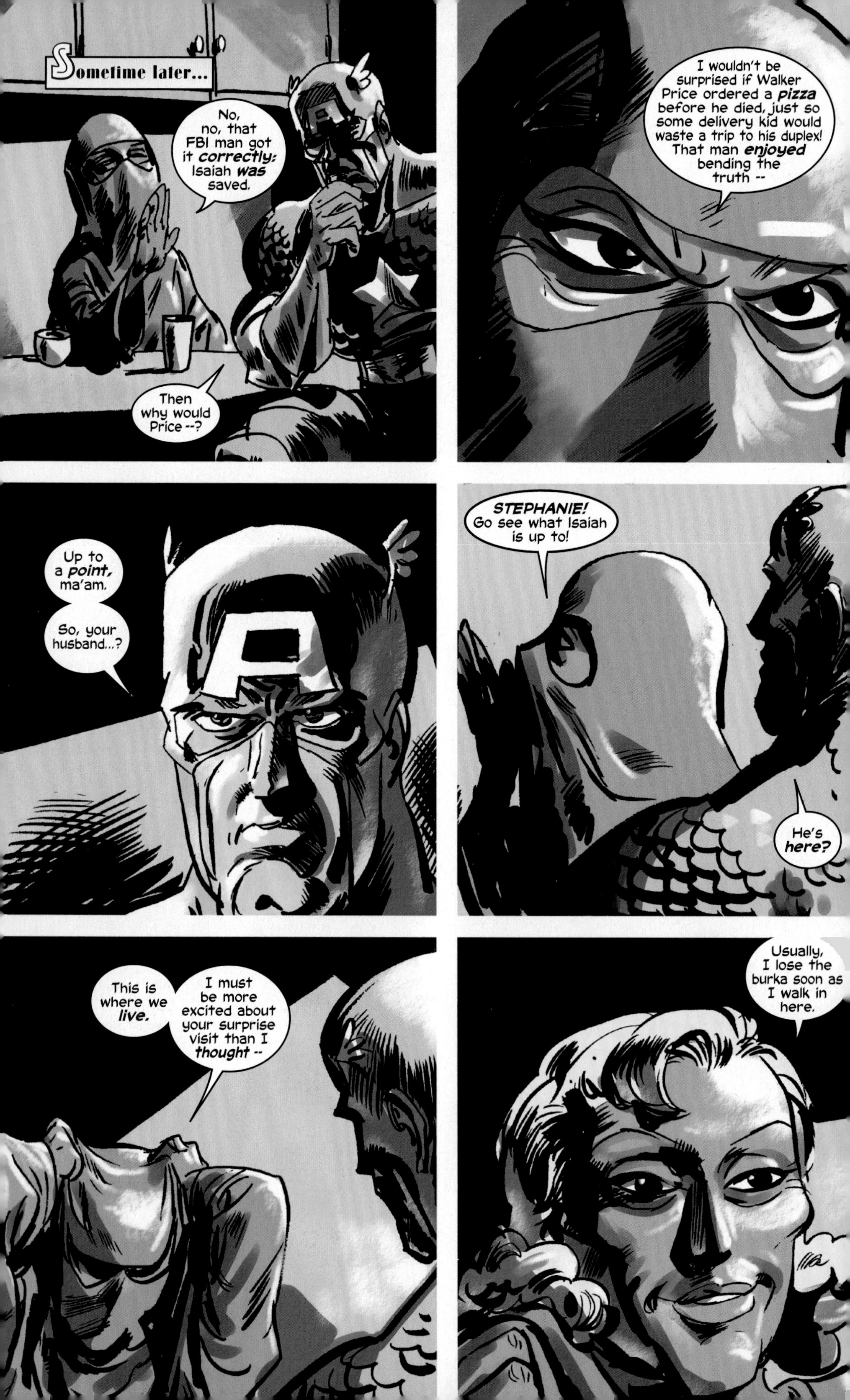
Sometime later...
No, no, that FBI man got it *correctly:* Isaiah *was* saved.
Then why would Price --?
I wouldn't be surprised if Walker Price ordered a *pizza* before he died, just so some delivery kid would waste a trip to his duplex! That man *enjoyed* bending the truth --
Up to a *point,* ma'am.
So, your husband...?
STEPHANIE! Go see what Isaiah is up to!
He's *here?*
This is where we *live.*
I must be more excited about your surprise visit than I *thought* --
Usually, I lose the burka soon as I walk in here.

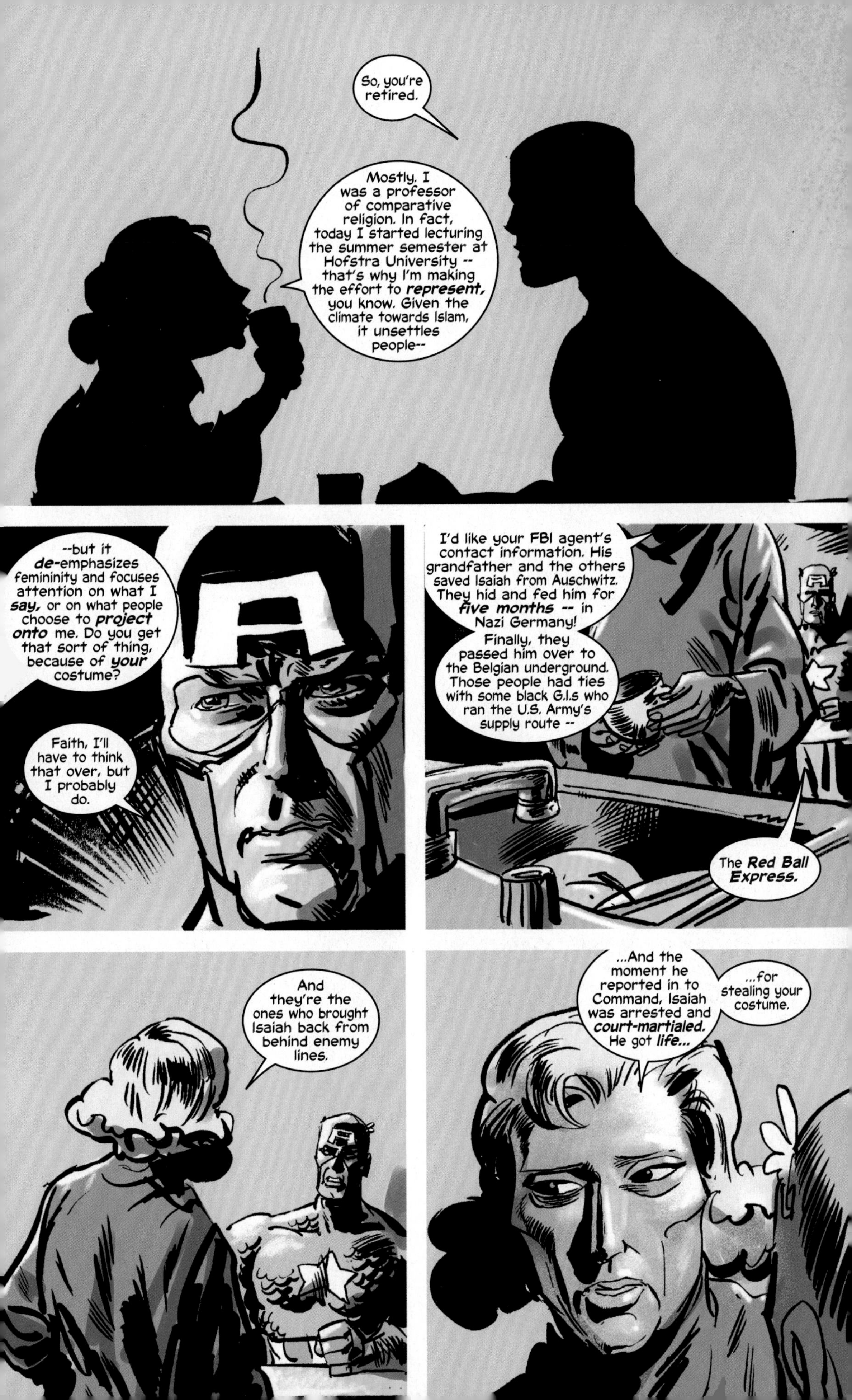
So, you're retired.
Mostly. I was a professor of comparative religion. In fact, today I started lecturing the summer semester at Hofstra University -- that's why I'm making the effort to *represent,* you know. Given the climate towards Islam, it unsettles people--
--but it *de*-emphasizes femininity and focuses attention on what I *say,* or on what people choose to *project onto* me. Do you get that sort of thing, because of *your* costume?
Faith, I'll have to think that over, but I probably do.
I'd like your FBI agent's contact information. His grandfather and the others saved Isaiah from Auschwitz. They hid and fed him for *five months --* in Nazi Germany!
Finally, they passed him over to the Belgian underground. Those people had ties with some black G.I.s who ran the U.S. Army's supply route --
The *Red Ball Express.*
And they're the ones who brought Isaiah back from behind enemy lines.
...And the moment he reported in to Command, Isaiah was arrested and *court-martialed.* He got *life...*
...for stealing your costume.

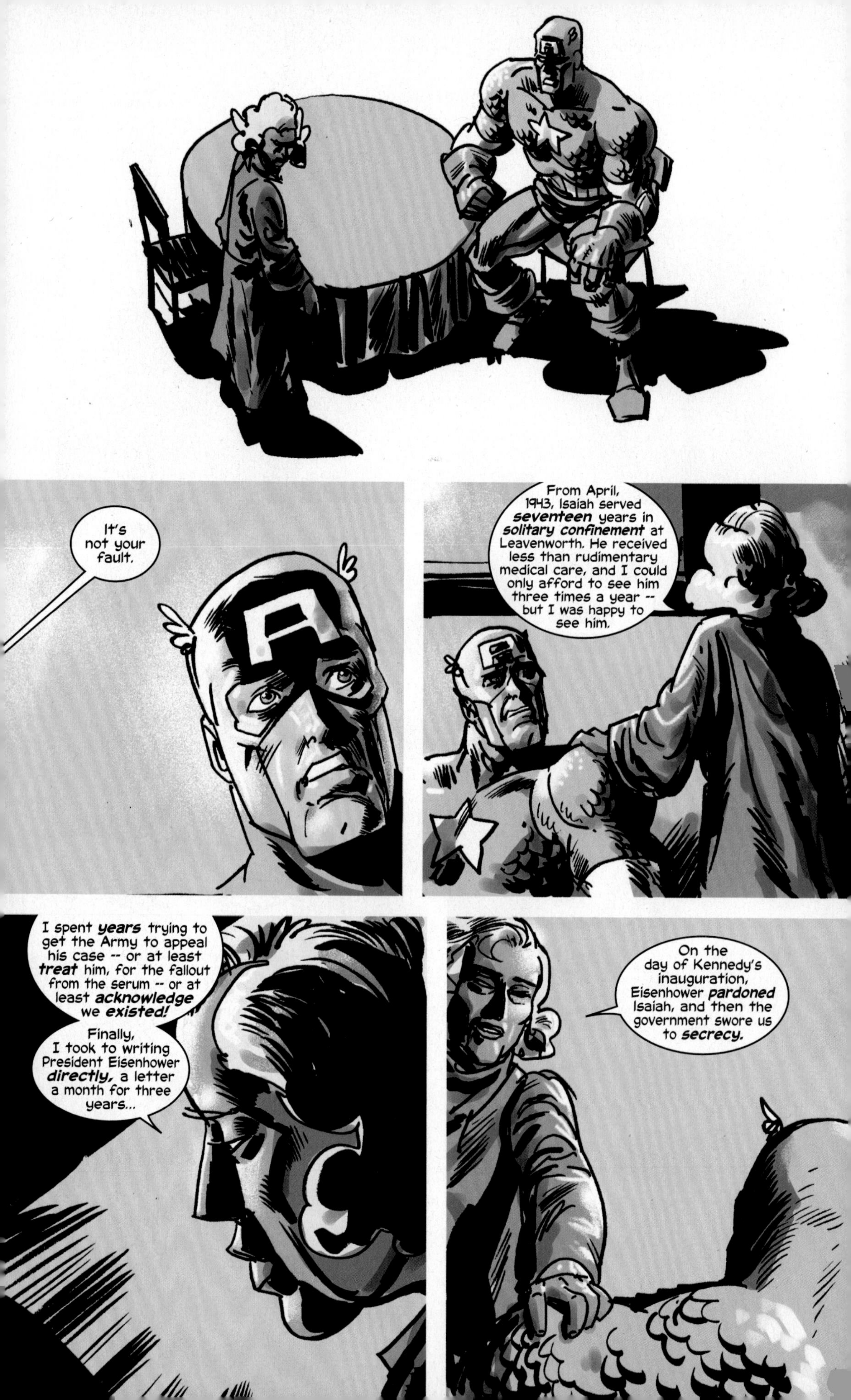
It's not your fault.
From April, 1943, Isaiah served **seventeen** years in **solitary confinement** at Leavenworth. He received less than rudimentary medical care, and I could only afford to see him three times a year -- but I was happy to see him.
I spent **years** trying to get the Army to appeal his case -- or at least **treat** him, for the fallout from the serum -- or at least **acknowledge** we **existed!**
Finally, I took to writing President Eisenhower **directly,** a letter a month for three years...
On the day of Kennedy's inauguration, Eisenhower **pardoned** Isaiah, and then the government swore us to **secrecy.**

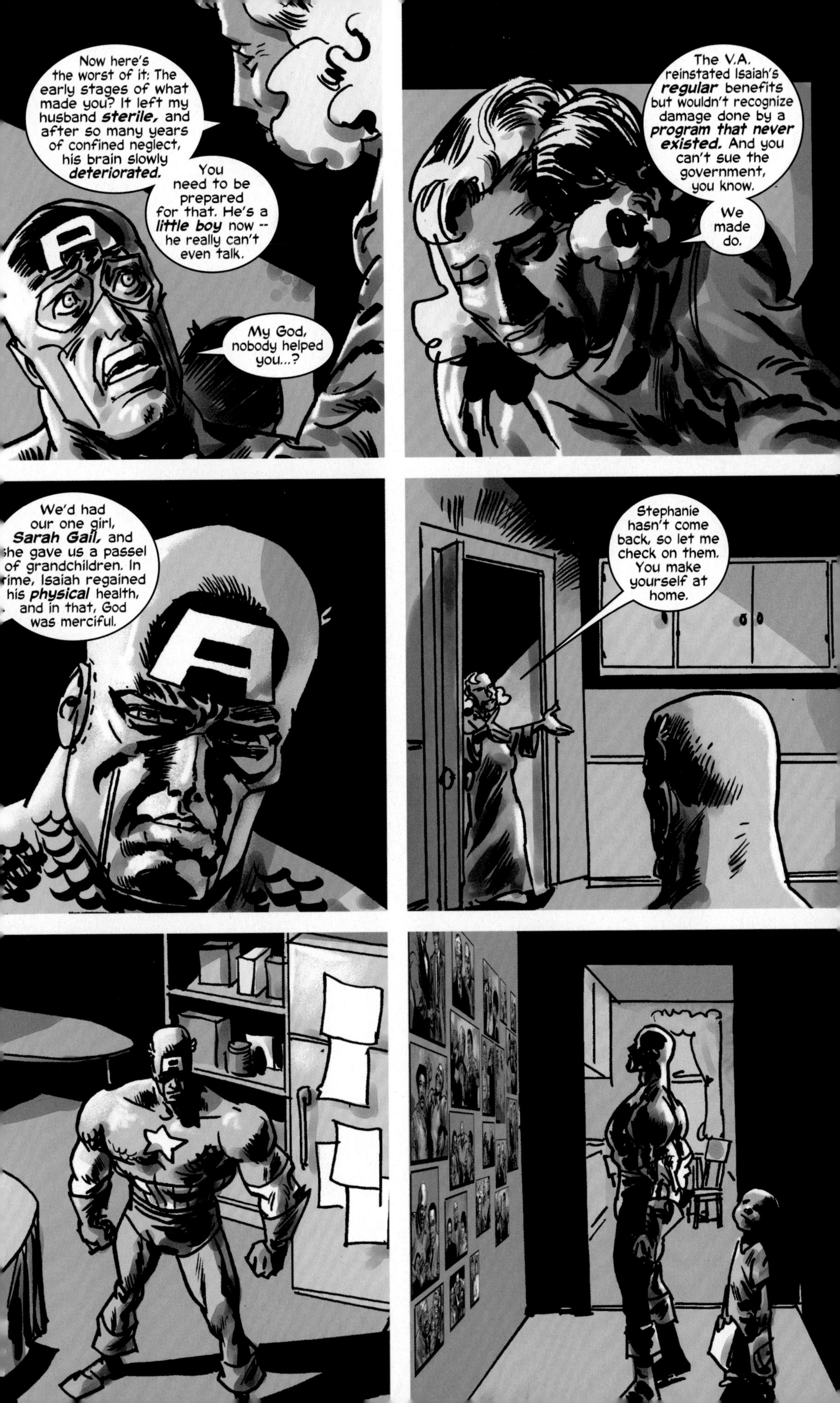
Now here's the worst of it: The early stages of what made you? It left my husband *sterile,* and after so many years of confined neglect, his brain slowly *deteriorated.*
You need to be prepared for that. He's a *little boy* now -- he really can't even talk.
My God, nobody helped you...?
The V.A. reinstated Isaiah's *regular* benefits but wouldn't recognize damage done by a *program that never existed.* And you can't sue the government, you know.
We made do.
We'd had our one girl, *Sarah Gail,* and she gave us a passel of grandchildren. In time, Isaiah regained his *physical* health, and in that, God was merciful.
Stephanie hasn't come back, so let me check on them. You make yourself at home.

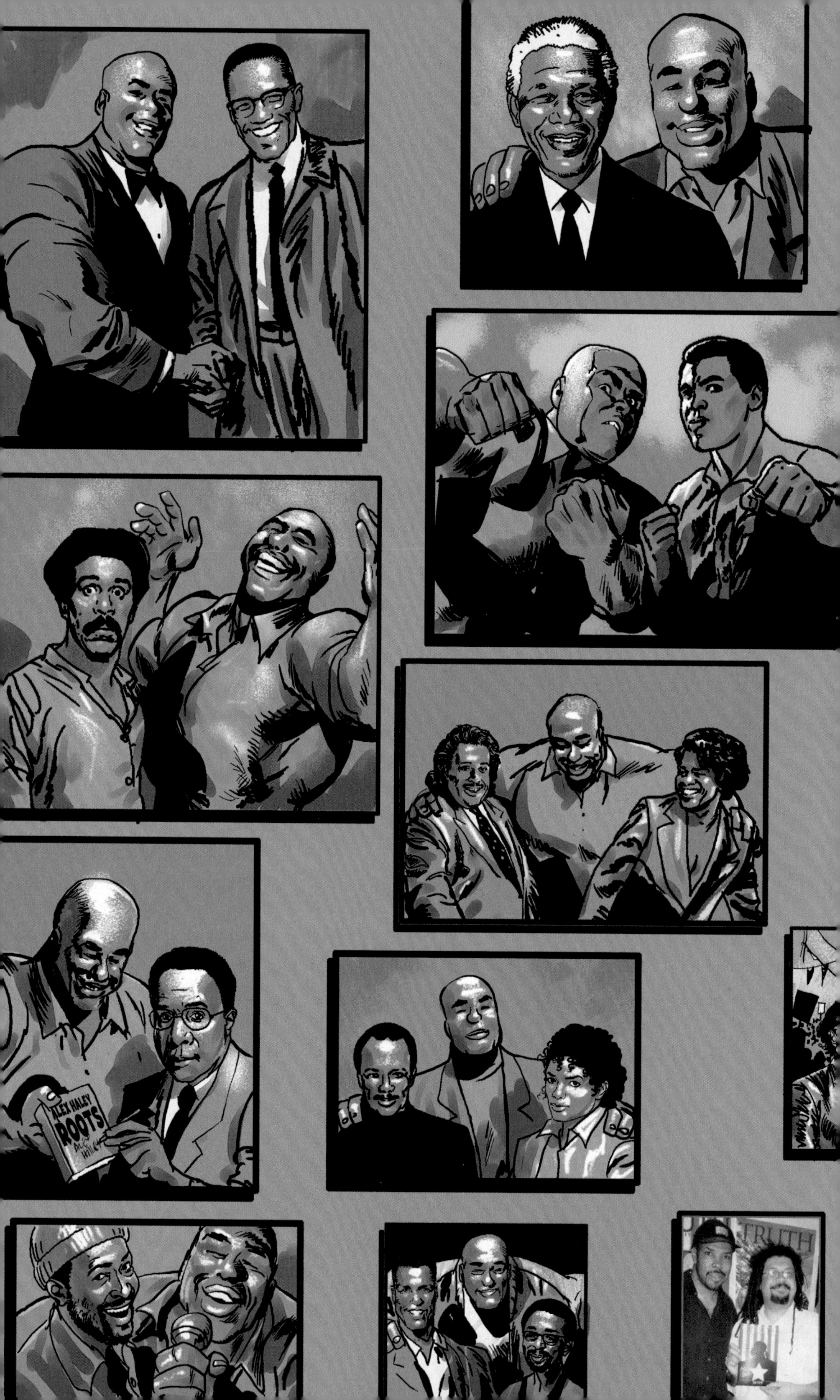
ALEX HALEY
ROOTS
TRUTH

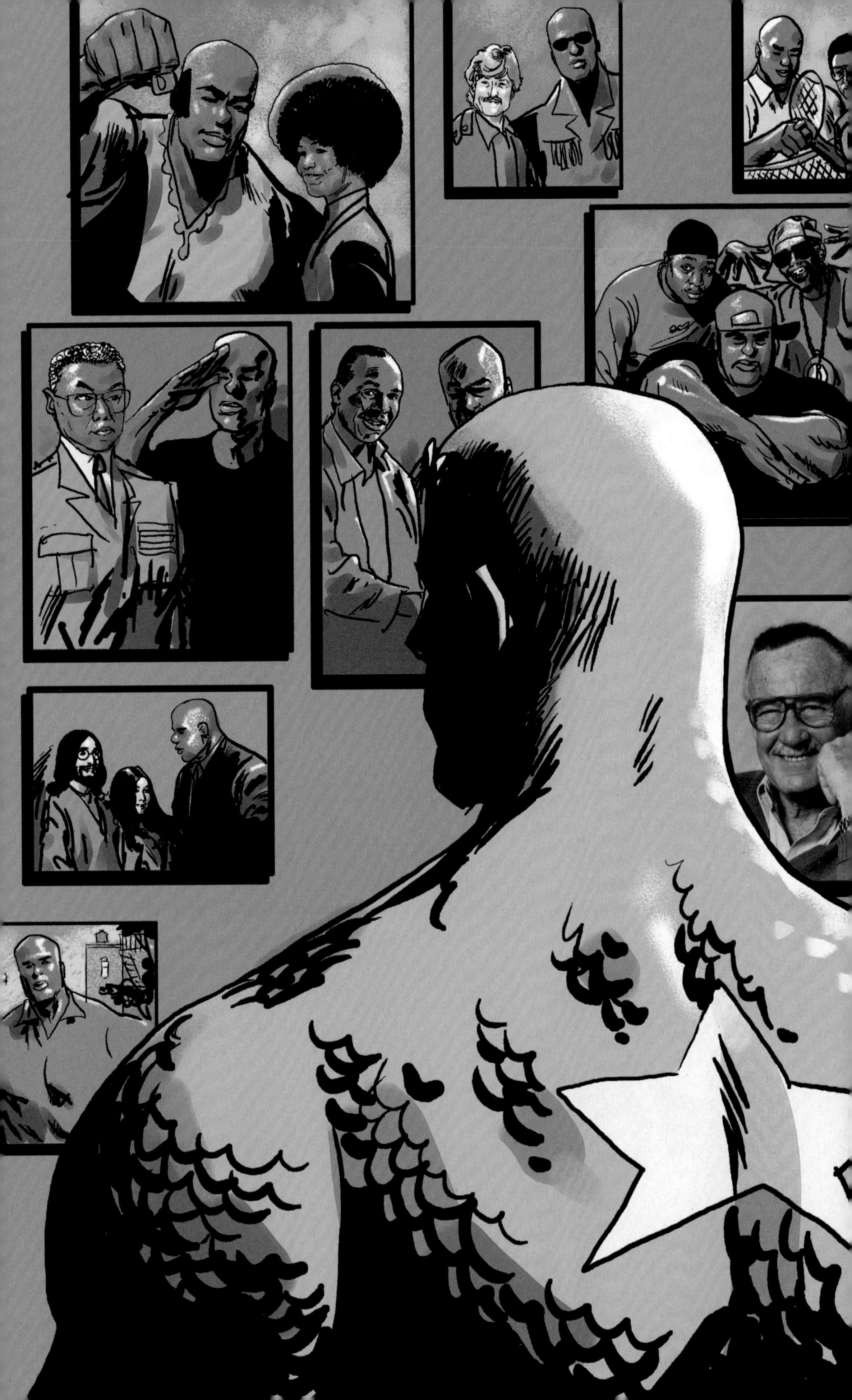

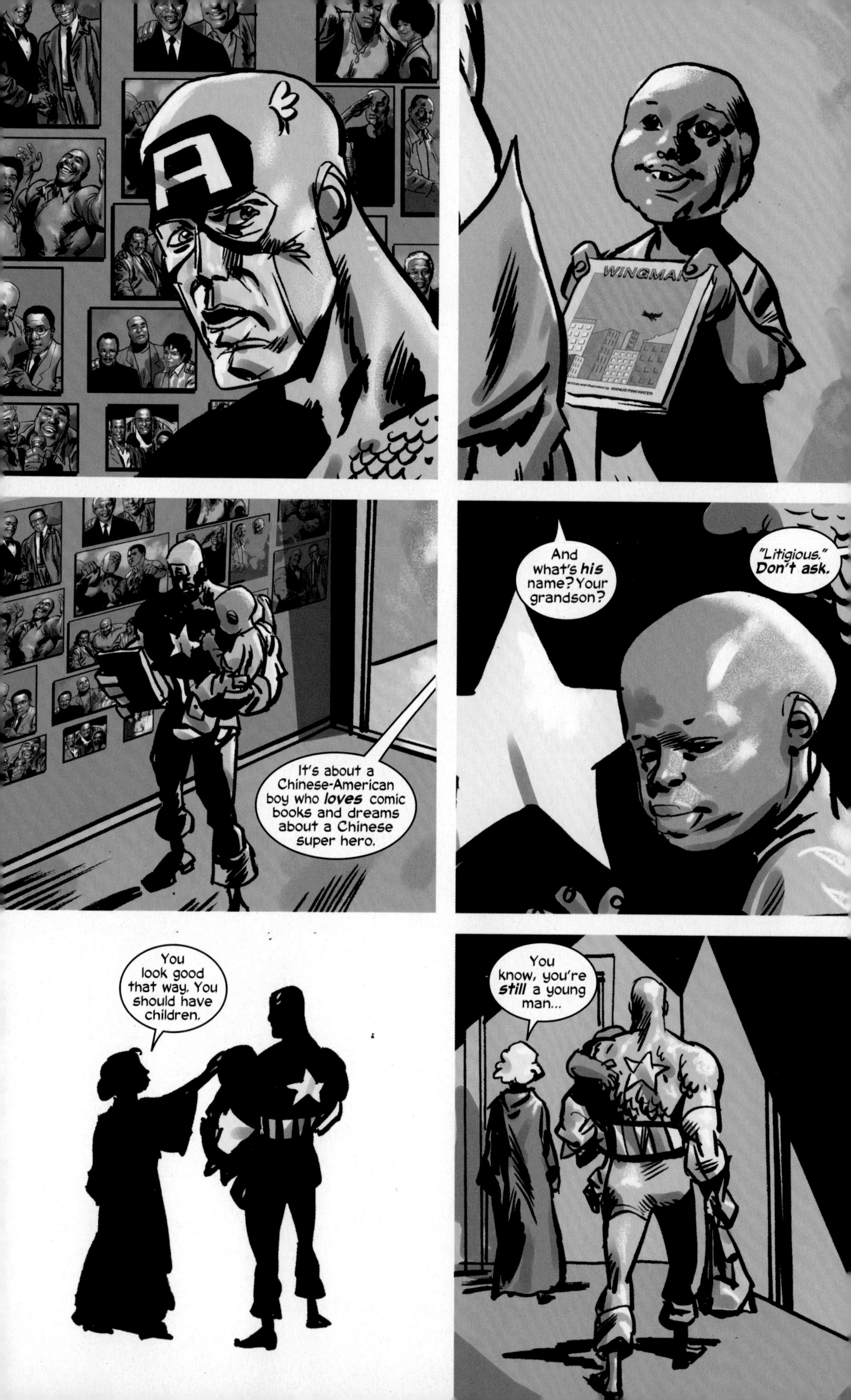
WINGMAN
It's about a Chinese-American boy who *loves* comic books and dreams about a Chinese super hero.
And what's *his* name? Your grandson?
"Litigious." **Don't ask.**
You look good that way. You should have children.
You know, you're *still* a young man...

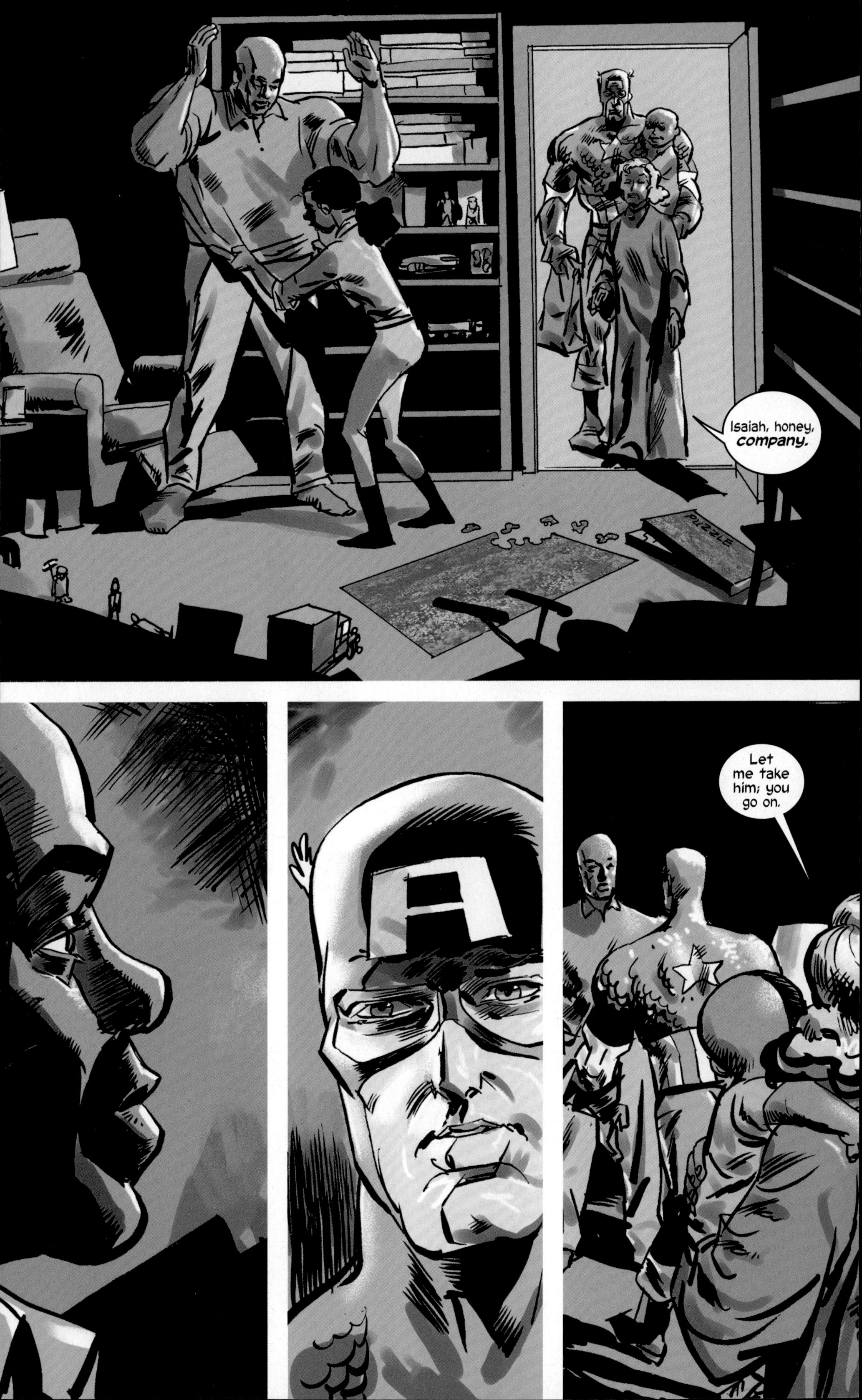
Isaiah, honey, *company.*
Let me take him; you go on.

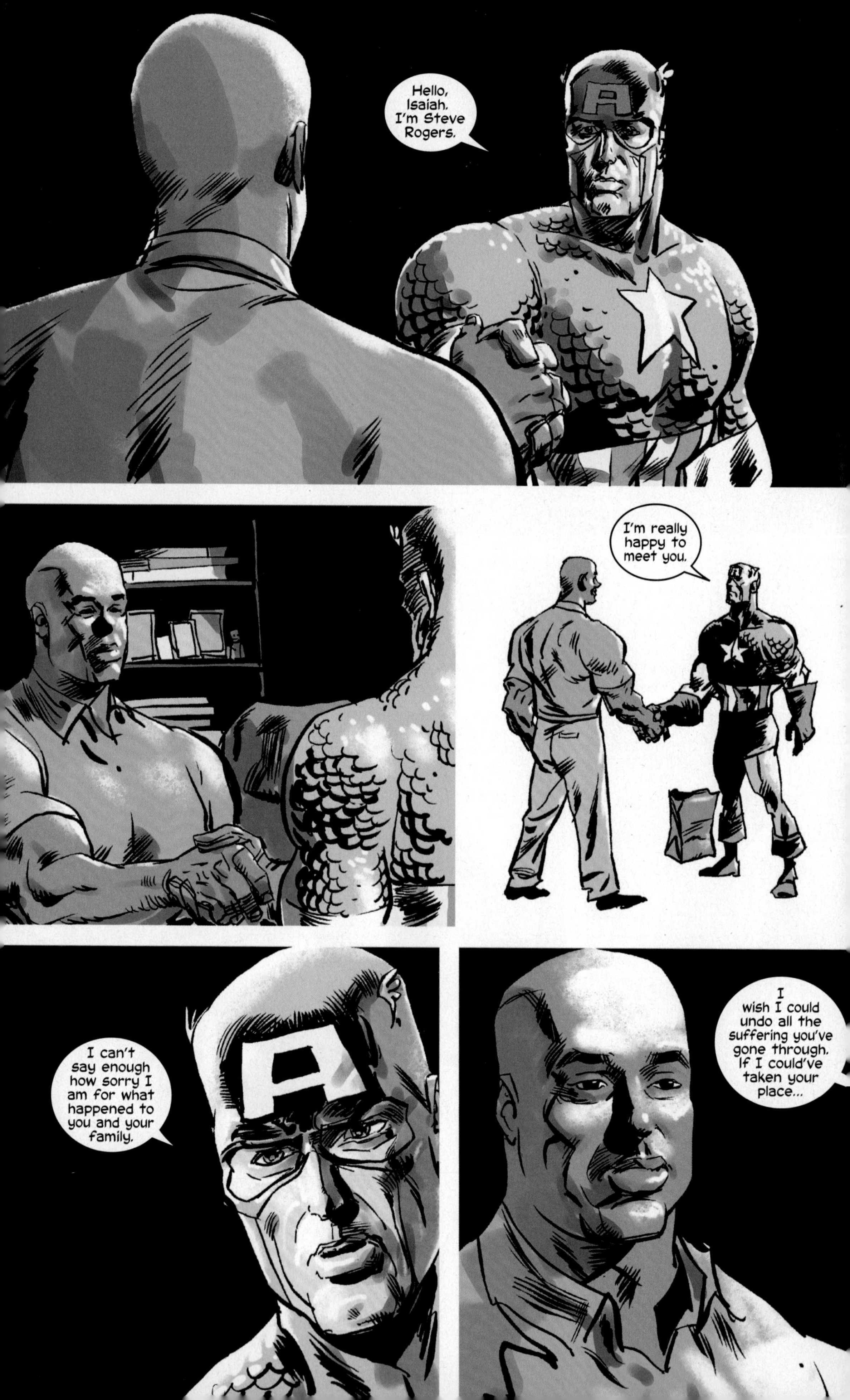
Hello, Isaiah. I'm Steve Rogers.
I'm really happy to meet you.
I can't say enough how sorry I am for what happened to you and your family.
I wish I could undo all the suffering you've gone through. If I could've taken your place...

duty, Isaiah. To you and everyone else. That's why I'm *here*.

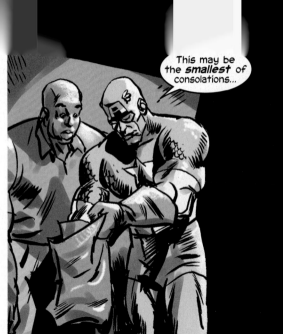

This may be the *smallest* of consolations...

...but I believe this belongs to *you.*

Mind if I get a picture of you two for his collection?

Anything, ma'am, any time.

Say *"cheese"!*

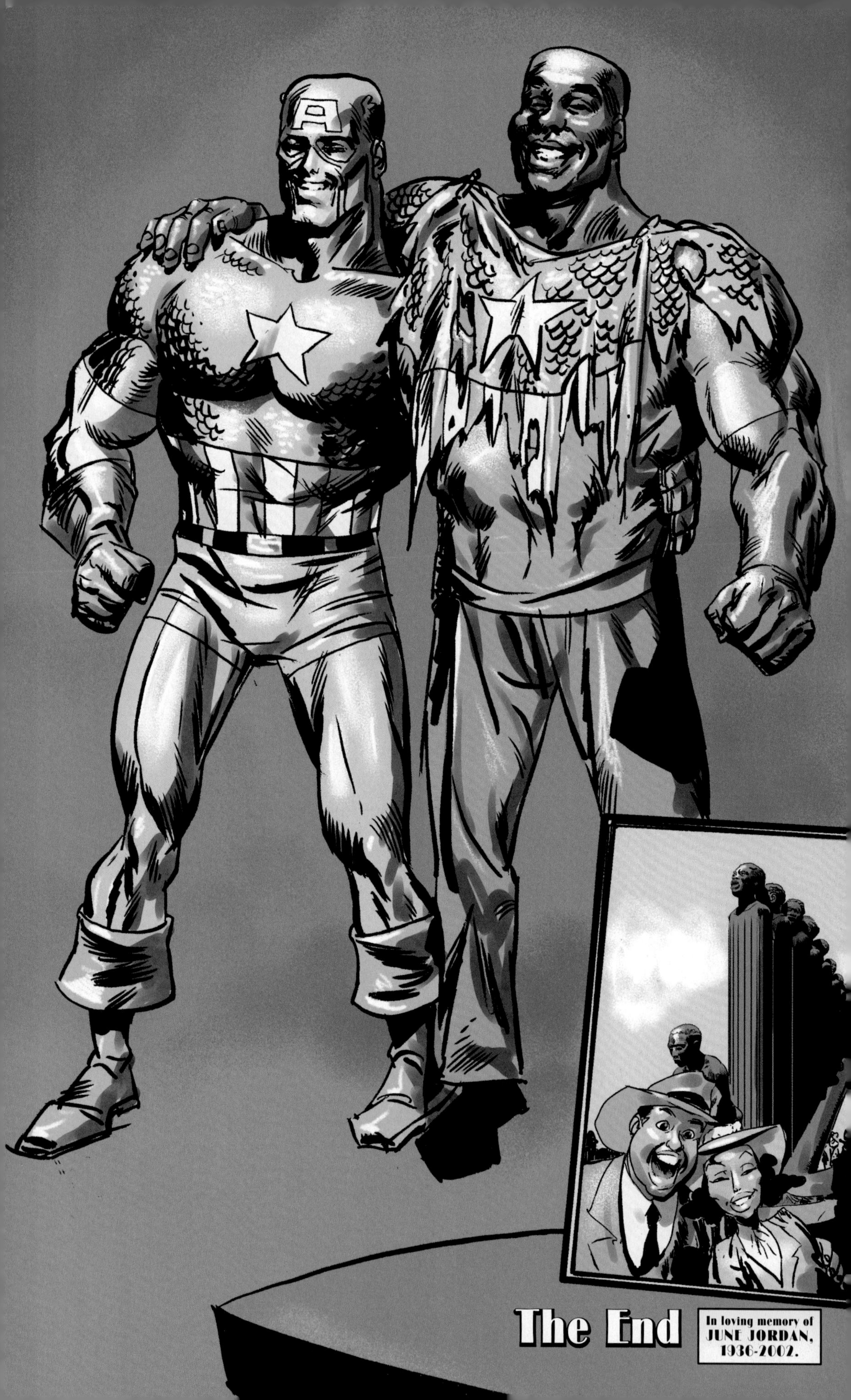
The End
In loving memory of JUNE JORDAN, 1936-2002.